Sam M. Jones

Christ In His Suffering

CHRIST
In His
SUFFERING

K. SCHILDER, Ph. D.

Translated from the Dutch
by
HENRY ZYLSTRA

SECOND EDITION

WM. B. EERDMANS PUBLISHING CO.
Grand Rapids   1942   Michigan

PRINTED IN THE UNITED STATES OF AMERICA

Many of the merits and none of the defects of this translation are owing to Dr. Henry Beets, who carefully read and edited the manuscript.

—*The Translator.*

FOREWORD

THE author of this volume on the suffering of our Redeemer ought to become well known in English-speaking countries. He is one of the most talented theologians of his day in the Netherlands. He is a deep thinker and an author whose writings are scintillating. They abound in paradoxes, which may not always be easily understood at first, but when thought through, like the well-beaten oil of the sanctuary they bring about keen intellectual satisfaction, discover new exegetical treasures in the Book of Books, and cause the reader to admire the exegetical keenness of Dr. K. Schilder.

Born in 1890, he graduated from the theological school of Kampen, his native city, in 1914. After his graduation he served several churches. But in 1931 the way opened to him to be enrolled as student at the University of Erlangen from which he graduated in 1933, as Doctor of Philosophy, summa cum laude. In 1933 the General Synod of his denomination, the Reformed Churches of the Netherlands, unanimously elected him to the important chair of dogmatics and ethics of his alma mater, which he is serving to this day.

For quite a number of years he has been the editor-in-chief of a religious weekly, "De Reformatie." He has published several books, the chief of which are three volumes on the Suffering of our Lord. Each of these three books is complete in itself. The first one describes the suffering of the Lord Jesus in its initial stages, ending with the Garden of Gethsemane. The second covers the Lord's passion, till He was condemned to be crucified. The third one relates His suffering from the last named stage, ending with a chapter about His burial. The rendering of the present volume in English was done by Mr. Henry Zylstra, a graduate of Calvin College, who received his A. M. degree at the University of Iowa, and who spent last year as graduate student in Comparative Literature, at Harvard University. At present he is assistant professor of English in the English department of Calvin College.

While the writer was requested to supervise the translation and tried to carry out his charge, he was enthralled increasingly by the fine, stimulating, and edifying contents of the volume now submitted to the English-speaking public.

Dr. Henry Beets

Grand Rapids, Michigan, August 19, 1937.

PREFACE

IT is a source of great pleasure and of gratitude to Him, the preaching of Whose name is the most beautiful task on earth, for me to know that this work, which I greatly enjoyed writing, is appearing now in English translation.

Acknowledging a sense of great gratitude to those who took the initiative in promoting this translation, and to those who devoted painstaking care to it, I express the wish that the work also in the large English-speaking world to which it is now made available, may, with the blessing of God, keep that confession alive of which Charles Hodge gave this epitome: "Christ saves us as our Priest"; and: "Christ saves us as a Sacrifice"—a confession which induced him, a learned man, to pray, in the words of Toplady's precious hymn.

> Let the water and the blood,
> From Thy wounded side which flowed,
> Be of sin the double cure,
> Save from guilt and make me pure.

K. SCHILDER

Kampen, September 3, 1937.

CONTENTS

CONTENTS—Continued

Satan at the Pulpit of the Passion

CHAPTER ONE

Satan at the Pulpit of the Passion

● *But he turned, and said unto Peter, Get thee*
behind me, Satan; thou art an offense unto me.
—MATTHEW 16:23a.

WE shall study the Man of sorrows, the Mediator of our confession, Christ Jesus. We shall see Him as He surrenders Himself in the night of His passion, and as He, clearly conscious of His purpose, moves straight to His death.

How else could we observe Him, then, except as He is in His threefold' office of Prophet, Priest, and King? For it is as the absolute and only true bearer of that triple office that He passed through the whole course of His suffering. There is no spot so small in the temple of His passion that it has not seen Him suffer and triumph as one always discharging that threefold responsibility.

We see Him as Prophet today. Observe and listen. He has Himself stepped to the pulpit[1] from which He will teach. Yes, He will teach, for He is to instruct His disciples, to demonstrate[2] to them that His suffering is the most imperative need of the world.

We see Him here as Priest. For, as you notice, even as He stands at the pulpit, teaching the ignorant and the foolish, a "satan" comes, a satan in the form of flesh and blood, it is true, but a satan, nevertheless. He comes, ascends the rostrum, and places an interfering hand upon the very pulpit from which the highest Prophet of God is giving instruction. That human satan makes

---

[1]. This word has been selected advisedly; it supports the connotation of the Greek of the New Testament, and points out the prophet's or teacher's office, which Christ, "seated" as a rabbi, fulfilled.

[2]. Such is the meaning of the original word, translated "shew" in Verse 21 of the King James Version.

a diabolical statement and a satanic gesture by which he hopes to thwart the spirit and counteract the influence of Christ's teaching. So he tries to conceal the cross, which Jesus already holds up before His disciples' eyes, behind a veil of satanical perversity and blindness. But observe closely now, for in this we see the Priest in Him assert itself: Christ briskly thrusts that interfering hand aside, so that His prayers and sacrifices may go on unhindered. Truly, He cometh, O God, to do Thy will. As a Prophet He will say what He must, and as a Priest He will in all things be sensitively alert and helpful.

Finally, we see Him as King, here at the entrance to the temple of suffering. For, as He sets out to execute the deed which is the one thing needful for the world, He moves straight to its realization, though there be as many satans around Him as there are disciples within His heart.

Depart, behind me, Satan. That is a statement of the Prophet, Priest, and King. It is His response to the greeting of those upon the way who would lead the Servant of the Lord to God too hastily. In fact, He greets no one along the road, for He goes to greet His God, the God who sends Him into death.

To see Christ active thus in the capacity of His threefold office, surely that marks a high point in the Gospel history. It marks that by the objective fact of grace revealed in Christ's Messianic presence. But another high point, this one in the subjective life of grace, is also attained on this occasion. Whoever reads the Gospel report of this event painstakingly will see that the disciples of Jesus reached such a summit. The chapter at present open before us tells us that these disciples, Peter at their head, now came to make the full confession that Jesus of Nazareth was indeed the Messiah. What had long lain dormant within them finally stirred; what had never broken through to overt expression was proclaimed aloud. The conviction burst through, patent and undisguised, in the language of the Christian confession: Thou art the Messiah, the Son of the living God. Yes, there are two heights of attainment here, the one objective and the other subjective.

Remember, however, that he who scales mountain heights and reaches lofty peaks finds breathing difficult. And it is especially true of the Kingdom of heaven that summits of achievement are also climaxes of anxiety, acmes of conflict. Whenever, therefore, we with true Christian mysticism want to sing the "introitus" to the hymn of Christ's passion, we do well to remember that heights of attainment in the life of grace are places of awful tension.

With true mysticism — for there is also a false mysticism. The false mystic struggles hard to scale a mountain top, supposing that when he reaches it he will find a pleasant arbor there and a smooth plateau ahead. But the true mystic knows that when he has attained a ledge on the steep ascent he will meet struggle there, will be confronted by the rock of offense and by the cross which he must take up and bear. A map charting the acclivity of the mountain is the false mystic's only guide. The ways beyond the peaks? Why, those are easy plains. But true mysticism knows that the cross is waiting at every mediate goal.

The true mystic knows that conflict so accompanies achievement, and he trembles at the thought of it. So we tremble, too. For we are compelled to notice that the first disciple who in his spiritual experience ventured to leap to the pinnacle, and who rejoiced at being able to say, "Thou art the Messiah, the Son of the living God,"—that this very man is also the first, having reached the apex, to stumble over the rock of offence, and, what is more, also to cause the Christ to stumble, were that not eternally impossible.

Simon was a Jew. And every native Jew, the moment he has composed the song *We have found the Messiah,* wants immediately to swell the music into the jubilant refrain: *Peace in heaven, and glory in the highest.*[1] So Simon Barjona, seated on a new ledge, wishes to enjoy that peace at once and to raise his voice in a hallelujah chorus. In fact, he has it all composed.

But on this day he, the exuberant singer, finds himself under the discipline of the Master of the musicians. True, Jesus, the First Conductor, has Himself elicited that Messianic hymn from the spirit and soul of His pupil. But, once the theme *Jesus is the Christ* has been faithfully recited by the elated student-precentor, the Master's voice drops. It suddenly falls, so to say, from the

---

1. Compare the story of the triumphal entry into Jerusalem.

eloquent heights of poetic song to the lowest level of didactic prose. The lesson He teaches in that voice is hard, is exacting. The disciples are eager, are all agog to sing, to rejoice, to praise peace and shout hosanna. And Jesus? He quietly begins to expound matters. He undertakes to "show"[1] them that He must suffer and die.

In a flash Peter interrupts that discourse: "Be it far from thee,[2] Lord: this shall not be unto thee." And then it happens. Jesus turns sharply around. His voice, calmly discoursing before, rises in tone as it raps out the rejoinder: "Behind me, Satan. Thou art an offense unto me. I called thee a rock, a man of granite, upon whom one can lean; but now, so far from being a foundation stone, thou art a stumbling block."

Just what does it all mean? How must we take this? We who were not witnesses to the event ask naively: Was it really that serious? And even if we are alert enough to remember that the word "satan" by no means always refers to the awful spirit of the pit, and that in this sense it means nothing more than "adversary," we know, nevertheless, that these considerations do not affect the truth that Jesus' harsh epithet fixed a wall of wrath and of righteousness between Christ and Peter. For Jesus cannot apply the name Satan to a human being without thereby thinking of the great spirit of revolt who dwells eternally in darkness. The question therefore lingers: How is it that Jesus suddenly addresses Peter so?

We may as well be honest. We shall never answer that question adequately. Our ignorance embarrasses us even here at the entrance to the temple of suffering. We cannot grasp half of the significance of what happens; we cannot understand, for instance, how the sinless soul of Christ reacts to satanic temptation, from whatever side that may come. Such a phenomenon, the second Adam, without sin, on the one side, and on the other a satanical being,—that we have never measured with the eye, nor fathomed with the mind. Who, in fact, would dare to make the slightest

---

1. Verse 21.

2. The same expression or a very similar one, sometimes rendered "God forbid," is used in the Greek translation of the Old Testament in such other passages as are found in: 2 Sam. 20:20 and 23:17; 1 Chron. 11:9; Josh. 22:29; 24:16; Gen. 44:7, 17.

comment about the sinless soul of Christ, which lived on earth unstained and responded purely to every stimulus?

But, even though we can never completely answer the question why Jesus on this occasion spoke so, we can say something about it and that according to the Scriptures.

This first of all: Jesus in this circumstance proves to be very man. As such He is subject to every psychological law of action and reaction which is not the effect of sin. Moreover, He is not only truly but also completely a man. Therefore, in this ultra-human existence before God, He sees great significance in all small things. The whole process of His mediatorial career is concentrated as a unity into each moment of His life. Every point within the circumference of His circles is seen only and always from a single focal center and consequently in harmonious relationship to the whole. Hence it must be that the satanic statement which at this time tears its way through His prophetic discourse hurts Him grievously. It recalls to His mind, very likely, that other moment in His life, when, at the conclusion of His baptism, the Spirit drove Him to the wilderness. Again that panorama in the desert rises before Him. Again He lives it, as though it had just happened. Again He experiences how, after the baptism which had been His objective for thirty long years, the Spirit drove Him into the wilderness to meet Satan. There the great Satan, the very prince of hell, hurled his temptations into the pure, human desires, the manly virtues, and the mediatorial passion of His soul. That Satan also said in effect: "Be it far from thee, Lord: this shall not be unto thee."

Now Christ has reached another mediate goal, another milestone. Again He is to be baptized, not with water but with consuming fire. That pulpit at which He stands here in Caesarea Philippi and from which He as a Prophet teaches is, in a sense, the beginning of the end and the end of the beginning of His mediatorial state of humiliation.

Again satan is present, a satan of flesh and blood, but a satan none the less. Again there occurs that influx of hellish passion: What God wills and declares inevitable need never take place! That, surely, is suffering. It explains the brusque reprimand.

But more can be said. Christ who always sees the organic unity in the mission of His life also sees the climax in God's purpose. After that other summit of attainment, His baptism, the Spirit drove Him into the desert to meet Satan. Now, at this second level of achievement, that same Spirit drives Him out to meet another satan, Simon Barjona. How terribly effective are the several repetitions in the fugue of God's wrath! The Holy Spirit Himself places Peter's rebellious hand upon Christ's pulpit. And for the Saviour, fully aflame as He is with love for mankind, it is far worse suffering to meet a satan of flesh and blood than to confront that one great Devil who is sheer spirit. Jesus Himself is human. He called Simon Barjona a friend. And a friend's opposition to the task which God placed upon the Son of man is a burden outweighing a thousand times the enmity to Him and the Father breathed out by the Demon of the pit. Hearing His *bride* speak and act satanically, seeing a human being, one of those for whom He is giving His life, become an instrument of Satan, observing the flesh in Simon Peter assert itself to take exception to heaven's law of atonement through fulfillment, and all that, mark well, at the moment of Christ's prophesying — that must have been Jesus' severest suffering up to this time. For He knows all the while that this same rebellion of flesh against spirit will presently nail Him to the cross.

Hence we do not wonder and we do not take issue with Him as Jesus curtly declares, "Get thee behind me, Satan." Silence is the response befitting this spectacle of the terrible grief which the Son of man, as a true, complete, and sinless human being, felt at this time. Silence, and an offer of thanksgiving as we notice that the pure and perfect Mediator takes uncompromising issue with as little even as the mere idea that God's counsel shall not be fulfilled in Him, or that the heavenly plan of redemption, bearing with it the gift of eternal peace, shall not accrue to Peter and to us.

Tremulously we place our fingers upon our lips at seeing this consuming fire of holiness, these flames of love, the quick lighting of this prophecy, which leaps out at the slightest contact with satanic will and spirit, and which by that very spontaneity of its reflex action proclaims the immutable law of, and wonderful fidelity to, God's determinate counsel. We worship and praise the quick response which sensitively obeys God's justice and promise of faithfulness; we bow before the perfection which never profanes the flawless round of God's righteousness and truth.

What besides? Well, you and I are standing at the entrance to the temple of suffering. What if we should sometime be told: Behind me, Satan?

The question strikes us dumb. Full well we know that we, too, have earned that black and ugly epithet. As often as we fail to believe, to serve the Prophet, Priest, and King, we are satans to Him. O yes, He is no more with us as He once walked beside Simon Barjona, but His Spirit, we know, has returned to dwell with us; and as often as we do not believe Him, as frequently as our hearts ponder some other way of redemption, we grieve that Spirit. And that familiar phrase, "grieving the Spirit," is the New Testament term for what before the day of Pentecost was called "being a satan to Jesus."

Yes, in us, too, flesh wars against spirit. For us also the entrance to the temple of passion is a place of amazement. There the Spirit of God begins battle against the flesh. There the atmosphere is oppressive. Fortunately, if we are really troubled, if we grow awfully tense within, the Worker of our salvation reprimands us for our overbearing impatience.

We shall have to make amends for such conduct long. It will be so throughout life. Even though we love the Lord, our experience will be that of Simon Barjona, who was sent back into the place of instruction one moment and who the next minute again spoke satanically upon the mountain of transfiguration.

Our course, then? Shall we turn back, depending upon our inadequate selves?

By no means. You remember that we pointed out two high spots. The one was a ledge on the slope of the subjective life of grace, of the experience of faith, of apprenticeship with Jesus. On that level we, like Simon Barjona, have spoiled everything.

But when the vapors of hell have lifted, when the wrath of Christ's words has dispelled the nebulosity of Peter's misconception, we look up to that other height. There on that second summit, on the mountain of objective grace, Jesus still stands, untainted by our pollution, Prophet, Priest, and King in purity and virtue.

To us, here at the beginning of the passion history, it is incomparable comfort to know that He stands so adamant on the threshold of the temple of suffering that not even the violent gusts of hell can cause Him to waver.

Satan on the Mountain of Transfiguration

CHAPTER TWO

Satan on the Mountain of Transfiguration[1]

● *And Peter answered and said to Jesus: Master, it is good for us to be here: and let us make three tabernacles: one for thee, and one for Moses, and one for Elias. For he wist not what to say; for they were sore afraid.*   MARK 9:5, 6.

JUST as in all things God's revelation evolves progressively and each new day marks some development of it, so in the history of Christ's suffering there is a gradual evolution which leads to a definite climax. And, precisely as in a well-motivated drama, so in this history that climax presents the sharp contrast of diametrically opposed forces.

The text before us illustrates such a climax. Before we note that, however, we must pick up the thread of events we dropped in the preceding chapter. In it we saw that Christ had been driven by the Spirit into Caesarea Philippi, and we found Him there in the company of the "satan" who tried to hinder Him from fulfilling His function. Now we are to observe Him again. This time the Spirit drives Him up to the mountain of transfiguration. But the remarkable thing in this circumstance is that this satan accompanies Him again. Accompanies Him? No, the fact is more striking than that: Jesus Himself takes with Him the very man whom He had called a satan; in fact, He names him one of the three favored disciples who may see at close range. It is that which, humanly speaking, gives this story such stirring dramatic effect.

Satan in the person of Simon Barjona, by placing his hand upon the pulpit from which the Master taught, had tried to inter-

---

1. This chapter does not comment on the conversation carried on by Moses, Elijah, and Christ; Chapter 6 treats wholly of that.

fere as Jesus was teaching His disciples the inevitability of His suffering and death. Jesus had done that teaching in a calm, conversational manner and in the language of the day. But now—prodigious difference—heaven itself opens to explain that inevitability. Moses and Elias come down from the skies to a high mountain, and there they show Jesus, not men, the way of His passion and death.

Nevertheless, even in this hour, in which the dazzling effulgence of heavenly glory forms a sharp contrast to the shadows of the cross, even now that satan of flesh and blood may accompany Jesus. No, not may, he *must* accompany Him. Jesus selects him to go along; the Spirit drives Christ to take Simon along. That is because the Son of man must carry out the choice of His sacrifice straight against the satanically protesting voice of His bride, the church.

In Caesarea Philippi Satan, called Simon Barjona, had in a negative way objected to the concepts of suffering and death. Now in a positive spirit he is to ask for a prolongation of life. But in both instances he will prove to be a satan.

It is very likely that in this contention of spiritually opposed forces and powers, nature, too, had to contribute in her own way to depicting the awful contrast. God, who is the Artist of artists, always knows how to make nature and Spirit speak the same language in a given moment. He reveals that art especially in the history of Jesus' passion. We can readily understand, therefore, why some have supposed that Christ's transfiguration upon the mountain occurred at night. According to Luke's account Jesus had gone up the mount partly to pray, and we know that Jesus more than once chose the evening for prayer. Besides, we note that the disciples, later, have fallen asleep. That too suggests a nocturnal scene. And if we remember, moreover, that the Master and His disciples, upon coming down from the mountain, were confronted by the spectacle of a despairing father and his mortally stricken son, that fact, too, confirms the opinion that the event of transfiguration took place at night. Such an interpretation, at least, leaves room for the time which must necessarily have elapsed during the journey downwards, and between

Christ's metamorphosis and His confronting that pathetic scene in the valley.

If it is true that God Himself planned that the events on the mountain should occur after dark, that circumstance enhances the dramatic effect of the story still more. For then we recall Christmas eve, that night "more beautiful than days." When that night settled upon the fields of Bethlehem the angels came to dispel the darkness with the light of heaven. But there is this difference: on that occasion angels brought the heavenly light, but on this one those who bear it to earth and lavishly shed its radiance abroad are men. Angels are much, but men are more. Besides, the angels on Christmas spoke *about* the Christ, Himself a child at the time. But now two men appear, men who stand in the presence of God daily and, as do the redeemed of mankind, stand nearer Him than the angels. These men, Moses and Elias, appear not merely to talk about the Christ but to talk with Him about "his departure at Jerusalem." And that Christ is no longer a child but a man, ready for the great deed.

Heaven exerting itself to give unusual distinction to this scene! We blush in shame at the thought of it. Heaven leaving nothing undone to create an atmosphere of translucent radiance as a fitting medium for the event — and men, as always, imposing what is ugly upon the perfect beauty. A satan in Caesarea Philippi is bad enough. But a satan upon the mountain of Christ's transfiguration is worse. Sinning tomorrow is always worse than sinning today, for each day proffers more abundant grace and therefore aggravates transgression.

There is no need to speak at length of what Simon Peter said. The story is well known. Heaven opened itself and two lustrous forms, later recognized as Moses and Elias, appeared upon the mountain on which Jesus wanted to meet God. They enveloped the Son of man within the aureole of their glamour. It was still their hour. Because darkness still obtained upon earth and every where surrounded Jesus, therefore mere men — rare privilege — might share their glory with the Son, and let Him shine in their light.

The three disciples, Peter, James, and John, are suddenly shocked awake by the superfluity of heavenly light. Their eyes have been heavy with sleep. Now they rub them and, in their astonishment, say nothing. But Peter cannot be silent long. "Master," he says, "what a happy circumstance that we are here; let us make three tabernacles, one for Thee, one for Moses, and one for Elias. Yes, we will make three shelters for Thee and Thy guests." For that is the sense of his words. By "tabernacles" he means make-shift shelters, quickly constructed from such branches, twigs, and foliage as were at hand.

It would be wrong to say more about this desire of Peter than is actually warranted. Some have speculated very boldly about his impromptu utterance. Some have said that Simon would by his proposal unite the Old Testament, represented by Moses and Elias, with the New Testament, represented by Christ, without the intervention of a legally adequate event. Others have supposed that Peter was pleading for escape from the world. That interpretation, significantly enough, would make of his improvised huts a kind of prototype of monasticism and the monastery. And many have inferred much besides, much more, in fact, than the words justify. We shall not indulge similar conjectures.

That is not saying, however, that Peter's speech, because it was uttered on the spur of the moment, was insignificant. True, he was unaware of its content, for he "wist not what to say." But God freighted his words with meaning. By this spectral miracle God elicited from Peter what was latent in him. God who even now shapes history, who by the Spirit brought Christ, Moses, and Elias into Peter's company, He it was who imparted profound significance to Peter's words.

Studying those words in the light God sheds upon them, we immediately notice two things. The first is the folly of Peter's proposal. Think of it: he wanted to build huts for heavenly visitors, to erect rudimentary tents for heaven's messengers. As well try to catch fluid sunlight in a mold. Yes, Peter would actually have prepared a kind of welcome, a reception for the children of heaven. As though earth could welcome heaven to itself! How differently Jesus Himself had taught. He had told of a celestial reception, a welcome at which heaven would receive earth. He assured the believers that one day the redeemed will receive them, the children of the earth, and will wlcome them, not to Peter's primitive lean-to's, but to the eternal mansions above. Really, how foolish this disciple's suggestion was.

Foolish — but that is not all. His words were sinful. Christ did not actually pronounce it, but Peter's speech again deserved the reprimand: Behind me, satan.

At this point we must, of course, digress to say that Simon's words also manifested great love. Note his readiness to serve. And how unselfish he is. He gives no thought to shelters for himself and the two other disciples; his only regard is for the Master and His guests. Truly, this is a love which gives itself unstintedly precisely because it wells up so spontaneously from a naive source. To such love it goes without saying that all must be given for Christ. For Peter assumes, you notice, that the moment he begins picking up twigs and branches, the others will immediately and eagerly assist him. Let *us* make tabernacles, he says. How fortunate that *we* are here. Indeed, this is an expression of the pupil's delight in serving his Master.

So far the digression. The fact remains that Peter's proposal was sinful. And the sin in it was this: he wanted to perpetuate the sheer bliss he saw. By that desire he was registering exception to the great theme Christ and His guests were discussing. Elias and Moses were placing the cross before Christ, were confronting Him with death. And in this awful hour Simon Peter wanted to cling to this dazzling crown, wished to possess forever this translucent beauty, to hold eternally this lavishment of light. Sun, he would pray, stand still beneath this mountain, and, thou moon, be fixed forever over this billowy refulgence of glory.

While Christ, and that in the very atmosphere of heavenly light and life, chooses voluntary death and hell's darkness, that satan of flesh and blood comes up to hinder Him and say: Master, prolong this hour of life and light; make the moment eternity; let us forget the world and its people, forget the temple, the myriad millions of men, forget Israel and the deep, dark valley of human suffering; come, consummate the present bliss; say to this passing moment: Ah, still abide, thou art so fair.

It would be unsympathetic in us to suppose that Peter's desire did not constitute a very real temptation to Christ's human spirit. His perfect humanity loved the light and longed for the life abundant. His soul, too, had it but for a moment severed itself from its official calling, would have yearned to eternally retain this heavenly vision. Therefore Peter's words were so characteristically those of a satan, a tempter. If the Saviour had, even in His thoughts, wanted to escape from the avalanche of suffering God was to loosen over Him at Gethsemane and upon Golgotha, He would have proved unfaithful to His office; such an attitude would have put a breach into the course of His obedience, and we all would have been lost with Him. Christ glorified after the cross, that is God's triumph. But a Christ who could have wished to be glorified before the cross would have been a victory for Satan.

How pronounced the contrast represented on this mountain, then. Here is Christ, surrounded by His church. Both branches of it, the militant and the triumphant, are represented, the one by Peter, the other by Moses and Elias. The triumphant church acts from eternal principles; the militant from the whims of the moment. The one lays bare before the Son of man the fixed decrees of God's eternal justice; the other the momentary desire of a poor, misguided, human heart. Heaven would make haste. See how it labors till all be fulfilled. It sends its own best representatives to the place where Jesus waits and prays. But Peter has time to spare. While all that is spiritual in the universe drives Christ to His death, Peter tempts with a prayer for delay. Surely anyone who is at all sensitive to spiritual realities will admit that this is a critical moment, a conflict between time and eternity.

If any should ask what point there is in so seriously considering Peter's foolish fancies, we would reply with the counter-question: Why did the Holy Spirit record them for us in the Scriptures? Surely, that record was not entered to give some amateur a handy jumping-off place for psychological character sketches. The matter was written for those who are willing to view it in the light of Christ and the rest of the Scriptures.

We happen to be thinking of one of Raphael's pictures in the Vatican at Rome. The canvas presents a contrast of light and shadow. In the darkly shaded foreground are a lunatic youth, a despairing father, and a group of disciples, helplessly huddled together. But one of this group is pointing upwards, for the light is there. High on the mountain the Master bathes in radiance. So Raphael divided light from shadow, light above and shadow below.

But the Holy Spirit painted differently in the Gospel account. On His canvas light and shadow are simultaneously present on the mountain top. On God's side, and heaven's, and Christ's, all is light. But on the side of Simon Peter and the militant church all is dark. That is what we must learn to see. Only by seeing both sides at once can we learn from that canvas how necessary the Christ is for us. So we shall be able to appreciate realistically that we rebel against our own salvation, that we, like the typical satans we are by nature, cruelly go counter to God's determinate plan.

And so the night of transfiguration does indeed transcend Christmas eve in significance. But the more we think of that superiority the more we should blush. For the distinguishing feature of this as compared with that other night is that now Christ has mankind, His church, His bride, with Him. But that church is pathetically divided. To the extent that it is already in heaven, its desire merges with heaven's and shows Jesus "his departure which he is to fulfill at Jerusalem." But the militant church, represented by Simon Peter, neither sees nor understands. Planted squarely in the center of the enormities of God's plan, it remains impervious to their significance. No, not impervious; it ventures an appropriate remark. And when it comes, the comment is full of folly and sin. So are things in pathetic contention: militant against triumphant church, flesh against Spirit, human naivete against heaven's law.

There is but One who can substitute unity for the confusion. He is Christ Jesus.

We should be willing to learn personally from this event. If we have in us some of the good characteristics of Simon Peter, we must accept a discipline of them. And we must be purged of the evil which we share with him. We noted that there was good in Peter. An additional comment on that is in place, now that we want to profit from his conduct. The text gives us a helpful hint by the discriminating use of a word. Peter, it tells us, in making his proposal, *"answered* and said." To what, pray was he answering? He had been asked no questions. In fact, he was rubbing the sleep from his eyes when he spoke. Still, the word has a definite connotation. It is this: Peter knew that all of these events upon the mountain concerned him personally. And that is the simple truth. Every redemptive act, every message from heaven, every manifestation of grace, every herald of judgment, in short, every token of revelation concerns us personally. Peter can serve to teach us that the moment God does something we must do something. Events are God's words. And when God speaks, we must answer.

But how, how make an adequate response? How convert the love and fervor we know into an intelligent zeal? Perhaps we can learn by following the narrative to its conclusion. Remember, it closes with the words: Hear Him! Hear Him!

Precisely that had been Peter's error up to this time. He had not listened enough. And as long as we fail to hear, to listen intently to Christ's words, our love and fervor will remain pathetically unintelligent. So long, too, we will continue to taint the atmosphere of God's immaculate holiness.

If anyone, indeed, could have prophesied some worthy thing without the arduous discipline of listening to the preached word, Peter could have done so at this moment. Think of his qualifications. He had the zeal, he had the love, he had that spontaneity of response, that disposition to answer when the facts speak. Besides — and this is remarkable — he had clarity of insight. God Himself illuminated his vision. For you must not fail to take note of one thing. No one had told Peter who were with Christ on the mountain. Yet he recognized them at once. He was sure of it: that one, he said, is Moses, and that other, Elias. He had never seen either. His certain knowledge was owing to the fact that God, as by a sixth sense, clarified his vision, gave him a privilege granted men only in moments of apocalyptic insight, moments in which eternity goes storming through time. Surely, these are special privileges, these which Peter enjoys above all others. Yes, if ever man could immediately have intuited truth, and that without having listened to the preached word, that man was Peter in this hour.

The issue of it, qualifications and all? — Folly and sin.

Now, however, *we* must bare our heads and tremble at the voice from the clouds: "This is my beloved Son; hear Him." The Satan who so summarily profaned the pulpit at Caesarea Philippi is embarrassed now. He has not listened to Jesus' exposition of the inevitability of His passion and death, the one needful thing for the world. Hence he cannot understand heaven's haste. Therefore God's voice thunders through the murkiness and nebulosity of Peter's mind and through that of the militant church. And its burden is: hear Him. Never forsake the pulpit, it admonishes, never leave the prophetic chair at which Jesus sits and explains the dire necessity of His death. Hear Him till He has done.

So God unites the Word which became flesh to the Word of the Scriptures, isolating neither from the other.

And you, religious enthusiasts, are you listening? Mystical souls, impetuous natures, naive children, are you? You, worshippers of spontaneity, gropers-about in your own nebulosity, do you hear the voice from the clouds? Hear Him! That extrasensuous insight, that immediacy of knowledge by which Peter at once recognized heaven-sent guests — perhaps you have often wanted that. But you must hasten to the Word. The Word is more than Peter's intuition. You are jealous of his impromptu utterance, are you? You thought that mood of transporting fear and astonishment the best possible for receptivity to heaven's verities? Hear the voice from the cloud. You must go back to the Word.

If that is the plain teaching of the matter we must be content to have it so. We will let the pulpit stand beside the cross. So only can we keep undisciplined impulse and foolish naivete from saying unbecoming things in Jesus' holy presence. For spontaneous expression we shall have to wait until heaven has welcomed us (and not we, heaven) to the eternal tabernacles. That will be the better day when folly and sin shall be completely purged from the militant church.

When that day comes, we shall be allowed to follow impulse spontaneously again. Then the law will be written upon our hearts. Then that right of impulsive conduct which once made Paradise a delight will be returned to us by God. Any form we chance to grasp will express the essence of holy things. Peter, having heard and heard all the Master's teaching, will by the living Christ be completely conformed to Moses and Elias. And he may build tabernacles then as quickly as he pleases. For in that realm every single tabernacle will exhibit the form and be characterized by the dominant tone of the one great Father's house. "And the Lord will create upon every dwelling place of Mount Zion and upon her assemblies, a cloud and smoke by day, and the shining of a flaming fire by night: for upon all the glory shall be a defense. And there shall be a tabernacle for a shadow in the daytime from the heat, and for a place of refuge, and for a covert from storm and from rain" (Isaiah 4:5, 6).

We leave the picture, knowing that we shall not see the significance the Holy Spirit sought to embody in it if we fix our eyes solely upon Peter, or solely upon Christ. We must, in short, be as charitable to the Holy Spirit as we are to Rembrandt when we go to see one of his canvases. When we look at a Rembrandt we take in light *and* shadow at a glance and so let the spirit of the artist possess us.

Let yourself be captivated in that way by the Spirit of God, who depicted Simon's folly and Christ's glory, both, the one beside the other; depicted, that is, the folly of the sinner and, over against it, the wisdom of our great Prophet; depicted the naivete that invites damnation upon itself and, in stark contrast to it, the inevitable progress of God's determinate counsel, which leads us into life, through Christ Jesus, our Lord.

The Ministering Angel Among Satanic Wolves

CHAPTER THREE

The Ministering Angel Among Satanic Wolves

> ● *Then took Mary a pound of ointment of spikenard,*
> *very costly, and anointed the feet of Jesus. Then said*
> *Jesus, Let her alone: Against the day of my burying*
> *hath she kept this.* —JOHN 12:3a. and 7.

THERE are those who regard the passion of Christ as a progressive series of intensely dramatic events, a series occasionally relieved, however, with God's permission, by a lyrical interlude or two. Such an idyllic intermezzo, they suppose, introduces a pleasant pause into that epic pageantry of blood and sweat, of struggle and tears. To some the legend of Veronica's handkerchief is just such an entr'acte; to others it is the account of the angel who ministered to the Saviour in Gethsemane; and to many it is the story of the anointing of Jesus' feet by Mary at Bethany.

If such an interpretation truly represented the significance of the passion history, that history would very likely contain ample material for a sensitive novel and for a gentle lyric of love. Here is a woman who, from a heart overflowing with love, offers the Saviour a vial of costly spikenard. Here is a house permeated with incense and a priestess who anoints the clothes of the High Priest of our confession with the very aroma which has already suffused her own garments.

However, this construction of the meaning of the Scriptures does not satisfy us. Whoever chose to write a novel, based on this experience at Bethany, and employing only the meager information recorded by the Evangelists, would find, unless he gave his fancy free rein, that he had too little material. And for him to let his imagination run riot would in this case be to profane the story.

The point is that so much is uncertain. We do not know precisely how to fit the account of the anointing at Bethany into the whole structure of the story of that last passion week which Jesus spent on earth. We do not know definitely the date on which the anointing occurred. Nor are we sure of the cost of the spikenard. True, Judas names the value of the gift in round numbers, but his was a rough estimate, albeit by a qualified observer, and, besides, we cannot be sure about the value of the currency of that day or about the standard of living. Furthermore, whether Mary, who anointed Jesus, used all of the ointment in the vial or only some of it is still a matter of dispute. Commentators differ in their interpretation of Jesus' statement, "Against the day of my burying has she *kept* this." Some say the "keeping" has reference to only a part of the ointment; others suppose it refers to all of it.

You see therefore, that any novelist who might care to convert this material into fiction would get little assistance from the Gospel writers. The Gospel is neither a novel nor a sequence of the fragments of one. The Gospel is not a short story. It is the record of God's work in Christ Jesus, given by revelation.

Others there are who cannot take up the Bible without raising psychological problems and proceeding then to solve these in their own way. The account of this anointing very likely provides these with much material for a long and fascinating study. They will have as a "given" this woman who has been bound to Christ by a very intimate relationship of spiritual love for several years, and a small company of people visiting at the home of Simon, once a leper, but later probably healed by Jesus. Whether he is dead or alive now does not affect the matter; his home, at least, remains the meeting place of this group of friends whose common attraction is Jesus. Moreover, the head and the heart of everyone in the company still ponder the—miracle, for it was at Bethany that Jesus not long before had raised Lazarus to life. Yes, there is matter enough, there are complications enough, and there is sufficient impression and expression for an involved psychological study.

Yet, even they who follow this course will find that the biblical data is unsatisfying. They can only guess at much of what happens. In fact, the very deed of sacrifice itself, significantly involved in this, leaves several questions unanswered. Most important of these is whether Mary fetched the vial, broke it, and poured the contents over Jesus in an uprush of affection or whether she had long planned to do so, and, accordingly, had bought the ointment specifically for the purpose. The King James Version, it is true, has Jesus say, "Against the day of my burying hath she *kept* this." Such phrasing does indeed suggest that a deliberate plan rather than a spontaneous impulse motivated her. But in this connection it must be remembered that the rendering of the text at this point is not known to be accurate. It may be that for days and weeks Mary had felt a premonition of Christ's suffering and death. But certainty is lacking. It may also be that the sombre word "burying" was first introduced into the conversation and into the home by Jesus Himself.

In short, the person who is given to making psychological analyses will find the Bible very intractable material. And again, it is no wonder. The Gospel is not a compilation of data, either theoretically or empirically assembled, is not a source-book filled with striking illustrations of psychological phenomena. It is a record of the redemptive work of God in Christ Jesus, a record given by special revelation.

There are others again who follow a third course in "dealing with" this story. As these see it, the Bible is not a unity in which one continuous, progressive history of God's special revelation is recorded, but simply a succession of edifying spiritual treatises. To these the one Word of God becomes many words about God. Accordingly they dismember the one Work of God into several works in some way related to God and religion. Consequently one of their favorite activities is to look for analogies, parallelisms, and allegories among the holy fragments into which they have shattered the Bible, and among the sacred histories. So they discovered, for instance, a story parallel or analogous to the one told in our text in the Song of Solomon. Since that time they write over John 12 this caption from the Song: "While the king sitteth at his table, my spikenard sendeth forth the smell thereof." And so they manipulate similar expressions in other parts of the Scriptures.

And readily we admit that in the love life of the bride of all ages, gifts are proffered in the hands, yearnings breathed from the heart, and songs sung from the lips which all issue from one law, beat time to one rhythm, and are in consonance with one song. To this extent, in this case, too, there most certainly is room for seeking out striking correspondencies and analogies.

But it is important not to forget that a happy comparison of Mary's anointing with an episode in the Song of Solomon, in some other book of the Bible, or with an experience elsewhere recorded, positively does injustice to the Divine meaning of the Gospel, provided the analogy is taken as the whole significance. God's work progresses, passes from stage to stage, from beginning to fulfillment. What He does in reference to Christ today has never been done before in the world. It is a new event, a unique act, occurring now, never to occur again.

Hence those who read the Bible solely to find comparisons and analogies can give no satisfactory account of the narrative in John 12. For instance, the spikenard referred to in the Song of Solomon must, if it is to be made applicable to this chapter at all, be immediately "spiritualized." As a matter of fact, however, Mary's ointment and its vial are both sensuously apperceived objects. And as for the King? He who is here in Simon's house is not seated in royal state at a round table, encircled by twelve knights, but is standing for the moment en route to the cross. No one, therefore, has the right to wrench the account of the anointing at Bethany out of its setting; that is, out of its relationship to Christ's humiliation and death.

No, that method is as wanting as the other two in explaining the significance of the occurrence. And—to repeat a third time—it is no wonder. The Gospel is not of a piece with the noblest book one happens to recall. It is and will ever remain the revelation-given record of God's one, progressive, redemptive work in Christ Jesus, His Son.

We, therefore, must take a different course. Trying, then, to keep this narrative of ointment and love related to the whole history of the passion, we see two things: first, Christ, active in the capacity of His threefold office; and, secondly, God, fulfilling His work and consummating history.

First we observe Christ again accomplishing His threefold task. Moreover, we note that He is both receptively and productively active in each of these offices. He takes and He gives. He takes from God who sends Him and He gives to the people to whom He is sent.

Christ again appears as a Prophet, and as such He is, first of all, receptively active. He absorbs into His being the light of His God. With His whole human soul He eagerly basks in the rays of revelation. He drinks at the fountain of the Scriptures, puts His lips to the sparkling water of the truth of God. He attaches Himself to the source, from which God's truth gushes forth, so securely that He receives it directly, views it from within and without, saturates Himself with it, lives it. That is why Christ, here in Simon's house, so thoroughly lives by the Scriptures. A hymn of Isaiah echoes in His being, and not a single chord, not one note of the song is lost in the God-hewn auditory of His soul. The song is, of course, the very familiar hymn on the "Servant of the Lord." Isaiah sings of Christ's suffering in it, but he also speaks of Christ's glorification. That song depicts the Christ as bearing the sorrows of all men. But it also pictures Him as a victor who shall "see his seed," as one to whom gifts will be brought, one for whom all treasures in heaven and on earth are reserved. And these two lines, that of humiliation and that of glorification, parallel for a while in Isaiah 53, merge at the point where the prophet sings: "He made his grave with the wicked, and with the rich in his death." Isaiah had already seen that men would assign His body to a place of shame, that the people and the government would select the grave of the Man of sorrows, would deliberately seek it out among the wicked and despicable. But he had seen also that the finger of God, the will of the angels, and the hand of justice would share in naming that burying place of the Lord and that these would designate it among the rich. There would be luxury, extravagance, and distinction at His burial because of the righteousness of His soul.

Therefore we honor the Prophet of our confession for so deeply immersing Himself in revelation, for living by it so faithfully, and letting His Messianic consciousness so completely conform His conduct to the Scriptures, that He accepted the costly spikenard and the vial. These probably represented the savings of a lifetime[1], but Jesus accepted them and referred them at once to His burial. He knew that His grave and luxury were appropriate to each other. Here at Bethany He already saw "his grave with the rich." Twice, as we noted, in Caesarea Philippi and on the mountain of transfiguration, He traveled the way of humiliation irresistably in spite of satanic opposition. Thus He experienced Isaiah's prophecy of the fact that men should designate His grave among the wicked. But, in this same moment, as His attitude toward Mary's gift shows, Christ is also absolutely sure that He will be assigned a burying place among the rich. Surely, that is living by the Scriptures.

Or note this other approach. When Zechariah has completed his prophetic work, he asks, "Give me my price." That request is a symbol of the demand the Chief Shepherd makes for His wages, for the reward the grateful soul is willing to give for the tender care of that Shepherd who in Zechariah, later in all of the prophets, and finally in the highest Prophet, Christ Himself, comes as the Good Shepherd to the true Israel. Zechariah pictures God, his sender, as One who insists that His right to wages continues in force and who exercises that right, even though He receives only thirty pieces of silver, the remuneration of a slave, of an outcast. Just so Jesus Christ, the greatest of the prophets, greater too than Zechariah, unhesitatingly accepts His price, here in the house of Simon the leper. Judas, who is present, quickly reckons the value of the ointment and concludes that such a wage is too high for Jesus—he himself being willing to betray the Great Prophet for thirty pieces of silver. But Jesus willingly accepts the reward of three hundred pence, very likely worth about two and a half times as much as the thirty pieces. And He accepts also the love of Mary's heart which is His entirely. He takes His remuneration without demur. Living by the Scriptures, the Great Prophet fulfills His office by laying claim to His reward from every soul to whom He has been the Good Shepherd.

Mark now how Jesus, having receptively done His duty as a Prophet, also becomes active productively. Have you ever con-

---

1. The amount approximately equalled the wages of a common day laborer for a period of three hundred days (one year). Compare Dr. F. W. Grosheide. *Kommentaar op Matteus*, p. 311, note.

sidered how Jesus by accepting luxury as becoming His burial must have astonished His disciples? He had just been teaching them that He was to die as a criminal, as One despised and rejected by the people and government. And in that situation it is more natural to think of the "burial of an ass," to use biblical language, of a being hauled away and thrown out than of an expensive funeral. On the mountain of transfiguration, in fact, these disciples had been exhorted to "hear Him." Now, having tried hard and painfully to get used to the idea of Jesus' curse and humiliation, they marvel to see Him accept extravagance as befitting His death.

Really, this Prophet is a hard teacher. He proposes riddle after riddle. A person has hardly grown accustomed to one thing before He suggests another, apparently contradictory to it.

And, looking at the matter thus, we, too, are inclined to regard the story of the anointing, at first hearing it, as a gentle idyll in the drama of the passion. It seems to be a lyrical episode, attractive to all who hear it. But, viewing it in its great setting, we say of it: This is a hard message; who can bear to hear it? Ah yes, Lord, there is but one answer: Hear Him, hear Him!

In the second place, Christ appears as a Priest. Again He is receptive first; that is, His priestly soul lives in and is sustained by God, who created it. As a Priest, He is so thoroughly imbued with the spirit of His office that He Himself is the first to mention the word "burial." It is priestly to pause, when the sun is shining and love is beaming from Mary's eyes, to pause on the bridge that arches the passion and to peer into the chasm where God's wrath lowers continually. Furthermore it is a readiness typical of the priest to relate every event that occurs immediately to suffering and death. Look: a pearl is being given the Saviour, very costly—vial, spikenard, tears, and a very great love. But before it can actually be extended to Him He is already holding out His handbag, laced with the crepe of mourning, to receive it. How sensitive He is to God's program, how He absorbs truth from the fountain of God's will, now beginning to be active in the matter of the great sacrifice. Most compassionate is this holy heart which anticipates God's hours of sacrifice with a pure and delicate humanity.

As Priest, too, the Saviour becomes productive. A good priest understands the frail, and leads the hesitant tenderly to the altar of thanksgiving. So this High Priest shields Mary's modest demeanor from the cruel censorship of the bystanders. He protects the dove from the vulture and then gladly accepts the offer of gratitude. He comforts the soul He is compelled to wound. Yes, Jesus also wounds Mary. Even if she had anticipated the coming drama of suffering, burial, and death, it was still terrible for her to hear the shocking word "burying" from His lips. We anticipate so many things which, when they come in their naked, undisguised actuality, nevertheless hurt the soul cruelly. But this Priest is kind to console. He takes Mary's gift. He assures her that her good work will become memorable, that the perfume of her spikenard will escape from the four walls of Simon's house and permeate the world. As a Priest he recites to her the words:

> Nothing remaineth,
> Nothing remaineth.
> Even the beautiful succumbs to the stain;
> But whatever in love was given to Jesus,
> That keeps its worth and will ever remain.

And this, above all, is priestly: When, in anticipating His burial, Christ allowed God's will to be realized in Him, He fixed the attention of His heart and mind upon His death, and so He began to make His own great Sacrifice.

Again, Christ proves to be King; receptive first, and productive then. So inextricably has His kingly function become a part of Him that He is absolutely convinced of His uniqueness, of His distinctiveness. It is a royal speech to say, "Ye have the poor always with you, but me ye have not always." In making it, Christ manifests the right of kings, for it is a king's prerogative to declare, "I first, and then thou." Now Jesus steps ahead of all of His brothers and sisters and says, as once Elijah did: "Make me thereof a little cake first . . . . and after make for thee." Meanwhile He is, of course, leaving room for the priestly service of benevolence—ye have the poor always with you. But as a King He wants the choicest things, the sheerest luxury to be reserved for Him. He is insistent upon the fact that there be no psuedo-democracy in the "civitas dei," the kingdom of heaven, no democracy in which the citizens help themselves and leave the

chance scraps of the table for the king. In His kingdom He would
eliminate the friction between the people and the monarch. But
note also that as a Ruler He is also a Priest. He gives as well as
takes. He is a Monarch who is also the Head of the body. Therefore His demands upon the citizenry are never independent of
His services to them. Serve them He does; else He were not the
Head. But He also makes demands. Otherwise He were no
King. It is His inalienable right to tax the people. "An expensive ornament," sneer some when they hear the word "king"
mentioned in our day. Precisely. Our King is an expensive ornament and He knows it. But He is also the very foundation
and—He paid His price, He gave His own life. Surely a King
who on this basis accepts as His due even the extravagant gifts
which love offers Him in rich profusion is thoroughly conscious
of His royal office.

The King is productive. He takes the gifts which rightly belong to royalty. He restores harmony to His quarreling subordinates, the disciples. As the Creator of the world, coming into
His kingdom, He now asks, in the language of the 50th Psalm,
for the "gold" and the "silver," and for "the cattle upon a thousand hills." Even though He is a Great Candidate for the darkest of graves, He insists upon these as a Monarch.

And so our attention in conclusion looks up from Christ to
God who anoints Him. The anointing at Bethany is a subsidiary part of the whole work of God's special revelation and grace
as it has progressed up to this time. Do you sense the significant
harmony? Twice on the threshold of the temple of sorrows God
confronted His Son with a satan in the form of flesh and blood,
with the satan in Simon Barjona. But that same God today
places a ministering angel upon His path. Satan and angel, both,
appear in human form. In short, the whole world of flesh that
is in enmity to Him and the whole world of spirit that extends
offers to Him are impressed upon His mind in the form of common words and experiences.

Those, then, who are looking to this story to find an idyllic
respite from the passion of Christ will be disappointed to learn
that even this ministering angel, whose name is Mary, can execute her loving purpose only in a setting of evil interlocutors. Hell's

foulest vapors mingle with the incense of the spikenard. Mary's gentle worship clashes with Judas' critical censorship; his whole being is in resentment against her. And the other disciples, too, are critical in their attitude toward her, for they do not fully appreciate the fact that God is here preparing His Son for what must come. It is as though God is offering His Christ a diamond, but has had it set in a cross. If His Son is to take the precious stone, He must take up the cross also and go to do God's will.

So is the conflict between spirit and flesh aggravated not only in the Christ but also around Him. The satanic opposition coming from Peter's lips first and then from those of Judas, and the ministration of love fully informing Mary's gift—these show that the struggle of spiritual forces in the air has been carried over to the small company of people assembled at the house of Simon the leper. Ah yes, coming to Jesus means exposing oneself to conflict.

We bare our heads in reverence. Who among that group in Simon's house understood the purpose of the Lord save Christ Himself? And who called forth the spirit of the Lord save the Redeemer alone? Put off thy shoes from thy feet; for the place where the leper once lay is holy ground. Now has the Saviour's soul been caught between the spiritual forces of the air and the spiritual energies of the kingdom of heaven, and He is being tossed to and fro by them.

The two lines of emphasis in Isaiah 53, that of humiliation and that of exaltation, meet at a point and form a scathing right angle provocative of passionate conflict. But Jesus remains poised in this passion. And He proceeds straight from the threshold into the vestibule of the house of sorrows. Just as the cyclonic gust of Simon's satanic utterance could not make Him hesitate, so the sweet incense of Mary's ointment cannot entice Him back out of doors. Behold, He cometh, O God, to do Thy will. In that conflict of antithetical forces, of hate and love, of ministering angels and satanic wolves, He remains one and undivided.

That, for those who would read the Scriptures in the light these shed upon themselves, is a little, though not one-half, of the meaning of the Gospel which tells of Mary who anointed the feet of Jesus. For it is a Gospel which tells, not of Mary, but of Christ.

And this besides with reference to that anointing. Never in history has there occurred such another. For to what purpose had the oil of anointing always been poured except to mark externally and to strengthen internally the bearer of the office of prophet, priest, and king? Behold, He is here, discharging the responsibilities of that threefold office in full capacity. His name is Anointed, Anointed of the Spirit, Christ of God. To Him this pouring out of oil is a great comfort and an eternal mandate, and to us it is a sacred revelation. For now He, Jesus of Nazareth, whom no one in the great wide world would anoint with oil, whose official right and capacity is denied by all flesh, now He receives that ointment from the hand of His Father. Heaven lets it drip through Mary's hands upon His blessed body. So He was twice anointed: first by the incomparable Spirit; now also with the symbol of oil proffered Him as love's choicest gift.

Now, if anyone would care to ponder these matters further, he would perhaps soar no higher than to the exalted thought that the angels in heaven never knew a more blessed hour than when they witnessed this first true anointing. For this one was genuine, at least on one side. Previous pourings out of oil had always been doubly polluted, had never been perfectly holy. The ointment had been tainted by the hand of him who poured it; the anointed person had never lived sinlessly, not even during the brief process of the sacrament.

At this instant a miracle takes place. Yes, even here at Bethany love has not entirely cleansed the offensive odor of sin from the oil or from the proffering heart. But the Anointed Himself is true, and good, and beautiful in knowledge, righteousness, and holiness. This, therefore, is not an instance of anointing making rich the anointed. It is that of an Anointed One who takes the oil which has been consecrated to Him, purges it, and pours it again over love's trembling hands. To this end that love may confess Him thus: My oil is found in Thee. Thou art the Christ, God's Anointed, Thou alone, Thou perfectly, Thou who preparest thine own oil.

The Last Priest Pointing to the Last Sacrificial Lamb

CHAPTER FOUR

The Last Priest Pointing to the Last Sacrificial Lamb

● *And one of them, named Caiaphas, being the high priest that same year, said unto them, Ye know nothing at all, nor consider that it is expedient for us, that one man should die for the people, and that the whole nation perish not. And this spake he not of himself: but being high priest that year, he prophesied that Jesus should die for that nation; and not for that nation only, but that also he should gather together in one the children of God that were scattered abroad.*
                                                    —JOHN 11:49-52.

THREE times now we have seen the Father hurl His Christ into the concussion of spiritual forces. Twice we witnessed Satan's attempt by means of the spoken word to drive a wedge into the firm breastwork of Jesus' soul. Once we scented the incense of spiritual ministration. Both, the satanic protest and the loving service, came to Jesus by way of daily experiences and by means of flesh and blood.

At this point the Scriptures go farther and outline to us the relationship between that satanical element which is born in hell and that prophetic influence which comes from heaven.

Today we stand before the chair of Caiaphas. Joseph Caiaphas is the last high priest to whom God Himself still allows the distinction of being Israel's highest official. His heart ponders satanic thoughts, and in this the Sanhedrin is his ally. But the Spirit of prophecy still broods over the hall in which these are assembled. Therefore, although in its secret thrust Caiaphas' statement issues from the depths of hell, in its prophetic implications it reaches up to heaven. And—what is more important— the Spirit of truth impinges upon the Spirit of Caiaphas from above and, no thanks to him, of course, permits him to utter that profound phrase in which the whole system of God's providence and the whole scheme of His redemptive plan is epitomized: One man must die for all!

Again God's ways prove stronger than those of men. Simon Peter became a satan to Jesus twice. He did so unwittingly. Mary became a ministering angel, and did not know it. Caiaphas actually prophesies; and he is unaware of it, for he gives his advice and pronounces his prophecy *not of himself*.

Another point immediately strikes the attention. When Peter, the disciple, proved to be a satan to Jesus, his protest was not related to the deepest individuality of his believing and regenerate soul. The significance of Mary's ministration of love may have transcended her comprehension immeasurably, but her conduct certainly was related to the quintessential attitude of her soul and was an organic outgrowth of it. So it is with those in whom the Spirit of Christ is active. When they speak Satan's language they play in a grotesquely unsuitable rôle; when they speak the language of the Holy Spirit they do not act but live the part in congenial responsiveness.

Not so with Caiaphas and his subordinates. When Caiaphas says things born from the spirit of hell, he speaks in conformity with his essential individuality. The satanic in his words is vitally related to his real self. That is his condemnation. And conversely, his prophesying of the Christ is not in its broadest implications, in its profoundest sense, and in its God-glorifying reference, a true expression of the disposition of his soul. That is because there is a great gulf between the *delight* of this prophet, parading there before his God, and the *burden* of the Lord which still allows him his exalted seat. That, too, is his condemnation.

Caiaphas prophesies today as once Balaam did, when, in spite of himself, he praised the "Star out of Jacob" and named blessed all those upon whom its rays fell. Thus Saul prophesied at Ramah while seeking David, the true king of the morrow, and Samuel, the true prophet of the day. Saul too was compelled to prophesy; he did so in spite of himself because the Spirit of prophecy seized upon and overwhelmed him.

Draw your own conclusion. When Saul wanted to prevent the theocratic king in David from coming to the fore, and to kill the theological prophets in Samuel, he thereby shattered the oneness in that memorable trilogy: the sacred priesthood, the true prophecy, and the theocratic kingship. By prophesying he dug his own grave; that is, the corrupt official, Saul, was compelled by the Spirit of true prophecy and of heavenly irony, to make room for the official to come, one appointed by God, and one who would discharge the duties of his office in purity and virtue.

Tremble, O man, and mark how God does precisely that but in fulfillment now as Caiaphas prophesies today before the Sanhedrin. Caiaphas is another such office-holder. He is a "called" official. He, too, prophesies about the only High Priest and the eternal King. Again that Spirit of prophecy is present. Again the same terrible, holy irony manifests itself. Caiaphas also, making his prophetic utterance against his own will, digs his own grave. The Spirit of Christ compels him at his own expense to make room for Christ Jesus, the highest official of God and man.

That in itself is another great mystery. Christ must come to the world over the graves of Israel's dead office-bearers. But before He comes, God calls upon heaven and earth to witness that the grave in which Caiaphas will be interred, and with him the last remnants of Israel's official-spiritual existence, will not be digged by God but by the mummied traditionalists of a dispossessed generation.

It was a noteworthy session of the Sanhedrin, that of which John tells us something. We read of its meeting, presided over by Caiaphas, at the close of Chapter 11. The chapter first tells of the great miracle that had occurred to Lazarus. He had died in Bethany and had been buried, but the voice of Jesus, the Good Shepherd, had called him from the grave and returned him, a living man, to Mary's love, to Martha's cares, and to the astonished gaze of a multitude.

Came the question, of course: Just what is this? What is the meaning and what are the implications of this redemptive event? Everyone was asking it, in Bethany and also at Jerusalem. By no means last of all the query came to the Sanhedrin, Israel's official information service. There especially it pressed for an answer.

The question comes to us, too. We know that we could not answer it without the Scriptures. A fact remains a mystery unless God discovers its meaning in His Word. As it is, we have that prophetic word, and it is very sure. It clearly indicates the real meaning of Lazarus' being called from the dead. The Divine thought revealed in that astonishing miracle already was expressed in Isaiah's prophecy when he said that the Messiah and His coming could be recognized hereby that the blind receive their sight, the lame walk, the deaf hear, the *dead are raised up,* and the poor have the Gospel preached to them.

Christ, before He raised up Lazarus, applied this prophecy to Himself and so signified its meaning. Between the time of Isaiah's pronouncing it and Lazarus' being raised from the dead that significant hour intervened in which Jesus told the messengers of John the Baptist that, to those who have faith, He can prove Himself to be the Christ by the fact that the blind see, the deaf hear, the lame walk, the dead are raised, and the poor are comforted by the Gospel. Hence Christ, before He called Lazarus from the grave, had become Isaiah's highest interpreter and exegete. Now the whole world may determine His genuineness by asking whether the things predicted of the Messiah by all of God's prophets, Isaiah foremost among them, are true of Him.

Consequently the God of majesty, the God of Psalm 50, the God of truth, exhorts Israel in firm tones and with the plea of love to look upon the open tomb of Lazarus and to acknowledge in their own day that Jesus of Nazareth is the Christ. He calls upon them to testify that the Messianic prophecy has been fulfilled, here before their own eyes and ears, in Lazarus' stumbling from the tomb, in Mary's cry of joy as she rushes to receive him, and in those words of Jesus: "Father, I thank thee that thou hast heard me: And I know that thou hearest me always."

That was the divine thought expressed in the raising of Lazarus, and by that miracle God now knocks at the door of the Sanhedrin, and for the last time asks for admittance and acknowledgement. By that miracle the powers of a coming age rushed to the rescue of a people almost lost. It was a bolt of God's lightning. It came to lick the world with its cleansing tongue, to burn the earth clean, to consume the chaff of unbelief and obstinacy, and so leave a soil in which the spiritual seed could grow again.

The Sanhedrin saw the lightning. Its dazzling brilliance penetrated the thick curtains with which they had hoped to keep the rays of truth shut out of their assembly hall. The scent of its smoldering crept into the closely shuttered house of Israel's last tribunal of justice. The nostrils of Caiaphas and his fellows sensed it. They must take careful thought. They must answer the question that presses all for answer.

What will that reply be? So much is certain: The issue is clear-cut: Jesus of Nazareth is the Christ or He is the Antichrist. He is the Messiah or He is the Beast. Either He is chief of the magicians of the kind that withstood Father Moses in the country of Egypt—and, if so, He far excels these in proficiency—or He is the legal fulfillment of Father Moses. If that is true the powers of revelation and gifts of grace have passed out of Moses into Him. Those are the alternatives. One or the other is true. The miracle that gave life to Lazarus cannot be "neutral" or void of significance.

But the Sanhedrin does not know that. Israel's official rulers, priests, and prophets cannot understand the meaning of events any longer. They do not see the significance of facts.

That they do not understand is not the worst of it. Intellectual comprehension of objective truth, and that alone, justifies no one. Therefore failure to rationally understand objective truth condemns no one. Such failure is not the cause of the condemnation. It may be one of the symptoms, may be one of the means by which the curse realizes itself in man, it may even be one of the items in the verdict, but intellectual error, solely, can never be the cause of a person's degeneration. No, the logical formulation of problems, of their rationalization, is not the quintessence of sin, for that essence is a self-assertion of the flesh in the deepest heart of man. It is a self-assertion which musters all of the energies of the heart and soul into its service in order to escape from the embarrassment of God and prophecy.

The Sanhedrin confesses to such self-vindication. What do they say? Why, that "the whole world goes after him."[1]

And that is the simple truth. Now that He has done "many other miracles"[2] and has raised Lazarus the whole world does follow Jesus. But—we should like to suggest to this group who are seated to have justice done—but just that fact should provoke you to anxiously hasten to the Scriptures, to God, and to the Holy Spirit. For it is quite clear: Jesus is anti-Christ or He is not that. If He is that, you, when you see that the world is following Him, should sound the alarm before your God and for His sake. You know Him as the God of your fathers, the God who, when the prophets, confronting false prophecy, asked Him for a sign to vindicate their genuineness before the world and before the covenant people, never left them without such vindication even though the miracle sometimes came as a judgment of God. If He is the Antichrist, sound the alarm!

If this Nazarene has accomplished the miracle at Bethany through Beelzebub, the prince of the devils, and if this Antichrist has ignited the fireworks of "signs and wonders of deception" at your very door, you can do only one thing: Raise holy hands to heaven, if you can. Call to your God! Make your session hall a miniature Carmel (although in a sense a large one)! Petition your God to tear the heavens open and to reveal at last the promised, true Messiah! For, if the Antichrist has come, the hour of the true Messiah must have struck. This, then, you know with strictest certainty: Here are the powers of the coming age revealed. Act accordingly and you will at least be eschatologically active. For the ends of the ages rest with you.

Or, and this is the other alternative, you can say that the Man who defeated the grave at Bethany is not Antichrist or one of his precursors, but the Christ Himself or His herald. Of course, if that is true, it is plainly your duty to ask Caiaphas to come down from his chair, to open the scroll of prophecy, and to have him point out to you all that the Promised One of the fathers has come "unto his own."

---

1. John 12:19; compare also 11:47.
2. John 11:47.

The crisis has come. The chair of Caiaphas is being threatened by the judgment seat of God. Who is to occupy it? The forces of the coming era are here. Let the Nazarene be Antichrist or one of his a hundred times, this much is plain: God is even now coming into His kingdom.

Really, it is a difficult matter for the Sanhedrin. To questions of such momentous importance no one can give a nicely formulated answer off-hand. Nevertheless, at any such time as that in which this body finds itself, the needful thing is to open the Scriptures, to let prophecy shed upon the events of the day the light of special revelation. That is their duty and they must undertake it for two reasons: first, for Israel's sake; and, secondly, for their own.

For Israel's sake, O Sanhedrin, you must explain Jesus' miraculous signs in the light of special revelation, of prophecy. Have you not read of the prophet, Zechariah, who classified the shepherds and separated the false ones, who abandoned the people and fed themselves, from the true ones who come not to be served but to serve, from those who will find their crown in the one Good Shepherd, who will sacrifice Himself, will seek the young ones, will feed the sheep, will heal them, and rescue them from the claws of death. Well, then, you who read the scrolls and officiously claim to "expound" prophecy to the people, say now, and that in unmistakable tones, who is this Nazarene, this sheep of Israel's flock, this "Son of Abraham," who rescued Lazarus from the claws of death and greatly comforted Mary and Martha? Are His the features of the false shepherd? Or is He the good Shepherd or one of His precursors? Surely you who claim to explain prophecy may leave nothing undone until you have pointed out the precise relationship between those prophetic visions and this recent miracle. Rise to the occasion. Be shepherds of your people. The false prophet, says Zechariah, will not "wear a rough garment to deceive" as long as the true prophets remain alert. If the Nazarene has done the signs of deception through Beelzebub, obviously you must rush to the aid of your poor, misguided people, and, in the name of the Scriptures, must tear the rough garment off the shoulders of the imposter. Or, in the other case, you must summon the people to come and, to-

gether with yourselves, to bow down before and become subject
to His leadership. Whatever the case may be, it is your inescapable duty to discover the criterion by which the true prophecy
may be distinguished from the false. Either you must punish
the false prophet or you will be forever rejected from the shepherd's office. Then the good Shepherd will feed His flock alone.

That touches on the second reason for which the Sanhedrin
must do the necessary thing: consult the Scriptures. Its members must do that for their own sake, because their office, their
position is being threatened. Note the distinctiveness of that
position. Caiaphas is in the presiding officer's chair. The spot
which that chair occupies has, by God's own direction, up to this
time been the highest point of the whole spiritual world. Israel
leads the nations spiritually. In Israel the Sanhedrin is the highest tribunal of justice to which the treasures of God's revelation
are still entrusted.   In that body, in turn, Caiaphas holds the
ranking position. Hence it is making no sweeping statement to
say that Caiaphas' chair rests on the very vortex of the spiritual
world, on the pinnacle of the nations. Caiaphas' own aristocratic
self-assurance knows that, too. The Sanhedrin knows and prides
itself on the fact that it stands at the glistening top of the religious life of the world.

The Sanhedrin knows that, but . . . there is one thorn in the
flesh. From the plateau of secular life, not in Jerusalem but at
Rome, another peak is rising. It is the dome of the Capitol. Beneath it is Caesar's throne. Just as Caiaphas wants his presiding
officer's chair to rest on the apex of the spiritual world, so Caesar wants his throne to represent the highest authority in things
secular, especially in those derived from physical might. The
position of Caiaphas is spiritually both at the center and top of
the world, and he would therefore have all things subject to it.
But Caesar's throne, central and paramount in the whole secular
world, would subject to it all that moves and has being among
the peoples.

Just what status, then, does the Sanhedrin still enjoy? Rome has
overshadowed Jerusalem, and Caesar's secular authority laughs
haughtily and derisively at the spiritual pretenses of Caiaphas and
his fellows. What gathers at Jerusalem today looks very much

the mangled remains of what was once a flourishing body. So pathetically little is left of the three offices which Israel once possessed. Prophecy has been still these many years. The priest who presides here now has not been able to keep the bond uniting him with Aaron unimpaired. Only by long and arduous competition with foreign tyranny and inner self-decay has the priesthood been able to rescue its cloak from the burning embers of Israel's existence. Really, if the Sanhedrin, frail as it is already, is hesitant in this critical moment in which the whole world goes after Jesus, it is altogether lost. True, the hour has not yet spent itself in which that body can say, by reason of God's voice in Israel's history: We are the legal office-holders; this place is the top of the world; here God's foot touches on the earth.

But now they must know what they are doing. That matter concerning Lazarus affects them personally. Can they annex for themselves the miraculous sign at Bethany and the language God speaks in it? If so, they are safe for the time being. Far be it from them, then, to cut the knot God Himself has tied for them with the dumb power of the sword. Prophecy alone, not Rome's brute force, can save them today. To kill Jesus with the sword is to summon the aid of the Caesar on that other world height. To call in the help of the Roman sword is *ipso facto* to surrender their offices; by that act they automatically sever themselves from their international distinctiveness and official rank. No, no. Let Rome keep her secular sword. They have another, the two-edged sword of the Word of God. Ah, Sanhedrin, do not look for a weapon in Rome's arsenal, but search the Scriptures!

Alas, Caiaphas does not and the Sanhedrin does not. They can see only one thing: the world goes after Him. And by that they mean: the world is leaving us.

That is more than they can countenance. So they begin to look for arguments. They play a rôle. They try to rationalize their self-assertion, to give their self-vindication the color of piety. Hear the president: Surely it is expedient that we put the Nazarene to death, for only by that method can we save Israel. Even though He be a legitimate child of Abraham—we will not discuss that now—it is better that this one member be cut off from the body than that the whole organism perish. You know the logic of every Pharisee—if we save Israel there is still hope for the world. But know this, that if we do not kill Him, the Romans will come, fearing the riot which the Nazarene has already provoked, and will rob us of the last vestiges of self-government which we still possess. Gentlemen, it is plain: One must die for all, one for all!

Apparently that was not the language of an oracle; it was just good diplomatic prudence. But the Holy Spirit who writes the Gospel points out something else. He tells us that behind that diplomatic speech, matter of fact and adapted to the occasion as it was, lay the one great principle common to all bearers of the prophetic word. When Caiaphas announced that one must die for all, he closed the peroration of the last offer-seeking, priestly speech with the words which from the beginning of time were written in the Book of God as the *ultima ratio* of the Counsel of Peace: One die for all.

In this meeting at a point of the line of God's thoughts with that of Caiaphas' fleshly argumentations, which are plainly satanic, we taste, by reason of God's own direction, the sweet yet bitter taste, first, of heavenly, holy irony, and secondly, of hell-born and sinful sarcasm.

That heavenly and holy irony is sublime but perturbing. Is it not unconscionable? To kill Jesus in order to save "Christ"? The Sanhedrin decides to put the Nazarene out of the way in order that the people of Abraham, that indispensable leaven in the loaf of civilization, may not be eliminated from the nations. They suppose they are doing God a favor, by safeguarding Israel and preserving unimpaired the eschatological realm over which the Messiah is to rule. Israel's last great tribunal of justice, you see, does not want God to be of service to it, but wants, instead, to serve God. It wants to serve God by making sure that the place designed for the Messiah is kept vacant, and by saving His realm for His kingship.

This had constantly been the prevailing motif of the Pharisaic, fleshly theology. Time and again that emphasis on a gospel of self-righteousness has tried to build and decorate God's throne for Him so that at His coming He could sit down passively and rest. The legions of Israel's secular children were placed at the service of Prince Messiah, who could hardly be expected to rule without the help of His faithful soldiers. It is in that spirit that the Sanhedrin now lays down, as a practical rule, the law: one must die for all. And it punctuates its pious intent with this prayer of thanksgiving: O God, Israel's God, we come here not to be served, but to serve.

Meanwhile God is giving a different meaning to that profound principle of conflict which Caiaphas employed. He explains the meaning of His secret counsel for our redemption in a diametrically opposite way. For the Son of man comes not to be ministered unto but to minister and to give His life as a ransom for many.

This is the awful, the holy, the Divine in heaven's irony. Heaven and hell simultaneously grasp the pen and write, each on a separate scroll, the great law of every epoch, the basic principle of time and eternity. One for all. Satan's revolution and God's reformation employ the same first principle. That principle is the conclusion of Caiaphas' false prophecy; it is also that of all of God's true prophets. Balaam pointed to the Star of Jacob. Isaiah also pointed to it. A cry rises from the depths of hell; a cry sounds from the heights of heaven. It is the same cry: One must die for all.

But when hell flings these fascinating words into the world and has them taken up into the minutes of the last great but fleshly tribunal, it thereby pronounces a principle opposite in meaning from the one God proclaims when He gives to the world the same rule for healing and acquittal. At both tribunals, that above and that below, the verdict reads alike. But the reasoning of the cases is different.

When God announces the principle that one must die for all He thereby introduces the concept of substitution into the world, an idea derived from Himself in His exalted counsel and embodied concretely in the Man, Christ Jesus. By sending that man into death as the one sacrifice of that law of substitution, God affirms that Jesus is the Christ. But by that same token God also declares that Jesus, because He is the Christ, takes with Him into the grave and afterwards into life the whole body of

His people. In life and in death, says God, Jesus fulfills the concept of Christ.

But when Satan by way of Caiaphas announces the same law, it is precisely his intent to charm the idea of substitution out of the world. For, according to his clever rationalization, Jesus is not the Head of the body in whom the whole organism dies and is buried, but He appears in that body as the one defective spot, the tumor, which must be cut away so that the body may live. By virtue of God's attestation, Jesus is the embodiment of the true spiritual Israel. According to the argument of Caiaphas, Jesus, so far from being the root which gives rise to the tree and sends its fructifying juices into it, is the parasite wasting Israel's organism. "One for all," says the Gardener above, as He sees all branches grafted into that one root, first with the curse and then with the blessing. "One for all," says Caiaphas, flattered by the nicety of his solution, as he, the Chief Pruner, cuts off that one wild branch in order to save the others. For Caiaphas does not know that Jesus Christ is the root of Israel's tree, absorbing curse and blessing, death and life, rejecting all of the dead, and taking with Him into His humiliation and exaltation only the true branches. Believing that Christ is the one parasite on Israel's precious cypress tree, Caiaphas prunes that branch away. Let that one die for all, he says, and the God of Abraham, Isaac, and Jacob will substitute for the Nazarene thorn Abraham's memorial fir tree, and the offensive brier of Nazareth will give rise to the myrtle tree of Father Jacob, and it shall be to the Lord for a name, for an everlasting sign that shall not be cut off.

Two interpretations, then, of "one for all." The one deduces from it the concept of substitution; the other reads into it the hypothesis of elimination. God declares: no reconciliation without fulfillment; and Caiaphas protests: no perfecting without pruning. Both interpretations, therefore, diametrically opposed as they are, conclude with the same epitome: one for all. And both commentators, the one above and the one below, sing as a grand finale to their verdict that refrain of Isaiah: Instead of the thorn shall come up the fir tree, and instead of the brier shall come up the myrtle tree: And it shall be to the Lord for a name, for an everlasting sign that shall not be cut off.

Whether one takes the way of Caiaphas, the way from below upwards, or the way of the Word, the way from above downwards, one arrives at the same world-principle: one for all. None can escape that solution. But it is the interpretation given it which determines everlasting weal or woe. The phrase condemns whoever explains it according to the flesh. But whoever accepts it from the mouth of God Himself, interprets it in the light of the crucified Christ, and believes, he shall be given eternal life abundantly.

Such is the irony that fills us with awe and demands of us who we are, members of the Sanhedrin, asserting ourselves against God, or children of the spiritual Israel, bowing our heads and saying: Lord, help me lest I perish!

We said that there was also a manifestation of satanic sin in this concluding statement of the next to the last Sanhedrin[1] session in which, by the grace of God, that body was permitted to sit. That sin still infests the world. Even today Caiaphas' solution to the problem of conflict is still in vogue. Let one die for all—that is the battle cry of every revolution. The world still wants to wade through the blood of a minority to a blissful state for the majority. When revolution so gluts itself with human blood it is still pointing its sword at the heart of Jesus Christ. For now as well as then He is an obstacle in the way of every Sanhedrin, a hindrance to all self-assertion. Mankind, therefore, would still brush Him aside.

Now, too, however, righteousness always punishes sin. The history of the Sanhedrin repeats itself. Today they would put Jesus out of the way in order to quell a riot; a few years later they are themselves the cause of rebellion. So it will ever be in the world. Each revolution carries the seeds of its disintegration within itself, for each tries to drive out the devil by means of the devil.

And now, with respect to what concerns us in this tragic conflict, we will care to see the thread of God's prophecy unraveled,

---

1. The last was that in which Christ was condemned; after that the veil of the temple was rent: the Sanhedrin was dismissed.

care to be led out of the maze of our thoughts safely by His hand.

Certainly what we have witnessed was tragic enough. But there is room, too, for great joy. Not the Sanhedrin, but Christ and His Spirit dominated the scene; in fact, they made this history in their own power. Jesus Christ did not darken the sun of Israel's sages. He did not trample the crown of the rulers into the dust. He let these accomplish their destruction themselves. He came to His own not as one who had broken law and office, but as the One person who fulfilled both of these. The priesthood committed suicide. Prophecy allied itself with Balaam and with Saul. The kingship ignored Israel's prophets by viewing the nation not in a spiritual, theocratic light, as that was so vividly illustrated at the grave of Lazarus, but by solving a spiritual problem with the coarsest weapon of the flesh—the sword. The last priest pointed to the last Lamb, and he said of it: Unclean, unclean. He sacrificed it not by way of satisfying the altar, but by way of protecting it for a future already lost. So did Israel's officialdom annihilate themselves.

The true Prophet, Priest, and King therefore comes to the world fully authorized. Now it is His hour and that of the power of darkness and of light. He will have to die, yes, for so heaven's law also declares. But the angels of God know already that His death means *life*. And he who listens to the law *one for all* in fear and trembling will not say that this doctrine annihilates the will; he will not repeat the words Ibsen allowed his Brand to utter:

> Will, the weakling, hides his head;—
> One man died for them of yore.[1]

Nor will he cast himself down the precipice and say in despair:

> Not for us the cup He drank,
> Not for us the thorny wreath,
> In His temples drove its teeth,
> Not for us the spear-shaft sank
> In the side whose life was still.
> Not for us the burning thrill
> Of the nails that clove and tore.[2]

1. *Brand*, Transl. by C. H. Herford, Scribners, 1894, p. 256.
2. *Ibid.*, p. 259.

Instead, he who has listened to this law proclaimed in an evangelical spirit will write beneath it the prayer:

> I thank thee, Father, that thou hast given me these words with thine own lips. Take me into Thy heart and cleanse me with the blood that satisfies Thee and reconciles my soul with Thee for all eternity. O God, the minutes of this next to the last legal session of the Sanhedrin were probably burned in the fire that destroyed Jerusalem. May the journal of my life not be its sequel, for that certainly would be destroyed by the fire that shall presently destroy the world. Nay, Lord, I would not keep my own diary. Teach me to read instead the *Acta* of the Counsel of Peace for thy Name's sake.

One for all! For me, too, my Lord and my God.

Christ Evaluated

CHAPTER FIVE

Christ Evaluated

● *Then one of the twelve, called Judas Iscariot, went unto the chief priests, and said unto them, What will ye give me, and I will deliver him unto you? And they covenanted with him for thirty pieces of silver.*
                                        —MATTHEW 26:14-15.

● *And I said unto them, If ye think good, give me my price; and if not, forbear. So they weighed for my price thirty pieces of silver. And the Lord said unto me, Cast it unto the potter: a goodly price that I was prised at of them.*   —ZECH. 11:12-13.

IN commenting on the words written at the head of this chapter, we shall not just at this time speak of Judas Iscariot. We shall give him our attention later.

First we want to point out the relationship between these passages and the episode upon which we centered our attention in the preceding treatise. We observed there, you recall, that Caiaphas and his Sanhedrin actually prophesied without being aware of the fact that they were doing so. We saw, moreover, that he and the other members of his solemn council refused to take the one way by which they might have returned to the road of sound prophecy: the way of believing, restrictive, and honest searching of the Scriptures.

The consequences of such spiritual indifference are never negligible. If we are not conscious, willing, wholly consecrated bearers of the prophetic word, we become its victims. If we refuse to become the subject of prophecy, we are compelled to become its object. If we are not vitally related to the content of the Word, our life becomes the pitiable victim of all of the forces and influences of the kingdom of heaven, which are expressed in that Word. When we are in enmity to these, they destroy us. We must live by prophecy, or we will most certainly die by it. And it never misses a victim.

The point is that the Spirit of prophecy cannot possibly leave anyone in a neutral position. God has sent His Word into the world: its effects are irrelevant to none.

This inescapable relevancy of the Word of God becomes especially obvious from a consideration of the present texts. Judas Iscariot has appeared before the Sanhedrin[1] and presented to them his proposal offering to deliver Jesus to them in exchange for a given sum of money. Asked how much they will give for such service, the chief priests reply that they will pay thirty pieces of silver. That amount, the exact value of which we do not know, but which becomes a considerable sum when we remember that it equaled the wages of a laborer for a period of 120 days,[2] apparently satisfied Judas.

This disgusting piece of business on the part of Judas and the chief priests naturally repulses us. But we must admit that to the feelings of anyone who thinks of Jesus as one of a number of heroes, thinkers, preachers, of anyone who gives Him a purely human status, far more shocking things have occurred than this betrayal by Judas and its confirmation by the gentlemen in toga. History tells many another tale of atrocity, of virtue, love, and truth sold into the hands of murderers for even less than thirty shekels.

But this instance of treachery brooks no comparison with any other. We acknowledge this Christ Jesus as the very Christ of the Scriptures. He is unique and cannot be named in a breath with other world reformers. He simply is not one of countless disillusioned ones who, because of their devotion to this or that ideal, were trodden into the mire. Christ admits of no comparison: He stands at the center of history as the Son of God and as the Son of man. He is the foundation and the crown of every responsible office in Israel and in the whole world.

1. Really before the chief priests; but compare also Schürer, *Gesch. d. Jud. Volkes*, Vol. 2, p. 251.
2. Dr. F. W. Grosheide, *Kommentaar op Mattheus*, 311, note.

Hence it would be folly to try to measure the shameful commerce of Judas and the chief priests by some quantitative standard, and to compare it then with other instances of treachery and murder committed against faith, in the world. The only appropriate question is to ask where prophecy is being fulfilled, where the Spirit of prophecy, with greater impetus or less, courses through those murderer's dens, temples though they be, temples in which the tables of the exchangers are a perpetual hindrance to the reformation of the sanctuary according to truth and right.

Considering the event in that way we know that nothing more ignominious ever occurred than happened here when Israel's official leaders, who by reason of their office were shepherds of the people, appraised, bought, and paid for the blood of Jesus at the price of thirty pieces of silver. Even that is not putting it nicely enough. This is not a "happening," is not an "instance." It is the one knot of history. The ignominiousness of it does not arise from the assessment as such, or from the person of Judas, or from the machinations of the chief priests. The awful significance of this event arises from this fact: those thirty pieces of silver are bandied back and forth by the Spirit of Prophecy. They never rest. They roll on through the ages. And the cause of their restlessness is that they cringe under the glaring searchlight of a harsh prophecy already five hundred years old. It had foretold how every unfaithful disciple of the Israel of the flesh would once agree that thrice ten shekels were ample compensation for the services of the good shepherd.

Really five centuries? Yes, approximately that many years had passed since Zechariah had been compelled to make that pronouncement. That long ago he had declared that carnal Israel would sometime evaluate and sell the Chief Shepherd at the price the chief priests gave the betrayer.

Those priests have degenerated so far that they manage to live in an atmosphere of Messianic prophecy only in an unconscious, and as such in an antagonistic, way. How astonishing, how preposterous almost, that these who are learned in the Scriptures should now quite unwittingly prove the validity of that time-honored prophecy in such a strictly literal manner.

These leaders of Israel reënact the deed of Hiel, the architect of Bethel, who, at Ahab's behest, had rebuilt the gates of Jericho. Almost five hundred years had elapsed then, too, since Joshua had threatened with a curse any who should dare to rebuild that city. Whoever ventures to do that, Joshua had said, shall give in return for his audacity the lives of his eldest and youngest sons. But Joshua had died and the winds of five centuries had blown the cadences of his voice out of hearing. Then Hiel came and, in as strictly literal a fashion, fulfilled the pronouncement of the prophet-judge.

Joshua uttered the curse at the time of Israel's first immigration into Canaan. Five centuries later God sought it out and fulfilled it. Zechariah voiced his declaration at the time of Israel's second immigration into Canaan, just after the captivity. Five centuries later God realized it in the session hall of the chief priests, those architects of the school of Ahab, graduate students of Hiel the Bethelite.

Do you see the meaningful parallelism? For why had God chosen to leave Jericho in ruins? Because over the debris of the gateway to Canaan, over the desolation of Jericho, spiritually discerning eyes might see this superscription written: *Canaan is the inheritance of a people who live by faith, not by works.* God had demolished those walls by the impetus of grace, not by that of the sword, of Israel's own power. God loved those ruins. The very lifelessness of those stones was a living testimony to the Gospel which preached free grace and justification by faith without works. Therefore the Word, therefore the curse, took its effect. Therefore prophecy is inescapably relevant to all.

That same God is here at Jerusalem, and that same Word is here. The superscription over Jericho, "Not by works, but by grace alone," continues to be an offense to every self-righteous Ahab. And since Christ —that Good Shepherd— is preaching precisely the same message, everywhere, continuously, day and night, that Christ must die. See how in Him God is taking vengeance on Ahab and Hiel. The message faintly preached by the dead stones of ancient Jericho is being perfectly taught by the living lips of Christ. His life is the resurrection from the dead of Jericho's ruins. But Ahab is alive. Hence Christ must die.

Because Hiel still practises his profession, he will ever try to chisel the work of grace out of the entrance to Canaan. See how the chief priests and Judas are busy perfecting the work of Ahab.

Remember, however, that the curse still obtains and that it must take its effect. It comes now to confirm a prophecy five hundred years old. Tremble before God, whoever can, for the majesty of God is sure; such is the prophecy which no one can oust from the world.

Do not marvel at the fact that the Holy Spirit, who wrote the Scriptures, has in this way flung a bridge from Zechariah, the prophet, to Matthew, the evangelist. This is not the first time He has done this kind of thing. Such inter-ramification is, in fact, the dominant characteristic of the Scriptures. All the words of God constitute the *One Word* of God. Without interruption the story of redemption progresses from Zechariah to this turning point and high point of history, to Jesus' being summoned to judgment. It is according to that rule of prophecy, according to that progressive law of the history of special revelation that Zechariah first revealed in principle the event which God makes actual in Matthew's account of the Gospel.

Concerning that prophecy of Zechariah this must be said first of all. In chapter 11 he shows us — as we pointed out, in passing, in the preceding study — that there are two kinds of shepherds in Israel: the hirelings and the good shepherds. The hirelings are the false ones who prophesy selfishly for the sake of personal gain. The good shepherds are those who bring God to His people in His word, and who draw the people to the Lord by His word. But the true prophets are hindered in their work by the hirelings. Zechariah states that, and adds also that the unfaithful people prefer the charming, captivating lessons of the false shepherds, to the austere, strict discipline of the true prophets, even though it is an evangelical discipline. And Zechariah becomes so resentful at the thought that the people should reject every good counsel that he proposes a catch-question to these unfaithful ones. Whether he himself actually puts the question or simply sets it down as a symbol of what was to come does not affect its significance in this particular. He asks for his wages: "Give me my price," he says.

The catch question is a unique rhetorical device. It can be utterly reprehensible. When used to take advantage of an ignorant or hesitant person in order to enmesh him in one's own net, it is simply detestable. But the catch-question can also be most admirable in its effects. When employed in the spirit of love to force an issue which is constantly binding anyway, to precipitate a decision which can and must be made, it is a perfectly legitimate device. More positively — this kind of question is born of God. Such a question points to the high seriousness of each minute of the life God gives us. For we should be ready at any moment to give a clear-cut answer to the great issue of time and eternity as it affects us: What think you of the Christ?

Such was Zechariah's question: Give me my price. It presented two alternatives. And, if any residue of spirituality had been left in the Israel of the flesh, if a modicum of the original theology of its psalms and prophets had still been active in them, the people would forthwith have given this reply to the question of the good shepherd: We refuse thee thy price.

They would have returned that answer for three reasons. *First*: We are unable to get along without your cares. Payment, you see, means dismissal, implies termination of service. And we cannot live without you; for our own sake, we cannot. *Second*: We cannot pay you a price because your work simply does not lend itself to such quantitative appraisal. The services of the good shepherd defy evaluation. They are of infinite worth, for God is active in them; by means of them evangelical grace is given us. Who, pray, can compensate for such boundless good? It is patent folly to reckon the value of the grace of God in terms of dollars and cents. *Third*: We may not give you your wages because such payment is no affair of ours. If you are a good shepherd, you are God's true prophet. Your mission, then, comes from Him. You are not our hired man, but a servant of the Lord. God is responsible for your wages, for He appointed you and called you to this work. How foolish to suppose that the sheep should or could remunerate their own shepherd. Payment is no matter of theirs; it is the business of the owner. We cannot give you your price. God alone, the great Owner of Israel's sheep, is in a position to reward His prophets.

Ah yes, if only Israel's leaders had replied in that fashion. Then they would have remained the spiritual Israel. By that answer they would have affirmed their belief in that fundamental, threefold doctrine with which the spiritual had always gloried over the fleshly Israel, a doctrine corresponding exactly to the reply given above. Note that doctrine and the correspondence. *First*: God's people are able to live only by the continuous grace of God (the shepherd is indispensable). *Second*: The gifts of grace are of infinite, not of limited, worth; consequently, these cannot be assessed or adequately paid for (the services defy compensation). *Third*: God alone sends and rewards His shepherds. His grace, therefore, can never accrue to His people except by way of the *transcendent* miracles of the Counsel of Peace (the relationship between the shepherd and the owner does not concern the sheep).

Whoever stops to think a moment will recognize at once that this threefold concept is the core of the Gospel of grace as contrasted to that other gospel of self-redemption. These three fundamental ideas constitute the formal pattern of the grace which has appeared in Christ Jesus as contrasted to the self-righteousness to which the Judaism of the flesh will succumb; they are the theme of the gospel of righteousness by faith as contrasted to that other righteousness which would build Israel upon a basis of good works.[1]

But Israel did not make that one, true reply. It turned a false answer to the "catch question" put by the prophets. That answer not only denied and did injustice to the element of grace and of justification by *faith* but also gave blatant expression to a pride which would redeem itself. Abraham's children, having abandoned his faith, *actually* paid out the stipend. When they did so they sinned, for by that act they were virtually saying three things: *first,* that they can get on very well without the good Shepherd and the true prophets (They choose to be guided by their own light; they strike the element of grace from their gospel of redemption); *secondly,* that they do not tremble in awe before the wonder of God's gifts of grace as men do before a

---

1. The Letter to the Romans.

thing of incalculable worth, but that they, instead, rank everything the prophets do in a class with general cultural benefits, which, like other cultural things, can be adequately *evaluated* and *paid for* (The element of grace has been completely abandoned; the notion of *infinitude* has been stricken from their gospel of redemption); *thirdly,* that they no longer want to play the rôle of sheep, but wish to do what is the prerogative only of the Owner of the flock (They lower the work of redemption to the plane of men, as if salvation were not God-sent in its coming to man. They were the sheep, but would be their own lords and masters. In other words, they strike the worship of God's *transcendence* from their gospel of redemption).

But they mocked the prophet, and in mocking him, mocked God himself not only by the fact that they paid the stipend but also by the amount which they paid. For they hit upon the sum which they paid facilely enough. Thirty pieces of silver, that was the price. Now re-read what is written in Exodus 20:32 and you will learn that thirty pieces was the price for which a slave could be bought. In short, the stipend represented the price of scorn, the price of disdain. God asks His people what value they place upon the services of the prophets, and they reply that they believe these to be worth no more than a slave, than a valet, who can be bought "for a song."

It is therefore no wonder that God, in turn, mocked this disgraceful compensation. The prophet receives the burden of the Lord to take the thirty pieces and to "cast them to the potter."[1]

Even if this casting of the stipend to the potter, probably a symbolical act, is not entirely clear to us, we can say this much about it: It is an expression of the disgust the prophet feels in his soul at the thought that the people are perfectly willing to pay him and to pay him so little. It may be that the correct explanation is this, that a potter just then happened to be busy in the

---

1. Some think that no reference to the potter should be made here. These maintain that, by a slight alteration, the text would read: "Cast them into the treasury" (of the temple). As we see it, however, this question must be determined in consideration of the references in Matthew 27 and Acts 1, and in these passages the potter is actually named. With respect to the question in general, compare Dr. F. W. Grosheide, *Hermeneutiek*, Amsterdam, 1929, pp. 231, 232, 237; and with respect to the context in question, p. 238, note 12.

temple and that he had the habit of sweeping all the refuse concomitant to his trade into a heap. By adding the thirty pieces to this pile of trash the prophet publicly demonstrated how worthless he regarded his reward. Be that as it may, for we cannot be sure, it is certain that only in an ironical vein could those thirty shekels be called "a goodly price." We can also be sure, moreover, that God flung His resentment full in the face of His people for their disgraceful lack of appreciation of the sensitive cares tendered them by the prophets.

He who follows the course of the Scriptures closely will understand that Zechariah said these things in prophetic reference to the Christ of God. Yes, his prophecy, too, rooted in the circumstances of his day. But an element of theocratic, Messianic reference constantly inhered in it. Precisely because of that element, Zechariah could penetrate to the deeper meaning of Israel's life, vacillating as it continually did between the pole of Messiah-expectation and that of Messiah-rejection. And it was that deeper significance of Zechariah's prophecy which had to be fulfilled in Christ, the chief good shepherd.

Therefore Matthew had to come as a complement to Zechariah, in order to show that the words of the prophet of the Old Testament were actualized in Christ Jesus. Zechariah came at a turning point in time, almost at the close of the Old Testament prophetic day. So in Matthew's account of the Gospel, Christ appears at *the* turning point of history, in the fulness of time, at noontide of that one "day of the Lord" the rays of whose sun Zechariah had seen shimmering in the distance. Thus Zechariah's prophecy is fulfilled in the council of the chief priests and scribes, and in Judas Iscariot.

There they are — on either side of the counter over which the best of blood is changing hands — greedy, money-grabbing Judas, and the leering, lecherous chief priests. Externally viewed, that is all of it; even to the purely natural eye it is repulsive. And that is all. But the spiritual vision discerns a third person in that place of ignominious bargaining, sees Christ Himself. See Him. Hear Him. Give me My price, He says. In Him all the prophets shout: Give us our price. Through Him that cry issues from every martyr killed at the altar, from Abel to Zechariah. God

Himself rises in this place and shouts to His people, to the seed of Abraham: Give me My price.

And . . . they count out the change, thirty pieces, the price of a slave.

The roof did not crash down upon these merchandisers. That it did not is not due to any "semen religionis" still hidden in some corner of the arid souls of these traitors to God, to prophecy, and to Christ. That is because of the will of God which selects these dark ways to the redemption of His people. God deliberately lets the thirty pieces of silver roll through the ages over the market-place of the world. He does that in order that men may choose between free grace and self-redemption.

That choice is still the liveliest option of men. The conflict between those two contenders is uncompromising. The way of a legalistic, "good works" salvation leaves that of the preaching of free grace: the way of the Judaistic, *pharisaic* "earning" of salvation is incompatible with the New Testament Pauline Gospel of redemption by faith. On this question Rome and the Reformation part company too. For Catholicism, though but in part, would buy salvation, and, though not intentionally so, would by its system of absolution again put thirty pieces of silver upon the table. Luther and Calvin, in bidding farewell to the Roman Tetzel, must protest: by faith alone; by faith, not by works, lest any should glory.

No, this is seeking out no false antithesis. The terms of that same ancient conflict still divide the true from the false. The Christ of God is very "particular"; the Gospel is very painstaking. There is nothing fantastic about those thirty pieces: they are the logical outcome of fleshly Judaism. Think again, in this connection, of those three elements:

1. Man can save himself.
2. Redemption is a limited thing.
3. Man does God's work.

And place over against it this confession of the spiritual Israel, of true belief, of the Reformed faith:

1. Redemption is eternally beyond our own capacity. God must justify and sanctify us anew each day. We cannot live without the Shepherd of our soul one moment.

2. Redemption transcends the possibility of compensation. We cannot by drawing on the resources of the whole world amass money enough to pay God. His gifts are of inestimable worth. And the gift cannot be separated from the Giver, who is infinite.

3. We can never put ourselves in God's position. We want to remain the sheep of His care, following, believing, and listening to the Shepherd's voice.

The thirty pieces are the tangible embodiment of the spirit of self-redemption. Grace allows no glorying in the self. Redemption is from Thee, from Thee alone.

If God is so exacting as to keep the thirty pieces perpetually rolling across the world, right on through the centuries, life is very serious. Those restive pieces protest that at any given moment each and every human being may be called upon to consciously choose for righteousness by faith and against righteousness by works.

What can be more moving than to put Zechariah's declaration next to the narrative of Matthew? Reading Matthew alone, I am disposed to say: What a giant in sin that man Judas was! Compared with him I am a dwarf, a Lilliputian, te Deum ... But when I hear Zechariah say that it is very natural for all unfaithful sheep to dismiss the Shepherd of Israel for thirty pieces, Judas becomes as small as I. And at second thought I become as great as he in transgression. Lord, as often as I do not believe, I dispatch the Good Shepherd, I grow to Judas' size, I attain the stature of the scribes in sin. O God, be merciful to me, a sinner! Reading Matthew alone, I think of Judas as I ponder Lord's Day 31 (the keys of the kingdom) of the Heidelberg Catechism. Reading Zechariah also, I think of myself, of the incriminating power of the Word, of the ultimatum of God's shepherding.

It is a serious matter to have a God who asks catch-questions. And we are unembarrassed by these only if we live by the Word, if we are able each moment to completely apply to ourselves the key-concept of our confession: living by faith through grace. It is our duty to work out that concept consciously and unconsciously each day, in our theology, in our dogmatics, and in our mysticism.

Never did Israel so abuse the treasures which God allowed them to take from Egypt as when, by means of Judas, Israel used these to pay for Jesus' blood. By that act Israel surrendered the office of stewardship. When it took the capital it had brought from Egypt and had amassed in Canaan and, for its own aggrandizement, used it to pay for Jesus' cross, Jerusalem, to speak in the language of Revelation 12, became the city "which spiritually is called Egypt."

As for ourselves? In fear and trembling we must admit God into our houses, our shops, our studios, and fields. Listening attentively, then, we shall hear Him ask: Give me My price. The question must come to all: what think you of the Christ? In that sense all must make an appraisal, all must return an answer. He is fortunate who can be quick to reply: Lord, I cannot appraise Thee. Thou only canst place a value upon me, O Lord, and include me with those for whom Thou hast given the inestimable price of Jesus' precious blood, flowing through the infinite, eternal Spirit.

Christ's Passion Announced from Heaven: The Realization of the "Glory of the Lord"

CHAPTER SIX

Christ's Passion Announced from Heaven: The Realization of the "Glory of the Lord"

● *And, behold, there talked with him two men, which were Moses and Elias; who appeared in glory, and spake of his decease which he should accomplish at Jerusalem.* —LUKE 9:30-31.

WE shall at this point discuss the transfiguration of Christ while in the company of Moses and Elias upon the mountain. We are aware of the fact that to do so is to depart from the historical sequence of events in the passion story. If we were to follow a strictly chronological order, we should have to insert this treatise between chapters 1 and 2.

But we have a reason for placing it here. You will remember that each of the preceding studies treated of what was introduced into the drama of the passion by human agency. On this side of the matter we discovered that nothing was certain, nothing sure. Simon Peter was a satan twice but he did not know it. Mary was a ministering angel but did not recognize herself as such. Caiaphas and his Sanhedrin prophesied but did so unconsciously. The chief priests counted the thirty pieces into Judas' hands, and did not understand that the curse hovered over the hall in which they plotted with him. Very uncertain, indeed, this human part in the passion program, very uncertain and indefinite. Men saw nothing and heard nothing, but, like blundering school boys, they spilled ink upon the blue-print spread out before them, thus marring the plan of God's justice and grace, and of his evangelical temple.

Hence, it is in order now to notice that the story of the Gospel proceeds to contrast with that human dubiousness the absolute

Certainty of heaven. The children of the earth, mere men, mere "flesh and blood" may not be aware of or may but faintly understand the powers of the coming age now swirling about their heads, but heaven does understand. When Moses and Elias come from heaven's side to discuss Christ's approaching death with Him, absolute certainty enters in. Now conscious prophecy obtains. The bearers of the energies released at this time know that their active influences are real and effectual.

The wind blows and men hear the sound of it, but they cannot tell whence it comes nor whither it goes. But heaven knows both its origin and its destination. And the certainty of heaven as revealed in the Gospel counter-balances the uncertainty of men.

That is the first reason for discussing the transfiguration now— to point out heaven's attitude, after we have lingered over that of men. And a second reason is this. After this chapter we shall accompany Christ out of the vestibule of the temple of passion into the building itself. Christ is about to take into His own hands the cord which will lead Him to Golgotha. Deliberately, calmly He will loosen the very winds and storms over His head.[1] Hence it is fitting to complete the discussion of the suffering in that vestibule first. Having seen the earth placed in heaven's light, we proceed now to get a glimpse of heaven itself.

We remarked just now that when heaven speaks, Certainty ensues, and that Christ in this moment passes from the medium of human nebulosity to that of heaven's lucid clarity.

There are some who deny that heaven on this occasion is unmistakably clear in its intent. These maintain that Christ, while He was on the mountain, was given the privilege of a choice between two alternatives: to enter heaven forthwith, without the antecedent passion and death; or, to enter heaven eventually, but only after the great sacrifice.

Now to the extent that this construction of the significance of the transfiguration intends to say only that Christ was being tried, that He saw those two possibilities exposed before His mind's eye, and that He then chose the better course — to that extent we have no objections to the interpretation.

---

1. "What manner of man is this, that even the winds and the sea obey him" by coming at His beckoning?

But that is by no means the same as saying that Christ was given the privilege to choose either an immediate ascension to glory, or such an ascension only after a sojourn in the pit of hell. When it is maintained that heaven left Him perfectly free to choose either the one or the other, and that it then would have been perfectly satisfied with whatever decision was made, we must seriously object.

To interpret the event in such a manner is to forget that behind it lay the binding pronouncement of the Counsel of Peace, a decree agreed upon by the Father, Son, and Holy Spirit. Remember that from eternity that immutable decree of the Trinity, outlining the Divine plan of peace and salvation, was constantly in force. How mistaken, then, it is to suppose that heaven should now come to the human soul of Christ, daily still learning as it was,[1] should come to the frail, humanly susceptible flesh of Jesus and offer it a choice between the divine inspiration of the Father and His own aspiration to life and glory, to peace and joy. Can it be supposed that God actually asked Him whether He felt disposed now to annul that eternal decree, single end of world history as it was? And would God, then, be satisfied with whatever choice was made?

That can not be the case. When the Father, Son, and Holy Spirit have exchanged their precious oaths, the man Christ Jesus may never rescind the decision. That is not putting it too boldly: He *may* not do it. As Man and Mediator Christ is subject to the law of obedience. Not by mere accident is He called the "Servant of the Lord." He subjected Himself to that law at His own baptism, and was never permitted to do anything except what was done in subservience to it. Surely, then, by giving Christ the privilege of a free and independent choice in the matter, God Himself would have been tempting Him, and "God tempteth no man."[2] It is true that God gives the first Adam a probationary command, and that He also puts the Second Adam to the proof. The same God who showed the first Adam a tree and a fruit which was "pleasant to look upon" and "to be desired to make one wise" also reveals to the second Adam at this time a beauty that

---

1. "Yet learned he obedience by the things which he suffered." Hebrews 5:8.
2. James 1:13.

is pleasant to enjoy and desirable for wisdom. Hence, to talk of a trial, a proof, a test, on the mountain of transfiguration is unobjectionable, but of a temptation — that can be allowed only if it is immediately added that such temptation is always Satan's doing, as when he prompts Peter to speak foolishly or in some other diabolical way tries to tempt Christ's human soul.

As for the rest, we refuse to believe that God Himself tempted the Christ to evil by letting Him choose freely in a matter inextricably related to His eternal Counsel, a matter which in time was attached to the law and to the oaths of fidelity. God never allows the world which He governs according to His plan, to balance precariously on a needle's point, held in the hands of a free, independent human being, even though that person be the Second Adam Himself. That would be paradoxical. The concepts "second Adam" and "free, independent human being" are mutually exclusive. Christ is not a man; He is "the" man; He is the covenant Head. He became that with the sole purpose of attaching Himself to the law of the Lord with all of the tentacles of His being.

Moreover, the facts at the transfiguration also make the idea that Christ was offered a voluntary choice on the mountain an untenable one. These indicate very clearly that heaven does not give Christ one moment of freedom. Just what are the heavenly visitors really doing? Why, they are talking with Jesus about the great theme, His "decease which he was to accomplish at Jerusalem." There is no obscurity in that wording. Moses and Elias do not regard the approaching "decease" as a possibility, but as a fact. Christ intended to, was almost to, had in mind to accomplish it— that is the connotation of it. And such nonchalant "taking for granted" of the departure at Jerusalem leaves no room for the hypothesis of temptation.

Satan's temptations and God's trials are very different. When Satan tempts man, he not only tries to conceal what is the main issue of contention between him and us before the throne of God's justice, but also tries to give a false impression of things. He presents an illusion as a reality. The Tempter always tries to conceal the main objective of God's justice.

That is very different from what God does when He puts humanity to the test. He may conceal, temporarily, the end He has in view, may for a while withhold from us complete certainty about the "main issue" of our life-conflict, but He never gives a false impression. He never encourages a subjective apprehension which is at variance with what is objectively essential to our knowledge. On the contrary, every trial which God allows man to experience is designed to induce him to re-direct his wayward feet to the main highway, to see the central illumination of God's truth clearly outshining the nebulosity of peripheral matters. God always moves towards and always influences us to urge our thoughts and lives into the direction of that ultimate goal.

And it is in that way that Jesus is not being tempted by God, but is being tried. That is the word. The transfiguration is a trial to Jesus in the sense that He sees a heavenly beauty, feels the influences of a celestial blessedness, breathes a divinely rarefied atmosphere, and yet may not enter into that marvelous glory.

That word "trial," however, suggests only a half of the significance of the transfiguration. To the trial God adds a revelation. This revelation Christ as a Man could and had to receive, so that His soul might be enlisted into complete and active coöperation with the whole revelation of God, and also with the whole God of revelation. God by means of it forces Him into the direction of the climax of His Mediatorship, to that point in the center of time and eternity, where He will stand — will hang — all alone, before His God.

It is this revelation which constitutes the real meaning of the transfiguration. The Church of God has long confessed that an extraordinary providence of God actively surrounds the Christ. See how real this mysterious influence becomes at this time. At just this stage in Christ's career as Mediator, God intervenes and, through the Spirit, gives Him a word of revelation, accompanied by a sign, and it is remarkable to observe how very appropriate this is to this particular moment of the sacred *history* of revelation.

In order to understand that appropriateness we must remember that three characteristics are common to every act of revelation to which God commits Himself *in time.* Those properties are:

1. Such revelation is always a true one.
2. Such revelation is never a complete one.
3. Such revelation is always a growing one.

Such is the threefold nature of every revelation given by God in process of time. Moreover, because of this essential nature, it makes a threefold demand of every person who receives it. That demand is as follows:

1. Because revelation is true, man must accept it.
2. Because it is incomplete, he must amplify it by turning to God with a consecrated soul and spirit.
3. Because it is constantly developing, he may not rest satisfied with it as given, but must press on to perfect it.

Observe how each of these moments characterizes the revelation that comes to Jesus upon the mountain and His acceptance of it. Those two considerations are an appropriate outline for our study:

1. True revelation comes to Jesus.
2. He willingly accepts it.

True revelation comes to Jesus, yes. By means of the Word and the Spirit, heaven speaks to Him, and what heaven says is true. The painful message it brings is that Christ, even though He is in this moment enveloped in glory and steeped in bliss, is nevertheless still the object of humiliation. Humiliation on the mount, you ask? Yes, because the robes of radiance and the glistening garments that He wears are borrowed. He is sharing in a bliss which is being lent to Him. It is no self-engendered beauty, this, which, unlike that which characterizes Him on Easter morning, on ascension day, and will emanate from Him at His return, has been externally thrust upon Him. He gets His glory from Moses and Elias; He shines in their light. He who has the right and the capacity to be the sun of the universe appears here as the moon. The sun is self-illuminating, but the moon, the weaker of the two, has no individuality of her own, depends for her light upon the other, and is therefore not constantly luminous. Jesus senses this reversal of the situation keenly. It is painful to Him, for He never sees a part at the cost of the whole, and can never dissociate one moment of His life from the cen-

tral purpose of His career.   He knows full well that Moses and
Elias have brought this glory with them from above, that they
are taking it to Him.   They also, of course, have derived their
glamour from God.   Nevertheless those aureoles of splendor
which surround them, those halos of bliss, are not mere embell-
ishment, not superadded adornment, but an outer expression of
an inner beauty, a beauty made apparent because their redeemed
souls had wrought a glorified body before the throne of God.
But Christ is not yet intrinsically glorified.   O yes, He is the Son,
but a Son who may only for a moment borrow the garments of
two of His Father's servants.   When these go, He must again
stand in the guise of a slave, naked and dismantled.

This we call revelation, and also true revelation.   It is true
revelation because by means of this experience heaven eloquently
preaches the truth about Jesus.   It tells Him that as Man He is
dependent, finite, in a state of humiliation.   It fairly shouts into
His ears the fact that not by such external adornment, not by
such superficial ornamentation, can or may His great metamorphosis, His ultimate transfiguration, take place.   For heaven cannot receive into itself a human Christ who has thus been endowed
with light and presented with glory.   By accepting Him so, heav-
en would itself have become the agent responsible for introduc-
ing sin into its immaculate holiness.   We know that no one can
enter God's mansions except He who radiates an intrinsic, organically evolved beauty, rather than a mechanically superadded
one; that none can enter heaven but he who has grown rich and
beautiful, ready to meet his God, by reason of the gradual growth
of a seed planted in him at his regeneration.   And although this
principle of glory applies only in part to other men, inasmuch as
their sanctification is realized in the last analysis only by an intervention of God's hand, for Christ the law of glory holds completely and unconditionally.   This Second Adam can not be satisfied with an external beauty but must by travail achieve the
living, active principle of it, and must, through the Spirit, develop
that to final fruition from within.   Heaven, then, by letting Christ
feel the inadequacy of a borrowed, mechanical translation to the
Jerusalem above invites Him to desire an organic departure from
the Jerusalem below.   So, in the fulness of God's own time,

when His law is satisfied, Christ will also arrive at an organic entrance to that other Jerusalem which is heaven. Only by dying to the law in the earthly city, by fulfilling every demand placed upon Him, can He achieve that glory which is not derived but is His very own and which, through grace, He can then, as a greater than all, pass on to Moses, to Elias, to Adam, and to all of His own eternally.

Such is the nature of the true revelation which heaven discovers to Jesus upon the mountain.

We must observe in the second place that Jesus willingly accepts it and that with His whole individuality. Never before in His life was He so much the servant as He is here in these moments. Although He is the Son, He borrows from the servants in His Father's house. He bows His head; He acknowledges His humiliation. Moreover, He promises obedience. Moses gave the law, Elias enforced it, He will fulfill it. He bows His head in obedience to the law. Moses led Israel out of heathendom, Elias extracted heathenism out of Israel, Christ will do both. He will rescue His people from the grasp of Satan; that is, He will justify them. But He will also draw every satanic element out of them; that is, He will sanctify them. So He will become the complete Mediator, fulfilling every requirement of the law. He will assume the awful burden of the moment, will be glorified only by suffering. He bows low, accepts the revelation completely, pain and all. He accepts everything that God reveals to Him without demur. And to the extent that God withholds anything, He waits patiently upon Him.

Does God, then, withhold something from Jesus, and does the Christ suffer because of that? Yes, the grief owing to what is not revealed far outweighs for Christ the joy in what is received. Precisely *what* is withheld, you wonder? Well, Moses is here, and Elias is here, but where is Jesus' God? Moses spoke with God upon the mountain, had a long conversation with Him, talked with Him again and again, as a friend talks with a friend. And Elias also, upon another mountain, heard His voice, a still, small voice, after it had passed by in the earthquake, the storm, and the fire. But Christ is not allowed to converse with God at this time. Three times, it is true, a voice is heard speaking about the Christ, but not once a voice speaking to Him and with Him. We remember that Jesus has climbed the mountain as one whose seeking soul longed to meet its God in prayer, and we know also that He did that, conscious of the fact that He was greater than Moses and Elias, and more than all the saints together. But God who condescends to speak with Moses and Elias recedes from His Son. This is the beginning of that appalling loneliness which He later expresses in the bitter cry: My God, my God, why hast thou forsaken me?

That, certainly, is a willing acceptance of God's revelation, of what it includes and of what it excludes. Christ here, in the face of Moses who gave it and of Elias who enforced it, accepts the full burden of fulfilling the law. Before He lays the cornerstone of the temple of the Gospel, He allows two standard-bearers of the house of the law to show Him the blueprints of the evangelical building He envisions, and to teach Him the plans according to which it must be built.

That takes us to our second major consideration. The revelation which comes to Jesus is incomplete. It is not conclusive, is not exhaustive. The revelation of God is always the truth but never the whole truth. What He says is all true, but He does not say all. He cannot reveal everything for the simple reason that God's infinity cannot be comprehended by finite man. And He does not want His revelation to be exhaustive, because He chooses to discover it by means of history; hence it will not be complete until the end of the world.

That the particular revelation given upon the mount is incomplete is quite obvious. Of course, there is much here in which to rejoice. The bearers of the light of heaven are dazzling creatures, and their brilliance is in striking contrast to the surrounding darkness. Moreover, this is all being done for Jesus. How ineffably beautiful, we say, looking at it from the human point of view. But if we look at this radiance against the screen of heaven itself and if we view it in the very light of God, it becomes less glorious. Seeing it in that way, we are inclined to make two observations:

1. These *bearers* of revelation reflect only the minutest part of the glory which they "see and hear"[1] daily before the throne of God.

1. John 3: 31, 32.

2. The *manner* of this revelation, too, merely hints at its real potentiality.

Yes, Moses and Elias reflect only a little of the heavenly glory which they daily see and hear. Even if for us mere human beings this sublime translucence seems most unusual, we must remember that for heaven it represents a diminution of the customary glory. Seeing the halos of radiance emanating from a lustrous Moses and Elias, we are prompted to say: Ah, yes, so those are who dwell before the throne of God. But that precisely is not the case. They are far more glorious there than they appear to be here at this time. Theirs is a tempered brilliance, there in the house of the Son. The earth cannot absorb the full glory of heaven. Moses must again veil his face because man cannot bear the intensity of its light. Accordingly, we get only a glimpse into the golden palace; its door has merely been set ajar. Behind Elias and Moses, behind these subdued reflectors of glory, we know there is the song of the angels, the very throne itself, the wondrous "four beasts," and the voice as of a great thunder. No, no, heaven's riches are not extravagantly poured over the earth. We can safely say, in fact, that these two giants accomplished more wonderful things and made a stronger impression while they lived upon earth. Elias in his day caused a vineyard to tremble, called fire from heaven, and quite upset the age in which he lived. And Moses moved over desert and sea like a tornado, drawing all the powers of a coming era in its wake. Compared with such stirring achievements, this one is rather weak and ordinary. A faint glimmer appears for a second. Then heaven closes again. And the earth has not even noticed it.

Just so, too, the *manner* in which the revelation comes to Jesus clearly represents a restraint of energy. Moses and Elias simply *talk* with Jesus. It is remarkable that in the original of Matthew 17:13, Mark 9:4, and Luke 9:31 a word is used which suggests a very casual conversation. The connotation is that Moses and Elias simply "have a talk" about His decease at Jerusalem. There is nothing striking, nothing unusual about it. How different matters had been before. Moses' eye had shot flames, his hand had struck fire from the rock, and his voice thundered awesomely. Elias, too, had been able to shake his people, and his coming and going was like that of a whirlwind. But now both the symbol accompanying the word and the form of it are usual, simple, ordinary.   Can we say that heaven opened and spoke with Jesus about the awfullest subject named among men, more awful even than—hell?

Such simplicity is, however, very appropriate to the occasion. Those signs, terrors, and awe-inspiring tokens which accompanied the words of Moses and Elias as agents of revelation during their lives belonged to the Old Testament.   By means of them they sounded the alarm and heralded the coming of something better.

That something better has come now.   The New Testament, the reality, not the prophecy, is here.   And now that it has come Moses and Elias too, are eager to get a glimpse of it.[1]   Yes, as far as external glamour goes, Moses and Elias are the sun and Jesus is the moon, reflecting their light.   But in reference to the hidden influences, to the concealed energies of the kingdom of heaven, Christ, as the Son of man and as the Lord of glory, is the very Sun of righteousness.   And when Christ Himself appears as such, the "moon" of the Old Testament pales in comparison and glides into the shadowy background.   We know from daily experience that visible and invisible forces are not the same. When electrical storms threaten, such invisible but potent influences penetrate the air that our radios are rendered useless because of them.   So the lightning of God mocks the frail energies mere men can release.

That figure applies to Moses and Elias in this instance.   In the final analysis these are only God's loudspeakers.   What they say is therefore the truth.   But Christ, who, as an innocent Man, will sacrifice Himself through the eternal Spirit, has in Him spiritual reserves as puissant as those of God's lightning.   He has that capacity with Him there upon the mountain, and in comparison with it the revelation which uses Moses and Elias as its agents appears weak and fragmentary.

Revelation is always incomplete but never was it more so than when its lesser potentialities were here revealed to its greatest Hero. God, who at sundry times and in divers manners spoke to the fathers by Moses and Elias, has in these last hours taught

1. Compare Luke 10:24.

them to be silent before the Son. Yes, Moses and Elias talked, we said. But never have men kept such silence, never left so much unsaid. In a sense the revelation upon the mountain was incomplete, was pathetically meager. In another sense it was never so profusely abundant, for its very inadequacy in these heroes of the Old Testament significantly points to its completion in the Son, who realizes God's words.

We notice, accordingly, that Jesus' soul is in accord with what Moses and Elias present to Him. The revelation is incomplete, but He will develop the inadequate data of the heavenly instruction by directing all the energies of a consecrated heart, and soul, and will upon God. He will bring the whole of His devoted individuality to bear upon realizing that revelation until it ends in the ultimateness of God's perfection.

It is by that very realization that He proves to be our Redeemer. The reception we disobedient creatures give the revelation of God is never completely appreciative of the riches of God's grace given us in it. But Christ always appreciates what God gives in a way that is appropriate to its nature and content. When God gives the Man Christ Jesus an incomplete revelation in the form of one talent in order that He may trade with it, Christ goes, His face fixed upon God, and toils relentlessly until He has gained all the other talents. He gives revelation its just due by concentrating his whole effort upon bringing it to its final fruition. It is true that heaven's door is hardly standing ajar. But that is enough. In God's own time, Christ will swing it open. Just so the influences of that coming age are released; Christ will then distribute them all so that they may flood the world until that day when His foot will again touch upon the mountain, and He will judge the living and the dead.

And in reference to that very ordinary manner of revelation of which we spoke, we see that Christ responds perfectly to that also. Moses and Elias simply talk to Him about the awful event to come; they merely tell Him of it. But the telling is enough for Jesus, is more than enough. Contrast His immediate and eager response to the Word with the pathetic reception which men are wont to give it. Christ Himself had previously pictured the pathos of that. When the banquet table of the Gospel is prepared, God first asks His servants to *tell* the guests that the table is spread. But they do not come. He then bids His representatives to *bring* them in. But that, too, does not suffice. Finally He must compel them to come.[1] Telling, bringing, compelling —that is the cycle of persuasion that must be brought to bear upon them before men will receive the Word that blesses them with the life of the Gospel. But Christ who at this time receives an invitation to appear not at the communion table of the Gospel, but at the place of execution of the Great Tribunal, goes when He is told. Bringing and compelling . . no, no: I come, O Lord, to do Thy will.

Naturally His soul, too, is grieved and depressed by it, but He nevertheless receives the incomplete revelation purely, and precisely by doing that proves to be our Mediator. He takes it and develops it until it reaches its fulfillment in God. The mere telling is as effective as the voice of judgment. To Him announcement and commandment are synonymous.

The third emphasis we were to consider is that the revelation of God is a growing one. It is constantly in the process of becoming, is always developing. And that aspect of it also is illustrated very clearly in the law of transfiguration which is introduced at this time.

Christ, as we noted, was enveloped in a medium of glory. His "raiment was white and glistening." He therefore underwent the same kind of transfiguration which Moses and Elias experienced in the course of their lives. Moses was transfigured when he visited with God upon the mountain. His face was so resplendent that the people could not bear to look at it. And Elias was similarly changed when he was taken up to heaven with horses of fire.

But neither Moses nor Elias attained perfection by their metamorphoses. They did not reach that resting place, that ultimate point in the being of a God whom all prophetic souls address with the words: Arise, O Lord, into Thy *rest*. Moses by his transfiguration bore the light of celestial glory from heaven above to the people below. But when that glory arrived in the

---

1. Luke 14:17, 21, 23; see also J. J. Knap, *In de Schuilplaats*, Kampen, J. H. Kok, 1913, p. 50 ff.

valley at the foot of the mountain, it was extinguished by the corruption of Israel. At first he had to hide his face, but later it again lost its lustre. And—what is more important—even while the radiance continued, Moses could not share the light with the people. Glory descends from above but it vanishes when it reaches the earth. In other words, the "glory of the Lord,"[1] which is the fulness of the revelation of God in the Old Testament, does come from heaven to mankind but it does not penetrate through, nor realize itself among, them. It is limited to Moses and he is powerless to distribute it among the people.

So, too, the glory of God takes a similar form but in a different direction in Elias. At his ascension he also undergoes a change. His features are transfigured; he bears heaven's glory from earth to heaven. When it arrives there it is, of course, not extinguished, for, so far from being destroyed, everything that enters heaven is ushered into abundant living. In heaven there is room enough for the brilliance which Israel at the foot of the mountain had not the capacity to receive. But when Elias carries heaven's dazzling brilliance upwards, the earth loses it and remains so much the poorer. Elisha must continue alone and the whole militant church must carry on alone. The transfiguration of Elias does not help them. In Elias the "glory of the Lord" still assumes the Old Testament manner of revelation; there is an ascension to heaven but no realization of glory below. Elias, also, is impotent to bring about that "realization," that changing of men from glory to glory even as by the Spirit. By means of the glory these giants of the Old Testament displayed, they did indeed give mankind a hint as to the nature of the glorification of man by the Spirit. But theirs was a static beauty—it could not inundate the world with a flood of light. After they, the best of the representatives of the Old Testament, had gone, there was still no such reality as that described in II Corinthians 3:18. Who among men in that Old Testament era could say: But we all, beholding as in a glass the glory of Moses and Elias, are changed into the same image, and now possess our glorification?

---

1. Technical term for the manner in which the glory of God was revealed to man in the Old Testament.

Hence the transfiguration of each of these is essentially a looking forward to, and a prayer for a better thing. Moses, the mediator of the Old Testament, cannot make room for the glory of the Lord among his people. He can only enjoy it personally, and but temporarily at that. And Elias who devoted his whole life to his people can also receive that glory only in a personal way and cannot share it with them. Surely, this is not the true salvation. In the one case the glory comes from heaven to earth, in the other it goes from the earth to heaven, but in neither case does it organically unify the two, nor become the abiding property of the people.

Because of that appalling inadequacy Moses and Elias are in reality groping toward and reaching out to the New Testament. These bearers of a temporary, static, and purely personal transfiguration are extending their hands to Jesus. For He will in His own power be the Worker, and in His own person the bearer of a glorification which will bless all who are His own. Yes, that is the really important consideration: this realization of glory. In Christ that glory, that revelation, is completely present (for He is very God). In Him it is not yet completely unfolded, however (for He is still humiliated man). But in this same Christ that glory and that revelation will by way of suffering and resurrection and ascension burst into the efflorescence of a new life. And that life this perfect and complete Mediator will share with all of His people. They will undergo His metamorphosis with Him, and will with Him rise out of suffering and death to heavenly blessedness. Behold, a greater than Moses or Elias is here. He is the Mediator between God and man.

To this evolving character of revelation Christ also responded in the one appropriate way; that is, as a Mediator. Again He swears a precious oath into the ears of His God. He declares that He, with His face fixed upon the throne of majesty, will go the way of suffering and of descent into hell. As a Mediator, He, together with all of His people, will shut out the last faint shimmer of light, and will bury Himself under the avalanche of hell, will subject Himself to the curse of eternal condemnation. Because they could not supply that condition, Moses and Elias were unable to consummate effectual glory. Had they attempted to supply it, they would have been everlastingly swallowed by eternal death. But Christ is able to achieve the ultimate, active glorification. After He has gone down into everlasting death He will arise again, and will bear with Him, also in His humanity, the inner puissance of true transfiguration. By His resurrection and ascension He will take it with Him to heaven, and will share it with all of His people. So He will genuinely unify heaven and earth and make room everywhere for the "glory of the Lord." That will be when God's tabernacle descends to men, and the new Jerusalem comes to the earth. Then, by way of suffering, death, resurrection, ascension, and the pouring out of the Spirit, II Corinthians 3 :18 will be actualized.

Moses and Elias, returning to heaven from the mountain of transfiguration, will prophesy there of the coming of Christ's redeemed, saying: They all, reflecting not our glory, but that of the once exalted Christ, are presently changed into the same image from glory to glory, even as by the Spirit of the Lord.

Moses and Elias gave to the Lord, and they lent to Him. But they desired and received much more. Had it not been for Christ's perfect Mediatorship, the glorification of Moses and of Elias would never have been recognized in heaven. For they, too, were saved only by this same Christ.

Obviously, we, together with these representatives, must reach out our hands to heaven. We must give the true but incomplete revelation which we receive an active reception, pressing on to what lies before. Moreover, we must pause in holy reverence. Now Christ has seen the powers of hell and of heaven loosened over His head. Now He steps out of the vestibule of the temple of passion into the building proper. He pulls the sexton's cord, shuts out the world, shouts hosanna, puts His arms around the supporting pillars, and, like the Great Samson He is, pulls destruction down over His head, in order that He may die, not with us, but for us, Philistines.

Christ's Necessary "Circum-
locution"

CHAPTER SEVEN

Christ's Necessary "Circumlocution"

● *And it came to pass when he was nigh to Bethphage and Bethany, at the mount called the mount of Olives, he sent two of his disciples, saying, Go ye into the village over against you; in the which, at your entering, ye shall find a colt tied, whereon yet never man sat; loose him, and bring him hither. And if any man ask you, Why do ye loose him? thus shall ye say unto him, Because the Lord hath need of him.*

And they that were sent went their way, and found even as he had said unto them. And as they were loosing the colt, the owners thereof said unto them, Why loose ye the colt?

And they said, The Lord hath need of him.
—LUKE 19:29-35.

IN THE foregoing chapters we observed Christ as He stood in the vestibule of the house of sorrows. Now we shall see Him put His own hand on the latch of the door that leads into the temple proper.

The first incident to attract our attention at this stage of the history of the passion is Jesus' royal entry into Jerusalem. We all know that Jesus was given a great ovation as He rode into the Capitol. Had we not always known that He must be in His Father's city?

It happens that very many observers have a way of seeing only the human aspect of that triumphal entry. These like to tell us of the enthusiastic thousands, of the surging masses of people who shout hosannas, extend those symbols of honor, the palm branches, in their hands, and who, in short, turn the city topsy-turvy by their holiday abandon. The sole regard of these

observers is to that concourse of people. Jesus — to use a collo-
quial expression—is left to shift for Himself. The crowd becomes the subject of the predication and Christ the passive object of it, the Man to whom all these colorful things are "happening."

It must be very obvious to all who ponder this event very carefully that to emphasize the contribution of the people in that way
is to give the matter a false accentuation, quite out of harmony
with the dominant tone of the story of the Bible. We must remember that the history of the Scriptures has been organically
constructed and symmetrically planned by its author, the Holy
Spirit.

The Reformed thinker and Bible student must take exception
in general to any presentation of the Scriptures, and to any interpretation of them, which seems to assign a passive role to Jesus, one, that is, which only in a subsidiary and incidental way suc-
ceeds in including the Christ in the story at all. Christ Jesus is
peculiarly the great Worker, the great Doer. His Father works,
and He works. Hence He may at no time be presented as the
"passive object" of events, and as that only. For Christ is conceivable in that way only when seen in relationship to His Father,
and even as such He is as active as He is passive. Hence, when
the church, and, for that matter, when anyone, speaks of an "active" and of a "passive" obedience, an equal stress should be
placed upon both adjectives. Such balanced accentuation, as we
see it, is one of the first principles of a Reformed interpretation
of the Scriptures.

That the active obedience of Christ should be as sharply ac-
cented as His passive acquiescence becomes clear from a careful
study of the passage at the head of this chapter. The incident
related there illustrates quite plainly that in this triumphal entry
Jesus Himself is peculiarly the active party; He is the first to act
at every turn: it is He who initiates even the ovation. So obviously is Christ peculiarly in charge of affairs on this occasion
that we almost feel inclined to speak of a kind of circumlocution.
Were it not irreverent and illogical, we should almost say that
Christ is at this time taking a very "roundabout" way to attain

His ends, that He is making a superfluous detour. But to say that sounds startlingly irreverent, and is in no sense edifying. We can better turn our attention to the multitude again. Look at those surging crowds. Listen: they are shouting hosannas!

Nevertheless . . . it does look like circumlocution. And that on Jesus' part. Perhaps we shall understand it better after we have studied again the introduction to the event.

In the first place, this is a very exciting time. The great festival which annually brought thousands of people, Jews and Gentiles, to Jerusalem from hither and yon is almost to begin. A nervously expectant crowd is looking forward to the scheduled program of events. The atmosphere is tense. And the tension is aggravated when this one and that begins to tell of the wonderful rumors that were beginning to be associated with the name of Jesus.

As quickly as a prairie fire the rumor passes from those native to the vicinity to the visitors from afar that Jesus has just miraculously raised Lazarus from the dead at Bethany. That piece of news creates a furor and immeasurably raises the pitch of excitement. The feast itself has not yet begun but the tension usually at its highest pitch during the festivities proper has now reached its acme beforehand. Naturally, the new miracle at Bethany, unusually astonishing as it was, is added, during the course of the conversations, to those which are already associated with the name of Jesus. A fascinating aureole begins to encircle His person. Quite definitely He becomes the center of attraction.

Moreover, the excitement is not the least bit tempered as the conversations on this corner and on that drift to the subject of the well-known friction between Jesus and the authorities. The question has been asked before, as a matter of fact, whether Jesus would dare to appear at the feast.[1] It is being asked again: Will he dare to come? Will he be intimidated by the threat of the Scribes?

And now—how very remarkable—everyone has heard it said, each from a "reliable source," not only that Jesus is in the immediate vicinity—for He is at Bethany—but also that He plans

---

1. John 11:56.

to come up with the people for the celebration. It is practically certain: the Nazarene will be there.

That news does put little Bethany on the center of the stage. There life was brought to light by Jesus' grave-vanquishing power. Yes, life was called from the grave at Bethany. And this fact prompts the query: Can that life defend itself and Him who aroused it against the threat of death issued by the authorities?

We know that Jesus had arrived in Bethany on the Sabbath day. We can imagine how restless that Sabbath must have been. The little town, usually so quiet and peaceful, was in a tumult. Current rules and customs governing the length of a "Sabbath-journey" were not too strictly observed by those who felt like going over to Jesus' house to satisfy their curiosity. Moreover, the distances separating the towns and villages were short. And anyway, if those distances did exceed the limit of a legitimate Sabbath-journey, there were devices enough the people could resort to, and, still preserving the letter of the law, travel as far as they pleased. On this particular Sabbath day, we can be sure, everything concentrated upon the person of Jesus.

Meanwhile, what does He do: recede into the background, or come out into society?

He answers the question Himself, and without hesitation. On the Sabbath He takes His rest, for He lives by the law. But on the next day, which is Sunday, He leaves Bethany, in the company of His disciples. That in itself is unusual. Imagine the crowds it must have attracted.

But now something takes place which causes not a little surprise. This time, so far from avoiding an ovation, Jesus seems actually to invite one. How often He had avoided the crowds; how frequently He had offset a mass demonstration by saying that none should report what miracles He had done. Now He seems deliberately to arouse curiosity and to attract the attention of the people.

Observe in how roundabout a way He proceeds.

He tells two of His disciples to go to a small settlement, not specifically named, situated some distance away. He tells them that when they arrive at that village they will find the colt of an ass tethered there. That they must take to Jesus.

It is this which, as we first read it, sounds very much like a circumlocution, like an unnecessary digression. If Jesus really wants a beast of burden, He Himself certainly can go and ask its owners whether He may use it. He can, of course, and that He does not is unusual and significant. Besides, He chooses an animal some distance removed rather than one from the immediate neighborhood. His disciples must fetch it. They are asked to do something which, to say the least, will excite the curiosity of those who see it: they are asked to commit a kind of robbery. Certainly their act will create that impression. Bold enough, all this, we feel like saying: to simply take the colt away from the man who owns it. Naturally the nonplussed owner will ask them what they are about. That, in turn, will precipitate considerable excitement in the street. A knot of people will collect there. Some discussion will ensue. The man will let the beast go. The rabble, their curiosity provoked, will follow the colt and its drivers until these come to the place where Jesus is awaiting them. We can follow the whole procedure to a T, can figure out precisely what will happen.

And so can Jesus. That is exactly the troublesome feature. Why this beating around the bush? We ask the question timidly and with embarrassment, but . . . it persistently comes back for an answer.

And, startling as these circumstances are in themselves, we must remember that we have been looking at them only from the human point of view. There is another side. A miracle is taking place here: nothing short of a miracle. We notice that the moment we think of the strange coincidence of persons and circumstances. That coincidence persuades us that the Spirit is at work on this occasion. This is more than coincidence, more than accident. God Himself is active in the event. Jesus works toward God, but God also works toward Jesus. The significance of the episode is not only that Jesus' discerning eye sees precisely where the colt is tied, and that He can state in advance exactly what the owner will say, but it is that God Himself is here disposing everything according to His extraordinary providence.

He directs matters so, that the colt is at the specified place, that the owner is at home, that the discussion predicted is actually begun, in short, that everything occurs as Jesus has announced beforehand.

Whoever believes with a childlike faith what the church confesses concerning an almighty and ever-present power of God's providence, whoever knows that the "crisis"[1] is vitally present in every moment in which the sacred history of God's special revelation is realizing itself, will conclude that this providence is obviously active at this time. The miraculous in the event may seem to be limited to a beast of burden, to a moping owner, and to two disciples acting rather unconventially. But, as far as the significance goes, that miraculous element is not second in importanee to the smoking of Sinai, to the receding currents of the Red Sea, to the water issuing from the rock or to the attraction of the animals to the ark. This miracle is second to no other.

Hence, if we try to keep God related to the event, we see how foolishly stupid it is to ignore the divinely "intentional" aspect of the event. There is a Divine purposiveness in it which comes from two sources, from above and below.

On the other hand, we do not care to deny, of course, that Jesus had good reasons for doing as He did. To name a few of these, for instance. The Saviour specified that the beast must be one "whereon yet never man sat." This royal requirement was an expression of His own awareness of the distinctiveness of His position. And there is a good reason for His requiring a colt from a neighboring village rather than one from the immediate neighborhood. By that He demonstrated that as a King His is the right of confiscation. This privilege of the king had been declared a fact before the Spirit of prophecy by the mouth of Samuel had designated Saul as the first ruler of Israel. Now that Christ, as the last, the great, and the eternal, King has come into His kingdom, He makes use of that right at once, before the people thrust Him out of His empire.

But, even though such reasons tell us that the Christ had good cause for doing what He did, they do not satisfactorily account

---

1. John 12:31: "Now is the judgment, the "crisis," of this world; now is the week of the passion."

for our surprise at His circumlocution. That, then, requires a more specific explanation.

We must remember that once before in His life Jesus seemed to take a very roundabout way in arriving at His purpose. We read of that former instance in Luke 4:29 and 30. Jesus had just preached His first sermon in Nazareth. At its conclusion the populace wanted to put Him to death, for His words had rankled them. In a flash the little city rose in tumult, the people poured out of their houses in throngs, and the excited mob hustled Jesus out of the city, beyond the suburbs, and to the edge of a high precipice. But when the furies of Nazareth had driven Him to that point, Jesus became invisible and "went through the midst of them." Naturally the question arises in our minds: Why did Jesus permit the people to go to such lengths before He made His escape? If He carried the power to withdraw from the passion and brutality of the throng anyway, why did He not exercise it at once? This, then, is another instance of apparent circumlocution. First He let every man, woman, and child in Nazareth lose himself in the bustle of an incensed mob. And only then He disappeared. He kept back the miracle until. . . .

And now He does it again.

There is a relationship between these two instances of circumlocution. In both cases Christ purposely, deliberately incited the mass upheaval. He lured the multitude from the homes of Nazareth in order to impress indelibly upon the minds of all, the significance of that high point in His prophetic career at which He had just arrived. The sermon He had just preached in their synagogue was His public inauguration into the prophetic ministry of Israel. And Jesus felt that this initial prophetic moment with its pure and penetrating ministration of the Word of God had to be preserved in the mind of the people as a "testimony unto them." They had to be made to remember His word ever after so that they might recall later that He had said nothing amiss, that He had simply let the Scriptures speak, and that natural human nature had nevertheless rebelled against His true prophecy, even to the extent of wanting to put Him to death.

Now at Bethany, His kingly, not His prophetic claims, are the important issue. He is to enter Jerusalem today, and Jeru-

salem is peculiarly His city. He wants to make His debut as a
King to as many people as He can possibly attract to one
place. At Nazareth He had called a mass meeting to witness the
beginning of His official career. Now He assembles the multi-
tudes again, this time appearing in His official calling as a King.
And He does this in order that at that last stage, His priestly "decease," at once the height and depth of His official life, the
whole world may, through the Word, witness the fulfillment of
His calling.

In making these comparisons we get a glimpse of the artistic
architecture of Jesus' life.

The first time Jesus took a roundabout way He did so in order
to catch the people in their own nets. Nazareth had counten-
anced Him for thirty years. That long they had accorded Him
"grace and favor." Then He made His first public sermon and
attached a pure application to it. Thereupon the hosannas of the
citizenry were metamorphosed into the bitterest of curses: crucify
Him, crucify Him! And this time He invites the masses to choke
the roads so that the whole world may be witness to the fact-that
the people first shout hosanna, and then, a few days later, when
He refuses to become what flesh would have Him be, raise the
other cry: crucify Him!

There is a magnificent harmony in the vital interrelationship
of these events, a pattern of Divine perfection, an agonizing
beauty.[1]

The second Adam Himself saw to it that His passing from the
outer court into the holy place of the tabernacle of the passion
should not be forgotten for a moment. The Sanhedrin may be
watching for an opportunity to take Him secretly, and not during
the feast, especially not before the crowd. But Jesus precludes
the possibility of a secret capture by describing an arc around
the Sanhedrin, by making a circumlocution which, as we know
now, is not superfluous but necessary.

The roundabout way which Jesus takes at Bethany, even though
it seems to be a kind of self-advertisement, is essentially just the
opposite. Jesus' circumlocution is as substantial and as full of

---

1. "Mysterium tremendum."

eternal content as the advertising of the world is hollow and superficial.

The Bible also speaks of a famous piece of advertising. Think of Isaiah 23:16. There we read a pathetic account of the decay of the heathen city, Tyre. The prophet pronounces a curse upon the kingdom of Phoenicia, and the judgment he prophesies is aimed especially at its capitol city. Just now, says the prophet, it may, by reason of its hydraulic engineering, its learning, and its military organization, occupy a conspicuous position in the secular world, but judgment will come upon it after a while. It will be buried, and then forgotten. But the forgotten and neglected city, we read, will not be congenially disposed to its widowhood. It will advertise itself in a futile attempt to recapture the attention it has lost. Tyre will parade upon the streets as a painted harlot, with a harp in her hand, trying to recaptivate the people by an artificially entrancing voice, by songs and playing.

This discerning picture of the prophet Isaiah is typical of that superficial and repulsive self-advertisement which not the true bride but the harlot needs to attract attention. Jerusalem, the true bride of the future, rises gloriously out of Zion, and, by virtue of an intrinsic beauty outwardly expressed, effortlessly enjoys the attentions of God Himself. But Tyre, the city which has prostituted the love of God, must assume the role of a neglected courtesan, weeping for a lost youth, and trying to compel attention by artificial means.

We should almost like to say that our Lord Jesus Christ similarly despairs now because of His own past; that He too is caught in a tragic conflict of personality, born of disillusionment; and that He by promoting the triumphal entry is making a desperate effort to get the esteem of the multitude. We should almost venture to say that . . .

We shall say it. There is a sense in which we dare to make that statement. In fact, that is all we can say—if we look upon Jesus only from the outside. Whoever fails to interpret Him in the light of prophecy, that is, in His own light, must conclude that the circumlocution which Jesus describes upon this occasion is quite superfluous, and very human—too characteristically "human," in fact. That Christ was simply advertising Himself here in a last attempt to elicit esteem—that has been said. Friedrich Nietzsche said it. He once pictured Christ as a frail and world-weary Hebrew, who, doubting His future, bowed forward in despair and fell into death's arms as the last attempt to find reception with the people failed.

In this matter, too, of course, the interpretation of unbelief and of faith differ fundamentally. The efforts of the Tyrian harlot to circumvent despair, and the circumlocution of Israel's Bridegroom, Jesus, are in essence diametrically opposed. The advertisement Tyre employed was a caricature of the chaste wedding day of the true religion. But in Christ the true Bridegroom takes the legitimate way to His people. Tyre offers to give; however, she does so for her own sake. But the self-advertisement of Jesus is designed to give the great gift to those who have ears to hear, the great gift of love which does not seek its own. The promises of Tyre excite what is loathsome in those who meet her. But the charm of Jesus is designed to expel sin from His people, and to substitute for it righteousness and wisdom. The self-advertisement of Jesus, the true King of Jerusalem, is the swearing of an oath: Though ye may forget, yet will I not forget thee. Behold I have graven thee upon the palms of My hands.

Hence it was not a kind of fascination in seeking out false and idle antitheses, no playing with textual possibilities, which induced us to contrast Tyre with Jerusalem. For the Spirit of God which is the Spirit of Christ is active in both instances. Two lines of prophetic pronouncement, two trends of history, both issuing in the Christ, emerge from them. Always there are two lines running through the centuries. The despair of the Prince of Tyre is voiced in a cry which rends the night of a godless cultural world. That world is compelled to advertise itself because intrinsically it is devoid of love and life and truth. But Christ, the King of Jerusalem, still lives on, unforgotten, in the love acts of a church which is replete with beauty, truth, and simplicity.

Let us return, then, to the sublime beauty of the person of Jesus Christ as He manifests it here in all of its fulness. As we look upon Him we see that He is beautiful in His life, beautiful in His person, and beautiful in His relations to God and to man.

He is beautiful in His office. He instigates that mass ovation according to a careful plan; according to a specifically delineated outline, He calls forth a demonstration which will eventually force Him to the office of Caiaphas. Thus He illustrates that His active obedience is as great as His passive acquiescence. For it is in this very moment that He is entering His death, is assuming His passive obedience. Nevertheless He is very active, is obedient in point of deeds. Notice how He accommodates Himself to circumstances, how He, so far from letting things happen to Him, Himself guides the people and forces the authorities to the great deed to take place in God's appointed hour. Once He said that He beheld "Satan as lightning fall from heaven." But He is not content with the fall: He wrenches Satan out of heaven. Yes, the "sword is awakened against the great shepherd," as the prophet had announced. But that sword is not only awakened from God's side; Jesus draws its point to His breast with His own hands.

This harmony between His active and His passive obedience is sublimely beautiful. The two balance perfectly. *Simplex sigillium veri* — say that especially on the via dolorosa.

Christ is beautiful in His person. See how cautiously He carries out a previously carefully elaborated plan, and yet how organically, how smoothly that conduct is interwoven with the sequence of events. He embodies a simplicity which the people would almost call a naivete, and a systematic approach which makes Him strictly the Architect of God.

This vital interrelationship of the several parts of Jesus' life is astonishing in that it manifests a complete coöperation with God (the concursus). The Man Jesus makes an artistic pattern of His life. Each day of it He is working on a mosaic, a rich design, unified but elaborate, a perfect whole. Every new day introduces some new event into His program; but He always follows the old course. Successive moments provide successive changes, but no occurrence violates the form of the whole. Jesus' life to many seems to be a piecing together of incidents. It comes in that guise to all who do not believe Him, to all who do not understand Him according to His own interpretation of His words.

But he who believes sees Him always doing His Father's business.

His Father's business . . . Christ is beautiful, too, in relation to His God.

A well-known commentator[1] points out that the perfect prayer, the Lord's Prayer, presents a remarkable contrast of the first group of three petitions included in it to the second three. The first triad comprises three petitions in which some property of God, rather than God Himself, is the subject of each predication. God's name is the subject of the first prayer; God's Kingdom that of the second; His will that of the third. This feature becomes especially conspicuous when we compare that first triad with the second group. For in each petition of this second series, God is the person addressed and the subject of the predication, even though that nominative of address and that subject is, as the grammarians say, "understood" and not "expressed." Note that such is the case.

> Give us this day our daily bread (i.e., Do thou give...)
> Forgive us our debts (Do thou forgive . . .)
> Lead us not into temptation.

Now the commentator referred to has asked himself why this difference should obtain; why, in other words, God should be addressed directly in the second triad of petitions and not in the first. And the answer he suggests is that we human beings should have such respect for God's work done in reference to Himself that it is unthinkable for us to designate precisely what He should do for Himself and to outline concretely how He should proceed to do it. The mystery which informs the hallowing of God's name, the coming of His kingdom, and the fulfillment of His will is so awesome, so sublime a matter that the petitioner cannot conceivably name the ways and means by which these ends should be achieved. The Almighty forbid that any man should outline a specific program which the God of heaven and earth should follow in order to realize the great purpose of all that moves and has being.

---

1. Strack-Billerbeck, *Das Evangelium nach Mattheus*, (Komm. z. N. T. aus Talmud und Midrasch), 1, Munchen, 1922, p. 408.

But the same petitioner, says this commentator, does not hesitate to point out specific ways and means when the desired ends concern himself. Give us our *bread*, he prays; forgive us our debts; and lead us not into temptation, *but deliver us from the Evil One*. That is being very specific as to the "what" and "how." And that courage is lacking in matters concerning God and His awful majesty.

There is no particular point in trying to decide now whether this interpretation of the delicate distinction between the first and second triads of the Lord's Prayer is the correct one. Certainly it is beyond dispute that we human beings are perplexed in the extreme when it comes to naming the means God ought to employ in hallowing His name, accomplishing His will, and causing His kingdom to come. To creatures of the dust those exalted purposes are a mystery which eye hath not seen, nor ear heard. No human heart has appreciated that mystery, no human mind understood. The gulf which divides the Creator from the creature is wide, and no created mind has analyzed God's being or measured the ways of His counsel.

Such is human limitation. But Christ is not bound in that way. He is true man and very God, and as such He is an eternal party to the counsel of God. His eye has seen, His ear has heard, and His mind has understood every minute detail, for He Himself planned along what avenues and by what channels God's great purpose must be accomplished.

Moreover, Jesus' true humanity enters into real relationship with His essential Divinity. He is ready now to assume personally the fulfillment of those three petitions of the first triad of the Lord's Prayer. He knows the ways and means by which that must be done familiarly, He takes them into His hands, He looks them over, manipulates them. The King of supreme love, motivated by the perfect zeal of God, does not scorn to use human "tact" as He proceeds to hallow God's name, to cause His kingdom to come, to do His will on earth almost as it is done in heaven. He thoroughly knows the steps in the program; without misgivings He makes use of definite means, fully satisfied that they will bring His Father's purpose and His own to full fruition.

In setting out to achieve this sublime end, Christ proves to be not only our brother but also our Lord. As our brother He is a man among men; as our Lord He is exalted far above us, even in His humanity. He is simultaneously a servant and a king. As a servant He identifies Himself with the least of those who pray the perfect prayer. He uses common, human means to realize the great mystery of those first three petitions. A madding crowd, a colt, a man of the street—those are the media. But He is also the King, the first in rank among the people; first, too, in His humanity. In this double capacity He prays and explains the Lord's Prayer; prays it in inaudible words, and explains it in common, in ordinary terms.

He Himself taught this prayer to His disciples. He alone could teach it, for He is the only person in heaven and on earth who actually embodies and fulfills its content and its form in His life.

Finally, Christ is most beautiful in His relationship to men. Observe how appropriately He treats each according to his essential nature: the Sanhedrin one way, the masses another. He has respect for the individuality of everyone and responds accordingly.

Jesus, certainly, has the right to startle the Sanhedrin, to break into its secret session, and to cause panic there, even as He had done when He dispersed the traders in the outer court of the temple and swept that court clean. And of course, He is able to do that. One prayer to heaven and twelve legions of angels will appear beside Him. Or He can give the word to the people and a legion of them will support Him in an attack upon that Bastile of falsehood, the Sanhedrin. Being students of Balaam[1] its members may have little respect for hosts of angels, but they certainly will honor a few hundred of the people. People, soldiers, and many of them—that is an argument they can understand. But Jesus avoids them. He sees to it that its members hear of Him, but His course describes an arc around them.

To the people, however, the poor victims of hirelings, the subjects of traitors, to these He comes lovingly and patiently. He

---

1. See Chapter 4.

comes, eager to teach them one more lesson, anxious to ask them once more whether they choose to curse or to kneel. Such is the beautiful love which deals with each according to his character.

We must bow in reverence before this Man of sorrows, fully embodying perfect beauty as He does. We must bow, and remember that He goes up to celebrate a feast—but is meanwhile busy with His suffering.

And we must remember also that in order to achieve this service of love Jesus is compelled to resort to Tyre's methods of self-advertisement. It is that fact which constitutes His suffering in this moment. In Jesus Christ God comes to Israel as a Bridegroom, for it is as a bridal people that He looks upon those masses today. Consider the incongruity, then. He who wants to preach the pure and holy law of marriage to His people is compelled to attract their attention in a way not unlike that employed by the Tyrian harlot. O man, bewail thy awful sins . . . because of them the Bridegroom must resort to artificial tactics to court your attention. Surely His perfect love has a right to your response by virtue of its intrinsic beauty. And still, after the flaming passion of that love has flared up into an official service of thirty-three years, the Bridegroom must woo by superficial means! True, these do not defile His love at all, nor cast the slightest reproach upon it, but they are, nevertheless, a sad comment on human sin and perversity.

Fortunately, however, that need not be the closing thought. We conclude in worship. Jesus' circumlocution was a necessary one. What is necessary is not circumlocutive; what is circumlocutive is not necessary. It is true that Jesus takes a roundabout way. But He is busy in the things of His Father. Beyond that our thoughts cannot go.

We do not always see the perfection of that pattern. We do not always see that by means of the apparently confused intervolutions of His career, Christ was creating the perfect poem, His Father's work. It will require all our days to the end of time to see that steadily always. To get just a glimpse of it requires a consecrated heart and a quiet soul.

But whoever has caught a glimpse of the fact that Jesus in the mean and commonplace activities of His life is busy in the things of His Father—He has experienced a moment of great faith. Whoever has seen that Christ's by-paths never lead away from the highway of His official career will find rest in His spirit, rest and reverence and trust. To see Him in that way is to see Him perform a double duty. It is to see Him bear the suffering that comes to Him because of our transgressions. It is to witness His perfect poise, to see a second Adam whose attention is not distracted, and who keeps the garden of His soul beautiful and pure. This is the Saviour who suffered for what we did amiss and who achieved what we failed to do.

He will enter the temple of suffering now. But it is comforting at this point to take knowledge of both of Christ's burdens. It is a comfort to witness the passive obedience by which He atones for our sin, for the sin by which we made chaos of the cosmos. And it is a blessing to note His active obedience, reaching to the beauty of God, an obedience which converts the chaos into a cosmos again, builds it and preserves it in and around His soul.

Christ Welcomed — and Travestied

CHAPTER EIGHT

Christ Welcomed — and Travestied

● *And when He was come nigh, even now at the descent of the mount of Olives, the whole multitude of the disciples began to rejoice and praise God with a loud voice, for all the mighty works that they had seen; saying, Blessed be he that cometh in the name of the Lord; peace in heaven and glory in the highest.*
—LUKE 19:37, 38.

ON THE first day of the Feast of the Passover, Jesus left the quiet of Bethany and, as we noticed, had His beast of burden brought to Him. Thereupon follows what under the circumstances is quite inevitable: the King's triumphal entry into Jerusalem. He wears no crown on His head as He comes, is unarmed and lowly. As far as its officials are concerned, the city makes no effort to receive Him. The rulers of Jerusalem hold their breath as they watch what is going on with jealous eyes. But what of that? The King comes to His city.

We know the story well. A multitude of people, of disciples and curiosity seekers, suddenly swarm around the Christ. Some who have not previously enjoyed His lessons, who have not attended the school of the Master before, are eager now to join the others. Meanwhile Christ, who is almost hedged in by the throng, reaches the point where the road swings down to the valley of the Kidron, urges the colt in that direction, and moves toward the city. There the crowd swells to proportions beyond easy computation. No one can tell how it all began. But the fact is that Jesus is almost overwhelmed by the sweeping currents of enthusiastic thousands. As the royal cortege proceeds, it begins to take on a really festive character. The excited people begin to tear branches off the trees and to wave them in the air as a salute to the King. They throw their garments upon the road, just as the disciples had previously placed theirs upon the colt. Hence, in a few moments, by means of this eager improvisation of these tokens of honor, the whole road becomes a magnificent display of glory and great joy.

And there is much that is good in the ovation. Jesus acknowledges that Himself by the words: "If these should hold their peace, the stones would immediately cry out." O yes, it is a beautiful thing to see that a long-suppressed admiration of the mighty deeds of the prophet of Nazareth finally found an outlet in the exuberant gladness of this multitude.

In spite of that, however, we may not forget that the Scriptures at this point, too, are describing the severest suffering the world has ever seen. We must learn to see that this festive demonstration not only is in keeping with the tenor of the passion story but also makes a unique and additional contribution to the suffering of Christ.

A careful study of the event soon reveals that there are several elements of suffering, humiliation, and grief in what is commonly called the "triumphal" entry into Jerusalem.

In the first place, it must have grieved Jesus to see how fast and loose this people is playing with Israel's prophets. It uses them, yes. It even employs their texts and psalms in the doxology it is raising in Jesus' honor. But the people are willing to accept prophecy only in so far as it seems to be compatible with their own notions. The same prophecy they inject into their paean of praise today is forgotten the moment they discover that it is inconsonant with the best thoughts and with the prevailing theological opinions of the leaders of the day.

How often in the preceding chapters we have been compelled to notice that the prophecy of the Old Testament was fulfilled without the slightest awareness of it on the part of the people. We saw Caiaphas, saw Mary as she anointed the feet of Jesus, watched the chief priests as they paid Judas their traitor's fee, and in each instance we made the disappointing discovery that Israel was not living by prophecy. In fact, they could literally fulfill what the prophets had said — think of the thirty pieces, for example — without recalling the letter, to say nothing of the spirit, of what was written.

But if it suits them, the people can remember prophecy. They remember now, for instance, the words which Zechariah spoke about the kingdom of the future, the Messianic kingdom. They have his description on the tip of the tongue and are enthusiastic about it. Here is Jesus, lowly and defenceless, riding into Jerusalem upon the back of a colt. When they see that, the seething multitude immediately recalls the picture in Zechariah 9. Their intuitive apprehension of the sound and sense of prophecy issues in a spontaneous paean of praise: "Hosanna: Blessed be he that cometh in the name of the Lord."

It is a great grief to our highest Prophet to notice that the multitude takes from the Scriptures what pleases it and ignores the rest. Such distortion is unwarranted, for the canvas of the Scriptures is woven of one piece and is seamless. Those who divide the Word into parts do precisely what the soldiers did with the garment of Jesus. That garment, too, was costly, all-of-a-piece, and seamless. But they tore it up and raffled the several parts. Depend upon it that as often as someone dismembers the Scriptures, Jesus' perfect soul suffers. It is the same as tearing Him apart. A rent in the body of the Bible, which is God's Word made Scripture, is equivalent to a dismemberment of Christ's body, which is the Word of God made flesh.

Jesus therefore suffers acutely now. Remember that He comes to present the true exegesis of Zechariah 9. Even while He Himself is putting the candle in the candlestick, the nervously busy floodlights of the false interpreters of Scripture are concentrated upon Him. This distortion is an earmark of that basic sin which is leading Jerusalem to its grave. Israel wants to shed its light upon Him. But He must illuminate Israel. This He does as often as He opens the Scriptures and fulfills them. But whoever looks at the Christ in his own light withdraws himself from the influence proceeding from Jesus through the Word. He excludes himself from that influence, though he shout hosanna a thousand times. To see Christ in our own light is to sin terribly, for it is to deny Him the right to minister His threefold office to us.

Moreover, this misconstruing of the inner essence of Jesus' activity soon reveals itself in its true colors. Luke, by his usual, sensitively discriminating phrasing, tells us significantly that the people "began to rejoice and praise God with a loud voice, for all the *mighty works* that they had *seen."* Their admiration, you see, is based on the miracles. Moreover, they stop at the visible things. That is Luke's double emphasis: Jesus' *mighty deeds* appeal to the Jews; and, they accept these not for their real meaning, but at their face value.

Now no one can deny, of course, that Christ demonstrated great power, unusual might, in His deeds. But that power is not basic and it is not primary. And, as for the second emphasis, although it is true that the dynamic element, the active energy, in Christ's miracles, becomes visible, subject to sense experience, still those visible expressions are not the all-important thing. It is true that the "mighty deeds" which He did, in other words, that the miracles which He performed, were signs by which the Word of God confirmed itself, and events by which prophecy was fulfilled. But such confirmation and fulfillment imply that the miracle is not an end in itself in Christ's work. Christ never rests in any single demonstration of power. A miracle is always a moment in a process by which the kingdom of heaven does "come," of course, but in order to come farther and to penetrate deeper. Every sign is prophetical. Every miracle eschatalogical. By a miracle Jesus never expects to attain some special result completely contained in the act itself. His miracles are media of revelation, pointing from the visible sign to the living Word. And, even to the extent that His wonders were conveyers of grace, aqueducts through which the waters of salvation flowed, even to that extent, they were designed to lead the thoughts of the people from the visible symbol to the unseen meaning, from the primitive sign to the vision of faith, which is the evidence of things not seen and which therefore can discern God without a miracle.

Whoever regards Jesus' miracles as ends in themselves does them an injustice. Whoever dissociates the symbol from the Word, whoever glories in the wonder without relating its external form to its internal meaning — he is looking at matters from the point of view of the apocryphal letters. For in these too a sentimental imagination becomes the prey of appearances and tries to authenticate Jesus by human argumentation. But such is not the canonical viewpoint. According to it the miracle is subordinate to the Word; the visible sign of grace is in the service of the invisible influence expressed in it. The canon presents the miracle as a unique and passing moment,[1] as an exceptional instance, which we want to pass by and beyond, simply because it comes at the beginning and not at the end of the way of grace. There is a sense in which a miracle is like Sodom. It is attractive, entrancing almost, but alas for him who looks back at it. The symbol of the miracle beckons us to look ahead.

That is just what the multitude does not do. They look at Jesus' mighty deeds; they are caught up by the miraculous element in His work; they stop at the wonder itself. And they do that in the presence of the Highest Prophet, who is the Canon, who is the first principle for all Scriptural exegesis. In His presence they repudiate the Spirit of the canonical Gospels by an apocryphal misapperception. This is but one manifestation of the perpetual conflict between the canonical and the apocryphal descriptions of Jesus' life.

In addition, Christ also suffers on this "festival" because the misguided people over-emphasize the element of "might" in Jesus' work at the expense of the fundamental element in it: namely, the restoration of justice. Christ comes to do mighty deeds, yes; but He comes primarily to restore justice. The redemption He wants to achieve is juridical first of all; just because it is basically that, it is also dynamic. By His perfect sacrifice and by His completely satisfying the law He wants to lay a foundation of righteousness under the living temple of grace, which is the church. After that, and only after it, the living waters of salvation will flow from beneath the temple-gate out into the world. Then the active energy of the Spirit will proceed dynamically to all forms of spiritual and material life; by it souls will be sanctified, the world be renewed, the earth be born again and actually wedded with heaven.

But the Jews are so steeped in their Messiah-expectation that they misread their own Scriptures. They are looking for a Messiah who does miracles, and have long ago closed their ears to a

---

1. As the Germans have it, the miracle is *einmalig*.

Messianic sermon which preaches redemption from sin and the restoration of God's justice.

This misapperception of Jesus' significance is strikingly illustrated in the doxology which the people sing. That paradoxical hymn simultaneously praises and blasphemes Jesus. It praises Jesus, but it curses Christ. It exalts the *might* of Jesus; but it is conspicuously silent on what deserves the loftiest praise: the *rights* of God. We should no longer be surprised to hear the multitude shout hosanna one day, and a week later to hear them cry: "Crucify Him! Crucify Him" in spite of "Hosanna"? No, no. So far from being in contrast with that earlier declaration, the "Crucify Him" is the logical result of that "Hosanna," and occurs *because,* not in spite of, it.

That is the logic of sin. That simply is the dialectic of the flesh. Such is reason, cut loose from the Logos of John.

Such logic is, of course, quite incompatible with Jesus' own explanation of His function and purpose. You remember that He once sent out the seventy disciples to work in separate groups among the people. When these returned, and He had listened to their glowing reports, He made this significant statement: "In this rejoice not that the spirits are subject unto you; but rather, rejoice because your names are written in heaven."

By that statement Christ impressed upon the minds of His disciples the very same distinction which the Jews might well remember today. For those disciples were quite elated about their ability to perform miracles; they could do so much, almost everything, in fact; could perform wonders, show signs, and even cast out devils. The kingdom of heaven, they felt, had passed through them dynamically. But Jesus pointed out what was the really remarkable thing, pointed out what was worth being exuberant about. The praiseworthy thing, He said in effect, is not your works of might, but God's work of grace. Not what you *can* do, but what you *may* do is remarkable. Your dynamic power is owing to the favor of God; His grace, juridically considered, gave you the right to perform miracles, gave you that privilege by elective favor. To be satisfied with doing mighty deeds is to be satisfied with a miraculous faith. The man who desires and lives the true saving faith refers his own dynamic energy to the wonder-working power of Christ and to His fulfilling the requirements of justice; and that, in turn, he refers to the sovereign good pleasure of God who wrote his name in heaven before anything in him had begun to live.

In that way Jesus, the Logos, at the beginning of His official career, defined the theological first principle of faith. Now He is almost at the close of that career. Meanwhile the number of the disciples has grown apace. Look at the countless numbers. But the quality of this multitude is not equal to its quantity; its faith does not keep pace with its fervor; its spirituality falls short of its enthusiasm. For the multitude speaks only of Jesus' might and of its own, and not at all of His and its own privilege. The dynamic, not the juridical, appeals to it. While Jesus is performing miracles, raising Lazarus, distributing food to the thousands, suppressing demons, this people honors Him. But a few days later, when He will bring the perfect sacrifice of fulfillment, will supply what God's justice demands, it will be ashamed of its meek and lowly king. And that is the best, although it is the most horrible, proof of the fact that its hosanna comes from admiration of the miraculous and not from a saving faith.

Essentially, therefore, the cynical chief priests and this elated crowd, exuberantly swinging the palm branches in the air, are allies. Both do injustice to the essence of Christ's official calling. Superficially there seems to be a considerable difference between them: the chief priests, nonchalantly counting the traitor's fee into Judas' hand, on the one side, and this honest, ardent, spontaneous crowd, in their ecstasy casting their finest garments into the road, on the other side. Quite a difference, superficially considered, yes. But essentially they agree. The shape and features of the sin of each group are not the same. But sin is sin, and unbelief is always unbelief.

Consider again that doxology which the people sing. Hear its chorus: Peace in heaven, and glory in the highest! It reminds us at once of the song the angels sang at the birth of Christ. How strikingly similar!

But there is one small difference — no, it is a prodigiously large one. The angels sang of heaven; but they also sang of the earth. And these celebrating myriads make mention of heaven only. The great need of the earth does not enter their minds. Note the angels' chorus once more:

Glory to God in the highest, and on earth peace, good will toward men.

There is no mistake about that. The angels who constantly live in heaven think of the earth at Christ's appearing. Earth's crying need is peace. But the earth will never receive that peace, unless heaven condescends to send the great gift down from above. Such was the import of the angels' song.

Meanwhile Jesus has come from Christmas eve to the night of His passion. At this stage a crowd borrows some of the words of the angels. The multitude sings a song. The verve and enthusiasm they put into it they have gleaned from a source other than the temple. But its content, the dogmatic idea behind it, the theological principle underlying it — that they have learned from the Pharisees. True, they also speak of peace; besides, they echo the angels' sentiment in rightly ascribing glory to God in the highest heavens. But the peace which they are thinking of is not the gift of God. Theirs is a pan-Jewish peace which comes to bless the earth by means of the Messianic kingdom, and which, they suppose, will thereafter ascend to heaven to bless God.

This emphasis, too, is just another effusion of the basic idea of the pharisaic theology in which these people had been schooled for years. That much the Pharisees had succeeded in teaching the masses. They had taught less of the truth that heaven ministers to the earth than of the dogma that the earth can and does enrich heaven. Hence the heaven-saluting doxology of the people is in keeping with the tenor of their theology, is an expression of their doctrine of salvation by good works and holy living. How repugnant that doctrine must be to heaven's greatest theologian: Christ Jesus! "Hosanna, Peace in heaven!"—that, one day. "Crucify Him, crucify Him!"—that, not a week later. But this too easy and perfectly logical transition clashes with the announcement of the angels on Christmas eve and also with the dogmatics of the Apostle Paul. Paul, himself delivered from the shackles of the Pharisees, also speaks of a Christ who renews all things, also the things in heaven, and bestows peace upon them. But Paul does not dare to think that thought, much less to say it, except as he sees the cross of Christ before it, as the legal prerequisite, as the source of the dynamic influence, as the fountain of the all-suffusing, heaven-permeating peace.[1]

How it must grieve the Christ at this time to see the people repudiating the law of His approaching death, and ignoring, no, scorning, the fundamental principle of salvation which the Holy Spirit is at the point of teaching the first Christian church. That great principle is that we can take nothing from below into heaven, unless we first received it from the highest.

This distortion of the significance of the work of Jesus was the fault of the people themselves and not that of Christ. For He preached the truth simply. Even in this moment as He enters Jerusalem He is fulfilling prophecy.

Yes, prophecy is being fulfilled again. In Zechariah 9 it had been foretold that the King of the Messianic realm should come to His people. According to that account He would not come storming into the capital as the Oriental despots were accustomed to do, but would make His approach as a prince of love and good will. He would be lowly, the prophet had said; that is, He would not rise to eminence over the shoulders of His subordinates, but would condescend to them in the spirit of compassion. He would be lowly: would come not to be ministered unto, but to minister. He would be lowly: that is, He would not build His throne at the cost of the blood and taxes of the populace, but at the expense of His own blood, which He would pay to God as a toll for the sins of the people. Such would be the nature of His lowliness as Zechariah saw it in the King of the future.

And a second thing that the prophet had predicated concerning this King was that He would come unarmed, in a defenceless condition. He would not invade the country on a war-horse, forcibly subjugating all to His rule, as the heroes of battle do. Instead, He would come to the capital on a colt, on the foal of an ass, an animal used in agriculture and not in war. This King, then, would differ essentially from the secular tyrants according to His character and according to the means He would employ to maintain His kingdom. *Je maintiendrai* — that would be His motto

---

1. Colossians 1:20: "For it pleased the Father (and was not, therefore, the result of human nobility) ... having made peace through the blood of the cross, by him (Christ) to reconcile all things unto himself; by him, I say, whether they be things in earth (these, you see, are not excluded), or things in heaven."

too, but it would be written, not under a lion, or under an image of the cavalry, but it would be engraved under a picture of the foal of an ass.

That was Zechariah's vision of Jesus' coming into His kingdom. Jerusalem is witness now; let them answer: Does Jesus add to the picture or subtract from it?

He does not, of course. His advent to the capital is precisely as Zechariah had pictured it. He comes as a lowly man, one with the people. He is defenceless, so harmless, as a matter of fact, that Pilate feels no obligation to put a restriction upon Him. So Christ proves that Zechariah's propehcy is completely fulfilled in Him.

His Messianic consciousness knew at once that the features of Zechariah's picture represented the God-appointed plan for His appearing in Jerusalem. Therefore His Messianic obedience is perfectly faithful to the features of that portrait. His pencil does not alter a single line in the sketch which God has drawn. He simply stands beside it and asks: Is it I?

But a conflict arises now between Jesus and His superficial admirers. It issues from the question as to how one must interpret the data of prophecy. For there is no doubt at all about Jesus' resembling the picture Zechariah recorded. The identity is beyond dispute. The people have been saying so themselves for some time. But the question is how to interpret the features.

The crowd has one interpretation. Jesus' lowliness, they feel, is but a temporary, a transitional phase. He will be poor with the poor today, but tomorrow, they hope, He will be rich. Surely, He will turn against Rome, will strip the gold from its splendid Capitol, and will use it for Israel's glory and for His own. As they see it, that empty-handedness, that lowliness, is but one stage in a progress to wealth.

As for His unarmed condition — that can also be explained. Naturally He must come unarmed at first, for the people would object to a ruler who should use the point of the sword to get into power. The king, they are sure, is not the pride of Israel, but Israel is the glory of the king. Moreover, every true son of Abraham has the right to rule, because — well, he is the son of Abraham. Hence it is natural that He should come unarmed. Later, by means of a plebiscite, they will graciously endow Him with arms, and will name Him commander of the army of Israel. He will owe His position to the consent of the governed, not to His intrinsic authority. Later, when they have delegated that authority to Him, they will follow Him and give heaven a peace which they have achieved on earth.

But Christ's exegesis of prophecy is at variance with this construction of the Jews. To this extent they are right: the lowliness they see today is but a transitional phase of a process. To that extent the masses are right. But they err in supposing that this meekness is a transition to secular glory. Jesus does not take the road upwards to Rome; instead He swings down to the gulf of eternal death. The lowliness Jesus manifests today must reach its culmination after a while in a profounder humiliation. Today He mingles with the least of those who keep the feast, but tomorrow He must disappear beneath the lowest; stripped and naked, He must die the death in the form of a servant.

His defenceless condition in its present form, identified as it is with His riding on a colt, is but a transition to a greater defencelessness. The colt, too, will be taken away from Him and be supplanted by bonds and shackles. So far from sitting and treading upon the garments of others, His own garment will be torn from His body and divided by lot. Even that is not all: besides disarming Him, the whole world will arm itself to the teeth against Him.

The lowliness and defencelessness of Christ are transitions, yes — but they lead to Golgotha.

Just for a moment, therefore, Zechariah serves as a meeting point for Jesus and the Jews. But again we must make the observation we have had to discover so often before: Jesus' interpretation differs from that of the people.

The multitude wrote a commentary on the 9th chapter of Zechariah. It cannot be that they wrote it in the sand, for to this day the Jews read it, nod affirmatively, and say amen. And they seal their interpretation with the symbol of palm branches. Those palm branches are prototypes of the trophies which will hang in the temple after the Romans, and not the Jews, have renovated it.

Jesus wrote the other commentary. He wrote it with His own hand, dipping His pen in blood. He accepted the ovation, palm branches and all, for they had been spoken of in the roll of the book. Therefore He accepted them as indispensable signs of God's presence in Him.

Is it strange, then, that Jesus who had heard the crowd sing Psalm 118 early in the week wanted to sing it better Himself at the end of the week? *Blessed be he that cometh in the name of the Lord.* But the very people who sent that chorus echoing through the heavens are the builders who refused the stone God had appointed to be the head of the corner. They bless the King by it, but their blessing is also a blasphemy to Him. For they distort the psalm. They shout verse 26, the paean of praise, most exuberantly, but they omit the stanza concerning the foolish builders.

Jesus, comforted by their false song, atoned for the singing. He did so at the end of the week when He left the room of the Passover with Psalm 118 on His lips. He sang it incomparably better than they — then, when He sought out the valley of the Kidron and entered Gethsemane. That was the first real singing of the hymn of praise designed for the Passover. Christ is the only One—this study proves that again—who can read prophecy and interpret psalms right. He alone can do that, for He alone embodies and fulfills prophecy in flesh and blood, in soul and spirit, in time and eternity.

Christ Relating Children's Games to Universal Prophecy

CHAPTER NINE

Christ Relating Children's Games to Universal Prophecy

● *And when the chief priests and scribes saw the wonderful things that he did, and the children crying in the temple, and saying, Hosanna to the son of David! they were sore displeased, and said unto him, Hearest thou what these say? And Jesus saith unto them, Yea; have ye never read, Out of the mouths of babes and sucklings thou hast perfected praise?*
— MATTHEW 21:15-16.

WE have just seen Christ ride into His realm in royal fashion. We heard the masses honor Him, and appreciated to a small degree the great suffering that afflicted His soul because of the royal reception and its several implications.

Now we have the privilege of fixing our attention upon the majesty of Christ. Were His authority as a king dependent upon the consent of the governed, or subservient to the will of a chance aggregation of the people, that authority would fade out with the waning enthusiasm of the crowd. According to the notions of those who went up to celebrate the feast, the ideal king is one who accepts His jurisdiction from the hands of the people, one who in all things lets them take the initiative. But if Jesus were disposed to satisfy such requirements, His own initiative would disappear as soon as the excitement of the populace had abated.

Beyond a doubt the people did want a king who would take his orders from them. We indicated at the close of the preceding chapter that the Jews hoped Jesus would fulfill Zechariah's prophecy concerning the coming of a lowly and unarmed Prince in a way suitable to their own interpretation of it. They wanted Him to take with Him an unmistakably worded "Act of Con-

133

formity" to the will of the people, so that they might arm Him then in their own good time, and might 'delegate authority as they pleased.

But we also noticed that Jesus objects to such distortion of prophecy. In Chapter 7 we saw that He Himself always takes the initiative. And in Chapter 8 we discovered that Jesus defines His kingdom, not according to the notions of a mob of excited people, but according to the dictates and intentions of the Spirit as revealed in prophecy. He Himself directs the course of affairs. He accepts the kingdom at His own behest. He gets His authority to do things from God and not from men.

You see that this fundamental conflict between the will of the people and His own began early. It loomed prodigiously large at once. Jesus' own discernment saw it fully informing the triumphal entry itself. And in the course of the coming days it defines itself in still more unmistakable terms.

The tension occasioned by the events at Jerusalem relaxed after a while; the excitement subsided; the violent overture to the week of festivities came to an end. After all, such celebrating could not last forever. The people again scattered over the city and the neighboring community. As a matter of fact, a kind of embarrassment took possession of them. They had honored a King, and pronounced Him a Prince of peace. More than one of them had in their nervous excitement thrown a sidelong glance at the palace of the governor, secretly thinking that the effects of this day might spell ominous things for the praetorship. When the clamor subsided, however, a flush of shame crept over the faces of the people. Strangely embarrassing thing: there was nothing they could do. At the moment there was little to say. This did not seem to be quite the right time to start distributing weapons, or to begin delegating authority. They had welcomed a King into their midst but no one could say just now what they should give Him to do.

If Jesus in this circumstance had only yielded to their wishes, He would have bided His time, accommodated Himself to the circumstances, and passively have awaited some event which would make it necessary for Him to step to the foreground. So He would have ingratiated Himself with the public, for that too was looking for a favorable moment to put a sword into His hand, and to turn Him against Rome and against its representatives.

Instead, Jesus deliberately goes His own way. He does not wait for the people to take the initiative. His actions are not mass-motivated, but self-prompted. He is the great Automatist, and in no sense ever an automaton.

Again He goes directly to His work. He manifests His kingly office this time by means of a mass-healing[1] in Jerusalem, right next to the temple. All kinds of sick people are taken to Him there. The lame and the blind are specifically mentioned. Jesus heals them all.

This is not the first time that Jesus engages in such a group healing. But this does seem to be a kind of special occasion. Jesus figured prominently in the minds of the people just now. They brought Him many patients, presented these to Him with the burning desire that He should heal them. And it seems that by the prompting of His own Spirit also a will to perform wonderful things moved Him now more than ever before.

Jesus had a purpose in mind as He performed these miracles. He wanted to continue what He had begun. He Himself had, by personally inciting that triumphal entry, explained and fulfilled the prophecy of Zechariah. That prophecy, we remember, had pictured the King of the future, the Messianic King, as being lowly and weaponless. Now Jesus wants to push the explanation of that prophecy, which He had begun on Sunday, farther. The purpose of His present miracles is to continue to give the best conceivable explanation of Zechariah's Messianic portrait.

Two features were dominant in that prophetic portrait. One was the coming King's lowliness. The significance of that prediction was that the Messiah-Prince would identify Himself with the least, the most common of His people. Observe how He enhances that feature of the picture now. How tenderly He leans over the lame and the blind, the meanest denizens, likely, of the least favored parts of the city. By condescending to these miserable ones immediately after His royal reception, He illustrates strikingly that He is the lowly King that Zechariah saw.

---

1. The word is used by Dr. F. W. Grosheide: *Kommentaar op Mattheus,* Amsterdam, 1922, p. 250.

But Jesus as completely interprets and as fully actualizes the second feature of Zechariah's picture: namely, His meekness, His weaponlessness. The defencelessness proves that His kingdom is not of this world. His is a theocratic kingdom. It makes no use of the formidable phalanxes of the other nations. It disdains to use the sword. It refuses to compete with others in filling its arsenals. It neither safeguards itself nor extends its boundaries by legions of soldiers or flouting banners. Not that it is passive and indifferent. O no, it penetrates the restive, secular world. But it comes in peace, and grows along spiritual ways. Its generative principle is one of spirit and of fire. Its power is not the "right of the strongest," but is intrinsic might, the authority owing to perfect qualification for rule.

He demonstrates this intrinsic might, not by maneuvering it against the Romans, against the praetorship of Pontius Pilate, but by turning it to the advantage of the sick, of the lame and the blind. The King is in His residence now. It is His turn to distribute gifts, to show mercy, to fill posts of honor. Jesus begins that benevolence at the lowest rung of the ladder. He has precious gifts to give, the best, save one[1]: life itself. Now it is His hour to break the bonds of death in which the children of Abraham are shackled. See how He flourishes in kingly service. He takes the fatal force of death, the last great enemy, the wages of sin, out of the community life. So He begins the great task of destroying sin itself, and of distributing the greatest gift: God's lovingkindness.

Very soon now, God and the angels in unison will raise the chorale of a heavenly Peace which will fill the whole universe. It is the prelude to that chorale which the lame and the blind are hearing beside the temple.

Jesus did many miracles in His life, performed many and various wonders. Some of them were signs accompanying prophecy. He was prompted to others by a priestly heart and in these a priest's love revealed itself. But the miracle which He is performing at the temple today is a positive expression and confirmation of the kingship of Jesus. It is a crystal-clear commentary, done in legible hand-writing so that all may read, on what Jesus

---

1. "Thy lovingkindness is better than life ...." (Psalm 63:3.)

said of Himself at the ovation which He incited.   It is an objective illustration which Jesus gives of the prophecy of Zechariah.   Jesus' miracle at this particular moment, on this specific day, at this definite place has a peculiar significance shared by no other miracle.   Every wonder, remember, is unique, has a separate meaning, and is in no sense a copy, a duplicate, of any other.

This wonder, for example, occurs next to the temple, and is a mass-miracle.   It blesses the city of the great King.   By means of it, Jesus, being in His rightful residence, declares for a last time the law of His kingdom.   He heralds the millennium of that future Prince of Peace, who is present already, the prince who comes not with the pomp of glory, but with the will to annihilate sin and to subdue the great penalty of it, which is death.

Moreover, this healing of the lame and the blind occurred during the week of the passion.   In this last week of His humiliation Jesus lets power go out of Him, and so proves that He is in control of the energies of the kingdom of heaven.   And that is proof beforehand, too, of the fact that the cross, when it comes, will be a revelation of strength, not of weakness, will be a deed, not a death.   One who can give life and subdue death as Jesus does in this last week of His suffering cannot die unless He *wills* it.

The King of Jerusalem, therefore, remains faithful now to the initiative to which He gave expression upon His entrance into the city.   And he is just as faithful to prophecy.   Precisely because He is that, the city which gave Him that glad welcome must get into conflict with Him.   For Jerusalem is not at all inclined to give up its own interpretation of the prophecy of a lowly and defenceless king.   They will admit that Jesus' healing of the sick is a beneficial, rather striking, and altogether philanthropic service, but it is not exactly what they had had in mind for Him.   Their sense of respect for so moving a demonstration, their ecstatic wonder at it, and their rather shy gratitude for it does not last long.   A king who goes his own way, especially when it is not the one which the people want him to take, cannot expect to keep the torch of popular enthusiasm burning long.

When Jesus, therefore, responds to the ovation given Him by this comparatively harmless service of benevolence at the temple, the leaders of the people are quick to take advantage of the subsequent abatement of enthusiasm. They rush in to extinguish completely the flickering flames.

This is the situation. While Jesus is healing the lame and the blind a considerable number of people, naturally, are standing by. Among these are a large number of children. They form a circle around Jesus and begin to play at a game of their own invention, in which He is the central figure. They begin to play "hosanna." No wonder. They have just seen that grand march which, in passing through the streets, sent clouds of dust way up over the houses. Besides, they themselves followed in the wake of the dense crowd of hero-worshippers. By watching the "big" people they learned how to respond to that prophet of Nazareth who had been saying such good things and doing so many wonderful deeds. Meanwhile Jesus has actually stopped at a given point and seems disposed to stay there for a while. This is their chance. They form their circle. Very likely they are swaying branches in the air, good green branches, just as good as those of the palm trees. They remember parts of the doxology and begin to shout these. The picture is complete for them. Just like the grown-ups do.

It is very likely that when the families of the grateful patients come to shyly kiss the hand of the Rabbi of Nazareth, not a few of these children are among them. In all likelihood, too, more than one of these youngsters is a personal pal and confidant of this blind old man and of yonder cripple. There is therefore a sense in which the children's game is nothing particularly unusual, and in which their shouting the hosanna chorus is quite ordinary.

In point of fact it was very ordinary. Any charlatan might have been similarly greeted.

Therefore it is not surprising to notice that the leaders of the people, who are bent upon using every means to counteract the masses' growing admiration for Jesus, crowd in now to profit from this chance to cast an unfavorable reflection upon Him. They step up boldly and ask Him whether He cannot put a stop to all that yelling on the part of those children. He wants to be taken seriously, does He not? If so, He ought not to give the appearance of actually being affected by the prattle of the youngsters. A man who really wants to exert an influence upon the people, should disdain to pose for such popular heroism; should do so especially here, in the shadow of the temple, where the scrolls are kept, and where the sages of Israel each day meet in consideration of the profoundest of problems. If He really wants to prove His worth, let Him go inside. The times are too trying for such child's play.

By such assumptions the Scribes hope to entice some incriminating word from His lips. Of course, He may choose not to answer. Then the question itself, conspicuously unanswered as it will be, will snuff out the flickering torch of mob enthusiasm. It will show the crowd that this upstart Nazarene is not as great as they had supposed.

Jesus' response? Well, He knows, of course, that not everything the children say is genuine, profound, sincere. He who saw through the superficiality of the hosannas of the people must detect many a falsetto voice and monotone in this chorus of children. Yes, He knows that their praise is not significant as an index to their appreciation of His work.

But He refuses to silence them. Their shouting, He feels, is a gift to Him, a gift coming not so much from the children as from the God of Israel. The moment He hears their chanting He thinks of the 8th Psalm. He hums it to Himself, ponders its sentiment in His heart, lets it resound in His soul. He takes His answer to the Scribes from it, an answer which corners them at once.

Do they know what the Bible says? Certainly, they know that—they are Scribes. But even as they reply they begin to fidget around in embarrassment. Good, Jesus goes on to say. In that case they will know that God counts the voices of children among the very great things; that heaven takes notice of them. In the 8th Psalm, they will recall, the poet says: "Out of the mouths of babes and sucklings hast thou ordained strength."

The phrase "babes and sucklings" refers to all children, for "babes" refers to children in general and "sucklings" to the infants—and we may remember that according to the customs of the east the mother personally nursed the child for a much longer period than is the usage in the west. From the mouths of all of these, therefore, God has ordained strength. He listens and accepts "the sacrifice of their lips."

Jesus quotes from the 8th Psalm and that gives His statement a peculiar value. It is the Psalm of magnificent things. It has a sublime theme. It sings of the sun, moon, and stars, and asserts that these all praise the name of God. But these—be they ever so overwhelming, so sublime—are not as great as the human soul. Contrasted with the physical universe, man is very small. But as a spiritual being He is great, for He bears the image of His Maker. And in the community of human beings even the frailest, the least developed life is greater than all the constellations of heaven. Out of the mouth of babes and sucklings also God has perfected praise. Even on a natural basis such praise is pleasing to God, for it comes to Him from the growing human world in His beautiful creation. But the children's chorus gives expression to the life of grace as well as to that of nature. God, who not only creates but also regenerates, delights in young voices. From the children of the covenant come the hosts of the faithful who will curb the power of sin later, will raise the battle-cry of holy war in the world in order that God may triumph in it.

Why silence the children, then? Jesus asks the Jews—and His question is as simple as the playing of the children—if God Himself, as all Scribes know, delights in the praise of infants? How, indeed, dare a servant of the Lord turn His back to a choir which is compelled to sing in praise of the Lord?

The learned gentlemen next to Jesus seem to think that children's voices are not in consonance with the atmosphere of that lofty temple. But Jesus says that the temple is precisely the place for such praise. Even in the temple of nature, the lesser temple, that over which the sun, moon, and stars form a vault, a chorus of children, according to the psalm, is a delight to the Lord. But such music is especially pleasing to Jehovah and to the angels when it comes from the temple of regeneration where the scrolls are kept and the laws of the covenant are deposited.

By a doxology of that kind, according to the psalm, the enemy and the avenger is stilled. Surely, they cannot expect Jesus to regard that too common which is not too trivial for God! In the name of the third commandment of the law of Sinai: Despise not the day of small things.

That embarrassing answer, naturally, sent the shamefaced Scribes on their way.

We, however, choose to linger with Jesus a little, now that the others have gone. Again we must worship Him for living so completely by the Scriptures, for living in them every moment. His reference to the 8th Psalm leaves it unbroken and intact. With a fine delicacy and perfect harmony He sings the whole of it in well-rounded, full-bodied tones. Its theme develops itself in His soul as a fugue. Melody and measure, both are perfect, whole, complete.

This psalm therefore gives the apparently trivial game of a group of children the sublimely tragical background of the whole passion week.

In the first place, the Psalm unites nature with grace. In it general revelation, natural revelation, represented by the sun, moon, and stars, is praised for its beauty and strength. But special revelation, too, is paid a lyrical tribute in it. For when the poem speaks of children whose function it is to still the enemy and avenger, that allusion can only refer to the spiritual conflict carried on by heathendom against Israel, by the seed of the serpent against the seed of the woman, by the Beast against the Spirit. From the sphere of nature the theme of the psalm rises to that of grace, from that of creation to that of regeneration, from common grace to covenant grace, from general revelation to special revelation. And Jesus, as He perfectly sings this psalm in His soul, resolves to fulfill it, even as He fulfills all psalms and prophecies. He resolves to be the Propitiator for the sins of His own people, but also to be the Redeemer of a groaning creation. He resolves not only to give spiritual gifts to sinners, but also to exercise the curse from the domain of the physical creation, to burn it out of the sun, moon, and stars. As He hums the psalm to Himself, Jesus rises to become the Mediator of creation in the broadest sense of the word. As He looks at the flagstones on which He stands at the temple, He proposes to make them not only the foundation of the church of the New Testament but also the groundwork of a new earth. Nature and grace, matter and spirit, both need the cosmical Mediator to give them eternal rest.

In the second place, the 8th Psalm regards that choir of children as a camp of God's recruits, a reserve upon which to draw in the onslaught of the moral and religious war, in the ancient battle of the seed of the woman against the seed of the serpent. Jesus knows as He hears the psalm resounding in His soul that He brings peace on earth; but He knows also that He brings war. In one sense the voice of the children is like a lingering cadence from the "Peace on earth" which the angels sang at Bethlehem. But as the psalm develops in His being, that note develops into a martial air. It announces the warfare that He must fight for righteousness' sake.

In the third place, the 8th Psalm assigns a function, a definite responsibility to the sucklings, small as they are. They, too, as servants of the Lord have their tasks to perform. As Jesus takes note of that He knows that He, as the greatest Servant of the Lord, must assume the responsibility for the greatest assignment ever given. If the souls of babes are centers from which influences go out to all of God's creation, then Jesus, as the mature Office-bearer, now approaching the center of history, knows that He must fulfill as well as sing that song of peace and war. He must effect a universal peace in God's great world, and must promote and complete the pan-cosmical war between the seed of the serpent and the seed of the woman.

In the fourth and last place, Jesus' attention goes from the exuberant shouting of the children to His own bitter cry on the cross. By reciting the 8th Psalm at the window of the temple of God, by reciting it through and beyond the voices of the children, Christ assumes responsibility for what that Messianic poem expects of Him.

In the 2nd Chapter of Hebrews, this psalm again returns to the organism of the Scriptures. There the New Testament completely discovers its meaning. It teaches us to read in it a Messianic humiliation even unto hell.

The psalm tells us that according to the original status of things man is the lord of created beings, and that according to God's appointed hierarchy he may therefore regard the angels as being in his service. But it also teaches that in another sense man is less than the angels, for he was made a little lower than they. That is the incongruity which hurt the poet's heart, that man should be lower than the angels now. Experience, however, confirms his judgment. According to his rank in the state of righteousness, man was, indeed, the lord of created things, lord, too, therefore, of the angels of heaven. But sin has crept into the universe; an enemy, an avenger, in the language of the psalm, has appeared in the cosmos. Things are no more as they seem, and no longer seem to be what they originally, ideally are. Man also has been removed from his position at the top of the hierarchy of the beings that were made. His power has been broken, his beautiful body has become the prey of death, his soul subject to the curse. As far as his capacities and abilities go, lordly man has fallen below the angels. Ideally, originally he is above them; actually he is beneath them. And the justice of God swears all of its oaths to the truth of that fact.

The incongruity of the former glory of man and his present condition is the particular tragedy of the 8th Psalm. Therefore it is also that of Christ as He fulfills it in the week of the passion. He comes to His own city as a Mediator. Because He bears human life in Himself, He must identify Himself with its frailty, its mortality, its humiliation. In Gethsemane, where He will appear as the second Adam, that is, as "man," He will obviously be lower than the angels, for one of them will have to come down to strengthen the Son in the garden. Without such sustenance He would be too weak and would disappear in bottomless mud. And it will become still more obvious on the cross. For He will then be forsaken of God, though all of the angels remain in the Father's company. Then His flesh will enter the ground where no angel can come. Then He will commend His spirit into the hands of His God, hoping against hope that the angels will bear it to His Father's lap. For Christ will take upon Himself not the humiliation of a man, but of "man" as he is appraised in the psalm.

So the poem passes through Christ to the 12th Chapter of Revelation. There is the woman again, and the seed of the woman, and the sun, and the moon, and the stars. There is the suckling again, composite of human frailty, child of the woman. Cosmic forces are eager to go out to that child, but it is included in the great curse of the world. However, that child, as the seed of the woman, is also the one, who, in the language of the Psalm once more, will "still" the enemy and avenger, that is, the old serpent.

Pause now and ponder this thought: in the soul of Jesus the Scriptures are never broken. Think of the Scriptures and of Him. Hear Him claim the authorship of it as the Logos; hear Him name Himself the *raison d'etre* of the Psalm. Listen to Him claim authorship of it, again, as the Lord of the Spirit (the Spirit of Christ which before testified in the prophets). Listen to Him name Himself at once the interpretative principle and the content of the Psalm. When you have done that you will have touched the ends of His soul.

Then you will know that this trust firmly dwells in the Spirit of Christ: by going the way of humiliation He will also be taking the way of exaltation. That way, He knows, will lead past the cross to heaven. True, He will be made lower than the angels, but He will also regain the ancient lordship. In Him Man will arise again to become king of creation in full glory, having neither angel nor archangel above Him, but God alone.

Again we bow in reverence before this Saviour, who in these last days of His humiliation upon earth, always lived and thought and felt artistically, significantly, in terms of the Word.

To the prattle of babes He relates the great world-problem of the glory of the name of the Lord, sublime, cosmical as it is in its implications. To an alley game He relates the course of the sun, moon, and stars. These, in turn, He unites with the woman of Revelation 12, and with her seed which is He Himself. Such is the actuality which is eternal; such is eternity concretely realized. The kingdom of heaven takes its course right through the games of children and through the petty censureship of jealous Scribes. Such is the majesty of the King whom Zechariah saw in his vision. Such is the glory of Christ.

In concluding, we must revert to the beginning for a moment. We must gratefully acknowledge that Christ exercises a double prerogative against those who, although they are still awaiting their opportunity, definitely mean to put Him to death.

Christ exercises the prerogative of personal initiative. He does not yield to the wishes of those who celebrated by waiting for them to act. He receives the program for His passion and coronation week directly from the hands of His Father. He spends His glorious hours of palm branches and laurels of honor with the lame and the blind. They understand that He acts upon His own initiative.

The second prerogative which He exercises is that of self-interpretation. Christ explains the "lowliness" and "defenceless-ness" of the prophetic picture according to His own meaning. He asks no one what he thinks of it.

Such is our ideal King: One who vindicates His rule according to His sovereign good pleasure, and who brooks no interference as He proceeds to execute it.

Christ Going to the Room of the Passover

CHAPTER TEN

Christ Going to the Room of the Passover

● *Then came the day of the unleavened bread, when the*
passover must be killed. And he sent Peter and John,
saying, Go and prepare us the passover, that we may
eat. And they said unto him, Where wilt thou that we
prepare? And he said unto them, Behold, when ye
have entered into the city, there shall a man meet you,
bearing a pitcher of water; follow him into the house
where he entereth in. And ye shall say unto the good-
man of the house, The Master saith unto thee, Where
is the guest chamber, where I shall eat the passover
with my disciples? And he shall shew you a large up-
per room furnished: there make ready. And they
went and found as he had said unto them; and they
made ready the passover. —LUKE 22:7-13.

CHRIST goes to the room of the Passover. The way there
is the way from the sign of the old sacrament to the reality of which it is the sign in the new sacrament. The road
to the room of the Passover is the road from the symbol to
the thing symbolized. A cloud of mystery envelops the Christ
as He goes. Our Passover goes to His Passover. Angels and
devils follow Him.

There is no unanimity of opinion about the details implied, and
the circumstances referred to, in the passage quoted above. Since
early times men have interpreted the data variously. Just where
the Passover was celebrated, for instance, is one of the questions
which has perplexed students, and to which these have given no
common answer.

We know what the Bible itself tells us about the manner in
which the guest room was reserved. The account given of it is
a very general one; few specific details are included. By com-

paring the several narratives of the Gospel, we learn that Jesus, early in the day, told two of His disciples, Peter and John, to go into the city. Obviously, therefore, Jesus and His disciples were still outside of it. At a given place, they were told, they would meet a man carrying a pitcher of water. He is the man they must ask about the place in which the Master can celebrate the Passover. They will find him perfectly willing to direct them to a house, where a guest chamber, suitable for the purpose, will be prepared for them. Some infer from the indication that the room was *furnished,* that the floor was carpeted, and from that, in turn, that everything was arranged for their convenience, even to the last detail. This may or may not be true; at any rate, the room was not a make-shift affair quickly pressed into service for lack of a better. God in His Providence supplied an apartment whose atmosphere and convenience suited the sanctity of the purpose.

This manner of reserving the room interests us particularly. Jesus sends out Peter and John to take an option on another man's property, and that without anything resembling a formal transaction. The occasion naturally reminds us of that other day on which Jesus sent out two of His disciples to take possession of a colt. On that day the King made use of the right of confiscation; on this He does so again. He boldly steps up to a man who is walking around somewhere with a pitcher on his shoulder, and arranges matters affecting the man's property quite as He pleases. That is one of the resemblances between this and the previous instance. There is another. We remarked then that God actively coöperated in the preparations for the entry into Jerusalem, saw to it, for example, that the colt was at the exact spot which Jesus had indicated. That God of providence shapes events in a similar way now. He does His part. He goes out to meet the will of Christ and the burden of prophecy in order that both of these may be fulfilled. It is God who induces the man, particularly predestinated for the purpose before time began, to leave home with the pitcher at exactly that moment, and to cause him to return at a similarly appointed hour. God makes him stop for a few seconds at the specific corner where he is arrested by Peter and John. God Himself spreads the cloth over the table at which the Son of man will lie to partake of the Last

Supper. One can never feel strongly the vital reality of the providence of God unless one observes it closely as it is concretely active in the drama of Jesus' suffering. . . The temple and its altar are far away but you need not ask where God now reveals the mysteries of His altar. A ripple of movement disturbs the curtain of the temple. Behind it those are ministering who are the official bearers of the right of confiscation. Levi takes his "tenth." Alas for him—God makes His demands through Christ and for Him.

There is also a great difference, however, between that seizure of the colt and this reservation of the guest room. When Jesus demanded the colt, He was making His appearance in the city in the capacity of a King. As such He took what He needed, irrespective of who the owner was according to the records. In the account which tells us of the preparations for the entry into Jerusalem there is no indication which leads us to believe that the man whose colt He required definitely belonged to the limited group of the disciples. On the contrary we get the impression that he was a man who was not particularly intimate with Jesus. The special assurance given him to the effect that the colt would be returned promptly is one of the factors which suggests that Jesus regarded and treated him as a stranger.[1] At least Jesus felt that He could not make demands upon the owner of the colt by reason of a tie of friendship.

But in this instance the man whose house Jesus and His disciples want to use seems from all indications to be a member of the more intimate group of friends and believers. This, too, is not surprising, for Christ appears now not as a King of the city, exercising the prerogatives He has to use the property He needs in it. Instead, He arrives now as the Mediator of the New Testament. He comes to partake of the Passover and to sit down at the table of the Holy Supper. On the other occasion the people massed around Him in throngs; now He isolates Himself from them. He goes to perform a holy task which, although a thousand others are also performing it, He will today make super-

---

1. Notice, in this connection, the correct sense of Matthew 21:3: ". . . straightway he (the Lord) will (after using the colt) send them"; cf. Mark 11:3: "revised" text, Grosheide, *Kommentaar op Mattheus*, p. 246.

fluous by substituting for it the better gift of grace: the Holy
Supper.

Jesus had deliberately proceeded in a roundabout way that
other time in order to attract the attention of the people. As He
did then, so He now gives His disciples a sign: there will be a
man bearing a pitcher of water, and they will find him at such
and such a place. Why this sign, we wonder? Was it to attract
the attention of the interested masses again? Was it to plant
the disciples more firmly in the faith? Yes, very likely it was for
the sake of the disciples, too, for Satan had greatly desired to
have them, in order that he might sift them as wheat. But we
must not forget that the sign obtains primarily for Jesus' sake.
Jesus' soul and spirit goes out to God by means of these signs.
And by means of them, too, God is working toward Jesus. His
trusting but tormented heart seeks a sign, not to dispel doubt, for
doubt does not exist, but to show Him by means of this true Passover that He is pleasing God. Christ yearns to know that the
place provided for Him in which He may eat the Passover is
given to Him as a symbol of the favor of God. By *demanding*
the colt, Christ manifested to all who saw Him that His was the
right to property; now by *asking* that simple conveniences be arranged for Him, Jesus reveals His poverty, not to all, this time,
but to the faithful. There is not a place in that whole city upon
which Jesus can take an option and say: "This is all my own."

Therefore the two events which we have been comparing must
be regarded as contrasts, or rather, as complements, to each other.
The first sign proclaims His wealth; the second gives expression
to His voluntary poverty. The first maintains: "By right the
whole city is mine." The second announces: "The son of man
hath not where He can lay His head." The first anticipates His
glory; the second acknowledges His passion: listen to the heavy,
heavy phrase, "My time is at hand." The first sign sounds the
trumpet for the Prince of the House of David: it demands that
all attention be given to the Stem out of Jesse. But the second
sign requires that some attention be given to the darker side of
that Stem. Mind you, the great Son of David must *ask* for a
room in that city of David in which He may eat after the spirit.
Jesus leaves the world, you see, as He entered it. A number of

years have passed now since two others, Joseph and Mary, hunted for a place in which the Son of David might be born. That poverty, too, was a token of the disintegration of the House of David which permitted its last children to wander over the world, homeless, naked, unwanted. Well, just as the House of David came into the world then, begging for a favor, so the great Son of David, even though He has been sworn into His office, even though He has persisted in kingly services, and even though in this same hour He will discover the very essence of the kingship of David, nevertheless must hunt[1] for someone who will do Him a favor, in order that He may eat the Passover and introduce the Holy Supper into His church.

"Even though" is the conjunction we used. Should it have been "because"? Be still, my heart! The King makes requests wherever He goes, and He must answer them all Himself.

The Man of sorrows is oscillating continually between these two poles, that of glory, and that of utter poverty. Between them lies the passion which He accomplished at Jerusalem. The truth about Jesus Christ consists of a unity of both of these elements.

Up to this point everything we have touched on in the account we are studying was definite. That is not true, however, of the remaining circumstances of the story.

The place where Jesus celebrated the Passover, especially, is not certainly known. Yes, if we go to Jerusalem, the dwellers there will direct us to a place, where, as they believe, the supper was served. They call it the *coenaculum,* a place where the so-called "en Nebi Daud" is at present located. This consecrated piece of ground is situated on the southern side of the hill which lies just west of the city and which is called "Zion."[2]

Naturally, we are rather suspicious of its authenticity as the people of Jerusalem direct us to this place. And it makes very

---

1. Even if we think of a prearrangement on the part of Jesus and the owner of the house (as, for instance, M. Van Rhijn believes, *De Evangelisten Marcus en Lukas*, Adam, p. 13), this word is appropriate, for it is a question of "favor," of "borrowing" in contrast to "demanding" or "taking." However, we have some objections to the theory of "prearrangement," objections which, because of the nature of this book, we will not mention here.

2. According to P. G. Groenen: *Het Lijden en Sterven van Onzen Heere Jesus Christus*, 2nd edition, Utrecht, J. R. Van Rossum, 1919, p. 23. However, he himself raises some objections. Cf. Zahn (TH) in commentaries and brochure.

little difference. What is more serious is that we cannot even reconstruct the plain data of the biblical narrative with certainty. The guesses may come and go—no one will ever indicate with complete certainty the exact house in which the Passover was celebrated.

There is, however, one supposition which is a very plausible one. An old tradition, which in recent years has been regarded as authentic by many respectable scholars, for very strong reasons, tells us that the house in which the Saviour celebrated was that of Mary, the mother of John Mark. He, in case the father were dead, would then be the "goodman" referred to in the text.

We cannot name all of the reasons at this point which make it very likely that this was the house. A few will suffice to illustrate. It is obvious from the biblical narrative that the man who was asked to reserve his room was one of the circle of faithful friends. Mark was indeed one of these. Later he appears in the first Christian church, and we note that as time goes on he gradually comes to the fore. If his mother actually did so at this time, it is not the first occasion on which she lent her house to the disciples. From Acts 12 we learn that Mary had a commodious house, containing a large reception room which was always open to the Christians which gathered in Jerusalem. Besides, Mark was an intimate friend of Peter, and Peter was one of the two whom Jesus sent out to reserve the room. Moreover, it is significant that Mark, who later wrote the account of the Gospel which now goes by his name, hardly touches upon these particulars; it naturally occurs to us to ascribe this fact to a modest reticence in matters affecting his own house. The man who carried the pitcher of water might, therefore, very well have been John Mark, or, as some conjecture, a servant of the house, one who knew about Jesus, and who understood at once the circumstances of His need.

We must confess that this identification of the place of the last Passover with Mary's house strongly appeals to us, especially because it makes possible such pleasant and significant perspectives. If it is true that the Mediator, the Head of His church, celebrated the passover in Mary's house, then it is pleasant to think that this holy ground was preserved as the property of the church for many years. Such a construction of the facts will explain, too, why Mary does not sell her beautiful home, when, after Pentecost, the first members of the little Christian church sold all of their goods and brought the receipts to the apostles for the benefit of the persecuted believers. The place, then, was too filled with sacred memories to sell. It was a delight to the little congregation to meet in the place where their glorified Head had eaten the Passover for the last time and the Holy Supper the first time. If we accept, in addition, that the house of Mary is referred to in Acts 4 as well as in Acts 12, the associations become more significant still. Then the place where Christ ate the last Passover, and from which He sent the command to eat and drink out over the whole world is the very same which was shaken by a miraculous influence that day after the prayer of the congregation.[1] Then God Himself by that force pointed to it as a place of holiness, as the connecting link between the remnant of the Old Covenant which killed the Passover lamb there, and the communion of the New Testament, which introduced the communal feasts and broke the bread and . . .

So we might conjecture, so dream on and on.

We know, for instance, that the man later known as Barnabas, but at the time still called Joses, was a nephew of John Mark. He was a Levite. He was born in Cyprus, but had returned from that city, to which his parents had immigrated. It is easy to imagine that he was often a welcome guest at the home of his Aunt Mary, if not, indeed, a regular boarder there. If this datum as well as all the other data should be true to fact, we can more easily understand his conversion to the group of disciples than we otherwise can. For, in that case, he must have seen Jesus and His disciples go in and out of his aunt's house periodically. He may, in fact, have been sitting downstairs as these were celebrating the Passover and instituting the Lord's Supper overhead.

If we go one step farther then, and, as some do, accept the opinion that John Mark as well as Joses Barnabas was a Levite, the vista becomes even more attractive. It would be a significant thought if we could suppose that a son of Levi, the ancient tribe of the priests, had helped to set the table for the last Passover

---

1. Acts 4:31.

which by the favor of God was celebrated under the law. For many successive generations Levi had seen his sons standing in tabernacle and in temple, slaying the Passover lamb and officiating at the Passover ritual. Now Christ eats the last lamb of the Passover and afterwards distributes His own body as the true lamb of the Passover. If John Mark, assisted by Joses Barnabas, prepared the table to this end, then Levi fulfilled his priestly office by his service to Jesus. Then Levi bowed before the better Priest, not of the house of Aaron, that is, of Levi, but Priest after the order of Melchisedek. Then Levi, who was allowed to take a tenth from the people, would himself by this Levitical service at this turning point of history, have *given* the tithe, toll of love and respect, to Jesus. Then the place where the Lord's Supper was served would be a place of pure mysteries, where fingers of love had embroidered this proverb on the cloth: "Out of the eater came forth meat, and out of the strong came forth sweetness." The "eater" is Levi who exacts a tenth from the people. Now he himself gives his house and a tenth of the income. He gives everything; he gives himself to the better Priest, who will forever dismiss him from his service by making the sacrifice superfluous. Yes, if these things are true, Levi has risen up in judgment against Levi. Once he was poor, working with His God between the curtains of the tabernacle. Then he received the beautiful temple. He is still in it, for all of his sons are there, trying to keep the Christ out of it. But while Levi lives on in the priests and keeps possession of the temple, God again takes up residence between the curtains. Indeed, between the curtains Mary has made, Levi, represented not by the priests, but by John Mark who brings his offer, is active in the company of Joses Barnabas, son of consolation. For, is it not consoling to Jesus, when compelled to remain behind the curtains, to know that God and Levi are there with Him?

But we may not, of course, go a step farther than is allowed us, even though the perspectives such considerations permit are attractive. A person must take thought to check himself for truth's sake, lest he succumb to recklessness and present as actual fact what at best he could but wish were true. It has pleased the Holy Spirit to conceal the name and genealogy of the master or mistress of the house in which the Passover was kept. We may never remove a veil which has been thrown around the facts by the Holy Spirit. We may not make a novel of the Gospel, irrespective of how edifying the piece of fiction may intend to be. Hence, even though we know many historical facts which make the construction just presented seem very plausible, we, too, will bow before the *Auctor primarius* of the Holy Scriptures, refuse to push uncertain details into the foreground, and humbly limit ourselves to what God has definitely given us. Obviously it is the will of God that the particulars which Christian memory would fondly recall should recede into the dark background, so that the whole attention might be given the matter of first importance.

That important matter is this. Christ, the Bearer and the Fulfiller of the law, celebrates the Passover in accordance with the demands of the law. There, between the curtains, where God enters into captivity, He fulfills the law (and that not outside of it, understand) and fulfills it by and for the Gospel. This is the central, the primary, significance of the whole matter: Christ celebrates the Passover because it is meet for Him to fulfill all righteousness. Because He wants to institute the Holy Supper, the symbol of the New Testament, He must follow the way of the Old Testament obediently to the very end. The birth-room of the Holy Supper must be kept immaculately pure.

Two lines meet in the guest chamber where Jesus is seated: that of the Old and that of the New Testament. Now the switch is thrown over. Fleshly Israel will no longer go up to celebrate the Passover according to the old law. Instead, spiritual Israel will rise from the table presently, will go out to celebrate a better Passover of fulfillment, the Holy Supper.

Throughout it all the Saviour's whole soul and all of His senses testify to the absolute sanctity of the holiness which binds Him with the strictest severity. He may not and He does not want to give us the New Testament until the Old is legally fulfilled. Precisely where the switch is laid, the rails must be most true. Nothing can be out of line there, or the place becomes one of disaster. Nothing is wrong. Christ obeys the law perfectly. He prepares the Passover according to all of the rules the law prescribes for Him. Neither an ultra-fastidious Jew nor an eager angel can detect the slightest departure from the law in Him. The Gospel of the New Testament enters the hour of its birth; but the law of the Old Covenant prepares the chamber.

Had Jesus not celebrated the Passover our Holy Supper would have been an act of revolution. But since He did celebrate it, and did so according to the law, our Holy Supper is His gift of abundant fulfillment. How He "desired to eat this Passover with His disciples!" There is work for Him to do, and where His work awaits Him, there His soul "longeth, yea, even fainteth, for the courts of the Lord." The Mediator in Him longs, yearns, to fulfill His office. He enters the room of the Passover firmly committing Himself to an active and a passive obedience.

Firmly committing Himself to a passive obedience: As He sees the table on which the Lamb is prepared, He sees in it the compendium of all of His suffering. That lamb is the sign and the seal of the love of God, who once permitted the vindictive angel of judgment to pass over every door on whose lintel the sacrificial blood was sprinkled; death should enter the homes of Egypt alone. To all the children of Israel that lamb testified that if they believed they should escape the destroyer. Today the Great Son of Abraham enters the room, full of faith and burning with zeal, but the eternal doom will be His alone to bear. All the angels of perdition will gnaw at His flesh. As Jesus sees the lamb, it shocks His soul. He is the only One who believed without once doubting. But Him the destroyer will not pass over. He has no blood to show which is acceptable to God. What, pray, can Jesus do with the blood of this slain lamb? It condemns Him to the face. All the doors of God's universe would recede if He should try to put its blood on their lintels for His own sake. He, the perfect, sinless Son of Israel is slain as the great Egyptian. He must die. The dead Passover lamb will weep over Him as over the first-born and only-begotten who could not be purified by the blood of an animal. His own blood must open the way to God. Never was a lamb so small, so poor, as this one. Never did man suffer so while eating it.

Again His active obedience complements the other. See, with His own hands He cleans a space on the table for the slain lamb. He takes His disciples with Him, and, although eating the Passover will hurt Him grievously, He sits down in their midst, takes up the meat of the lamb, blesses it, raises His eyes to God, praises Him by means of all the forms for prayer prescribed by the law, and does that in such a way that every sentence and each separate word receives the sincere account of His consecrated soul. The flesh of the Passover Lamb burned in His mouth as He ate it. He bore the law of the Lord in His bowels. He took and ate. He ate the food which in the most meaningful sense of the phrase was sweet to the mouth and bitter to the belly. The sign and seal of Israel's cleansing mocked Him as One for whom there is no compassion. He bore all things because He exceedingly loved His own.

We have heard it said of old time that the lamb of the Passover had to be perfect, unblemished, young, and wholesome. Such is Christ Jesus as He goes to be slain. He satisfies the law perfectly, pays its penalty to the last farthing. Our Passover of the New Testament is perfect: there is no sin in Him. He is undefiled, for He keeps the law. He is young and strong as He leans over the slain lamb and absorbs every bit of its mortality into Himself.

We must step up now, put our fingers in His blood, and sprinkle it, not over the doors of our houses, but over those of our hearts. Then we must present ourselves, not to the Priest, for He has seen us already, but to the God of the Priest, to the God and Father of our Lord Jesus Christ.

Whoever understands this all-inclusive moment of salvation will have no reason to regret the vagueness of the Gospel account of it. For His soul will be illuminated as never before. On this occasion the mysteries of the altar, be it in Levi's house or elsewhere, but surely according to the order of Melchisedek, were metamorphosed into the mysteries of the communion table.

The altar is the Old, the table is the New Testament. Both exist by reason of His blood.

Ask no more questions now: whose blood, which Passover? That would be to profane this glory.

The table is spread. My Jesus prays.

Christ Constraining Satan

CHAPTER ELEVEN

Christ Constraining Satan

● *And after the sop Satan entered into him.*
  —JOHN 13:27*a*.

AS Christ enters the room of the Passover to celebrate the sacrament with His disciples for the last time under the shadow of the Old Covenant, Satan steals in beside Him.

This is not the first time that the satanic element has revealed itself in the history of the passion. But the feature that distinguishes the present manifestation of Satan from his previous interventions is that it accentuates the contrast between the divine and the satanic influences upon the human life of Jesus. Formerly the satanic element imposed itself upon Him; now He Himself beckons it to come out, constrains it to reveal itself. Then Christ said: Get thee behind me, Satan. Now He says: Satan, come forth. It is almost midnight now, and each stroke of the clock sounds a heavier note than the one that went before—that is, to those who have ears to hear.

There are three dangers against which we must be on guard as we study this subject.

The first danger is that we limit ourselves to Judas Iscariot as a person, that we interest ourselves solely in the psychological complications of his character, lose ourselves in the drama of his trying life. As we see it, a highly important principle which is binding in such studies is that we may allow no subsidiary figure on the way of suffering to dominate our thoughts to the exclusion of the central figure. Christ is always the one for whom, to whom, and by whom all things on that road move and have being.

The second danger is that, inasmuch as the character of Judas *is* a consideration, we tend to make him as wicked as we possibly

163

can. Since early times men have fairly exhausted their imaginations in an effort to find terms vindictive enough for Judas. He has been presented as the most flagrant example of the sheerest delight in sinning. Hence it was not a treacherous play of Dante's own creative imagination which induced him to put Judas in the nethermost pit of hell in his *Vision*. Dante's judgment had the confirmation of many observers before his time, and of as many after. Nevertheless, it does not require long argumentation to point out the inadequacy of this supposedly rightly calculated distribution of justice. There are people in whom sin reaches a profounder degree of wickedness and insults God worse than it does and is in Judas Iscariot. He was not guilty of what Jesus calls a "blasphemy against the Holy Spirit." Therefore there are those who sink farther into the slough of wickedness and guilt than Judas did. We happen to recall a woodcut on which two wasted figures are depicted. The man on it has a high silk hat, set rakishly on his head. A big cigar protrudes from a lecherous mouth. He wears white gloves on his hands, and an expression of fatuous disdain on his face. The other figure is a strumpet whom the wastrel is escorting on his arm. Both are pictured against the dark background of a large city. As they proceed they throw a sidelong glance at the naked body of a tortured Christ on the cross, lying athwart the very street in which they have been soaking themselves with liquor. The woodcut depicts how haughtily indifferent the ungodly life of many people is to the presence of Christ; how terribly blasphemous the coarse, presumptuous laughter is of those arrogant ones who do not even have time to take a cigar out of the mouth in the presence of the Crucified, and who fall asleep indifferently after seeing such a spectacle. We believe the kind of people typified by this woodcut do far greater violence to Christ than Judas Iscariot ever intended to do. Paul spoke of himself as "the chief of sinners" and he did not add the qualification, "except for Judas Iscariot."

The third danger to which we had reference is the tendency to regard Judas solely as a traitor, to wholly identify his transgression with treachery. The betrayal of the Master for thirty pieces of silver has become a symbolical, almost a mythological, phenomenon and motive throughout all ages in history. Too often we fix our attention on that aspect of Judas' transgression alone. To do so is unwarranted. First of all, we can say that if the essence of Judas' deed was a betrayal of confidence, many other men, known or unknown by name to history, have been his equals in such treachery, and many other people have proved more intrinsically despicable than he. Moreover, if we see only the betrayer in Judas, and fail to relate the crucial conflict of his life to the very special significance of Jesus, and to the critical time in which He made His appearance in the world, then we, too, wholeheartedly agree with Dante in his assignment of guilt. For Dante in his *Inferno* placed the betrayers of Julius Caesar, Brutus and Cassius, in the same circle of condemnation in which he placed Judas. Yes, this notion of guilt is fair, is the only right one, if one identifies the whole of the sin of Judas with a betrayal of confidence, of trust, of loyalty, of a high spiritual ideal, or of one of the heroes of such spiritual vision. But, for those of us who believe the Scriptures, such ranking of Judas with those two past-masters of treachery is an effective warning against the very dialectic which is being applied in arriving at the conclusion. The peculiar sin of Judas is not properly defined as a betrayal, but is better circumscribed as a self-reliance, a self-assertion, in matters affecting the deepest needs of his life. His was a self-assertion which caused him to reject the vision of the Messiah which Jesus presented to him, against which he could say nothing, and to substitute for it his own conception, a notion compatible with his egocentric, materialistic, Judaistic character.

If we look at the subject in that light, we are immediately prompted to a profound humiliation. We keep back all vindictive words which we might otherwise feel inclined to fling at Judas. For, looking at it in this way, we see him standing dangerously close to us. However, there is this to gain from the humiliation: we learn to see the Christ, the *central figure* in the room of the Passover.

As we see the soul of Jesus engage in battle with that of Judas, as we see the Spirit of Christ take issue with Satan, who, although previously present, now enters into Judas, we are interested to learn the answer to this question: Does the struggle between the Spirit of Christ and the Satan in Judas begin now, or is it a struggle which now comes to overt expression for the first, or for a repeated, time, but which has been present constantly?

The answer to that question can be an unequivocal one. It is true that according to John's account Satan entered into Judas as this disciple sat over against Christ at the table of the Passover. But we also read, and in an earlier passage, that Satan had revealed himself in the soul of Judas before.[1] It was not, therefore, the first time that the satanic element appeared in Judas and came to expression in acts of betrayal and unbelief. The Bible itself tells us that "Satan had put it in the heart of Judas" to betray Christ.

A long history of sin antedated those earlier words, too. They represent the culmination of an anxious spiritual conflict. We shall not say much about that history, for much has been written and is available about it. There are a few particulars to which we must refer.

We proceed on the assumption that what comes to expression in Judas at this time in the hall of the Passover was latent in him from the beginning. When a person is regenerated by the Spirit of God, something reaches expression in him which previously was no part of him, for regeneration introduces a new and perfect principle into his human life which was utterly alien to him before. But in the life in which regeneration has not taken place evil branches can grow from the evil root which is there. Whatever in such a life reaches eventual fruition was present in it from the beginning.

The Scriptures teach us that the basic sin of Judas was not unrelated to his love of money. We may not ignore that bit of information. Because of a pronounced craving for wealth, his character becomes one-sided. It was not centered in God, the chief Good and only Owner, but in himself. However, this fundamental greed was suppressed for a time. The longing for wealth persisted but did not come to external expression. Some force acted upon the life of Judas which checked for a while that inclination to evil.

That force was Jesus' entrance into his life. We believe that Judas, when, at the beginning of his responsible, mature life, he

---

1. John 13:2; Luke 22:3.

met Jesus and followed him, was acting from honest motives—
using the word "honest" in a strictly human sense, as designating
the relation of one person to another in the common, popular
way. It may even be the case that to an extent the experience of
Judas was parallel to that of Jesus. We know that Christ had
Judas come to Him after prayer; who can say whether he in response may not have come to Jesus with a prayer in his heart?
There was so much in Jesus that captivated him, put him into an
ecstasy, perhaps (the Greek of the New Testament is by no means
stinted in its use of that word). In the first place, the preaching
of Jesus must have made a strong impression upon him. For
Jesus in a strong and aggressive way preached the coming of the
new Kingdom, the Kingdom of Heaven. And Judas was eager
to hear of that.

Remember, Judas was a man of Judea,[1] and Judea was the
home of orthodox Jews. In comparison with Galilee it could
justly be called the fortress of Jewish orthodoxy. It was the
country of the scribes and rabbis. There the law was interpreted;
there scholars tried to catch the spirit of the national history;
there, in a chauvinistic and Pharisaic manner, the traditions of
the fathers were taught in both lower and higher education. They
who must teach and explain the traditions of Israel and hold
them up as a model were stationed there. In short, Judea was
the cultural seat of the nation, the center of theological and political thought. Consequently it was in Judea that the will to
revolution was secretly fostered. In Judea the grim animosity
of Jewish nationalists, theologians, and professors of history
was constantly being nurtured. There, too, however, the unob-
trusive but determined Roman soldiers insisted by means of the
sword that Rome should retain the leadership. There then
Jesus came, preaching a virile message of a new Kingdom, bringing purely eschatalogical ideas to bear upon Israel's inert and
wasted spirit. No wonder that Judas, a Jew of Jews, an ultra-
orthodox Judean, a man who loved his country passionately and
was eager to see her future glory realized—no wonder that he
was quite enamored of Jesus' teaching.

---

1. Is-Cariot: a native of Cariot.

Moreover Jesus performed miracles. Energies of the coming era were being abundantly and powerfully revealed. Judea became a stage on which the whole world might see heavenly forces at play.

Add to these features the nobility of Jesus' soul. That must have captivated Judas altogether. Consider the pedagogical wisdom of the Master. He gave His disciples work to do. Judas, also, was allowed to go as a kind of missionary to the "province," the country of sleepers, to shake them out of their lethargy quite properly, to perform miracles, to preach, and to fight demons. Really, it was a glorious time. Things were going wonderfully. Never had Judas lived with such zest as now.

And the disturbing thought lingers that at some time men will thank God for what Judas meant to their spiritual and eternal lives.

But matters could not remain as favorable as this. Jesus never rests at any one point. Each day His course seems to veer into a new direction. And as Judas observed that, He gradually arrived at the disappointing conclusion that at bottom Jesus and he were growing estranged from each other.

One large issue on which they simply could not agree—a very live one to any orthodox Judean—was that matter of the Messiah concept. Of course, their difference of opinion on that count did not become apparent to Judas immediately. It did not, for—fatal tendency!—Judas kept his ponderings to himself. He said not a word about any conflict he felt to anyone around him. But in his heart he grew more alien to Christ constantly. As time went on he saw more and more clearly that what Jesus did and did not do was incompatible with what he himself dared to hope and expect of the coming Messiah. The theology that Judas loved was that unbroken series of false prejudices which so conspiculously characterized the orthodox wisdom of the scribes and rabbis. Nor was that emphasis at all peculiar to Judas. All of the disciples of Jesus at first nurtured in their hearts—even more than they rationalized in their minds—a materialistic conception of the hope of the Messiah.

At first only a very slight difference distinguishes Salome, the mother of James and John, from Judas. You remember that it was she who asked positions of honor for her two sons in the kingdom which, she supposed, the Messiah would soon establish. She, too, assumed that Jesus would, within a comparatively short time, build an earthly kingdom, which would assert itself against Roman authority, and fling a broad national banner to the skies. In such a kingdom, naturally, honorary functions would be assigned and positions of importance filled. Salome's wish was that each of her sons be given one of these prominent offices.

It was a similar notion of the nature of the new kingdom which had made Judas eager to get an eminent position in the new state. However, at the beginning of his association with Jesus and His disciples, this yearning to be a ranking office-holder in the nation was temporarily suppressed in favor of the ideal which charmed him so irresistibly in Jesus. The "charm" of Jesus appealed to him with such captivating force for a while that he temporarily restrained his greed for money and base love of power.

Temporarily—for when the novelty of the new association became routine, when he became acclimated to the actuality of discipleship with Jesus, he reverted to his old ambition, never absent but dormant the while, and concluded that this new kingdom might prove very profitable to him. Just think: a seat next to the new king. He was not always clearly conscious of that desire perhaps, he may not have formulated it for himself in so many words, but it, nevertheless, lingered as a dream in his heart. The semi-conscious hope persisted that the coming of the kingdom would mean the great promotion for him.

As time went on, however, that inner hope came to a tragical overt expression. As life with Jesus became more common and matter-of-fact, the secret passion of Judas began to assume a more concrete shape. Months passed, and Judas became convinced that what he wanted most was a prominent position in the new kingdom. While that ambition was gradually taking shape in the breast of Judas, Jesus, from His side, each day indicated more clearly that He was quite unsympathetic to that view of the kingdom, that He was, in fact, definitely opposed to it. Judas may have been present when Salome presented her petition, may have heard Jesus reply that a cup of passion needed to be drained first, and that, besides, the assignment of positions of honor was no part of His jurisdiction, but that of the Father. Yes, Judas may have been present then. We notice, at any rate, that what at first seemed a very slight difference betwen the two sons of Salome and Judas now appears to be a large one. Salome's sons were frank, were outspoken about their ambition. That of Judas was a subjective matter. And when Jesus by His words frustrated the ambition of James and John, these gradually but consciously adapted themselves to the answer. Their love and faith prompted the adaptation. But Judas said nothing, and continued nursing the ambition in his heart. In other words, he turned his back to Jesus and sank more deeply into himself. That was his second sin: He did not surrender; he had no faith; he trusted himself.

Naturally such unbelief and greed constantly drew him more deeply into condemnation. Each day the conflict grew more clearly defined. No wonder! Jesus kept doing less and less of what Judas wanted to see accomplished. Just think: after all this time, not a single giant of the forest planted by Roman hands had been felled. Not one lance had touched Roman blood. Moreover the entire legacy of the rich sons of Zebedee had gone for provisions; not a cent had been devoted to arms and ammunition. Jesus' program seemed bent on decentralization, for He went hither and yon, from one part of the country to the other. But of centralization, the ABC of organization, He knew nothing. In Jerusalem He had not so much as a cellar or garret with a loophole pointing toward the palace of Pilate. Now that He wanted a room for the Passover He actually had to borrow one. A characteristic way that was, too, of His "method" of doing things, a method which frowned upon any kind of secret preparation for an armed protest against Roman authority and which delegated everything into the hands of the twelve disciples.

The conflict between the ambition of Judas and the conduct of Jesus was even more sharply accentuated when Christ refused to accept the crown that was offered Him. To Judas that refusal emphatically declared that his slumbering desires did not have the slightest chance to be realized in Jesus. Would he had said so then! But he locked his longings inside himself and nursed his disappointments in secret. In the company of the highest

Prophet he put the lock upon the windows of his soul and drew the shutters down. Even when Jesus asked His disciples whether they, too, now that the masses, their enthusiasm waning, had turned their backs to Jesus, would not prefer to go—even then Judas said nothing. In other words, he braced himself anew against Jesus' instruction, against Jesus' hunger for souls, and sank more deeply into the old self-reliance.

Crisis followed crisis. Again and again the words of Jesus gave Judas an excellent opportunity to disclose the conflict in his heart. But he as frequently refused to surrender himself to Christ. Surely, in the sight of God these three years of steeling himself against the compassion of Jesus are more than the few moments in which his fingers clutched at the traitor's fee, and his lips allied themselves with Jesus' enemies. Not his taking the thirty pieces from the Scribes, but his clinging to their doctrine, when he might have yielded to the other, was his transgression. This especially was his sin: He did not accept the Gospel of Christ.

As he isolated himself from Jesus, so he also became estranged from the other apostles. Remember, he was the only Judean in the group. The others were all Galileans. In this respect alone, the man from the cultural center may have felt superior to the simple fisher-folk from the back-country. Certainly his Judaistic, ultra-patriotic point of view and his rabbinical theology tempted him to think meanly of the eleven laboring men from Galilee. He must in time have despised them for their inclination to accommodate themselves to a king who had no dispatch about him and to a kingdom which had no "teeth" in it.

Such was the genesis of what is called the sinister betrayal of Judas. So Satan imposed himself upon Judas' soul first in order to *enter* it later. Thus Judas, from his side, more willingly opened the doors of his soul to the satanic influence. We can therefore easily understand the reference in the Scriptures pointing us to the fact that after numerous crises in which Judas persistently shut out the light of Jesus, Satan gained the mastery of his soul.

Now we are in a position to consider the scene in the room of the Passover once more in its relationship to Jesus and to Judas.

Jesus has entered the guest room and has entered as a host. He is presiding at the supper. As He eats, He conducts the conversation, sometimes in general, sometimes by means of remarks addressed to specific persons seated next to or over-against Him. In the course of this conversation He reveals also that one of those will betray Him.

In response to that perturbing remark, all of the disciples reply: Is it I, Lord? To that query Jesus makes no general response. Later, however, when one of the guests has asked in a whisper whether He will not say who the betrayer is, Jesus replies that the disciple to whom He as a host gives the next bit of food is the one who will betray Him. (For it was the custom of the host personally to give a bit of food from the bowl to each of his guests as a token of personal friendship.)

Thereupon Jesus takes the bread and gives it to Judas.

And after the sop Satan entered into him.

That bit of bread burned Judas' lips, just as the thirty pieces scorched his fingers later. His restless soul, fully conscious of the fact that Jesus saw everything, knew that now too Jesus was seeing quite through him. In fact, Judas had feared for some time that Jesus would publicly unmask him. However, each passing moment indicated that He would not. Even at the time when the disclosure seemed most imminent, and Jesus seemed intent upon publicly laying bare his sinister intentions, Judas had been left alone.

After that time every minute that passed in the room of the Passover was burdensome to Judas. Every minute in which Jesus made no mention of him, but let him live his own life as he chose to live it, was a torturous martyrdom. From one point of view this reticence on Jesus' part demonstrated that His kingship, even as it extended itself to the intimate group of the disciples, disdained to use force. To Judas, however, it was a pointed and shaming revelation of grace, which, while it spared him, was inviting him to repent.

Was inviting him to repent . . . but that precisely was the essence of Judas' sin: he did not want to live by grace. And when Jesus then, as though nothing were amiss, performed the office of host without discrimination, treating him as He treated the other eleven—then the conflict became unbearable for Judas. His rebellion against the love of Jesus reached its acme. His disgust with that pacifistic group and their doctrine of non-resistance grew beyond bounds. He remembered his contract with the chief priests, promising a stipend the equivalent of three months of work. And then "Satan entered into him."

Satan *entered* into him. That significant word is one of the strongest the Bible uses to designate satanic influence. The Scriptures use several different words to indicate the several gradations of the influence of Satan as it realizes itself in man! It speaks of *temptation*: Lead us not into temptation, but deliver us from the evil one. It tells of Satan's *filling* the hearts of men: Ananias, why hath Satan filled thy heart? More serious still— the Bible mentions an *indwelling* of Satan. When the evil influence which has temporarily been exorcised from the habitat of the human soul later regains mastery of it, that demonic power "dwells there." But the connotation of the phrase "entering in" is the severest of any. There is only one designation in the Bible which conceivably can suggest a stronger meaning. For that, one looks in the historical books in vain. One must turn to the *Apocalypse*. There, in diction unfamiliar to common experience, we read of Satan who lends the Antichrist his ability and his "horns." "Entered in"—that is the phrase used here! And it is used here only!

The fact that the phrase "entering in" is employed in this connection does not mean so much that Judas was extraordinarily eager to let Satan in as it means that Satan never previously made so determined an attack as now. He realized that he had to exert every effort in this moment of world-crisis to preserve the soul that had almost been touched by the flames of Jesus' love; he knew that he had to try hard to preserve it as a torchbearer of hell, so that it might set fire to "both Herod, and Pontius Pilate, with the Gentiles, and the people of Israel."

Now we can understand what Christ was doing at this time. Yes, we have often and carefully scrutinized Judas Iscariot upon this occasion. But have we ever paid close attention to Jesus Christ? He proves Himself to be the Willing in obedience, the Willing to work in the house of the Father. See His hand dip in the bowl and hand it to Judas. When He does this Judas knows that the host is still treating him as a guest, still giving him His hand, still showing him the sign of affection. There is the silent question: What do you wish? He knows the Master is not ignorant of his thoughts, is not greeting the betrayer unsuspectingly. He knows that Jesus is reading his soul.

Judas must choose now. He must weep or he must curse. Or, if he can restrain the tears or the curses for a while, these at least must be born now. Which will it be, Judas? What has the proffered morsel wrought?

And after the sop Satan entered into him.

Mark that this is not the first time that the devil has influenced him. It has happened before.[1] That former invasion, also, was called an "entering in" of Satan.[2] But something intervenes between the first and second invasions — that something is the sop. In other words, an act of Jesus interposes itself between the antecedent and the final entering in of the devil.

Man is what he is. Judas belonged to Satan before he took the morsel. But man always tends to become more of what he is, and he becomes that after Jesus has given him to eat. The sop does something. It does not inject the poison into the blood. But it does — and that is Christ's fullest right — cause the blood to course faster through the veins. The poison is in the blood vessels already. But the sop makes it do its work more quickly.

Have you observed that Christ fulfills His task as Mediator, now also, in relationship to Judas. As a Mediator He *releases* spiritual forces which are extant already. Christ sees these words written on the wall of the Passover in handwriting as startling as that which Belshazzar saw. He that is unjust, let him be unjust still. An angel responds antiphonally: He that is filthy, let him be filthy still. And the community of all the saintly dead replies: He that is righteous, let him be righteous still. He that is holy, let him be holy still. Christ, fan all the fires aflame! Fan all the fires in the smithy of the world. Force the antithesis.

Christ fans the fires. He gives the sop. It sanctifies every believing soul. Again He gives it. It proves filthy the filthy soul.

1. Verse 2.
2. Luke 22:3.

The morsel Jesus gives calls in Satan and the Spirit of sacramental grace alike.

The food that Jesus gives does something. After Satan entered Judas that first time, Judas could still bear having Jesus wash his feet. He could withstand having a holy hand touch his foot. The washing of the feet, the least intimate of contacts — Judas could bear that.

After that he is offered the bit of food. But as one who eats, too, man becomes more essentially what he is already. The sop quickens the pace of the development already in progress. The blood which flowed sluggishly before, races through the veins now. Now the holy hand that touched the feet before, touches his mouth. This is the second, the more intimate contact. Again Judas can bear it; the morsel does not scorch his mouth.

After that bit of food Satan "entered into" him. Previously he had only "put it into the heart of Judas" to betray Christ. Satan waits for the sop to take its effect, for he knows that Christ is sovereign. After the sop the sin in Judas quickly realizes itself. Judas arises. And the parcel of food is the occasion which leads to a third act, this one an act of Judas. That food is the occasion —by no means the cause — of the kiss of betrayal.

The washing of the feet: the least intimate contact; the hand touches the foot.

The sop: a more intimate touch; the hand brushes the lips.

The kiss: the most intimate contact; the lips touch the lips.

And that is the end.

It is very difficult to read these matters in the Scriptures without bursting into tears. But before we can weep about Judas and about ourselves, we must be willing to see Christ, to see Him in His majesty. We must be willing to see Him in the power of His Word and in the power of His deed. For if we have not learned to see the Christ, what good can all our weeping do? Our tears would fall to the dust futilely as did the bitter ones which Judas wept.

But we are willing to see the Christ, and are willing to see Him in majesty. For He is always doing something. His sop, His gift, and His touch are never ineffectual. His act makes an apostle or an apostate of a man. The bit of food which He gives in a moment of crisis is the transition to a first Holy Supper, or it is a catalyst, whipping years of sin into final culmination. When Jesus gives us food, whether by means of the organs of sense, or by means of the Word, the life process is quickened, whether it be good or evil.

As Judas sat at the table with Jesus, he whispered to himself: I eat what I please. Spiritually I eat what I choose. I "eat the roll" of prophecy, the prophecy of orthodox Judea. My food is to do my own will. I select my own food.

But on this day he is *given* something to eat. Jesus constrains Judas. Judas is compelled to eat. Jesus' friendly but earnest gesture has all the force of an ultimatum. He does not eat what he chooses. Spiritually his food is given to him.

When he had eaten that food, Judas realized that the bread of all men is to do the will of their father. Such is the bread of all men, for all men have a father. He is God or he is Satan. He whose parent is the Father of our Lord Jesus Christ, who does His will, has eaten His bread and will live eternally. But whoever is born of "the father, the devil"[1] eats the food of Satan. Such a son may say that he eats what he pleases. But when the bread of God is given to him, he so much more obstinately eats death to himself from the bread of hell. He, therefore, does not eat what he wants. He eats death to himself, not because the food of God cannot avail to counteract death, but because the food of hell is desired by all those who use it as an antidote to life. That is the food such a person chooses after he has been given the bread of life. He eats quickly. His haste is the haste of madness, a madness which clutches at what it supposes is an antidote when good food is presented to it. But the antidote, coming from Satan, proves to be poison.

The sop which Jesus gives has the same effectiveness and the same effect as the Word which God gives. That Word, also, never returns void; it achieves whatever pleases God and quickly effects the purpose for which God sent it. That Word forces choices upon men. It converts men, or it hardens them. It makes men bow, or it stiffens their necks in haughty obstinacy. Both,

---

1. John 8:44.

the sop and the Word, send out the Spirit unto repentance, or Satan unto a hardening of the heart. Take the sop; listen to the Word. Afterwards men can say of you: Then entered the Spirit into him; or they can say: Then entered Satan into him. The one or the other effect will follow.

It is profitable to make this discovery. For, when we despise Judas utterly because, perhaps, he immerses himself in sin a few inches farther than we, we are making odious comparisons and missing the truth. Not so if we have seen the Christ. Whether we be in the same room with Him in Jerusalem or, now that He dwells on high, in the same universe with Him, does not matter. For He is always present with us. He was present in the sop. He is present in the Word.

Remember, it was not the sop so much that did it. It was the force emanating from His eyes, the majesty of His glance, it was His utter compassion which made the finger He placed on Judas' lips the conductor of the vital energy of the Word. The bit of bread, the finger—both were charged. They were charged with a force more potent than that which we now call electricity. The Spirit was present. The purpose of centuries was brought to bear upon that parcel of food. The moment of contact between the soul of Jesus and that of Judas was a moment of "discharging" of spiritual energies. Lightning broke loose. Satan felt the shock and could not rest any longer. Christ had constrained him, had made him restless to the point of death.

Christ constrained Satan, not by the sop, but by the Word which proceeds from the mouth of God. "Man shall not live by bread alone, but by every word that proceedeth out of the mouth of God." Christ kills Judas now — for he was dead already — and He does that by the Word alone. And if it was solely by the Word that the sop quickened the invasion of spiritual forces into Judas' soul, we do well to pay close attention. That Word is still active.

The pressure of the Word upon the world increases every day. The outward sign of the Passover or of the Holy Supper may remain as it was. But the presence of Christ, the power of the revealed Word, develops, grows, comes to a fuller fruition every day. Really, life is difficult after one has kissed the feet of Jesus.

Difficult as it may be, however, it is safe. Just as God conceals Himself behind the humanity of Christ, so on this occasion the majesty and power of God were concealed behind the ordinary gestures of the goodman of a house, of a host. But behind that external gesture faith discerns the omnipotent and omnipresent God. Faith finds rest in that Presence. The Holy Spirit enters in. A hand extends a bit of bread: it is the mystical union; it is the holy communion.

Christ Not "Suppressing" Satan

CHAPTER TWELVE

Christ Not "Suppressing" Satan

● *Then said Jesus unto him, That thou doest, do quickly. He, then, having received the sop, went immediately out.* —JOHN 13:27b and 30a.

IN the preceding chapter we attempted to gain an appreciation of the conflict that lowered in the soul of Judas. We discovered that in the earlier part of his discipleship he had forcibly suppressed certain sinister desires and wicked passions.

We concluded that this suppression was an effect of the temporary influence of Jesus Christ upon his conscience, of Jesus Christ, that is, as Judas understood Him. The "figure" of Jesus had elicited a strange admiration from Judas at first. Jesus, when He first captivated Judas' ambitions, had caused him almost fatal grief. In response he, with all his gifts and abilities, his fervent aspirations and passions, had yielded with a kind of mystic wonder to the charm of this new Master, who seemed to know and to be able to do almost everything. It was a halcyon time in Judas' life, an exciting, pious period.

But the outcome had not been favorable for Judas. The issue dividing Jesus and him was never resolved. Judas lacked the one thing that mattered. He wanted the needful thing: regeneration. Really, therefore, he lacked everything. True, he had enjoyed halcyon days when he first met Jesus. He had been able to suppress his evil desires and passions — even his greed for money. Jesus had been just that entrancing.

But . . . yes, he had succeeded in inhibiting his wicked ambitions, his avarice, his self-assertion, but these had not been destroyed in principle. He had suppressed his old nature, his old man, for the time being, but that old man had not been crucified, put to death, buried. All of his fleshly drives, all his wicked motives had been temporarily subdued, but they had not been expunged, not even vanquished in principle. Judas lacked the one necessary thing: he lacked *regeneration*.

Regeneration and suppression are not synonymous. The person who suppresses merely transposes; he puts the beautiful in the place of the ugly, the good in the place of the bad; he simply subordinates his wicked impulses to his better aspirations. The evil, the sin, being merely transposed, still occupies the house of the soul. It is moved from the upper to the lower story of that house, but it still dwells there. And the good, the better aspirations, to which the evil must give temporary stead, is not a spiritual substance; it is a kind of natural nobility, a product of common grace, rather than of the renewing of the Spirit. Hence suppression is doubly inadequate: first, because the inhibiting influence is not a spiritual good; and, secondly, because suppression merely transposes; it does not expel evil nor destroy it.

Regeneration, however, is a work of God, a gift of grace, achieving much more than to remove evil from the conscious to the subconscious mind. The renewing of the Spirit effects a different and a greater result. It annihilates evil in principle; it severs the root. It overcomes evil with good; it does not displace, but it supplants death with life. Regeneration is the entrance of Jesus Christ into our personalities in order to conquer death in us by the new life which is this life.

This event of conversion through regeneration is, of course, a process, and therefore not completed at once. We know, and we confess that the conflict of the old with the new nature perseveres, even after regeneration. Consequently we know too that even after regeneration there remains room, in a sense, for a "suppression" of the good by the bad and of the bad by the good. Such interchange of dominance and subordination is the experience of the person renewed by the Spirit, during his progressive conversion. In a limited sense, there is some room after regeneration for the old personality to temporarily suppress the new; for the new then to re-assert its predominance over evil drives, for the old, in turn, again to attain the ascendancy . . . Alas, it is true, even after regeneration.

But in allowing for the possibility of such an interplay of suppression by the good now and the bad then in the personality of the reborn, we must make this qualification: the old nature will never permanently suppress or inhibit the new; victory is sure for the new man, for it is Christ who conquers in him.

Again, therefore: Suppression and conversion through regeneration are essentially different in kind.

To return to Judas. When a human soul such as his was remains untouched by regeneration, he has in the home of his soul only such furnishings[1] as bear the trademark of Satan. Consequently, Christ can enter the house but He cannot enter it as a Mediator; He can enter only as a person whom we respect, find fascinating, marvel at, and whom, to an extent, we are even willing to obey. But He cannot come into such a soul as Mediator, as Conqueror, as the Quickener of life through the Holy Spirit, as the One who takes us with Him into His death and afterwards raises us with Him in the resurrection. The suppressing, the inhibiting, which takes place in such a soul can merely be the psychological jugglings, the natural "up's and down's" of the old personality itself. At best a soul of this kind can only be aware of the least essential, of the most superficial, aspects of Christ.

The heart of Judas, the heart of the unregenerate man, refuses to be searched and renewed by Christ and His Spirit. On the contrary, it puts Christ, and even Him according to His least individual distinctiveness, under the searchlight of its own inquiry. And only in so far as such a Christ is seen and appreciated in that way can He enter into a regenerate soul of this description. His ideality can then serve to suppress for a while various base desires and evil motives (think of the influence on the greed of Judas) but it cannot *vanquish* sin, nor annihilate the wicked heart. The result is a personally, temporarily effected improvement. By virtue of an idea, of an ideal, of Christ, personally engendered within himself, such a man has temporarily corrected, improved, civilized himself. But he has not been smitten down by the *person* of Christ, he has not been *converted*.

In such a hapless circumstance there can be but one issue, one outcome. After a while that which was inhibited for the time be-

---

1. An allusion to Christ's analogy of the human soul to a house containing "furnishings," "goods," "vessels." Matthew 12.

ing, and forcibly suppressed into the dim recesses of the subconscious life will with redoubled vehemence rush to the surface and surge into the crest of the conscious life. Because of the inhibition it will assert itself so much more violently. Long suppressed desires eventually cry for release with the vengeance of vultures. When that happens the person who embodies them does what he does *quickly*.

Such is a tragical evolution. But it is inevitable, is terribly logical, unless God intervenes unto repentance. For the unregenerate man may live in Christ's company, may accommodate himself after a fashion to Jesus' program, but essentially he will continue to live by self-assertion. Christ cannot be a Mediator to this man, for he keeps pushing the offer of the Mediator out of the center of his unrenewed personality. Yes, Christ can enter into the restive, striving, self-consuming soul of this man but only as a noble person with a pure, strong spirit, and a poised will. Yes, as a Man among men Christ may even set the man's spirit aflame and evoke a crucial psychological conflict in his soul by placing all the unregenerate's inhibitions under the rays of His penetrating insight. But in the crisis which Jesus arouses in that way it is not grace which triumphs. Instead the feverish process of sin and self-assertion will be quickened until the man yearns for death.

That makes the matter one of dead earnest. The crisis comes. Something must bend or it will break. The imperative of action asserts itself absolutely. The sole resource of that tragically enmeshed personality then, fatigued, exhausted as it will be, is to the dark speech issuing simultaneously from Jesus' lips and from his own soul: What thou doest, do quickly!

Nothing now is added to what was already present in this life. Christ introduces nothing into it. What happens is this: that which is present already manifests itself. The temporarily suppressed, the momentarily inhibited, now, and this time finally, demands its rights. Its *rights*—precisely, for this man has never denied these. He has simply ridden rough-shod over them. He has never "operated on" his own heart, never said to it: You have no rights whatever.

Then Satan invades the soul. And the soul goes out to meet Satan. For it is the peculiar majesty of Jesus that He can conquer man without man's first approaching Him. But Satan's frailty is proved by this, that he cannot approach a soul unless that soul has first turned to him.

Jesus, the Mediator, introduces a new element into the regenerated person. Satan can only jostle old elements, can only agitate what is native to man.

Perhaps it will be worth the while to scrutinize this matter more closely.

We must not suppose that such spiritual inadequacy as we have just described is applicable only to such peculiarly evil natures as those of Judas and his ilk. To yield temporarily to a kind of spiritual enchantment and consequently to "suppress" base passions and desires, and at the same time to let sin assert itelf is not conduct peculiar to Judas alone. To a certain extent every human being is partly subject to the same laws. Hence, his "suppression" concerns each of us vitally.

As it happens a relatively recent school of psychology has been especially attentive to precisely this phenomenon of "suppression," of "inhibition." This school goes so far that it, if not actually basing the whole science of psychology upon that phenomenon, does try to explain most psychological processes in terms of it.

This is not the place to name the scholars who are adherents of the school, to say how much of truth, how much of falsehood we detect in it, to indicate to what extent we agree and to what extent we oppose the philosophy propounded.

This can suffice. Generally speaking, we agree that in every personality there is an unconscious, inhibiting influence exerted by one desire upon another; further, that this repressing influence is an activity of our deepest seat of conduct, of a secret will, that is, which, by reason of sin, chooses to face realistically only those data of experience which please it most; a secret will, therefore, which avails to make a service of self (that prominent alternative to the service of God) quite possible even when God pursues and Jesus charms.

Now it is remarkable to notice the remedy which this school of psychology proposes for a person as thoroughly unwholesome as that described. He will escape fleeing from himself, we are told, only when he takes each of the instincts, drives, desires, and passions which he has suppressed into the subconscious and, one by one, discloses them to the light of day by impetus of a calm mind. He must, in short, stop fleeing from the naked, terrible reality which is his self. He must stare his inhibited desires full in the face. He must confess aloud to himself that all his fears really are the product of his own personality. By unsparing self-disclosure he must learn to fear nothing that is actual.

And if he cannot achieve such self-unmasking in his own power, he must be given the assistance of another. That other person must teach him to discover his soul to his mind, to tear the veils from his unconscious life. In short, the psychiatrist must come to direct the man, who is groping blindly in his way, through the dark recesses of his personality. A psychiatrist worth the name will simply hold a mirror before his patient; he will let the searchlight of self-knowledge play unmercifully upon the personality, especially upon its obscure corners. Acutely realistic self-knowledge — so goes the theory — is the only, and is an adequate remedy for the unhealthy soul. Just so he acknowledges himself as he is and quits the attempt to circumvent such acknowledgement, he will find rest and peace in his soul. That is the contention.

We can name many objections to this theory. According to this philosophy, man can save himself; the Mediator is superfluous. We concede that self-knowledge of the kind described can improve, can civilize a man to some extent; but we know with certainty that it cannot in principle destroy the evil will of the old nature. The interpretation has no use for the terms regeneration and conversion. True, when put in practice, it makes an attempt to push aside the unsuitable "furnishings" of the soul;[1] but it makes no effort to supplant these with such new equipment as comes from above by the renewing of the Holy Spirit — furnishings which bear the trademark of God and of His Word. Hence we conclude that this new psycho-analytical doctrine of redemption is antagonistic to the Christian faith and to the one name given under heaven whereby man can be saved.

---

1. See note, p. 183.

We shall say no more about it. The subject of this book is not conversion, nor psychology; the theme of this book is the suffering Christ.

We alluded to the position solely in an attempt to set Christ in clearer relief. Christ is in the room of the Passover. So is Judas. And Judas, though daily following Jesus, has been "escaping" from Him for years. Yes, Christ is in the room — therefore the crisis is pending for Judas, the great Inhibiter. The fact that these two are together in the same room makes the case of Judas with his complexes and inhibitions an exceptionally fruitful study.

For we must remember that the Christ who is present here is, in the strictest and in the broadest sense of the word, the physician of all souls. In the strict sense He is that as a Mediator for all His people by special grace. But humanly speaking, He is also a physician in a broader sense. He is the sinless man. His spiritual life is perfectly wholesome. The activities of His mind are perfect. Well, should He not then, and simply as a man, influence all He meets and influence *perfectly?* This Jesus is here in *Judas'* company. He is a sacred fire of motive energy and intellectual energy, of pure, humanly genuine desires. Moreover, He is righteous and incriminates no one.

And how does He affect Judas? What is Judas' experience in the perfect presence of the man Christ Jesus?

So much is obvious. Christ does not function as a psychiatrist, as a physician according to the ideal of the school of psychology to which we alluded. He did not say to Judas: what thou doest, *discover* that quickly. Then you will be a free man. Then you can look me in the face, and will be converted. Then the sword of the archangel of an accusing conscience will vanish. No; Jesus said: What thou doest, do quickly!

Jesus by that remark fully acknowledges the fact that a man's *knowledge* does not alter his *being.* He asserts that, in the last analysis, only two kinds of life are possible. There is the life which in the profoundest essence of its being turns to God and lives by His will through regeneration. And there is the life which in its essential reality turns to and lives by itself, a life whose dominant motif is not derived from God but is the self-engendered product of its own natural state.

Back of this dual possibility lies a profound mystery; a mystery which abundantly manifests itself in the facts of experience. We trace it back to the foundations of eternity when we tremulously speak of *election* and *reprobation*.

Christ bows to the majesty of the law of election and reprobation in the room of the Passover, and He at the same time fully vindicates that of the responsibility of man, even of the man Judas who eats bread with Him at the same table. Yes, it is precisely *his* responsibility which Jesus respects.

For, while Jesus is seated at the table, He appeals to Judas' sense of responsibility. Jesus lets His penetrating searchlight play upon Judas in a final attempt to evoke a· self-disclosure. How often Jesus had invited, constrained, almost compelled Judas to fall on his knees before Him and to confess everything to this Lord! Repeatedly Jesus used every possible means to recall from the sombre depths of the disciple's soul those things which he had suppressed into his unconscious life.

If Judas had responded to that invitation, he would thereby have proved that his perverse will had been broken already. Then the Spirit of Christ would have "entered into" the soul of Judas triumphantly "after the sop." And upon that basis good would have overcome evil in Judas.

But Judas kept still. He locked himself inside his own being. He moped in secret.

The chicken was invited under the wings of the hen but it would not.

Both are in the room of the Passover. The sacrament has been prepared. Centuries look on. Spiritual demons are in the air; the angels of God are watching. But one influence is more potent than that of demon and angel, the influence of Jesus' soul. By means of this influence Jesus lets Judas burn once more in the white-hot flame of his own smoldering passions. You ask how Jesus achieves that, how Jesus constrains Judas to walk through the flames he himself has set afire? The answer is: by letting His will, moved by God, enter into that of Judas, and by fixing His searching eyes upon those of Judas.

In spite of the pressure, Judas still chooses to ally himself with Satan.

The measure is full. Trembling in its august presence, Jesus acknowledges the law of personal responsibility, respects it even in Judas. He abandons him, yields him to Satan. What thou doest, he says, do quickly.

This matter is a profound revelation of the essence of the Man of sorrows. At the same time in which He fairly constrains Satan to come into the room of the Passover and virtually compels him to construct the frame of the cross, He assumes the double law of election and reprobation, on the one hand, and that of human responsibility, on the other.

This event is not an isolated or peculiar incident. Soon Christ will be hanged between two murderers. He will be sensitively aware then that one is the object of eternal election, the other of reprobation. Just so the soul of Jesus now experiences that double law in reference to His apostles. As He looks into Judas' eyes He lives with him the drama of his reprobation and responsibility; simultaneously He experiences the drama of election and responsibility of those others lying at the Table, chosen vessels to tell His honor, who will presently see their names written in the foundations of the heavenly city.

This synthetic, this comprehensive awareness in every indivisible second, this uncoerced and broad perspective is the justification of Jesus as man before God. It is also His human vindication before God in reference to Judas. For Judas suppresses oo very much: his base passions first, because such inhibition profits him; his better aspirations then, because that profits him. But Jesus suppresses nothing. At the beginning Judas suppressed election ("your names are written in heaven!") in favor of responsibility ("He casts out devils!"). Now he suppresses the concept of responsibility in face of a false, Judaistic notion of election (God's appointment of Israel as a fleshly people of Abraham: — hence Jesus must die). But Jesus suppresses nothing, inhibits nothing. Each moment of His stay with this small group of disciples in the house of the Passover He is simultaneously aware of election and reprobation and of the human responsibility of each to God.

This sensitive and comprehensive awareness imparts a profounder tone to His words: Ye have not chosen me, but I have chosen you. Moreover, a consideration of these facts also compels us to give closer attention to that other statement, that of the high-priestly prayer, in which Jesus acknowledges that those whom He has chosen are the same as they whom the Father has given Him.

In the expression "I have chosen you" Jesus is the *subject* of the electing; He Himself does the choosing; He rises and falls by an act of His own will, by a self-expression. And because He does the choosing Himself He influences all, including Judas; He brings the whole weight of His human soul to bear upon Judas, and upon the other disciples. He exercises the full force of His ethos upon them. "Have I not chosen you twelve for the work, twelve elect, to assist me, to stand at the fire?"

But in the expression acknowledging that they whom Jesus chooses have been given Him by the Father, Christ is the object of the election. As man, therefore, according to its import, Jesus must accept what is given to Him. He is completely subservient to the one Will which moves the earth, effects God's pleasure, and brooks no interference. In its presence all must be silent. Even the Son of man must be still. If Judas is not among those given Him, Jesus cannot receive him. Jesus can do His duty to the disciple as long as there is breath in Him, it is true. He can bring the full force of His sinless, dynamic, beautiful personality to bear upon him. He can always welcome him warmly, let him bathe in the blessed sunlight of His own perfect, patient spirit, but, unless Judas has been given Him by the Father, Jesus can only effect a suppression, and never the needful conversion. He cannot because of Judas' unbelief.

So much for Judas. But when we try to relate the austere mystery of the laws of election and reprobation and that other law of responsibility to Christ Himself, the significance of the issue in the hall of the Passover penetrates our hearts and lives with a constricting vehemence. Both of these laws confront Christ simultaneously. He senses the minutest implication of both. Yes, He sees both represented in the twelve who are with Him. He is aware of the force of both laws especially in Himself. He senses it and knows that God is awful.

As man, He knows He is a servant, and subject to that one law of election and reprobation. If He did not know this He could not bear to sit in the same room with Simon Barjona and with Judas, could not eat the same lamb as these, nor breathe the same air. But He can bear to do so. He can, because His conscience is faithful to God. He, by especial appointment, is the Elect of God, the Chosen above all others, the appointed Head of the covenant of grace. How profoundly and how intensely He feels that fact! Now, in this room, and at this hour His thoughts go back to the prophets, to each, to all, to Moses, to Jacob, Isaac, Abraham, Shem, Noah, Enoch, Abel, and Adam. He is very certain, humanly He is very sure, that He is the Head, the appointed Head of the covenant of grace. He knows . . . for He has seen Judas, and behind Judas, God.

That is a part of it. But there is another side to the matter. He is aware of His responsibility. He has seen Judas, and behind Judas, God. He knows that He is responsible to the highest degree. For He has seen Judas and He has seen Simon Barjona and both are an obligation to Him. Yes, God stood behind Judas. But He stood behind Simon, too. God stood behind Simon as Lord, and as Lord He pleaded for him. No, the Lord — a friend talks with a friend; think of Abraham and Moses — talks with Jesus now, and tells Him to plead for Simon.

Simon, Simon, I have prayed for thee. Alas, Judas, I could not, I simply could not plead for thee. I could not because of unbelief. You harbored unbelief. You still embrace it. But Simon —in him grace dwells. Grace means election. Election, grace, comes in the form of a covenant. And a covenant always means responsibility. Sacred responsibility.

Entering the community of all the prophets, of Moses, of Jacob, Isaac, and Abraham, of Shem and Noah, of Enoch, Abel, and Adam, Jesus Christ swears that He is responsible to God, that He is the responsible Mediator of the covenant of grace.

Election and responsibility; O God, O God!

Election, chosen Head of the covenant of grace!

Responsibility! Responsible Mediator of that covenant!

Election!

Yes, Father, such was Thy good pleasure. The best I can do for Judas is to stimulate "suppression." For him I can at best be mere man, be a certain Jesus, a civilizing influence. To the ex-

tent that I am a Mediator, my office can only aggravate his condemnation. But — should I demur to sing psalms for Thee on
that account, Lord my God? The angels praise Thee, the apostles,
all the hosts of heaven praise Thee, O God, Thou who dost elect
some and they come, who, as is illustrated by the best effects of a
purely human influence dost cause others to suppress, to flee.
Lord, my God, Judas is here. He must go now, for I must celebrate the Passover, and eat the supper, and break the bread . . .
Lord, I am Thy Chosen One, am one with all Thy elect, and that
is burdensome knowledge; it weighs very heavily. The prophets
spake of "pressing" issues. They spake of Me. See how I am
driven till all be fulfilled, till I can see behind the clouds. It is
hazy here; no, it is awfully dark here in this hour with Simon and
with Judas; O God, it is so very dark. Dwellest Thou in darkness? Yes, Solomon knew it. God dwells in darkness and is One
who must choose, must select, reject. Yes, God of Abraham,
Thou who didst accept Isaac and reject Ishmael — and who didst
appoint the fortunes of Jacob and Esau before they were born—
yes, of course, I stand aside for Thee. I was not interfering,
Lord, I simply peered into Judas' soul, simply let my eyes burn
their way into his soul. I did not gainsay Thee. Ah, I know full
well that I can do nothing for Judas: it was my fate to be a man,
and that was Thy pleasure; it pleased Thee that I should be human. No, I shall not confute the Word pronounced over Jacob
and Esau before birth, over Simon, over Judas, and over Me, my
God. Father, how beautiful Thou art. Was that sound just now
not the song of the angels? Ah, yes, the hymn of praise is there;
the book of psalms lies open. Very soon we will sing the ritual
and with sincerity of heart. We will sing the hymn of praise for
Thee, O God; even though Thou dost elect, we will sing. I shall
say that those knives must be put aside. It is enough. Election
is just enough. It is so very simple, so inevitable: it is enough.

This only I know, Lord my God, Thou alone doest things. I
am a man: man cannot break the walls Thy counsel hath established. Once I could do no more miracles because of their unbelief. I could not, Lord, not then, not at that place. I was very
tired. And I cannot do any now. Unbelief is present in the room.
Its fumes rise up against the sacrificial lamb. How that hurts.
Could I rest, satisfied, here in Thy election and reprobation?

Must not those fumes be removed? Lord, what that man doeth, let him do it quickly. But Thou art holy; Thou dwellest in the praise of Israel. The hymn of praise is read: the knives must be put away.

Judas, Judas, what thou doest, for thou doest it, (I do it, God doth not)—what thou doest, do quickly.

Lord, I can breathe more easily now. Election is a matter of fact because God is. But responsibility is fact also. God must be sought. God is and giveth reward; He giveth Himself to all those that seek Him. Yes, responsibility is real and binding, Lord my God.

Hence, I shall arise and do my work. Do all of it. Away with the knives. I go to address myself to Judas. Save Simon, Lord, sift him as wheat. I have told Judas already; he must go, must do it quickly. I did not ignore Satan. My eyes are open; I have my loins girded; the lamps are burning. I go to meet Satan with full awareness. I bear the lamp of watching in my hands. I see him there; I sense his presence. Thou sayest I must meet him, must confront him squarely. And I do it even now, my Lord. Thou has united me strictly; Thou hast fixed inviolable limits for all men. What can man do to melt the ice encrusting Judas' soul, to ply the brass that sheathes the souls of others? Lord, my love burns fervently. Flames of the Lord, flames of the Lord! But there are waters they cannot lick up: Judas is Judas still. I could not enflame him, nor set him aglow. I am man, Father; I am man. It is a palpable limitation to be man, to appreciate the need of Simon, of John, of the others — Thou knowest their names. I am bound up with them. Sweet bonds they are that bind me, though they hurt cruelly. But I go to do the work. Samson, Samson, hero of God, chariot of Israel and its horses! I am doing it already, Lord. I come, O God, to do Thy pleasure. I come to work. I have an eager will to achieve, Lord. I wrought with my whole human will and all my human energies upon the soul of Judas. I saw flames enveloping him: we burned in the same fire. Still, I have but the will, Lord, for I am human. Thou hast sovereign jurisdiction, for Thou art God. Thine is the kingdom, and the power, and the glory forever. Amen. I bow, I bow low in acknowledgment. I do the work. This is my body that is broken for many unto a complete propitiation for all of their sins. Broken — that is the word. Something is breaking here. Thou hast ropes which cut cruelly. The purest soul, the soul of perfect virtue cannot break the wall. The ropes of murderers cannot bind as firmly as Thine, My God, Thou who dost elect and condemn!

But I come. I take the responsibility. Allow these sheep to go, Lord. But I shall call Satan out from the dark. Satan, come. Do quickly what thou doest. Here is Judas, and here, Simon: sift them, sift them as wheat. May God have mercy upon the kernels of grain. Lord, be merciful to Simon. Come, Satan: now is the time.

Here, Judas; it is inevitable. God says so. God is standing right there. It is very light in the room now. A fire is burning. Judas, take it, take this sop. Go now: what thou doest, do quickly . . . .

No! No, of course not. Such was not His experience. It is difficult to think about Jesus Christ. But this there was in that experience, we may be sure: the burning of election, the fire of responsibility; the synthetic comprehensiveness: a relating of those twelve — with a gulf dividing them — to Himself, and a reference of all of them and of everything to God.

So much was in His experience. I believe that because I believe that Jesus was *very* man and *just* man. A Man of sorrows He was, stricken of God, but maintaining His poise as though seeing the Unseen. I believe this because the Scriptures exist and set me thinking. Is this a haughtiness? Yes, it is audacious to think about Jesus Christ. It also is haughtiness not to think about Him and nevertheless to pray tonight. To pronounce the name of God, that is haughty too. And I know that some such experience was His the night He was betrayed.

He was the Elect, the Responsible One.

He was the Chosen Head of the Covenant of Grace.

The Responsible Mediator of that Covenant.

And on a night in time, on a street in Jerusalem, where not long before a chauffeur cursed, a rooster crowed, a Mussulman yawned, and a woman yielded—it happened. God in the flesh, in typical human flesh. He looked out of human eyes. I was taught that this is called: revelation. God came into the flesh. Alas for me if I do not believe it, if I am not active in it.

Jesus goes out now. Close your eyes, people, but open your hearts. The Head and Mediator of the covenant of grace is here. He comes, He seeks. He is looking for the elect, searching for the host of prophets and apostles and for the cloud of witnesses which must still come. He comes to catch us up into life. See that He comes to take me up, for promises are resting upon me. He comes. His eyes are opened wide. He sees clearly, and is alert. He comes to snatch me from Satan's claw.

His eyes are open, yes. I see Him stepping over Judas' dead body to reach me. He does not ignore the corpse of Judas nor does he sidestep it. He does not push it aside. It is as Isaiah said, when at the close, I suspect, he could go no further: "They shall look upon the carcasses of the men that have transgressed against me." So Jesus comes over the body of the stricken Judas to say He has a promise for me. For He must come to me.

O God, do not let Him, and with that same thorough-going authenticity, stride over my dead body and my dead soul . . O God, be merciful to me, a sinner. For He blinks at nothing, suppresses nothing. My secret self, my Judas-heart is an open book to Him when He comes. O God, how painful is salvation?

How plainly we can see from the experiences of Judas that Christ cannot be satisfied when a person lets Jesus enter his personality only as an ideal man, as a preacher of a noble ideal, as an idealization of our own base instincts. For all these supposed features Judas loved Jesus at one time. In those forms Jesus actually entered the disciple's soul, and as such "suppressed" much that was impure and sinful there.

But Christ vindicated Himself in Judas, and that in holy wrath as a *Mediator*. He wants vindication as nothing other than as that. He is not satisfied with being merely "a man." For, as a man, He was appointed by the Father to be the Mediator. That means that because He is Mediator He is Man.

That is the one thing that matters. A solemn proverb tells us: all or nothing. And although we are glad to admit that the superficial side of Jesus achieves much good in the world and inhibits much evil, we must maintain and protest, confronted by the inner mortality of Judas, that Christ Jesus requires vindication in us *only as Mediator*. He may not, because of the Father He may not desire anything less.

Because Thou hast done this, hast wanted to be solely a Mediator in the room of the Passover, Thou couldst institute the Lord's Supper there; therefore, too, I am able to say: My Lord and my God.

We are raising these matters for consideration because of a specific reason. By means of them we can get some slight appreciation of the Saviour's human soul, of His Mediatorship as He actually experienced it in His flesh, and also of the way in which the life and time of Jesus is parallel to those of God's eternity.

We may not look at Jesus and at Judas, at the room of the Passover, at the hardening, the conversion in a fragmentary, piecemeal manner. For that is not seeing them the way Christ saw. What we have said thus far can be epitomized in this way: Jesus suppresses nothing within Himself. He does not scrutinize one part of the whole thoroughly and the rest superficially. He never sees things granularly; He under-emphasizes nothing. Therefore the Christ who includes in one glance the full round of God's election and reprobation has a right to demand that we see the room of the Passover as a smithy in which the anvil is being struck by God, in which the hammer is propelled by the powers of eternity.

To look at Judas, and especially at his tragical end, first, and then uncritically to leap to the concept of the election and reprobation of God is to fail to appreciate the issue, for then these two will always stand in irreconcilable opposition to each other. But when we pause to see Jesus and Judas walking together, wrestling with each other, exchanging influences each moment, each hour, each year of their association with each other, and when we see the conflict between them increasing in vehemence, and then relate the experience to election and reprobation, and responsibility—then we can appreciate that these two, the eternal Decree and the experience of life in time, are one.

Then Christ stands behind everyone who reads these lines, whispering articulately into his ear: What thou doest, do quickly. In the essence of the matter, son of man, you are doing but one thing: by faith you are doing the work of God, *or* by indulging sin you are doing the work of Satan. But what you do, do quickly.

If those words really reach us, the Mediator has spoken to us. In that moment He comes to effectuate in us the conflict which he wrestles with us all His life, and tries to spare us a foolish flight from His awesome actuality. Very often He pronounces those words and every time He does so He drives the process in us farther.

One day He will pronounce them a last time. Then the culmination for us will have come; we will be ready for death or for life. Hence there is but one pertinent question: Are you one who fears Him or one who does not fear Him?

If we want to ward off the Christ in our deepest being, then He, His whole soul and every desire, clings closely to God when God rejects us justly. That is the case, not because Christ loves our condemnation, but because He loves God, also the God who judges.

Therefore, it is an awesome truth to know that Jesus never delivers piecework to God; that He suppresses nothing; that He drives all to its organic conclusion. His whole soul spoke when He said to Judas: What thou doest, do quickly. With those words the conflict of Judas' soul with that of Jesus had an end. That word was the beginning of another, a word which Jesus spoke from the Cross: *It is finished.* May each of us fear lest that cry of triumph some day be the Father's recognition that Christ has done wrestling with His Spirit in us and that nothing more can be done for us.

Fortunately we can also state it the other way. If Christ is one and undivided in wrath, He is also that in the work of Love; if He suppresses nothing in reprobation, He suppresses nothing in the adoption unto children.

That is great comfort for us. Just as His whole soul participated in the relinquishment of Judas, without a hint of division between His conscious and unconscious life, so too the fullness of His unified soul pours itself into the prayer which He as a High-priest sends to the Father from the room of the Passover.

That prayer, which the profound apostle John included in his account of the Gospel, takes on greater significance for us when we consider that Jesus is different from Judas, different from the other disciples who are of the elect.

Judas suppresses Jesus: he crowds Him out; the better insight, the call to confession, these he suppresses. And the apostles and believers, even when they are born again, continue to suppress a great deal, because they are not yet perfect in love and do not yet live fully in and by conversion.

But Jesus suppresses nothing in His soul. He cannot crowd into the background anything which He finds there. His entire soul, therefore, one undivided as it is, is fully brought to bear upon every predication of the high priest's petitions. His complete personality fully informs every comfort His mouth utters. Hence He goes steadfastly to the cross, not demurring. That cross which confronts Judas and Simon Barjona, which faces all things beautiful and ugly, He accepts with His heart, with all His soul, with all His mind and with all His strength. With each and with all of these He desires God in the cross. And just as He drives Judas out before Him, without in any way ignoring him, so He drives the soul and body, the full humanity of Peter, James, John, and all the little sheep of His flock ahead of Him. He dies the death in an awe-inspiring love, which has a vivid sense of the justice of wrath, of the necessity of the dread decree. He believes God is One, and He trembles.

Was the comforting of a human soul ever so humiliating, so disarming and, conversely, was the humiliation and discountenancing of God's brilliant light ever so comforting?

We should, however, be losing sight of the dominant purpose of this book if we were to conclude this treatise so.

The conflict which obtains in this experience is at bottom not an issue between the soul of the Mediator, Jesus, and the soul of Judas, but is the struggle between Christ as the Word made flesh and Satan.

We must return for a moment to the point at which we began. Whoever thinks the word "Satan" thinks the concept "suppression." That is not mere word-play. It is beyond question that the sombre spirit of Satan is not susceptible to the same psychological complications as is the soul of a human being. In human life an antithesis appears between the conscious and unconscious life. Somewhere in the human mind a threshold has been fixed; above it the conscious life operates; below it those passions lower which even the person himself does not know.

Not so in Satan. In him, too, all is conscious. He sins in full awareness of himself. His are not the laws of human nature; he has not the fickle, vacillating passions of man. He is a Spirit of eternity. In any given moment he can name precisely what is active within him. In every second of his sinister business he sees below the work he is doing the image of the beginning of his existence when he lived with God and as a created spirit praised Him.

Hence in Satan suppression cannot be similar in kind to that which took place in Judas. When we call Satan the great Suppressor, in spite of that, we mean that he is in every moment of his existence pushing God away from him, God, and justice, and right. Satan knows God better than any man. He cannot, however, suppress God into the subconscious life, for he has none. But by means of his will he is always attempting to push God out of his being. However, in the atmosphere of eternity, the desire counts as the deed: *in magnis voluisse sat est.*

In that way Satan, by very definition, is the great Suppressor. He suppresses God. He knows He cannot succeed but he persists in the attempt. He knows he cannot circumvent the judgment but every energy of each moment of his life goes into the effort to escape that wrath. Not that he attempts to forget and ignore as men often do. This great Suppressor attempts always to throw off what he refuses to acknowledge, not what he refuses to consider. Hence the Scriptures say of him that he trembles.[1] That trembling is symptomatic of the strained passion, the perpetual restlessness, the relentless striving of the satanic essence.

Now look at Jesus in the Passover room. We know there are two in the room. Jesus is there. Judas and Satan are there, and they are one. Judas suppresses and trembles, Satan suppresses, and he trembles. But a third person is present, and He is really the First. He is Jesus Christ. He suppresses nothing, He knows everything, and He wills all He knows as God's truth—and He

---

1. James 2:19.

also trembles. He, however, trembles only before God. Judas trembles because his own passions perturb him. He creates his own restlessness; he is divided against himself; how can he possibly continue to exist? Satan trembles because God is against him and because he is against God: these two are divided against each other. Together they cannot stand. And Satan would not fear if only God were divided against himself: but God is one.[1] Satan trembles because God is not as Satan wishes Him to be. God therefore plants the fire in Satan's spirit. My Lord Jesus Christ also trembles. Is He, too, in a state of self-contradiction? No, on that count He can continue to exist. Is He divided against God? Again, on that score He is free. But Christ trembles because God is divided against Him, because He bears the curse of God in Him.

Even so He will embrace His God. He will desire God and that not blindly. No, no, Christ does not tremble, for, although God is against Him, God, Satan, Judas, Simon, and my soul will never induce Him to rebel against God. He suppresses nothing, and so He gains the great victory. No, in a sense, Christ does not tremble.

And see. Brace yourself firmly as you look. Deliberately, with poise, He raises His hand, extends the bread, speaks the word, relinquishes Satan, lives a millennium in a moment, dispatches Judas, meets His Father, passes God's sentence upon His accusers, takes up the cross, and dies the death, and at the conclusion of all: Father, into Thy hands I commend my Spirit.

This is sublime and very praiseworthy. Christ Jesus stands between Judas who suppresses, and Satan, the patron of all those who suppress. He is related to Judas. He has much in common with Satan. But He stands opposed to both in holiness, and in this He vanquishes them eternally.

We said that Christ was related to Judas. That is true. He shared with Judas His humanity, His activity, His growth, His progress in learning, His susceptibility to being tempted and to being proved. But Christ, in contrast to Judas, manifests a perfect obedience. Hence, although He shares His humanity with His disciples, His holiness sets Him apart from Judas' sin. Thus

---

1. James 2:19.

He conquers Satan who tries to make use of Judas in an effort to tempt Christ to do evil.

Christ has also some characteristics in common with Satan. For He, the Word of God, the Son of eternity, the Logos, is one with Satan in this that He sees all that is happening in the present in indissoluble relationship with all that has occurred in the past, and in doing it, relates all to what will happen in the future.

But Christ stands in opposition to Satan in that He desires God with a perfect holiness and invites God to Himself perfectly.

Thus it happens that this human soul, though it must live and learn and develop with Judas, nevertheless cannot expel God from itself for a second. Could God care to push God aside? The world could more easily pass away. Bow, then, and worship: Jesus Christ desires God, His soul longs for God. He will seek God early in the morning, will seek Him at dawn, when the cock crows; on that morning, too, when at the cock-crow, Judas destroys himself, and on that other dawn when Satan curses God as never before, and very sensitively aware of what He is doing, constantly wills to ward Him off.

And in this opposition of Jesus, who, as man, is both sensitive and poised, to Satan, the suppressor *par excellence*, Christ in every indivisible moment of His existence completely conquers Satan. Now Christ by the much more magnetic attraction of His soul, and by the irresistible lure of the active energy emanating from His life can charm Satan out of the secret corner in which he is lurking and beckon him to come to the table where He is eating bread, to His breast, and to His holy heart, and then can break out into psalms to God.

It sounds paradoxical but we set it down as significant truth: precisely because Christ can in any instant attract God to Himself with His whole personality He can so invite Satan to come to Him. Not because He desires Satan but because He loves God perfectly. And if God's clock can strike the hours only for the power of darkness, Jesus will move the pendulum of that clock of time with His own fingers. He winds the world-timepiece with His own hands. He calls Satan into the open, and says to him, suppressing nothing He needs to know out of His consciousness: This is thy hour and that of the power of darkness; what thou doest, do quickly.

If Christ had called Satan to Him without simultaneously beckoning God to Himself with a passion of perfect longing, His act would have been one of sheer haughtiness. He would have been rejected from God's presence as one who essayed to play with demons while riding a tornado of the wrath of God. We would have perished with Him.

And conversely, of course: if Christ had desired God alone, if He, raising the false prophecy of a God *an sich* to the plane of truth, had not beckoned Satan to Him, now that the time was fulfilled, His soul would not have responded purely to the dispensation of God's occasion and to the circumstances which God's counsel had appointed beforehand. Then the clock of Christ's human conscience would not have been regulated according to the sun of the counsel of God. Then the pressure of the atmosphere bearing down upon His soul would have been different from that obtaining in the heaven of God's counsel, in the sphere of God's law and Gospel.

But now that Christ beckons both God and Satan unto Himself, Christ with a perfect love and Satan with complete aversion, but both with perfect awareness, now the Saviour manifests Himself. This is He who can pray what actually was prayed in Gethsemane, who suffered an eternity in time. This is He who, although He is given but a square foot of ground on which to stand, sees all powers, those on earth and those in heaven, simultaneously; He sees all included within its meridian. This is He who buoys the great All up in His strong arms, in obedience and in virtue, as a Mediator of justice and redemption.

Thus we see Jesus standing.

The disciples suppress the old nature with the new, and the new with the lingering effects of the old.

Judas suppresses the better aspirations possible by common grace, a possibility in which Jesus' influence also assists, by the deeper passion of pride. He cannot, does not want to redeem or be redeemed.

Satan by his own will suppresses whatever he knows and exerts himself feverishly to oppose and hamper redemption. He suppresses the truth of the impossibility of victory by the seed of the serpent over the seed of the woman.

But Christ suppresses nothing and no one. He assigns everything to its place and leaves it there. He sees nothing *an sich*. Everything is related in strict organic relationship for Him: Christ and Antichrist, heaven and hell, God and Satan, Judas and —dare I say it—Judas and I, if I believe. So did the Saviour from moment to passing moment, conform Himself perfectly to God, who knows Himself perfectly (for the Spirit proves all things); to God, who knows the world perfectly also and all that is in it (for the Spirit is also called the Seven Times of God, running through the world). Since God and Christ are one now in ignoring nothing, suppressing nothing, Christ is proved the Saviour and Mediator of God and man.

Our poor souls may sometimes suppress the promise, but always it will arise again to protest: I love God, for He hears my voice: He will not forget me, nor suppress me in all eternity.

Christ, confronting the volume of wrath and the gateway to heaven, suppressing never—that is comfort. It is that which was impossible to man. That is God in the flesh. Now the Sabbath bell began to sound over a world lost in guilt.

Death too grasped the rope and began tolling, tolling . . .

The Mediator Washing the Feet of His Own

CHAPTER THIRTEEN

The Mediator Washing the Feet of His Own

● *After that he poureth water into a basin, and began to wash the disciples' feet, and to wipe them with the towel wherewith he was girded. Then cometh he to Simon Peter; and Peter saith unto him, Lord, dost thou wash my feet? Jesus answered and said unto him, What I do thou knowest not now; but thou shalt know hereafter. Peter saith unto him, Thou shalt never wash my feet. Jesus answered him, If I wash thee not, thou hast no part with me. Simon Peter saith unto him, Lord, not my feet only, but also my hands and my head. Jesus saith to him, He that is washed needeth not save to wash his feet, but is clean every whit; and ye are clean, but not all. For he knew who should betray him; therefore said he, Ye are not all clean. So after he had washed their feet, and had taken his garments, and was set down again, he said unto them, Know ye what I have done unto you? Ye call me Master and Lord; and ye say well; for so I am. If I then, your Lord and Master, have washed your feet; ye also ought to wash one another's feet. For I have given you an example, that ye should do as I have done to you.*—JOHN 13:5-15.

WE ARE aware of the fact that to treat of the story of the washing of the feet of the disciples, at this point, is again to depart from the chronological order we have been following. We allowed ourselves that privilege before. Again we do so with a specific purpose in mind. We have been looking at the dark side of the picture of Christ in the room of the Passover. Now we choose to see the brighter side. We were seeing the shadow, when, in the vestibule of it as well as in the temple of sorrows itself, we observed Christ struggling against the satanic element, and saw that element warring against Him. Therefore we must now devote some attention to the light, to the

Spirit of love and truth, to the Spirit of prophecy and of the official ministration of redemption. Christ surrenders Himself to death in the room of the Passover. Hence, Christ comes before us first of all in the guise of a servant, of a servant who washes the feet of his own. Thereupon He appears as the Mediator who ministers Himself unto them in the Holy Supper.

There was a perfectly natural occasion for this service of the washing of feet. A dispute had arisen among the disciples about who should be the greatest of them. Their thoughts frequently tended to linger over that question of the balance of power. It is possible that the argument on this day was conducted with an eye to a possible assignment of functions in that future kingdom, a kingdom which all of them had at first confidently expected in a temporal form, and which still haunted their imagination in that guise. Be that particular matter as it may, however—a dissension had arisen among them.

Christ undertakes to stop the argumentation. He lays His garments aside, takes a basin of water and goes about a duty customarily performed by the least of the household menials. He proceeds to wash the feet of the guests, whom, as a host, He has Himself invited to the sacrament. It is in this sense that the washing of the feet may be regarded as a perfectly natural service, fitting nicely into the day's program.

Nevertheless, no believer can suppose that Jesus' act of love is completely accounted for when it is regarded as a deed quite naturally evoked by the circumstances. Into this act of Christ as into so many others an element of necessity enters. The system of Jesus' life as Mediator again harmonizes perfectly with the prosaic forms and complications of the day's business.

We may not, therefore, regard the washing of His disciples' feet simply and solely as an item in Jesus' schedule of activities; still less as an addendum superadded to that program by reason of the exigencies of the occasion. We may not even consider it as a service which Jesus assigned Himself as an appropriate prelude to the Passover meal, and as nothing more than that.

The washing of the feet is more than a casual, more, too, than a special item in the program of activities for the night in which He was betrayed. Again the majesty of the eternal Spirit manifests itself in Christ's daily conduct. That is the majesty of a Spirit who gives His divine ordinances of regeneration form and color in the flowers which, figuratively speaking, burgeon forth spontaneously wherever He places His foot. It is specifically the work of the *Mediator* which gives eternal significance to all events which take place in the night of the passion. The mystery of the Messiah is revealed in them, also in the washing of the feet.

We shall not expose and refute at length those various exegeses of this event which tend to dissociate it from Christ's mediatorship.

There are those, for example, who interpret the washing of the feet as a mysterious preparation of the beloved disciples for the mystical marriage of the heavenly Bridegroom with the church.[1] Others suppose that this act must be regarded as a bathing, a purification, not unlike the so-called "mysteries" of the pagan world, by means of which, after so many ritualistic washings and purgings, a candidate was initiated into certain "mysteries" and raised to a higher degree in the religious order which had instituted them.[2] In the same way, these aver, by means of the water of cleansing—note that the holy water, not the holy person becomes the important matter—Christ now initiates His disciples into the Christian mysteries (supposing these actually exist). Accordingly, we are told, He prefixes this act of service to the Holy Supper advisedly, indicating in that way that the Supper, too, was one of those mysteries. The implication is that by means of the mysteries the religious life is emphatically differentiated and segregated from the natural life. By eating the holy bread and drinking the sacred wine the religious man retires into the secluded room of the mystery, there to meet with God in intimate, esoteric communion.

It would be inappropriate to dwell long on a refutation of these positions, so widely do they differ from our own.

Obviously the assumption underlying the theories outlined is that Christianity is but one manifestation of the general phenomenon called religion. Such explanations are designed to fit Chris-

---

1. Eisler, alluded to in Carl Clemen, *Religions geschichtliche Erklarung des N. T.*, Vol. 2. Töpelmann, 1924, p. 113, note.

2. Clemen, pp. 280, 281; also the standard literature on the subject.

tianity into the system of decadent paganism of the late-Hellenic spirit. They do not explain the Bible and the Gospel in terms of its own meaning—a requisite any honest scholar would set down as primary, even though he regarded that Bible as simply another cultural book. Such expositions distort the Scriptures, are the product of interpreters who have chosen once and for all to do all they can to fill in the gulf between Christianity and other religions, and—changing the figure—to melt Christ, and Buddha, and Mithras, and all other "saviours"[1] together in one crucible. They throw the Bible on the same heap with all the other "sacred" writings: this they do in order to show that the "one" spirit of the "religious" life gradually expresses itself through the channels of these various books, in order to prove that at best only a difference of degree, never one of kind, can obtain between the several religions, saviours, and systems of redemption that have evolved in the world.

The fundamental fallacy in these positions is this: they fail to acknowledge the significance of the *office* of Christ, and the *office,* too, of the disciples. Precisely because we wished to push the significance of the "office" to the fore we chose to allude to these other explanations of Christ's washing His disciples' feet.

Just what is meant by *office* in the religious life of the people whom God favored with His revelation? What is meant by it in the sphere of special grace?

Certainly that concept does not signify that as a result of the favor of grace a person is inducted into one of the "mysteries" where, in aristrocratic aloofness from men and affairs, he may have a passive, immediate communion with God. On the contrary, the term "office" implies service. The person favored with the gift of the office immediately converts the privilege of that into a calling. In him, *Gabe* (to use the nicer German designation for the gift of God) immediately is changed into *Aufgabe* (what he must do for others in God's name). "Office" implies a going out from the solitude of seclusion, in which one has met and been prepared by God, into the great world in order to share the blessing received with others. Not a greedy swallowing up of the waters of grace, but giving free outlet to the river of sal-

---

1. Drews, Arthur. *Die Christusmythe*, Jena, Diederichs, p. 99.

vation—that is what the concept "office" implies. It cannot mean an aristocratic seclusion from others on the part of the "initiate," a retreat into an "ivory palace" of religion, whose every window is shuttered from and every door is barred to the world in order that grace may be received "purely." In the Old as well as in the New Testament, office signifies an active power, a mission. This force throws doors wide open, presses out at the sills, blows the Spirit through crack and crevice into the great world outside. The office-bearer tears every veil asunder, forsakes palace and temple to reach the hovels of men, descends to the deep valley of common life in order that he may, in God's name, give the world what he has first received from God.

That is the essential difference between the theories to which we alluded and the truth to which we adhere—a difference not peripheral but basic in character, and a truth which is binding upon us who read the Scriptures in their own light, who honor Christ as the only Saviour, and who oppose Christianity, as the true religion, to paganism, as the false.

Dare we forget that Christ appears on this occasion as an office-bearer? God forbid.

The washing of feet which took place in the room of the Passover, which preceded the Holy Supper, which the eternal counsel and foreknowledge of God chose to actualize here and now— dare we lift that act out of its sublime setting? For behind that act and in it is contained the whole struggle of Christ Jesus in His official career as Mediator. In it is contained the struggle of Christ Jesus, who wants to perform the responsibilities of His office perfectly before God, who by His "official" example, by His "official" power, wants to constrain the Spirit of God, to speak the Word with a power derived from God, in order that thus the Spirit of Christ may convey the Word He speaks and the example He gives, to the apostles.

No, we dare not lift the account of that out of its context. We must refuse to cut the story of the passion into pieces, to make of it so many acts of a drama, whose tension is relieved by this lyrical entr'acte, this soothing episode, this gentle washing of feet.

In the name of our deepest conviction, in the name of the Reformed principle of interpretation of Scripture, we protest against any attempt to explain the washing of feet as a prelude to the Supper in such a way that both the washing and Supper are inveigled into a system of Christian "mysteries," supposedly extant. Whoever chooses this interpretation curses Christ with sterility. He overlooks the very significant spiritual meaning of Christ's act. We must remember that it is precisely John who records the act. And it cannot be denied that if this service of love were to be regarded simply as a token of friendship *par excellence,* simply as a supreme gesture of courtesy on the part of the gentlest host the world has ever seen, to a few, trusted friends, simply a demonstration of fellow-feeling, of intimacy—if it were to be regarded solely as such, it remains inexplicable why the other Evangelists say nothing about it[1] and precisely John emphasizes it so strongly.

That is a remarkable feature. For John is the Evangelist who, throughout his account of the Gospel, is continually pointing to the fact that the external acts of Jesus are so many revelations and evidences of the presence of the Word which was made flesh. He never permits us to see the whole significance of Christ's outward conduct in His external acts alone. His constant effort is to relate those outward expressions, those external forms, to the inner, infinite, spiritual, divine, everlasting being and life of the uncreated Word, of the Logos, the Eternal Son, who was with God in the beginning and Himself is God.

That emphasis points to the truth that the washing of the feet cannot (after the fashion of those who would relate it to the pagan "mysteries") be interpreted as a concealment, a retreat of the Divine to the comfortable shelter of an intimate communion, reserved for aristocrats by the grace of God, but that it, on the contrary, also is an illustration of what the prologue of John's record of the Gospel had revealed: namely, that in Christ, God comes into the world, and in that way sent out to the lengths of the earth—God revealed in the flesh, dwelling among men. Hence the office of Christ must become manifest and active in that mild

---

1. True, Luke (Chap. 22) records Christ's discourse, but says nothing of Christ's exemplary deed. We shall speak of this discourse later.

and unostentatious act of the washing of the feet. This account which John gives us is not a product of fancy, not an idyll, not an Arcadian play. The event it describes is not the embodiment of a supercilious aloofness on the part of certain "initiates" of a certain mystery. In the washing of the feet the great Office-Bearer of God goes out—to the apostles first, from them and through them to Jerusalem, Asia Minor, to the lowlands of the sea, where Batavians lived even in that age, out into the great, wide world.

The significance of the washing of the feet is not simply that by this token a gentle, gracious Master wants to teach a few of His best friends a lesson in humility. Such lessons can be learned elsewhere also. No, not that. In this service the Messiah takes up His Work, and, in doing that work, seeks the whole world. Is the room of the Passover small?—the Spirit will break its bounds. God Himself sets the pins of this tabernacle of communion far apart. Had He not done so that tabernacle would have become a tent of vanity.

Moreover, it is not only the prologue to the Gospel of John which suggests the basic principle that will explain the meaning of the washing of the feet to us: the chapter which narrates the event makes the same fundamental principle of interpretation binding. One writer,[1] consequently, has correctly observed that the token of love which Christ manifests to His disciples "is not completely contained in the washing of the feet. If in St. John's opinion that act itself constituted the whole token of love, he would have related the second sentence of the chapter to the first very directly by the use of the word 'for' or 'now.' As a matter of fact, the word used in that transition is the conjunction 'and,' a word designating sequence simply and nothing more. Hence, the evidence for the supreme[2] love Christ had for His own is not limited to the washing of feet, but includes everything written by this author in chapters 13 to 17. The discourses of Jesus, certainly, are an eloquent expression of the love of Jesus."

---

1. P. G. Groenen, *Het Lijden en Sterven van O. H. Jesus Christus*, 2nd Ed., Utrecht, 1919, p. 43.
2. The word "supreme" is used here because in the writer's opinion the line in verse 1 should be translated "he loved them *supremely*" rather than "he loved them unto the end." This opinion is a plausible one. Dr. C. Bouma (*Evangelie van Johannes*) also adheres to it.

That interpretation is the correct one. It is not merely accidental that in the Gospel account the washing of the feet is closely related to the discourses which Jesus spoke to His disciples in the room of the Passover. Such interrelationship is in harmony with the very form of the Gospel. Those discourses, too, certainly were not intended only for the few, were not a treat reserved for the secret delight of some few favored "initiates." If any one should undertake to measure the column-space devoted to Jesus' "public" addresses and that of those given to an intimate circle in the room of the Passover, that person would find that these private discourses, spoken between the washing of feet and Jesus' captivity, fill a very large percentage of the total space.

Can it seriously be suggested, then, that John the Evangelist is letting little flashes of mystery for him and some few others play before the amazed eyes of beginners in the faith, of "freshmen" converted to Jesus much later than he was, newcomers, who, alas, will never graduate to the level of the apostles, those favorites of Jesus, but who may in this secondhand way get a glimpse or two of the intimate secrecies enjoyed by the first disciples? No, no, not that. John is in his narration of this act, as he is in his account of all of the discourses of Jesus, himself *seeking* the world. In this instance, too, by means of the Gospel he seeks to make the office of apostleship productive for the world outside himself.

And, as we observe that the Word of Christ was given them for our sake in the room of the Passover, it becomes our duty to understand that Christ, so far from joining Himself in esoteric communion with a company of "initiates," personally not only officiates at the service, but also shares His official function with His apostles. In that way He makes the washing of the feet a subsidiary part of His official ministry in the world. And that is the reason for which the apostles in the succeeding discourses are designated as being not so much those persons who stand next to and live by virtue of Jesus, but as office-bearers of God, who *as such* receive promises, and are assured of the Spirit to inspire them in their official work.

In the washing of the feet, also, therefore, that emphasis on "office" must be discovered and accepted before any interpretation is attempted.

It is the High-priest, the Prophet, and the King who washes the feet, and who by that act sends His Word out through the apostles.

And that is why we insist upon directly relating the love of Christ, together with His sensitive care, to His office.

There are two ways in which we can do the Bible an injustice by a false interpretation of this event.

We are doing the Scriptures an injustice if for the sake of the office we lose sight of the love of Christ. To do that is to reduce the washing of the feet to a purely formal transaction, fruitful, perhaps, for teaching us rules of ecclesiastical manipulations bent on an official display of edification, but one which the Spirit has abandoned.

But it is also doing an injustice to the Bible to ignore the emphasis upon the office in favor of stress upon the love of Christ. To identify Christ with love, quite dissociated from Christ the Mediator, is to retain nothing of this narrative of John except a faint atmosphere of gentle enchantment. Such misreading of the account is to build the bridge between the episode of the washing of feet and the "mysteries" of India and of Greece. It is to invite the probability, no, it is to invite the certainty, of degenerating to that sick and sentimental attitude of those who look at the love of Christ as a purely erotic inclination, sublimated to a spiritual level, the kind of attitude, for example, to which Novalis succumbed in his spiritual hymns. Then, remembering the Indian mysteries, and regarding Christ's act in the room of the Passover as "parallel" to it, one is tempted to repeat with that poet:

> When Christ assures me I can be
> His own—assuring by his favor's light
> How soon a luminous life for me
> Dispels unfathomable night.
>
> Man only when I belonged to him
> Dark destiny gave daylight room
> And India even in the North
> For the Beloved burst in bloom.[1]

We repeat: if we look at the office, at "calling" in that way—rather, if we *overlook* it in that way—that is, if we force mediator-

---

1. From Novalis, *Geistliche Lieder.*

ship and history of revelation out of this scene of tender love, we are quite ready to enter, with a spiritual but altogether unbiblical eroticism, into those other words of that poet:

> Firmly grasp his hands in thine,
> Fix thine eyes upon his face;
> Flowers bend unto the sunshine
> Thou must bend so to his grace,
> Give him all, give heart and life:
> Thine he is, faithful as is faithful wife.

But the Scriptures place a very different concept of love over-against such confused eroticism.

We, too, certainly, we too, want to see a manifestation of love, and of tender love, in this episode of the washing of feet. But we refuse to define that love at the prompting of the spirit of our time.

For some in our day choose to think of love as the sustaining energy of every living thing, as the creative force, the prime mover, the first principle of a world and life view. Those who do so make two fundamental mistakes.

In the first place, they make all men equal in love. This one has more of love, perhaps, and that one less, but essentially all are born of love. Not one human creature, accordingly, nurtures hate, feeds enmity at the roots of his being. Love lives in all things alive.

And those who have this view are perfectly willing to let Jesus wash our feet, but that only as one possessing an *intenser* quality of love than other men. Over against this conception we postulate another: namely, that Christ is not one with other men by reason of His having been born of love, but that, as Mediator, He gives others something they do not possess in themselves. We refuse to look upon Christ as one differing from us simply in the degree of intensity of His love. We must regard Him instead as the Mediator who must offer us love as a gift if we are to have it at all.

In the second place, the conception alluded to is erroneous because it forgets that love can really grow only when it is rooted in regeneration rather than in natural birth. By nature we are not related to Christ. We cannot even emulate Him in the service of washing feet unless He warrants it. The example He gives us can not possibly be separated from His work as *Mediator*. We may not forget that by His washing of the feet He was calling attention to the fact that man must be "wholly clean," and therefore needs above all other things a cleansing which will purify him *in principle* and for *an eternity*. And such cleansing is the washing of *regeneration*.

Those, then, are the reasons for which we object to any sentimentalized paraphrase of this story, be it ever so charmingly done. We object to any version of it which separates the demonstration of love from the service of Mediatorship. If such versions were really based upon the Scriptures, we should have to agree with Novalis and acquiesce in his spiritual eroticism. Then his analogy of Christ to a "faithful wife" would have our assent. But, because it is the *office* of Christ which is completely pouring itself out in the *act* of His love, that love is spiritual, official, purposive, masculine, virile, and prophetic. It represents, not the secret delight of the Bridegroom and some few of His intimates in the seclusion of a bridal suite, but in an official love which blesses the world. It is as a faithful Mediator and not as a "faithful wife" that Christ, in the washing of feet, gives Himself to all as the servant of all.

"How friendly, how intimate this place seems!—" Should you like to write that over the door of the chamber in which Jesus is washing the disciples' feet? Well, you may—but not until you have understood first "How awful this place is!"

Once the key to unlock the meaning of this event has been given us, we have little trouble in manipulating it. In this story we see Christ as the second Adam, while en route to the wilderness of the cross and of death, prophesying the law of the restoration of Paradise, that law according to which the least and the greatest, the servant and the Lord, the one who blesses, receiving the tithes, and the one who is blessed, giving tithes, no longer oppose each other but meet and live with each other in harmony. As the second Adam, as the image-bearer of God, the Mediator in this instance too, is a prophet, king, and priest.

Christ is a *prophet* in this instance: He preaches the law of the Kingdom of Heaven to His disciples. He proclaims love, and in doing so declares the nature of its law with prophetic clarity. He demonstrates that love is not a natural life-function which is common to all, and that it is even less the inherent life-principle of all being, uniting all created things to each other and naturally relating the several members of any body to each other. Instead He teaches that love can have being only by reason of the mediatorship, which offers the greatest sacrifice not because of the pressure of sympathy but because of the imperative of the Will of God which grants reconciliation through fulfillment. Christ asserts that the expulsion of enmity from the world is not to be the product of culture, or an achievement which will follow naturally when the better impulses resident in man once are given free rein; on the contrary, He declares that the birth-chamber of love is the same as the place where justice demands its due. All reconciliation, including that between man and his fellowmen, can come only through *fulfillment*.

In order to preach that message Christ relates the washing of feet to the institution of the Supper, He preaches the Word in which the Mediator exposes His sacrifice to full view, and He promises the Spirit of Pentecost as a *gift* from *above*, for which He will pray the Father.

Those two emphases are extremely important ones in the prophecy of the gentle Jesus, menially engaged as He is in the service of washing feet.

The Spirit, the effectual principle of love, the prime Mover of it, can *only* come from above. Love, sympathetic coöperation, is not a flower which grows in gardens planted by men. That is the first emphasis of the prophecy. And the second "like unto it" is this: the Spirit of love proceeds from the mediatorship only, for it can come only after an anxious *wrestling* for it in *intercession* with the Father. Love is not possible, you see, without the *mediatorship*.

This prophecy which accompanies the *act* of Jesus exposes to us fully the significance of that act.

The man Jesus walks around the room with a basin of water in his hands, but—we may not forget it—the handles of that basin are being held in heaven. Take the Mediator away and Love's meanest article of furniture—a slave's wash-basin—will be drawn up into heaven. What remains of it on earth then is but a pathetic, empty caricature of it.

Is that not plain prophecy? Is not Christ teaching with shaming clarity that love is not to be regarded as the *sublimation* of elements of it with which the disciples were born, but is instead a *gift* from above, a very effectual power of love, and given solely upon the basis of His atoning and satisfying sacrifice?

In His preaching which accompanies the act of the washing of feet Jesus adds to the *objective* intercession on His part, the subjective need of regeneration, the indispensability of uninterrupted sanctification in His people. He enjoins the thought upon Simon Peter that love is not self-sufficient, cannot nourish itself, cannot guarantee its own fruition, but that God's almighty power must intervene to that end each day again. The soul must be purified again and again by an unintermittent, ever returning visitation of God's influence, which gives those who in principle were purified at regeneration, sanctification also, and thus guarantees that the fires of love will not die nor be extinguished by the stifling dust of sin.

That is Christ's prophecy about love. So He relates it to His own work, just as the fruit of sanctification is related to the root of justification. Thus He proves that love is impossible without mediatorship and regeneration. And so He asserts that every field of the merely natural, human world is arid and sterile.

And the sum of His prophecy is this. There is a love which is solely the product of *common* grace, *it is true*. This love is included in that eternal rotation of our natural life, in which love and hate, sympathy and antipathy, appetency and aversion, the day of marriage and the day of war continually exchange places and keep each other in balance, vacillating ever, ever, ever . . .

But the love which has worth in the Realm of Heaven lives by reason of other laws. It is not part of this vacillation of the natural life of common grace, of the tedium which the Preacher of the Old Testament deplored so sorely. For this love, arising as it does in the Kingdom of the Heavens, from the soil of special grace, entwines itself around the cross of Golgotha, the central redemptive fact, and derives its nourishment from the outpouring of the Spirit of Pentecost. It will never follow the circuitous groove of common grace, but will *undeviatingly* assist in the realization of the history of redemption until that history culminates in the youngest, the "last" day. This love is bound up with the cross and resurrection, is inter-ramified with the ever-progressing process of special grace and revelation, a process never disturbed, which will *fulfill* the world's times and bring them to rest in the day of Eternity.

That is the first emphasis. Christ the prophet does not ally Himself with love as the natural life principle; instead He allies love as the fruit of the spirit with Himself.

Peace foundations, humanitarian propagandists do like to carve Christ's water basin in wood, and to embroider it upon their banners. Against them Christ prophesies this: *What I have joined together, you shall not put asunder. Why do you accept my washbasin and ignore my bread and wine, my cross and .. my Word?*

Christ washes the feet of His disciples as a *King* and that is so much more evidence to show that His kingdom is not of this world.

At precisely the same time in which Christianity made its appearance in the world the *Caesarship of Rome was being deified.* It is not mere coincidence that at the very time of Christ's advent to the world the Caesar of Rome sent out the decree that he was to be honored as a god and be worshipped with the name "Lord." Thus the "Lord" of the world's realm rose to power over the shoulders of his subordinates; wading, when necessary, through their blood, he established his throne and somewhat later became the apotheosis of the glory of man. Such was the "Lord" who had himself anointed by the many as the great One.

At *this* same time Jesus anoints the feet of His disciples. The Lord of the Kingdom of Heaven enters the circle of those who are eminent in His Kingdom, His disciples. But He offsets any danger of His own and of their yielding to a blissful indolence of rest upon luxurious divans, breathing incense offered by others. He proclaims the law of that "Lord" who washes the feet of others in the guise of a slave although He is the Lord of all.

In doing this Christ explains further the fifth commandment, the one pertaining to respect.

There are many kinds of respect for authority—coerced respect, patriarchal respect, and spiritual respect.

Now there is no denying the fact that Jesus of Nazareth, simply as a teacher, as a worker of miracles, as a thinker, elicited the respect of men. Argue His mediatorship out of His life entirely: He still, in a relative way, enjoys the esteem of men. "They call Him master, and they do well."

But today Christ as the second Adam comes to preach and make binding upon the world as His will another message: namely, that all respect, cultural, patriarchal, that of an inferior to a superior anywhere, *may not be separated* from the mediatorship which is in Christ Jesus. Note that Christ accepts no respect, no honor, not even that which a teacher enjoys among his pupils, without first *earning* the highest possible respect by suffering the profound humiliation of slavery. What can He care for Socrates' respect among his students, what for the cultural superiority ascribed to their leader by the peripatetic school of philosophers, if He is not the Mediator? How can He care for any attitude of respect which arises from *common* grace? As long as the world endures there will be masters and servants, teachers and students, strong men and weak, culturally accomplished and culturally unfavored. As in the matter of love, so in that of respect: the riddle of the Ecclesiast inheres in it. He, too, looked upon *respect* as it operated under the fatiguing, maddening vacillations of the shuttle-like process of experience. Today he sees a lord riding a horse, a slave walking alongside; tomorrow the slave rides, and the lord, poverty-stricken and dispossessed, goes on foot. A king builds a palace today; tomorrow rebels destroy it. In such matters, respect, honor, acknowledgment of authority remains a relative thing. In natural life, on the plane of common grace, there is no *absoluteness;* there nothing is conclusive about respect. And that is really saying that, truth to tell, there is no respect! Must Jesus Christ file His claim to respect in such a world and upon such conditions?

Of course not. Were it so, death would have inhered in the quality of respect forever. If Christ's superiority were based on common grace alone, He would be a mere man among men; then His respect would be subject to that eternal wheel of vacillation to which we referred in connection with the Preacher of the Old Testament.

In the interest of an absolute, thorough-going respect Jesus rises to His feet, throws His robe aside, takes a basin, and washes His disciples' feet. In the same hour in which the sacrifice of the cross will fulfill all other sacrifices, in which the Kingdom of special grace will mercilessly cut its way through all world relationships—in that same hour He reveals the fact that He desires no respect which arises from mere earthly relationships. He wants a respect which has its origin in heaven. It is a respect which dares to use a wash-basin and a cross. He files His claim to respect by appearing in the loin-cloth of a slave, by hanging naked on the cross. His Kingdom is not of this world, His honor not the product of the movements of this world. His authority comes from above. He does not wear the loin-cloth *"in spite of"* His crown. It *is* His choicest crown, save one. The cross only is choicer.

As long as men let Christ wash the feet of His disciples, meanwhile turning their backs to the cross, that washing may be ever so appealing as a humanitarian incentive to the false prophets of philanthropic enterprises, Christian or non-Christian, but will always be misconceived. In such attempts on the part of social reformers to annex the episode for their purposes, irrespective of whether they have Jesus' basin engraved upon their stationery and ballots or not, man remains the equal of his fellows, authority asserts itself over against the "underdog" today, and tomorrow itself bows to him. To and fro: the eternal wheel. The exigencies of the occasion determine. But Christianity will have no part in that scheme. That scheme will remain a philosophy and an attitude earthy and of the earth, will not represent an intervention of the Kingdom of Heaven.

But Christianity will escape the revolution of the wheel of things if it does its simple duty; that is, if it relates the story of the washing of feet to the history of the passion. It must insist upon that relation in social life too. And in the administration of the office in the church. By such insistence a genuine authority, a real respect, will arise, by which a reciprocal interchange of the service of love and of the pleasure of love causes the Spirit of Christ to be fruitful in the world, and the church to flourish. Then a relationship of authority and respect will arise, which still includes that obtaining between owner and laborer, between teacher and student, between the culturally strong who can stand on his own feet and the weak who must rely upon another. These relationships of natural life, thus, by virtue of common grace are sanctified by and put in the service of the Gospel of special grace through Jesus Christ our Lord. On that basis the washing of the feet is not an *example* or a *symbol* for humanitarian propaganda but is, as a subordinate part of Christ's official service, an act of royal jurisdiction, which *earns* the blessing that accrues to social service. God's kingdom is not merely portrayed in this act; it actually comes, realizes itself, in Jesus' gentle manner as He girds His loins, quietly restores Peter to his senses, and, with bowed head and holy calm, proceeds to wash the feet of twelve people. It was a mild, a mellow, a gracious service in a way, but it was also a constraining, a formidable, a more than magnetic potency of the Spirit of the strong will of the King, Christ Jesus. That slave's garb proves He is the coming King. The basin is not in contrast to, nor a preparation for, the crown: it is the *beginning* of it.

As King, too, then, the bearer of the basin of water understood and removed the difficulties weighing upon the Ecclesiast of the Old Testament. Today this Lord travels on foot, but sometime He will sit upon a white horse and yield the reins to none but God, so that God may be all and in all.

Finally, Christ washes the feet of His disciples in the capacity of Priest also. The same Person who by reason of a royal sense of personal worth accepted the luxury of Mary's precious ointment, now returns as a Priest what He accepted then, returns it twelve times, too, or better, innumerable times. As far as Christ is superior to Mary, so far is the deed of the hand that is disturbing the water superior to that which poured out ointment. Water in Jesus' hands is more precious than spikenard in ours. The difference is as great as that between time and eternity.

And this service of water is for our benefit. All have quarreled among each other. For all these He not only preaches peace, but also makes a beginning of peace. Blessed be this Peacemaker!

Christ in His priestly care is attentive to personal, individual needs also. Who does not think of Simon in this connection at once? Simon, too, had his difficulties in seeing that the relationships of the realm of grace begin and interconnect in a way diametrically opposed to those in the realm of nature. As often as Simon tried to draw Christ into his scheme of things, he became "a satan" to Christ. Now Jesus aproaches him and radically overturns all human ways of doing things. When Peter, confronted by this, becomes "satanical" again, and tries once more to dictate and prescribe the laws of Heaven's Kingdom according to those at the basis of human relationships, Jesus approaches him in a priestly way, and says: "Everything or nothing! Simon, accept this turning things upside down, or else: *You have no part in me!*"

Then Simon saw the lightning flash, the other world open itself to view; he bowed in acknowledgment and comprehended the thought that the revelation which comes from above does not accept the laws obtaining on earth. Revelation has its own law, the law of the mediatorship.

Yes, such service is priestly service.

As priest He preaches to them the need of a continuous repentance after regeneration. After all, there is a double washing. First there is that which immerses the whole man in water and cleanses him from top to toe; that is the regeneration of which baptism, presently, will be the sign. But the man who bathes himself completely at home, and then walks to the house of his host, will surely dirty his feet if he wears only a sandal, while en route. Hence, after the bathing of his whole body, he will be compelled to wash his feet repeatedly. And this may be regarded as fitly analogous to the need of a daily repentance, even after the gift of the principle of regeneration. That daily repentance, then, Jesus also enjoins upon them. And as a priest, Jesus serves as surety for it. He *too* washes feet.

He is prepared to do something now which He can do only once. It is a task which, once achieved, can never need doing again. That task is the cross, is death, resurrection, and ascension.

Not the justification only which takes place once for all, but the sanctification constantly being realized in us, as well, proceeds from Christ. See, He is washing feet! Not regeneration only but continuous repentance also, not only the root but also the branch and foliage and blossom and fruit proceed from Christ. Lo, He is washing feet!

Such is the perfect mediatorship. The cross as *single* redemptive event would not suffice without the washing of feet which points to the repeated gift of the promise and which repeatedly applies the strength of grace.

It is very comforting for us to know that, before the Holy Supper, Christ washes the feet of His own.

At that Holy Supper, remember, He presents Himself to us in a two-fold relationship: as the host, and as that which the host serves; as the giver, and as that which is received; as He who distributes the blessing and as the blessing itself. As a host He is in glory, but as the food on the table He is broken and annihilated.

That same double relationship holds true of the washing of the feet.

"Ye call me master, and that I am," Jesus declares confidently. In saying it, the host, the master, the first in rank is speaking.

But He also proceeds to wash the feet, and in this is the equal of a slave. As such He is the least; He disappears beneath all others.

When I sit at the table of the Holy Supper, I see the glorious King; I also see the slave, who has no outer garment. In the form of this dual unity He extends the bread to me. I take it and eat; I cannot think what to say, but He Himself speaks to me as a Prophet, buoys me up in His priestly arms, guides me as King; and this is a blessed experience known to none except the believer.

Once more — and this time with assent — we can listen to Novalis.

> If his love they only knew,
> People would be Christians all,
> Would abandon all their fears,
> Would adore the Only One,
> Would companion me in tears.

Nevertheless, yes . . . even now we cannot read Novalis with assent.

Would all men become Christians, if they "knew" His love? We must be Christians, born of the Spirit, included in Christ, in order to "know" this love. This love is folly and an offense to a natural student of human nature. Thank God for that; because it is, it can save us.

The water-basin is not the grail of knight-errants nor is the blood-basin that.

The hands of Jesus stirring the water are just as offensive and foolish to "the flesh" as are the spiked hands dripping blood from the crossbeam. But, in the loin-cloth of a slave, He is unto them that believe the power and the wisdom of God.

The *power*, too. He is the power of God, too.

Remember the service of washing feet took place on the side of the wall opposite to that behind which some were delighting themselves with sweet nebulosities, or yielding themselves to "naive and sentimental poetry."

Christ at the Communion Table

CHAPTER FOURTEEN

Christ at the Communion Table

● *And as they were eating, Jesus took bread, and blessed
it, and brake it, and gave it to the disciples, and said,
Take, eat; this is my body.*
*And he took the cup, and gave thanks, and gave it to
them, saying, Drink ye all of it; for this is my blood of
the new testament, which is shed for many for the re-
mission of sins.*   —MATTHEW 26:26-28.

IN the two preceding chapters we fixed our attention upon a
two-fold reality. We noted, first, that Christ, while seated
in the room of the passover, suppresses nothing. On the
contrary, He is sensitive to every phenomenon, visible and invisible alike, which confronts Him there. He *keeps everything in
mind,* acknowledges each detail completely, gives every fact a
full measure of attention. And, secondly, we discovered that
Christ appears in the room of the passover in the capacity of His
office, keeps His office constantly in mind, vitally preserves the
sense of His official calling in His own soul besides transplanting
it to the souls of His apostles.

We shall now observe that these two emphases become *one*
truth, that these two lines meet at a point.

The merging of the two takes place in the institution of the
Holy Supper. For if Christ is indeed the valiant Hero and the
pure and genuine Prophet-Priest-King, who ignores and suppresses nothing but in His soul acknowledges everything to the
full extent to which it can lay claim to His attention, He, having
achieved this, can rise in the assembly, take the cup in one hand,
the bread in the other, and say: I accept these signs in order to
relate them to My person: eat, drink, and do it in *remembrance*
of Me. By creating a memorial for Himself, Christ is telling His

people: Do not forget Me; do not put Me out of mind; carefully remember My person and My work, great and mighty as they are; do not suppress Me until I return. Do that till I come.

By that request, you see, Christ asks a compensation for His suffering as the Messiah who Himself suppresses nothing for His life's sake.

Besides that, however, we must know that in instituting the Supper He is acting in the capacity of His office. It is not as a man among men that He requires a memorial, and that memorial is not another one of the many monuments dotting the face of the world. No, no. He makes His appearance as office-bearer. His request for a remembrance in the world after His death is not like that of those mundane great, who, knowing that death will *rob* them of their office, try to keep some vestige of their meagre humanity alive in those who come after, by requiring monuments for themselves. On the contrary, He wants to continue ministering His office to the world: the remembrance of His death is a sharing in His Mediatorship. The memorial He seeks to create for Himself is not the remembrance of a person whose office ceases the moment memory begins; instead it is a communion with His person, a ministering of His office. He remains the living one in the thoughts of His own, maintains His office, and continues to be the Mediator to those who by faith support the communion.

Now you can see what warranted us in saying that in the institution of the Holy Supper two lines meet: that of Christ who never suppresses anything in the world — who can, therefore, lay *claim* to remembrance in that world; and, secondly, the line of *official* life and service.

The institution of the Holy Supper, at this moment, and in this room, consequently, places Christ in a four-fold relationship: to *God;* to *Himself;* to the *World;* and to the *Church.*

In the first place, Christ, at the institution of the Holy Supper, enters into that particular relationship with God which fully becomes Him now. On this occasion Christ confesses that He is perfectly conjoined with God. "I and the Father are one." "He that hath seen Me, hath seen the Father, Philip!"

Consider: what was God's primary will and intent throughout the Old Testament? What single word epitomizes, and that as early as in the books of Moses — what single phrase precisely designates the activity of the God of revelation as it operates in Israel's trekking through the world? What formula is the compendium of all liturgical ordinances and accomplishments? The answer is easy: the Bible constantly stresses the thought of *creating a memorial in remembrance of the name of the Lord.*

Those words epitomize the whole purpose of all of God's activity in Israel in giving revelation and special grace to that people and making it fruitful in their lives. The whole purpose of the busy, colorful public worship among them is just this: God causes His *Name* to dwell there.

The place where the tabernacle will stand is called the place where God will cause His name to be remembered. So also the place where the temple later rises from the ground, and even every altar which God Himself dedicated and assigned, rests in a place where God wanted to create a memorial to His name.

This same purpose now permeates the soul of the Servant of the Lord, the Priest in the house of God, of Him who has been faithful in that temple to the last detail.

He does just one thing: *He causes His name to be remembered.*

Such an emphasis is an *idolatry,* deserving the curse; or it is an *obedience* which will achieve the award of glorification for itself.

For it is true that the question might well arise: Does not this matter suggest idolatry? There is but one name in the world which may create a memorial for itself. That one is the holy name of God. All thoughts must rise up to *Him.* If God, from whom, by whom, and to whom all things are, creates a memorial for Himself and for His name, He is sounding a bugle-blast over the world, which emphatically declares: I am the only One who has being in myself alone; I am the only One who can completely express My being in Word; I am the One whose self-expression releases influences, so that through the Word I reveal my image and send My name among men. Therefore all thoughts will be directed to Me. Therefore all that has breath, and soul, and spirit will have to remember Me, saith the Lord.

God, who creates His own memorial, is a jealous God, anxious for His honor. He gives His honor to no man. He gives neither man nor angel the privilege of creating a memorial for Himself; He does not simply because God alone is memorable.

And Christ, seated at the table in the room of the Passover, declares in full, round tones: Do it in remembrance of Me. And it is sheer revolt, is satanic, is the great rebellion, is incarnate godlessness for Christ to create a memorial for Himself, personally; —that is, for Himself, isolated from His office or from Him who gave Him that office.

If Christ had designated His own name and person as the great goal of the journey of a "remembering" mankind, if He had wished to be remembered by man after He, be it only for a second, had expunged God from His soul, and had regarded Himself as greater than God, or if in instituting the Lord's Supper He had but momentarily done so independent of His Mediatorship, then in that instant Christ would have become the Antichrist.

Then the Supper would be the food of dragons. Then the table of the New Covenant would be impure. Then communion with Jesus Christ would be identical with sitting at meat with devils.

You see that this matter, like the several others we have studied, is again a delicate one. The issue obtaining in this room of the Passover is one of eternal right or of eternal wrong; it is a question of all or of nothing, of being a servant or of being a rebel.

But we can thank the Word of truth for preaching a Christ to us who never thrusts God out of His thoughts, and who never expels His own mediatorship from Him. He never does, and hence He does not do so in instituting the Supper — in remembrance of *Him*.

In this way we can understand how it is possible for Christ to institute the Holy Supper without hearing the world creak on its hinges and without seeing Christ obliterated as an Antichrist by a stroke of God's lightning.

That is because Christ in this moment appoints a memorial to His own name, solely thereby to create a memorial unto the name of God. He does so simply as a Servant of the Lord, who, by exercising communion with His people in the Supper, is by that means as a Mediator sustaining the relationship of that people to God. This He will do until He returns. As soon as is possible, He will take the Supper out of the world. He will Himself set fire to the last Supper-table, and gladly stride over its ashes in order, in the company of the Supper-celebrating congregation, to give up the kingdom into the hands of the Father, so that God may be all and in all. That will take place as soon as may be: Lord, thou knowest it; He desired no more than became Thy shepherd.[1]

This point of view helps us to see why Christ, in instituting the Supper, begins by saying "do it in remembrance of Me," designating His *own* name and constraining us to continue pronouncing that name, and, later, at the institution of baptism, continues calling that name when He says "make them all my disciples," but thereupon puts it into the service of the name of the *Father* and of the *Son* and of the *Holy Ghost*. "Baptize them," He says on that occasion, "in the name of the Triune God, in the name of the Father and of the Son and of the Holy Ghost."

Christ, who establishes a memorial for His name, establishes a memorial for the name of God.

He is able to do that because He is the temple of the living God, as well as the Priest of that temple. He can do it because He is at the point of supplying the altar with His sacrifice. God Himself is creating a memorial to His name by letting the Son institute the Supper in the world.

Consequently Christ stands over against this God in full consciousness of the mediatorship.

It is remarkable that Jesus does not hear a single voice from heaven in reference to instituting the Supper. The circumcision was introduced after a special command had come from God. Just so the Passover was instituted upon the expressed commandment of the Almighty. But the sacrament of the *New* Testament is introduced without any definite command to do so from above. Christ heard voices from heaven more than once. Even in the last week, when His lips uttered the prayer "Father, glorify Thy name (that is, create a memorial for it)" a voice was heard from heaven in answer to that petition. But now, here in the room of the Passover, no "voice" is heard.

---

1. Compare Jeremiah 17:16.

No voice is necessary. Christ is so permeated with the Messianic consciousness that He acts on a basis of infallible certainty as He takes the bread from the table and, by blessing it, segregrates it from any other bread in the world. And He takes the wine from the table, pronounces thanks over the cup, and in that way lifts that wine out of all other liquors of the world. Thus He accepts bread and wine as the means which God Himself allows Him to use, so revealing Himself as the Messiah, who knows unhesitatingly what He may do.

In that way Jesus Christ in His Messianic awareness not only directed all things to God, in order to culminate in God as the final cause of things, but also in that Messianic consciousness dared to superintend the gift of God, that is, God Himself.

As the servant of the Lord He wants to put Himself into the service of the Lord, and to create a memorial for Jesus' name only for the sake of God's name. That we have seen already. Moreover, this Servant of servants is confident that He dares to superintend the powers of the Holy Spirit, the full majesty and omnipotent activity of the triune God. Surely His taking the bread and wine at the institution of the Supper is taking them not merely as signs of His death but as coupled with the power of the Holy Spirit. Only when that Spirit joins itself to the eating of the bread and the drinking of the wine can there be a strengthening of faith and a mystical union of Him who eats and drinks at Christ's table with Christ, and in Him, with the living God. So does the confident spirit of Christ superintend the Holy Spirit of God. He does it because He can act from the complete certainty of His purity and virtue, because He is beforehand perfectly sure of His right to claim a reward. He superintends the Holy Spirit in order that this One may later keep the believers in relationship with God by means of bread and wine and may sustain the communion of human souls with Christ's body and blood.

Such is confidence in its highest conceivable form. Such is the confidence of my Lord Jesus. He dares to place His broken body and poured blood on the very apex of the world, right under God's eyes. He dares to say: Father, it is my will that the Holy Spirit work with this body and blood until the day of days. Father, I take Thy Spirit out of Thy hands. My brokenness, which stands over against heaven and its beauty, surely is the great unity and the most beautiful gem of purity and virtue. I come, Father, and my reward is with me.

No, *voices* were not necessary to Jesus as they were necessary to Abraham and to Moses when these instituted the circumcision and the Passover, respectively. *Externally* considered, the sacrament of the New Testament is less exciting, is weaker, is more meager than that of the Old. But in its essence it is infinitely stronger, ampler, more puissant than the sign and seal of the Old Testament, and it appears as both of these in the very manner of its institution. Christ carries the voice inside Himself. The thunder of voices occurs but it is so powerful that earthly ears cannot hear it. That thunder echoes in Jesus' soul. The sacrament of the New Testament does not get its approbation in thunder or theophany; it vindicates itself solely by the fact of its origin in the *Messianic* conscience.

Such "poverty," of course, constitutes great wealth.

In the second place, Christ consciously enters into a pure relation over against Himself upon this occasion.

It is an astonishing thing to consider that the very table upon which the slain Passover-lamb[1] has a place is the same at which Jesus is lying in the capacity of a host to His disciples; and to think that Christ removes that lamb from the table after it has served its purpose and He has accorded it full respect—removes it, in order to put Himself in its stead.

Christ does this on purpose. The moment in which He blesses the bread, and, giving thanks, also blesses the wine, is the moment in which the Passover of the Old Testament has to give way to the Supper of the New. As a matter of fact the food and drink of that supper had been "blessed" at the beginning of the meal also. But until Christ blesses them again these belong to the Passover-meal of the Old Testament. Christ does "bless" them *again*. A second time He blesses the remnant of bread and wine. The first blessing served to segregate this bread and this wine from its use in natural, daily life, to dedicate it to its ritualistic function in the sacrament of the Passover. But the second thanksgiving-blessing pushes the *segregation* farther; by it Christ separates

---

1. Compare note on page 272.

what belonged to the Old Testament from that Testament; this bread and wine He sets aside exclusively for the *New Testament*: "This is the New Testament in My blood "

You see that this second thanksgiving which was pronounced over the bread and wine throws the helm of the world completely around. That thanksgiving, that event, is momentously important. By it Christ recognizes that in brokenness and death, He must as the Messiah stand at the turning point of history.

Up to this time every eye looked forward to Him; from now on every eye will have to look back upon Him. Until this moment the lamb of the Passover had to serve as symbol and type of the coming Christ. By means of that lamb He taught all men to look forward to Him. But now that the end of the beginning of God's time has come, now, in this center of the world's time, now the beginning of the end is approaching. That is why Christ removes the lamb and places Himself upon the table. He places Himself there, and places there also the bread and wine. And He says: Do it in remembrance of me. Do it as a retrospective memorial.

So it is that He asserts Himself as the fulfillment of the lamb of the Passover, as the crown of the Old Testament, as the content of the Supper, and as the cornerstone, the sustaining power, and the Mediator of the new covenant.

Nor could it be otherwise. The Passover lamb was a mere *thing,* and a religion cannot, in the last analysis, get its support from a thing. We need a person, not a thing; not a shadow of the reality, but the personal reality itself. For that reason Christ puts Himself in the place of the lamb as a person, asserting Himself as the Messiah at the proper time.

All roads lead to this point, all the ways of the world had to meet at this place. For the laughter of mockery had cut its way through the world. The devils had laughed. The Passover had been slain and the blood of a thousand lambs had this very day reeked to the heavens. The true Lamb stood in the midst of the slaughter and no one noticed Him. Therefore hell laughed. The court of the temple was teeming on this same day with these shadow-symbols, with innumerable lambs. But He who was the absolute reality of those symbols passed unnoticed. So hell's demons laughed. A hundred priests appeared, each supposedly a connoisseur of lambs: these must be tender, unblemished, perfect. And these priests tested the quality of the lambs; that was their duty. But this whole service of testing had become a shockingly superficial routine. The priests did not understand the important meaning of it all, did not see that the requisite of a tender and perfect lamb was but a "shadowy" preface designed to point out the perfect tenderness of the better Lamb who should come, and who should be without sin. See, He is here now, He, the sinless, tender, perfect, unblemished, holy, and "innocent" one. Yet, no one sees Him. Because of the abundance of lambs, people can no longer see the one lamb. And Satan's sneering mockery shatters the atmosphere with derisive laughter.

Christ hears it; He takes note of the laughter.

He rises to His feet. He sees the vault of heaven arching high over the roof of His house. He counters the mockery of the devil's laughter, which is tearing the night apart, with His own solemnly earnest voice. His words go out to the spheres as heralds of a King's will: *This is my body, this is my bread, take, eat, do it in remembrance of me.* Does the whole world overlook God's one true Lamb—then It will elevate itself. It forces itself upon the attention of all the believers with a sovereign bearing. He who suppressed nothing outside Himself may impel everything unto Himself in purity and virtue.

That is His fullest right; it is His right to receive worship.

Christ also enters into a pure relationship with the world at the occasion of the institution of the Supper.

This Supper, you must know, is in no sense a private celebration. This most holy Supper is open to the public. Its holiness is not that of the Old Testament. The holiness of seclusion? In *essence,* yes, the holinesses of the New Testament are also secluded; for the rest this new holiness brushes all curtains aside, pushes every ladder of hierarchy away, and, although insisting upon a holy essence, it displays its holy *forms* to every eye. The public worship of the New Testament is conducted *in front* of the curtains.

For this reason the Supper is not exclusively an affair of the church, but affects the whole world. Christ does not take the bread and wine, turn His back to the world, and so in the company of a few "initiates" isolate Himself from the world. No, His actions are "open and above board." What He offers His disciples at this time, He later allows them as office-bearers to "take over," in order that they, in turn, may distribute it among others. The Supper is not a sacrifice for "initiates," conducted behind the curtains; it is a "breaking of bread" in the open court in front of the palace of highest Wisdom, who, while eating, continues to invite others to the feast. By the Supper Christ completely fulfills the priesthood in Himself. Therefore, by it the priesthood becomes general, spreading out among all the believers. It steps away from the curtain, displaying itself to every eye. The Supper is not a sacrifice; it is a breaking of bread.

Precisely, then, because the Supper is not a mystery for a cult but an exercise in communion with the living Christ by faith, that Supper affects the whole world. For Christ affects the world.

Just what is it that Christ tells the world by means of the Holy Supper? How does it happen that this sacrament, although it points back to the inauguration of Israel's public worship, at the same time has bearing upon the *world,* is actual, modern, if you will, and a sign and a word of the times?

To explain that we shall have to allude briefly to our preceding chapter. There we observed that the Roman Caesars were letting themselves be worshipped as gods at exactly the time of Christ's birth. And we pointed out that this coincidence, so far from being accidental, was quite according to the wise direction of God, Who Himself shapes history.

Such deification of kings and Caesars was a *religious* action. By such conduct the world of that day asserted that the Caesar-king was a kind of mediator capable of uniting the physical world of men on earth to a supersensuous world where God dwelt. Plainly, how very plainly, the world of that day was looking for the mediatorship, and in its own way giving expression to the mediator-concept. It elevated kings. Because the king is the apex of human attainment, it made him a mediator and a god. To call the king, as the most princely and accomplished of men, a god, is to call him the mediator. So a people raises itself up into heaven by means of its king.

In that fashion kings were raised to a position of divine prestige at that time. The lustrous cock upon the tower of Babel was none other than the king-god. The leaders of the people were the stones that went into the formation of the tower, and its top now touched on the heavens. In that way, you see, everyone was reaching heaven in the person of the king.

So did the Roman Caesars have their people name them Lord and God. Thomas says it to Christ: *My Lord and my God.* In Rome they address Caesar so. The church confesses of Christ that He is Lord. The same word is current in the courts of the dazzling Caesar and king. Herod in his circus paraded before the people in his silvered costume, scintillating from myriad facets under the brilliant sun, and let people burn incense before him with the flattering assurance: *The voice of a god, and not of a man.* That incident was not the exception but the rule. Such deification, such naming the king a God and not a man was the general practice of the time. Herod was punished; his body was eaten by worms. The penalty did not accrue to him, however, because he allowed himself to be named a god; the same God who has jurisdiction over worms had allowed such haughtiness to continue for years. Herod's penalty must be explained by the fact that he dared to accept such praise *in the shadow of the temple* of the living God—close to the supper-table of Christ.

Christ—and this is the point that has bearing upon our discussion—in instituting the supper asserts a kingship which is different in kind from the kingdom of the princes of the world. They can recognize as gods only such heroes as have been anointed with nectar and adorned with splendor. To be a god, the king must move in a medium of glory. God according to this interpretation represents sheer strength and beauty.

The King lurking in the room of the Passover is not so. True, He knows Himself to be the King, for He requests that a memorial be created for Him until the end of the world. No man can enjoin his will upon others more forcefully and strongly than by making a request. But this King, although He wants to be the center of all culture, and therefore bases culture upon religion, makes His appearance in brokenness. Broken bread and poured wine—those will remain the symbols of His kingship until the end of time. Observe that He does not present His brokenness as something that must be quickly overcome and soon forgotten. Standing before the cross, He does not advise His aides to engrave a crown upon His royal weapon, or to embroider a wreath of victory upon His floating banners. On the contrary, although He knows that within a few days His kingdom will be in glory and that the crown and laurel will be handed to Him from above, He nevertheless accepts the cross and desires that the memory of the brokenness of His body and the loss of His blood be perpetuated in the world until the end.

He wants His splendor as a King to be just such brokenness and loss. So Christ declares the law of His own Kingship and Kingdom in opposition to the deification of the earthly king who is able to live only upon the condition of wholeness. He makes His declaration by giving His broken existence, His broken shape and design, form and color in the symbols of broken bread and poured out wine. Thus He declares to the world that which He soon confirmed to Pilate: *My kingdom is not of this world.* Pilate's astonishment as expressed in the question, "Art thou, then, a King?" is in the essence of the matter an utterance of amazement prompted by the paradoxical meaning of the Holy Supper. In this way, then, that is, by the *sacra coena,* Christ denies the kingship of the world with its self-arrogated, divine privileges as well as the mediatorship which that world had conceived. So He preaches to the world the one truth about the real mediatorship between God and man.

Exactly because that Roman practice of exalting kings and Caesars to the plane of the divine was a *religious* action, the poverty of a paganism which must call its best and most accomplished man a god and mediator appears. The exaltation always took place, of course, by the grace of man. This, then, is just one more instance in which man *asserts* himself as a very god; he conceives the mediatorship as a self-prompted intervention between himself and the gods. In this case the *intervention for man* is merely an *invention of man.* But Christ Jesus, by holding up the picture of a broken King before the world, shows us that the mediatorship cannot be found where man asserts himself, exalting himself in his king, and that it can be found where man (as the Son of man) is crushed, broken, annihilated.

Such is the evangelized significance of the Supper. By putting this festival of a king, this sacrament of a mediator, into the hands of Galilean fishermen, rather than into those of ordained priests, Christ, from the privacy of the room of the Passover was also directing a message to the world. This was the message: Intervention with God for man can only be the invention of God Himself (I Cor. 2). May He forbid that the church should ever neglect to preach the world-message contained in the Supper. That Supper has bearing upon the church and therefore affects the whole world.

And, finally, the institution of the Supper affects the church. In instituting it, Christ places Himself in the position of a pure relationship over-against it.

In the first place, He immerses it in the communion with His passion. Notice how He is doing just that in connection with the specific matter we have just been discussing. The Kingship was being deified, the King being called to serve as a mediator. Obviously, therefore, the service of the state will honor the king from this time on only when, as a flawless hero, he is seated on his throne. Accordingly, you see how the Holy Supper of the first Christian church actually was a violation of state law. It represents the confession of a Lord and Mediator other than the pagan world of that epoch chose to honor. Precisely so the Supper became the incorporation of the believers into a communion with the suffering of Christ. From this time forth Christ is making martyrs.

He is fully conscious of the fact that He is doing so.

Only by entering into the communion with His suffering can the believer "fulfill the remnants of Christ's suffering and exercise communion with the Lord in it." As often as he wants to feel the power of the Holy Supper burning within him, he must seize upon his Lord, triumph in His death, rise with Him in brokenness to confess that to lose everything in the world's terms is equivalent to gaining God and His Christ for eternity.

Christ is seeking His church in the Holy Supper. Yes, He has seen the altars in Israel and watched the temple rising from the ground. But altars and temple, both, *stood still*. That is the pathetic thing, that the places where God creates a memorial to His name are quite static; the kingdom is still immobile, cannot yet *go out* into the world.

Christ, however, is not static. He takes the bread and He takes the wine; He sends out His fishers of men; He dispatches men and women; later He sends humble shopkeepers from the alleys and by-ways of Asia Minor—these He sends to the farthest parts of the world. Everywhere, now, bread is available, and wine can be obtained; the table is a static altar no longer; it can be set *everywhere*. Today, you see, the Old Testament almost passes into the New. The Old Covenant was aware of only a few wayfaring places at which God prepared a memorial for Himself; the New will make it possible to prepare such remembrance everywhere—that is, wherever "two" or "three" are gathered in Christ's name. Ours is a portable supper-table, a movable dish, a cup that can be folded and taken along. The catacombs can accommodate no altars but they can contain a supper table, and that is the blessing God gives His church in the institution of the Supper. The tabernacle traveled; that was a frail beginning of movement; the temple was fixed firmly upon stationary rock; that was the poor sequel. But the *highest* temple spreads itself over the world, accompanying God's royal priesthood wherever it may go.

Today the church is seeking the Saviour. Heretofore in moving through the world it waded through blood, the blood of lambs, of steers, and of bullocks. Even the blood of the Passover lamb saturated the earth, soiled the clothes of those who celebrated the feast, almost caused the angels in the presence of God to suffer, reeked up to heaven. The earth could not get enough of it; heaven, it seemed, could not get its fill of blood.

But heaven is satisfied today. In this unique hour the Holy Spirit broods over the room of the Passover and moves the soul of the man Christ, who Himself is also active to that end, to give the Holy Supper to the church. He takes bread; bread is that which has no blood in it. And He takes wine; wine, too, has no blood in it. He takes bread and wine, bloodless symbols both, as His signs. The agonizing bleat of the dying lamb will never rend the atmosphere again; every pain will be subdued by the one cry of the dying Lamb of God: it is finished! By this single shedding of blood every other stream will be effectually stopped.

So Christ puts His church at rest. He chooses His signs for her from the bloodless order of created things, and chooses them from the most ordinary of daily needs, the popular food and the popular drink! By these means He tells His church: The pain has been fulfilled, the grief infinitely multiplied. At My table I give you Myself in complete communion: Take and eat, and create an *eternal memorial* for Me as your Lord and Servant.

Thus the Supper becomes a festival for angels as well as for men. Of course, the angels do not actually taste of the food, but partaking of it with the lips is not the important thing. True, it is necessary for us to eat of it. But in this matter, too, the needful thing is that we sympathetically turn to God. The main issue in the world is not that *we* be saved, that *we* enjoy ourselves, that *our faith* be confirmed. The final cause, the chief end of all things in this matter also is that Christ create a memorial to Himself, that the one *name* given under heaven actually be declared among men, in order that so the name of God may be remembered and glorified. God created all things for His own sake. He prepared the Holy Supper for His own sake. If we acknowledge this as the intrinsic essence of the Holy Supper, that in it God enters into the remembrance of faith, in other words, into the community of life with His creature, then we can acknowledge that the angels also partake of the Supper, for it is also their "meat" to create a memorial to the remembrance of God, and in creating it to be edified, and built up in love.

Christ, then, proves to be the Man of sorrows precisely because He acts as a king of glory. The moment in which the sense of royalty and that of menial service meet in the same mind, the former in no sense suppressing the other, is a painful moment. At the same time in which he senses an unmitigated ambition for the kingship, which is whole and unbroken, He has to enjoin upon His disciples the task of celebrating that kingship until the end of the world in the form of His brokenness and humiliation. That conflict in His inevitably significant soul causes Christ a grievous suffering, an unutterable tension.

But the Man of Sorrows also bore this suffering at the institution of the Lord's Supper willingly and in love.

Rely upon it, His human soul felt crucial pain as He weighed the bread in His hands and poured the wine into cups. In doing so, He saw Himself before His eyes, Himself crucified. Only a few moments later Satan will dangle that placard before His eyes, "Christ being crucified," and that taunt will drive the sweat of anxiety, the sweat of blood, out of His pores. Here in this hall of the Passover, however, in this meeting-place for the first Holy Supper, Christ courageously and firmly depicts Himself before His eyes, Himself crucified. Although His soul trembles in longing for God, His hand does not betray a quiver. His eye is not darkened, although He offers Himself up to the inertness of death. A secret light glimmers in His eyes and plays upon His face, even while He is depicting Himself, and stamping Himself as a seal upon the heart of His own, the glimmer of light is there, even when He gives Himself away as one broken, when He pushes the *sign* of His death as close to the *moment* of that death as is possible. His doing that must cause Him unspeakable anguish, for the closer a thing approaches the thing symbolized, so much more eloquently does its form address, startle, or comfort the human soul. Yet, so profoundly did Christ love His own, that, although the sign and the event signified almost touched each other, He could, nevertheless, prophesy of the meaning of these sacrednesses, could command them, as a King, that they could do this until the end, and, as a Priest, could pray for the Spirit, to enjoin Himself with the sign.

Jesus' eyes rested calmly upon each of His disciples, yes; but they also peered out into the distance, out to the farthest horizon. There they saw the figure of another.

That other was the Antichrist.

It was the man of sin who taught the thousands to say at that other table, the table of the deification of man, the deification of the king of the world: He is the perfect, the whole, the unbroken one; his glamour will always be his; his flesh will not be broken, nor his blood poured out: Kneel ye all before him, for he is a God, man, and mediator. *The voice of a god, and not of a man.*

In that guise Jesus sees the Antichrist, he who prepared the festival for the deification of man.

When Christ sees him, wrath springs from the soil of His love. In that moment the zeal of His love, which by means of the Supper would strengthen His people till the end of time, burns ardently; but in it the will to revenge flows hot. Standing beside the supper table He takes it upon Himself to destroy the Antichrist by the sword of His mouth.

We cannot go farther than that.

And we need not go farther. Before our very eyes the Son of man stood in the presence of "the Ancient of days." His Messianic consciousness drove Him there. Thence He came as God and man.

We cannot go farther; we know nothing more. But what we know and have suffices. We heard His voice: the voice of God, *and* of man.

Now we know that this Holy Supper is both ancient and modern. It blesses the humblest and curses the proudest. It represents love and wrath, tenderness and force, antithesis and synthesis. We should be in a great darkness in which our feet would stumble upon all those murky mountains, if the *Person* of Christ had not given Himself to us with the clarity of prophecy, the steadfastness of kingly conduct, and the communion of priestly love.

His grace sufficeth us. Beyond that phrase we may not go: *it sufficeth.*

Christ Wrestling Before God Against Satan

CHAPTER FIFTEEN

Christ Wrestling Before God Against Satan

● *And the Lord said, Simon, Simon, behold, Satan hath*
desired to have you, that he may sift you as wheat;
but I have prayed for thee, that thy faith fail not.
*—*LUKE *22:31-32a.*

CHRIST received His own at the table of communion, yes;
but first He received them *in prayer.* True, the Priest
after the order of Melchizedek overturned the altar of
Aaron; but Aaron's breast-cloth, on which he bore the names of
the tribes of Israel over his heart, remained, and that is our comfort. Christ receives His own within His heart: He is their inter-
cessor before they know of it.

As we listen to Christ telling Simon that Satan wants to sift
the disciples as wheat, but that He interposes His intercession between Satan's desire and the Father's right, two things strike our
attention.

The first is that in these words of Christ we have what we
might call the *first* thanksgiving service. The church still continues in the custom of engaging in a brief thanksgiving service
immediately after the celebration of the Holy Supper. Sometimes
that service is called a post-communion meditation.

In a sense that is what we have here, a post-communion, a
thanksgiving service. It is really the first of its kind in history.
Luke shows us plainly that Christ spoke the familiar words of the
text at the head of this chapter after the ministration and institution of the Supper. And it occurs to us that Christ did not resort to this first post-communion meditation in order to gently
move the souls of those who had sat with Him up and down on
the passive undulations of a vague emotionalism — but that He,

249

after having mystically *concentrated* their thoughts, in the Holy
Supper, now lets these thoughts *scatter* again. The theme of the
mercies of Christ which had been enjoyed *synthetically* in the
Supper now breaks up into its component parts again. In the
Supper Christ bound up the souls of His own with His soul. He
intensified and intimately united theirs and His. Now that the
Supper is finished, however, they must be led from the heights of
faith to the edge of the cliff beneath which bottomless abysses
yawn; heaven and hell open before them — now, after the first
Supper. At the mystical table the theme of God's love was seared
upon the souls of the disciples as a unit. Now that theme breaks
up into its several parts again. The "concentration" of the heart
is followed straightway by its "expansion," by its diffusely comprehensive attention to God's highest heights and Satan's deepest
depths. After the intense and concentrated intimacy of that moment of mystical communion with Christ comes the shock of a
spoken word by which all the chasms of hell and all the forces of
heaven are revealed to them.

Satan hath desired to have you: see the abyss of hell in that.
He expressed that strong desire in words, and placed it as a definite demand against the disciples before *the throne of God*: read
in that of the heights of heaven.

Surely, this sermon of thanksgiving is a weighty one, setting
the universe wide open even to its most sublimely transporting
depths. But it is a comfort to know that Jesus Christ as Interces-
sor, as Intermediary, as Mediator, understood the profundities of
hell and entered His plea against Satan with the Father in highest
heaven. In this manner the drama of heaven and hell took place
in the soul of Jesus; to this we owe our gratitude for the fact that
this thanksgiving sermon, sublime and awful as it is, does not de-
prive us of the comfort of the Supper. In fact, this comfort is
infinitely intensified by the words of Christ.

Moreover, this first thanksgiving sermon is instructive as well
as comforting. For Christ at the end of the supper, not only the
entering into His communion but also the *remaining* there *is
entirely owing to Him.* In the conflict between God and Satan the
disciples have been thrown back and forth as corn in a sifter, and
they would have succumbed, Simon, too, would certainly have suc-

cumbed, if Christ's strenuous prayer had not borne them to and laid them down before God. The *preservation* of faith, too, is solely the product of grace.

That is the first thing that strikes our attention at once as we read Christ's words on this occasion.

A second thought is worth remarking upon.

If we may put it that way, we would call Christ's words about Satan's desire to sift and about His own intercessory prayer *the solution of the problem.*

Solution to which problem?

To the problem of all that occurred before.

Again and again we have observed that Christ confronts Judas and Satan as the one person who is absolutely authentic, who thrusts nothing out of His attention. Judas and Satan were two of those who wanted to suppress everything uncongenial to their wishes out of their souls' lives and out of the complexes of their spirits. Over against these, you remember, we placed Christ as the genuine Man who flees from no fact, even though brutal pain tears at His heart and wrenches His inner being.

Now Jesus says that He has seen beforehand what Satan wants to do with the disciples, Judas excepted. He has entered into Judas already; that is fact now. But Jesus knows with direct certainty that Satan is not idle now. Christ pursued what happened in Judas backwards to the verities of election and reprobation and followed it forward to the face of hell. Now He does as much. Christ includes Judas, yes, but also the other disciples, and you and I, in that sustained attention by which He refers all temporal things to the eternal, all visible things to things invisible, everything fructifying today to what was but a root yesterday, and will bear new fruit tomorrow. Moved as He was by what happened in Judas and to Judas, He did not let that perturbation of His soul cause Him to forget the *other sheep.* Even when one was lost, He kept His attention upon the other eleven. He let the dead bury the dead; He turned Himself to the living. So He suppressed nothing.

He celebrated the Supper with His own; meanwhile, however. He *saw Satan.* He took the bread: He saw the foul vapor of Satan hover over it. He lifted the cup: He tasted the acid of

Satan in the wine. He drank everything to the dregs and searched out eternal mysteries in every single thing.

Three of these mysteries He finds now, and He points to them.

One is the *Supper*. In it the quintessential "mystery" of man is ushered into the very life of faith by Christ and the Spirit.

Another is *Satan* who avidly desires to sift. That is the quintessential "mystery" of Satanic essence, which none can fathom or know.

The third is the heart of God. And that especially is the great "Mystery." As He appeals to it in interceding with the Father, He does so not as a hopeless one, but as a person confident and assured, one who *knows* what the Father is. It is in that manner that He pleads for His own.

All three of these mysteries obtain simultaneously in the depth of Jesus' soul: He says, *I have prayed for thee,* before God, against Satan, during the Supper. That is sublime holiness. That is the luminous light of clarity. That is the flame of love. He is a Christ who knows the "sorrows of Satan" in the moment of the Supper and whose most impelling spiritual drives simultaneously fight against that Satan. Again, you see, He appears as the one person who does not suppress; He comes, genuine and authentic in the harmony of His perfect soul. He has room in His heart for all, because He knows that they all (plural) have been required of God by Satan. But He also deals with each person individually. In an especial way a prayer stirs in His soul for Simon. "I have prayed for you (singular), Simon!" Besides the past and the present, the *future* has a place in His heart. Later, we know, Simon is given a task for the future, and in that charge to the *one* Peter *all* are again included and safeguarded: "and when thou art converted, strengthen thy brethren."

Such is the complete absence of the sin of "suppression." Past, present, future; individual and society; deepest depth and highest height; God and Satan; Judas and Simon; a plea for a sentence and a plea for acquittal—all these simultaneously and each in its place, found room in the one soul of the man Jesus Christ.

Truly, such a High-priest became us, was fit for us.

Cautious, bashful in the presence of such human majesty, we step nearer Jesus, and hear Him say: Simon, Simon! When

Jesus calls a name twice something momentous is to take place: Martha, Martha; Saul, Saul; Simon, Simon!

And this is tremendously important. Simon, Simon, Satan hath greatly desired to sift thee as wheat.

We must consider four matters: first, the fact that Satan desires; secondly, that Satan desires them all; thirdly, for what end Satan desires them; and, fourthly, in which moment of time Satan does the desiring.

Satan desires. Who can say even the least important thing about that? If the desires of one man can be understood by another only with difficulty, if human wants are hard to delineate, how can we possibly say anything of the depths of Satanic desire? To speak of the sorrows of Satan represents a kind of haughtiness.

Nevertheless, Christ has prophesied concerning these and has asked us to meditate upon them according to His direction.

In a general way, we can state that a sinister purpose, an ominous desire, an active life force which militates against God lowers in Satan's being.

But that is not saying all there is to say. God is intrinsically the immutable one, is never in process of "becoming," is never "evolving." God *is*.

Against this eternal fire of holiness beats the smoke of Satan's thorn-bush. His hate is constantly directed against God—against God as the eternal one.

But God who is immutable in essence reveals Himself also in changing works. The works of God in creation and in regeneration *are* in process of becoming, *do* develop, they *do* pass from strength to greater strength. His work strives to realize a purpose, is of eschatological character, for it is bent upon that catastrophic glorification of the work of redemption at the last day.

In this sense, God has a dual character: the God of being, and the God of action; God as from Eternity He is, and God as He is eschatologically in action, as He will one time show Himself to be in the perfected history of revelation, in the great harvest of His completed redemption work. And Satan desires to increasingly militate against this god who is *being* and who is *working*. The more God's being becomes manifest in God's work, consequently, the more that work becomes manifest in the world, and the more the teleological influences of the kingdom of heaven become active in the world, the more vehemently Satan nurtures desire against God. Satan's wrath is boundless, particularly when He knows his time is limited (*Revelation* of John).

Well, if that is so, the night in which Christ was betrayed is a particularly irritating goad at the heels of Satan.

On this night, we must remember, the holiness of God refuses to be confined within itself, or to reveal itself solely in the condemnation of Satan and in the perdition of those who belong to him. This night the holiness of God will extend itself. God's holiness will begin imperial warfare, designed for expansion. It aims to become manifest in the justification of sinners. By means of twelve apostles it aims to pour itself out upon the church, an institution whose holiness will appear *in the institution* as such and have its effect there until the last day. To that end God puts to work the eschatological potencies of the coming era. On this night storms rage, hurricanes howl. A whirlwind moves over the universe. Hence this night particularly rankles Satan. Life, this is thy sting.

Such is the genesis of Satan's desiring.

Just as Christ gave shape and words to His desires in the room of the Passover by expressing them in a prayer, so Satan puts his desires into language throughout the universe (even though that language can only be spiritually understood). His desires attack God's work. His hot passion burns the fringes of the seven stars. The seven stars are the seven churches. The seven stars represent the completeness of the church. The seven stars are in the room of the Passover, for the apostles are there with Jesus. Now Satan bestirs himself against the churches. He desires things against them — he pronounces his desires in words. He draws up a writ of complaint against the seven churches and turns it in at the Highest Tribunal. He delivers it into God's hands. Hence, there is a battle of words in the universe: the desire of Jesus (the Defendant) expressed in *word,* and the desire of Satan (the Plaintiff) also expressed in *word,* battle against each other.

Consider how significant this is. Christ puts the perfect desiring of the Holy Spirit (dwelling in Him) and that of the genuine soul (which was given Him as man) into words. And those words, the words of the high-priestly prayer, can be heard in every sphere, for they cause the universe to quake. And that word of Christ, rending the clouds as it does, moving the heart of God as it does, also stirs Satan, sets his zeal aflame, and kindles his fervor to such pitch of intensity that he too puts his desire into words. No, his language is not human language; he does not speak an earthly tongue, for that is impossible. God only was made flesh. Satan was not. But to the extent that he is able to do so, Satan makes his wants concretely known to God. He formulates a "prayer." Jesus says that Satan *desires*. He desires Jesus' disciples.

Just before this, in His high-priestly prayer, Jesus had prayed for these disciples. "Father, I pray for them; neither for these alone, but for them also which shall believe on me through their word." In that way Jesus' prayer unites the whole church—the seven churches—to the life of the apostles and so bears the whole church to the throne of God on the wings of prayer.

But Satan does not hesitate in this crucial moment. His desire is not created by that of Jesus, but it is fanned into a blaze by it. Precisely in that lies the proof of the fact that he is conquered already. Jesus was ahead of him, was first in desiring God. Nevertheless, irrespective of whether he is losing or not, he still tries to conquer. Such is the essence of Satanic being: to desire the impossible. Thus Satan's desiring militates against that of Christ.

If we may employ a figure of speech in our effort to designate the spiritual character of Satan's conflict against Jesus, we would suggest the figure of two broadcasting stations. We know that one such station can dispatch its waves, and that another can send out its waves against those of the first. Just so, a wave of Jesus' soul has been sent to God; it bears a petition of redemption, it is a fervent plea for those whom the Father has given Him. Meanwhile Satan dispatches His waves from another side of the world. His design is to interfere with the transmission of the message of the Son of man. This is the spiritual warfare, in apocalyptic language called the conflict of spiritual forces in the air. The two forces are two witnesses: the one accuses and the other defends. Both appear before the one Tribunal of God.

Satan desires. He dispatches his messages unintermittently. Gradually his desiring grows fiercer. Finally it becomes a demand.

The real sense of the passage is this: *Satan has laid claim on thee. He has asked God to deliver you up to him, my disciples.* He has filed his claim, and that claim takes on the absolute character of an ultimatum. For the whole world this is the hour of the *ultima ratio*. Satan wants God to turn the disciples over to him; he desires, begins to shout it, finally abjures. Is it not true that sin dwells in them? Is Simon essentially different from Judas? Was the Messianic kingdom properly received in their soul? The wages of sin is death, is it not? And death is universal? Yes, yes, Satan desires, claims; tries to drive a wedge into God with the help of God's own hammer, His *Word,* in which He binds up death with sin.

We see, in the second place, that Satan lays claim to *all* of those who are in the room of the Passover with Jesus. He insists that evil accrues to all (the "you" of the text is plural), to all who are of Christ.

As if Satan had no designs upon Christ Himself! Of course, he has: Him he desires most of all.

But Satan cannot avail against Christ. Christ is firm; He stands erect. For that reason Satan directs his attack upon the disciples, the apostles of the future. If he cannot sever Christ from the church, he can do the other thing: he can sever the church from Christ. Therefore he desires the apostles, for these represent the whole church. By means of their office that church will flourish and live. If these should succumb "the one seed of the woman" would be destroyed. Then the fountain of the church would be stopped. Then Jesus' side would bleed in vain. Then the four-and-twenty thrones encircling God's single throne would be vacant throughout eternity, as far as the twelve apostolic chairs were concerned. And — if those twelve apostolic thrones are vacant, the twelve patriarchs, too, will have no right to theirs. In that case everything in heaven and on earth will be confusion.

That is why Satan wants them *all.*

But Simon especially he would desire. For Simon has periodically been a "satan" in reference to Jesus. Satan knows that if he can tear this seal off Christ's arm and heart, if he can aggravate "the satanic" in Simon, and suppress other elements in him, then the fall of Simon will be very disastrous; then the foundation of the church will be torn apart at precisely the corner in which Simon's stone has been laid.

That point ushers in our third consideration. With what intent, for what purpose, does Satan file claim on Jesus' disciples with God?

That he may sift them as wheat, we read. He wants to *sift* them. What is the signification of that figure?

A writer[1] who has first-hand information about Oriental practices because he has been an eye witness to these, tells us that a woman generally manipulated the sieve. This is his record of the process. She "grasps the sieve, half-filled with grain, in both hands. She begins her work, which she carries out with remarkable dexterity, by vehemently shaking the sieve from left to right some six or seven times. Naturally, such shreds of straw and bits of chaff as were still mixed with the grain rise to the surface. Most of these she can take and throw away with her hand. Now she puts the sieve through the motion of a teeter-totter, raising this side first and then that, blowing hard over the screen of her tool all the while. This part of the procedure, executed with special skill, has three results. First: all the dirt, and all the shriveled kernels fall to the ground through the interstices. Second: such straw and chaff as still remain are scattered or brought to rest by her blowing in that part of the sieve which is farthest from her. Third: the good grain remains, heaped up in the center of the sieve, and the bits of stone form a separate mass in that part of the sieve which is nearest her. Thereupon she takes the stones, straw, and chaff out with her hand."

Sifting wheat in this connection, therefore, represents a violent shaking to and fro in an endeavor by that means to make the separation of the wheat from the chaff so much easier. By the figure which He employs Jesus is pointing to the fact that the awful import of the night which is coming will shake the disciples back and forth as violently as wheat is shaken in a sieve.

But the whole purpose of the sifting is to satisfy Satan's desire. His purpose is not to take the chaff from the wheat, but to

---

1. Neil, James, *Palestina en de Bijbel,* J. W. Kok, Kampen, first edition, pp. 77-78 (a second edition has been released).

get the wheat out of the chaff. He wants to shake the disciples so violently that they will lose their minds in the night of fear and anxiety. Then—that is, when they hardly know what they are doing, it will be so much easier for him to blow the wheat, to blow what was good in them away, and to retain the bad in them, to keep the chaff. By means of the sifting, in other words, of the suffering, Satan wants the evil, the chaff, to predominate over the wheat, which is good. In his presence the night of suffering now at hand becomes one of demoniacal *temptation*.

For this purpose he asks a writ of habeas corpus from the Father. He asks that the twelve be delivered into his hands. They are really his, are they not? Or did some one pay a ransom sufficing to buy these eleven Galileans out of Satan's hands?

The text discriminates nicely in pointing out that Satan desires this sifting as his *right,* that he files claim to his property now, demands them of God, as though he were their owner already. When grain changed hands in the East the sifting of it became a duty of the buyer, not of the seller. The buyer had to see to it that wheat and chaff, grain and straw became separated. And in this sense, Satan, from the very beginning, acts upon the assumption that he is already the owner of all the wheat which God wishes to gather into His granaries. The harvest is mine, he tells himself. God is not to gain possession of it for the price of the blood of Christ, in order that as buyer He may then take the chaff from the wheat in His own fashion. No, never, never shall God be the buyer of the grain. God, Thou are not warranted in paying Thyself the fee of ransom. The field of souls is the devil's property. And he will do as he pleases with the wheat and the chaff—such is the fundamental issue in Satan's conflict against God. The issue does not concern the right to put to the test, to prove, to try the disciples (a sifting designed to bless) nor the right to tempt them (a sifting designed to curse). The basic contention is this: whose *property* are the disciples? If, as a matter of fact, the field of the world has been sown with evil seed, may God appropriate that field to Himself, subject it to Himself, and proceed to sift its harvest, or will Satan cling to the field as to property legally his? And then—sift its harvest in *his* fashion?

Satan's warfare against God is a struggle for the deed of ownership to the world, and in it, to the church.

Jesus knows very well what Satan intends to do after that matter of the deed has been settled. If the field continues under his jurisdiction, the spirit of Rebellion will try to lift the good out of the souls of the heavily oppressed, to keep the bad, in order by such means to curse with eternal sterility the field, which God Himself once planted. *Satan hath desired to have you that he may sift you as wheat!*

The fourth question to raise itself is this one: At precisely which moment of time did Satan desire this?

The answer is obvious: At *this* very moment he desired it.

In order to appreciate the fine shade of distinction in the text, we must remember that in Greek a particular action can be designated in two ways. Sometimes the action is presented as one which takes place completely and instantaneously, and sometimes as one which continues. The Greek language has a way of indicating whether an action is instantaneous or continuous.

The remarkable thing is that in this text Christ points to Satan's desiring as occurring instantaneously, in a given moment of time. When Christ says: "Satan hath desired to have you," that form of the verb is used which indicates the instantaneous and not the continuous action. In other words, Christ indicates that Satan's sinister desires have reached a climax; they take on special poignancy. Even though Satan is not limited by time, he does act in accordance with time sequence because God is carrying out His work in time. The heights and depths of the historical process of God's redemptive work also describe the curve of Satan's feverish striving. The stirring of the clear water in the pool of redemption is reflected in the movement of the dark water of hellish passion and activity. In spite of himself Satan has to accommodate himself to God's times and circumstances. God throws His stone into the water; the circle of its wave goes farther and farther, and at last dashes against the devil. Satan cannot escape the force of the wave of God's power.

Such is the situation in this instance. First there was the fact of Christ's prayer. Hence it is impossible for the reaction not to set in; and that reaction is the Satanic "prayer." Is Christ's voice raised in prayer? Then you are sure to hear Satan's voice also, full of a wild passion, and full of that kind of pain which is the portion of him who wants action and can only attain to reaction. Now God's lightning rends the skies; His thunder roars through the world. It arouses Satan's spirit strangely, it makes him desire with a new fever; he raises a stronger voice in pleading for what he supposes are his rights.

He pleads before God. He pleads because God pleads. His plea represents reaction. When God makes His legal rights the order of the day, the business of the moment, that day and moment Satan must act. Right versus right, the claims of the one elicit the claims of the other. The counsel for heaven rises; the counsel for hell must jump to his feet. Christ has been named Counsel and Mediator for heaven's cause, has He? And the Spirit named as His successor after Him? Then Satan will present his own case before God. He lays down his claim; cites law versus law, but laws and precedents all designed to eternally counteract the laws of redemption.

See the line the Scriptures lay down. This, this is Christ's epilogue, written in response to the prologue of Job. And this is the prologue to Chapter 12 of Revelation in which Satan returns as the "accuser of the brethren."

No human fabrication, no spurious gospel can achieve such profound and moving depths of authenticity as the Gospel of God achieves in this matter. True, that Gospel tells us of Satan and his griefs, but primarily it tells us of Jesus Christ, who, while He is here in the room of the Passover, experiences the tension and sublime drama of the prologue to Job, of the Apocalypse, and especially of the book of the seven seals.

It is a great comfort to think that the same Goel, that same "one of a thousand," who had to witness favorably for Job, now is present in the flesh to participate in the spiritual litigation which is shaking the universe. The terror, the dread, suggested in the book of Job, is being fulfilled in our ears today. But the comfort of that book comes with the dread.

You must remember that the Messianic emphasis is very pronounced in the book of Job. Job, when he is surrounded by "devils" in the human form of evil friends, men who continually

accuse him, and afford no hope of acquittal, of compassion—
Job then speaks up himself, and appeals to the Witness who will
plead for him before God. Job is being sifted by both God and
Satan, is being hurled to and fro between the rocks of the ages.
He had to be placed in the sieve in order to prove in his self the
majesty of God. And the Counsel and Witness to whom he appealed will plead poor Job's cause in His plea before God; He
will implore Job's redemption there. Even when Job succumbs
to despair, complains against God, loses all sense of direction,
and argues against the Messianic element in his life, even then
Elihu appears and by pointing to the Messiah makes room for the
Messiah's Gospel. The Messiah will come and, as "one of a
thousand," will suffer and find atonement for him.

The tension between a Satan who desires to sift as wheat is
sifted, on the one hand, and the Witness-Advocate who lets the
sifting go on as He intercedes but meanwhile preserves and gives
a content to Job's faith, on the other hand—that tension is present already in the book of Job.

The comfort of that Witness and Advocate becomes perfect
now.

When the Jobiad was written the Goel had not yet appeared.
Job and Elihu simply strain their eyes in peering into the vague
distance where in blurred outlines they distinguish the figure of
the Mediator pleading His case in heaven against Satan. But now
the Goel, the Witness, the Advocate, the Mediator has appeared
in the flesh. Simon, Simon! Job, Job! Elihu, Elihu! See, I
am here. I have come today. I have prayed for Simon, I have
opposed My intercession to Satan's accusation. Behold, your
Saviour is here.

So Christ comes up through the centuries as the surety for His
own. In this moment of crisis, of world-crisis (John 12:31) He
experiences in His prayers beforehand the fact of His surety
which He will seal with His blood after a little while. He has
prayed for them; in the spiritual world the cross has already been
lifted high.

He prayed for them as a Man of sorrows. By that act He
manifested His *faith*. An attorney who wants to base his plea

for the client's acquittal upon a ransom still to be paid must be very certain that it will be paid.

In His plea for the defense, Christ's grace is as universal as it is particular. He prays for all those who are present, for He wants to enter them all as documents attesting the fidelity of God. But He is *especially* sensitive to Peter's case. For Simon, who spoke satanically at the beginning of the history of the passion will at the feast of Pentecost be the first to allow his spirit, driven by the Spirit of God, to express itself in words. I have prayed for thee, Simon.

Finally, what was it that Jesus prayed? Did He ask that the sifting might stop?

No, He could not pray for that. Job was sifted by both God and Satan. David was driven to action by Satan and by God simultaneously. Paul, later, will be hampered in carrying out his plan for the journey by Satan and by the Spirit, will in the same moment be beaten as with fists by both Satan and Jesus. Just so the disciples are now being sifted by God and by Satan. Simon, Simon, the Father hath desired to have thee, that He may sift thee as wheat. It has to be that way, Simon. Simon, this is the hour of the one great sifting and of the one great separation. Now the chaff will be separated from the wheat; hell will be completely separated from heaven. The syncretism that allows the tares to grow up with the wheat will be broken in principle. The moratorium called Common Grace, allowing tares and grain to flourish together, will be recalled in principle. This night, this cross, Gethsemane, Golgotha, and Christ Himself would be as vain as perfect vanity if the whole world were not bandied back and forth in the conflict between God and Satan.

No, Christ does not ask that the sifting be stricken from God's or from Satan's order of the day. Had He prayed that, He would have cursed His hour, would have blasphemed the hour of His death. Could He have asked calm and quiet for the day designated for turbulence and storm? It is true that the priest in Christ lets His love plead for the little ones, but His love for one of these never causes Him to thrust the whole community of His church or the sacred program of the great redemption out of His prayers. Therefore His priestly love does not ask that the dis-

ciples be taken out of Satan's sieve; had He done so the Priest
of our confession would have asked that He Himself might escape the anxiousness of that sifting. Then the world, then we,
would have been destroyed with Him.

Christ asks the Father for another, a different thing. He knows
that Satan is but the second, that God is the first cause of the sifting. Therefore He turns to God asking that faith may not
abate—May they remain in Thy hands, Father! Thou dost sift;
and Satan sifts. But Thy method is not his!—Satan wants to
keep the chaff and blow the wheat away. Christ would retain
the wheat and take the chaff out of it. By sifting, Satan wants
to suppress the good by the evil; Christ, also by sifting, would
overcome evil with good. And now — Father, into Thy hands
I commend their spirit. Let them go out now. Keep their faith
steadfast, guard over the field of their soul. Do it, O God, for
Thee, for Thee alone.

In that way Christ exercises His prayer over-against Satan. He
prays loudly, aggressively. His prayer, too, like that of Satan,
represents instantaneous, not continuous, action. His prayer is a
cry this time, cutting its way through the air. Father, it says,
they believe; help Thou their unbelief . . .

That prayer leaves only one way open to mankind. Jesus
prays. Who can refuse to pray with Him?

Our whole being must rise up to pray with Him now. We
must pray that He hasten to the cross. For that is plainly His
own desire. We must take Him at His word as He spoke it in
prayer. His intercession by means of the spoken word must give
way to the deed now. Christ in His prayer pronounced "Amen"
upon His own sacrifices, still to be made. May He make haste
now to draw the "Amen" out of the throat of the angels and of
the entire church, in order that He may stamp it as a seal upon
the deed which because of His faith is acceptable to God beforehand.

Jesus prayed. By prayer He took His own cross out of God's
hand, and loosed the Spirit from God's heart. The cross was
for His own use; the Spirit, who preserves the faith, was for our
benefits. Jesus prayed—how dire the need for that.

But we can be comforted. Each day Satan still pleads in opposition to Christ; he still tries to name that uncertain in heaven which is really fixed and assured. But his present efforts are as futile as the former attempt—he is trying the impossible.

The comfort is not such, however, that, because of Christ's intercession by word and deed, we can rest upon it, as we rest our heads upon a pillow. Moments of tension, crises—these remain in the world. Crises, we know, require *sifting*.

When the winds of Satan blow against the ark, threatening to crush its sides, God's winds, we know, also blow and quickly impel the vessel beyond the treachery of cliff and mountain. His love lifts the ark above danger—we know that, and it is certain —but it is blowing hard just the same!

In our day the breakers of Satan's jealousy and hate blow against the church, the tiny vessel which is the church; and again we know that God will cause His winds to blow it beyond the crags and rocks. But again—the fact is that it is blowing hard; there *is* a bad storm! Intercession and intervention point unerringly to the judgment, to a crisis.

As for Simon! And as for us? What must Simon do; what shall we do?

Simon does not know just yet. He needs a Mediator who prays for him first, and afterwards opens his eyes to see the nature of this spiritual conflict. Not until later will Simon understand.

And we, Lord, we are no better. Afterwards, not until afterwards, shall we understand.

However, since we know, since we are sure that Christ must still present His cross in heaven daily, as He intercedes for us, therefore each day is oppressive for us. We may very well count our days, for He who intercedes for us ascribes great importance to them. Intercession is inconceivable without a process of segregation. It introduces the principle of segregation into the world. Intercession puts the seven to work.

But let that suffice. All our thinking finally rests in the prayer of Jesus. Thinking, our thinking—that finally leads to supralapsarianism.

Job was sifted solely because God took delight in it. God delighted to demonstrate in Job His perfect fidelity to Himself, and to demonstrate that to the least deserving spectator. Precisely so the disciples and the whole communion of the church are thrown into the sieve for the sole purpose of demonstrating God's honor, of preserving His authentic dignity before the eye of Satan. Whoever traces the word "sifting" back to the eternal verities of God must end in what the church humbly calls supralapsarianism.

But if our thoughts are led to an impasse that way, we can listen to this infralapsarian utterance: *I have prayed for thee.* I have found atonement. I entered into thy need, my people; I lived it with you in my soul. I have gone through all the qualities of it with you, and I who speak am a man, like you in all things. But I am also the eternal God. Hence, God by me spoke to you today in an infralapsarian manner. In the direct need of your soul I was sensitive to the need. I have prayed for you.

Now everything is good for us.

When I look upon it from God's side I can only think of the sifting in a supralapsarian way. Then God experiences a peace which annihilates me, is the *alpha* of my sifting and the *omega* of all of my suffering. For that which was last in my suffering (the *omega* of my sifting) was the first element in His decision (the *alpha* of His counsel).

But when I listen to Christ, who is the Word become Flesh, praying for me, I hear in that the infralapsarian equivalent. Then that which was the *alpha* of God's counsel becomes an *omega* also, an *omega* in Jesus' *human* soul. My *alphas* are His; my *omegas* are His. His mouth learns to read God's sublime script together with my mouth. Perhaps I am a mere child: Perhaps I cannot read, but can simply spell. He spells out the words with me. In all my anxiety He is anxious—just now He prayed for me.

Now I want to rest in Him. Now supra- and infralapsarianism have merged in temporal and eternal union, have merged in the cross and in the prayer of the Priest of my confession, Jesus Christ. Now I would rest in Him.

The Author Sings His Own Psalms

CHAPTER SIXTEEN

The Author Sings His Own Psalms

> And when they had sung an hymn, they
> went out into the mount of Olives.
> —MATTHEW 26:30.

WHEN Christ leaves the room of the Passover to enter upon the night of His passion, He goes on His way singing.

You and I are not the first ones to meditate upon that singing of the Man of sorrows who is walking on the way of suffering. Long ago the contemplation of "the singing Christ en route to the place of slaughter" charmed the feelings of many, and induced some to begin singing themselves. In the middle ages, especially, many an individual sat down to compose a song about the hymn which Jesus sang as He went out to die.

Whoever takes notice of the many hymns which the spirit of the middle ages left us in its literature will observe that very frequently the theme of the singing Crucified One is expressed in the symbol of a nightingale pouring its exalted notes into the air from a May-tree. By this means the harsh brutality of the cross gives way to the rich luxury of a May-tree in blossom.

The arid voice of the Man of sorrows, whose blood is flowing from many wounds, whose dry throat can utter no sound save the scrawny cry of His Holy Passion for God, is by such artistic compositions deprived of all its terribleness. A different figure is substituted for it—the figure of the lyric nightingale which, because it loves so much, cannot help but sing. The seven words of the cross, we are told, are the seven high notes of the nightingale. And thus men have lyrically woven a poetic halo around all that Jesus said and sighed and suffered in the night

269

of His passion, by comparing Him to the nightingale which sings at the prompting of overflowing love.

We may as well say outright what must be said of this. Such poetry does injustice to the content and to the holiness of the Gospel of the Passion. We simply may not metamorphose the brutal outlines of Christ's wrenched body and forsaken soul into the lush sweetness of a nightingale whose pulse-beats are regulated by life and love and by these alone. For, although love and the will to live caused the Holy Heart of Jesus to beat faster— the finger of God's justice made it stop. Under the threat of that finger Jesus suffered terribly. That finger made His body writhe in pain, His soul bend to breaking. His utterances were not those of natural love gratified by the situation; they were those of justice, of the strenuous achieving of grace which would attain peace on the cross by passing through awful struggle.

To that consideration we must add another. Whenever the figure of the nightingale is employed to represent Jesus' love, that figure, irrespective of its lyric quality, always separates the love from *prophecy*.

The nightingale sings under the foliage of its tree. Its song does not carry beyond the boundaries of *nature*; it echoes back from these on reaching them. And that for nature and for the love of nature is quite enough. Surely, there is life, there is the throbbing pulse of it in the song of the nightingale and in the wonderful luxuriance of the green garden of the earth. But there is no prophecy in these. Nature is subject to prophecy, is part of its domain, but nature never yet sang prophetically. Nature is not the mouthpiece of the highest prophecy, and never prophesies, itself. True, the Spirit is active in it, and that same Spirit gives everything alive in it a tongue and language with which to speak. But the Spirit does not enter into nature to prophesy through it. That right, the right to prophesy, the Spirit has reserved for man.

Remember (we cannot tire of stressing this) that it is Christ who *prophesies*. He prophesies aloud of the deed He does for us and of its implications. And it is precisely by His prophecy that He carries the deed and its significance far beyond the bourne of nature, carries it up to God's high heavens. His deed, you see, is accompanied by the *Word* of prophecy.

Hence it is that when Jesus sings He always sings prophetically. Such singing is not poverty; it is abundance. The beauty of nature is less beautiful than the beauty of the Word. Yes, Jesus sings prophetically. But afterwards He also sings lyrically, epically, didactically. Therefore the song which He sings before the cross at the farthest end of the temple of suffering as well as that which He sings here at the threshold of it in the room of the Passover is a *prophetic* song.

That song lays hold on the Word. It fulfills the Word. It explains the Word. *When they had sung an hymn, they went out into the mount of Olives.* Jesus goes to God singing.

We must not say too many disparaging things of medieval poetry in its use of the symbol of the nightingale. For we must admit that we ourselves, generally speaking, have devoted more attention to the seven words on the cross, which are only derived from the Scriptures in part, than to the hymn of praise which Christ sang in the room of the Passover and which in each of its parts was entirely derived from the Scriptures.

Yes, we pay more attention to what Christ says during what we appreciate as His suffering, to what He says in a wild and plaintive voice and at the prompting of awful passion than we do to what He says in quiet recitative at a time when He apparently is still far from the cross. And such division of our attention probably characterizes us, and that unfavorably.

Do you suppose that we may abuse Christ's calm as He sings the Scriptural words by fancying more profundity into the words on the cross than into those of the hymn with which He left the room of the Passover? May we really think that a greater manifestation of love issues from those passion-wrought cries which we designate "the words on the cross" than from the prophetic appropriation of the Word of the Lord in Jesus' hymn?

To put the question is to answer it.

Hence we must re-examine our Reformed principle of the interpretation of Scripture as it applies to our confession about the soul and spirit and work of Jesus Christ. We must acknowledge that the hymn of praise sung at the conclusion of the meal

of the Passover is as worthy of our careful attention as are the
.words of the cross, taken singly.

We must say at the outset that the singing of a hymn obviously represents nothing *unusual*. At the Jewish Passover thousands
joined in the singing of the same hymn which Christ sang at this
time.

The singing of a hymn, the singing of that particular hymn was
a part of the official programme of the feast of the Passover.[1] In
other words, the singing and the song represent the usual thing.
The hymn was a familiar one, comprising Psalms 113 to 118.
Taken as a unit these psalms were called *the Hallel*. According
to the ritual for the occasion these had to be sung in two tempos
at the Passover. All Jews followed the customary usage.

Perhaps that is the reason for which so many people find nothing moving or extraordinary in that hymn, and find something
much profounder in a word spoken on the cross, one which none
but Jesus ever spoke.

Such reasoning, surely, is sheer foolishness. What Jesus does
is not affected by the fact that others also do it. The important
point is that no one in the world does a thing *in the same way
that Jesus does it*. Something entirely new inheres in the singing of the Hallel the moment it comes from Jesus' lips. That
new and different quality never was known in the world before
and never will be repeated in it again.

And that unique quality does not inhere in the tone of the
voice which sings the song but in the mystery of the fact that
now the Author, the Poet, is singing His own poem.

This is a beautiful and a holy matter.

---

1. Our belief to the effect that the meal, concluded by the Hallel, was indeed
the Passover meal, is related to this fact as well as to the argument of Chapter 10.
There is an opinion which asserts that the Passover meal was another, different
from this. The nature of this book does not allow us to expose the reasons for
our holding to the opinion that Jesus actually participated in the Passover meal.
We shall simply say that our opinion rests on arguments derived partly from the
history of revelation, and from its structure, but especially and primarily on exegetical bases. It can be very generally said here that the intimate relation between
Jesus' commission to find a room where the Passover could be celebrated and their
sitting down in (this) room (the one requested) immediately afterwards makes the
interpretation very tenable.

On the day of the Passover and on the day before and after it people sang the Hallel in every street, in every home. The heavens echoed because of it; the angels were greatly troubled by it, and also greatly pleased.

But no one ever sang it as Jesus did. In Him the poet was singing His own song.

The poet himself is the best reader of his poem. The secret of elocution is sincerity. And it is true that to understand a poem we must appreciate its setting. Moreover, in order to appreciate a poem fully, the reader must be able to enter into the poet's heart, must be able to read it, must be able to read the poem companioned by the author's feeling. In fact, the student of poetry must possess the poet's heart: Hear a hundred persons recite a poem; hear the author recite it then. And if he is a good speaker and can hit upon the inflections and cadences proper to his emotions and thoughts, he will read better than any of the hundred, simply because he created the poem. He it was who experienced its emotion; and he it is who can best express that emotion.

There are poets, of course, who are less talented as speakers than as poets. They are capable of significant emotions and can put them in words, but they are not gifted in the rhetoric of speech.

Jesus has no such inadequacy. Every form which He employs in speech or song is perfectly expressive of the significance of the particular, unique moment of time in which it is spoken. The form is *completely adequate* to the requirements of the moment in reference to the demands of His being.

Draw your own conclusion. Heaven hears all Jerusalem singing on this day of the Passover. The pious homes echo and re-echo the praise for the salvation achieved for them.

But among those singers one is unique. He is Jesus; He is the poet; He sings His own hymn.

Have you ever read Psalm 116? And stopped to ponder the meaning of the phrase: *He hath heard my voice?* Ah, but God hears so many voices. The whole of creation sighs to Him, the host of apostles sing, the chorals of the church rise, the shrill voice of cursing shatters the consecrated tones of praise; the peals of rebellion rend the skies and all these voices are directed to heaven. God hears an oppressive totality of voices. Nevertheless, we read: "He hath heard *my* voice." He distinguishes the one voice from the many.

Have you read the 116th Psalm?

Jesus sang this psalm also on the night of the Passover. Jesus' mouth pronounced the words:

I love the Lord because He hath heard my voice.

Do you agree that those words were never uttered with such certainty as then: *He hath heard My voice!* No, the song was never sung in this way before. The poet was presenting His poem from the foot of the stairs, to the throne of the Highest Majesty.

He was not a *troubadour* of love (as some by adhering to their "spiritual" eroticism suppose).

He was not a nightingale singing "he knew not how."

He was the Prophet, the Exalted One in the hymns of Israel, singing His own hymn before God.

The Passover ritual, like every other "ritual," is very significant, but it also was never observed in the perfection of its essence save by Jesus alone.

If we accept the fact that the singing of the hymn, although prescribed by the law, is harmoniously woven into the mosaic of Christ's life-work and that this hymn, imposed as it was by external dictation nevertheless was given an organically interconnected and genuine place in that life, we can readily see in what sense it is that the Poet Himself is singing His own psalm on this occasion.

Before Christ tabernacled among us as a man, He, as the Eternal Word of God, as the uncreated Logos, as the Angel of the Lord, *already prophesied* in Israel. This is the great mystery which Peter put into words by saying that the Spirit of Christ which was in the prophets of the Old Testament did signify, when it testified beforehand, the sufferings of Christ and the glory that should follow (I Peter 1:11).

In those words of Peter, the Spirit prophesies that, as the humiliated and exalted Mediator, Christ is the *content* of prophecy (including the Psalms) not only, but that He by His own Spirit was active as the Author of prophecy in Israel (again including the Psalms) also.

He who came to Israel was the Holy Spirit. But He was also the Angel of the Lord. The Eternal Word, the Son, *He also* came to Israel.

These two *are,* as they appeared to be then, *one* person.

It was the Spirit of *Christ* which poured itself out in Psalms 113 to 118. And now it is that *Spirit* of Christ who proceeds to sing His own hymn, and to sing it in the *soul* of the man Jesus.

This is the profound mystery which no one can understand. This is the mystery of God and man united in one person. Human nature, God alone knows how, was perfectly united with the Divine in single, undivided conjunction.

This mystery, this miracle, which we accept by faith in a general way was particularly applied to, was given unique application in the event of the day, in the singing of the Hallel. We do not know how the Spirit of God, which is given to Christ "without measure," influenced the human soul of Jesus of Nazareth as often as He prayed, thought, developed, and *sang*. We do know that the Spirit is present in all of the souls of God, that He works and prays there. Those words were written for us which say that the Spirit itself makes intercession for us with groanings that connot be uttered. But, save for the thrust of that "cannot-be-uttered" those words were written for Christ also. The Spirit prays in the soul of Jesus and the Spirit also sings in Jesus' soul. God's own Spirit, who is eternal, prays and sings in the soul of Jesus, who is a creature.

Jesus differs from us in respect, of course, to the fact that our souls carry sin and the lie within themselves and for that reason to an extent still pray and sing in opposition to the Spirit; and the Spirit, similarly, works in opposition to these. But Jesus is always without sin and always prays and sings in full consonance with the Spirit.

Moreover, a second difference distinguishes us from Jesus. Our human finiteness and limitation can never appreciate the influence, the words, of the Spirit in our heart as fully, cannot be as aware of these, as Jesus was.

But in one important respect Jesus on this occasion is like us in all things: though He is infinite according to His person, He is *finite* according to His soul.

We cannot say more about it. We may not say more. We may worship and believe. We may believe that the infinite person of the Son, and the infinite Spirit of God are two-in-one, and that this one is the Author of the Hallel of the Passover. These two co-exist in the human, created soul of Jesus of Nazareth. In order to fix the divinity of His Person, the profundities of the Eternal Spirit, and His own perfect human will upon God, the Logos, the Spirit impels Jesus' soul, drives Jesus' genuine, authentic *soul,* and all that is in Him, to sing the hymn of praise and thanksgiving. These three impel His soul and drive all His senses to present the hymn of God as a sacrifice of praise. Now the words have their fulfillment:

> I will love thee, O Lord, my strength.
> The Lord is my rock, and my fortress, and my deliverer;
> My God, my strength, in whom I will trust;
> My buckler, and the horn of my salvation, and my high tower.

The *Author* of them sang those words that day; sang them accompanied by finite music, of course, sang them "in proper time," for He was human. Nevertheless, the *Auth*or actually *sang.*

What we human beings could hear of it were the cadences of the voice, the purity of the tones, the sublimity of the hymn. But those who heard did not really hear, for their eyes were darkened. They did not see Jesus' eyes as He sang, for their own were blinded. And their ears were stopped; they did not hear the vibration of high feeling in that voice, nor how Jesus deepened it by His assent. Their hearts had continued to be "fat" in part.

Irrespective of who heard, however, Jesus sang thus. The Angels heard it even better than the disciples did. Their own song at Christmas, they felt, could not compare with this hymn of the Poet-King, Jesus.

But of auditors, one is most important. God heard His voice and supplications. God inclined His ear.

Thus the Author sang His psalm. Again, however, the general law, the eternal verity, the "great mystery," the fact that God is revealed in the flesh is applied to it.

We may not regard Christ in the form of a servant only when He wears the servant's loin-cloth at the washing of feet, or when He bears the cross on His way to death, or when He is forsaken of God. We must *always* see Him in His servant-garb.

Even when He sings the Hallel the eternal Poet of the Psalms does so in the form of a servant.

Observe Him a moment, observe the Author of the Psalms. He is reading them from a bit of paper; just as a priest reads the mass from a book, just as every Jew who goes up to celebrate the feast reads the hymn from a leaflet, so Jesus in obedience to the official prescription reads His own psalms. The Poet subjects Himself to the law of priests and rabbis, for so "it became" this poet to "fulfill all righteousness." The great Author must read and sing His own compositions as does the weakest singer at the feast. The little old woman who sings her psalms so brokenly in the church on Sunday, but who loves Jesus, is in this respect accepted by Him. Haughty as poets have been alleged to be, this One does not ignore the crowd "because the best they can do is to dabble with the beauty of a hymn anyhow." Our great poet is a prophetic Poet but He is also a *priestly* poet. He sings, *being under the law.* This manner of singing is as fully informed with obedience and humiliation as was the moment of baptism when Jesus told John: Suffer it to be so now: for thus it becometh us to fulfill all righteousness. O, boundless compassion!

The poet sings with the others, with the meanest and frailest in the chorus, sings with them in a more actual sense than even David did. Woe upon Michael! Now especially, now it is sure: she will remain barren. She will fall to the ground, dead. O boundless mercy!

We know who this Author is. He has more than twelve legions of angels at His command. He can tell them to raise a chorus in the skies, excelling that which appeared on Christmas eve, spellbinding Jerusalem. And that Author sings His own verses *under the law,* thrusts the angels aside, lets them stay behind the clouds, tempers His voice lest it cause the walls to quake, and patiently accommodates His singing to Peter's strident voice.

That is wonderful, is it not? Think, that voice will still be calling aloud when He is dead.

Can that be true which we rather tremulously suggested in Chapter 10?[1] Is Jesus, the later Barnabas, perhaps, sitting downstairs while this singing is going on overhead? If so, He must have struggled, and suffered, and prayed strenuously before he could understand later on, very much later on, that He who was singing in his Aunt Mary's house was singing His own hymn, that He was the Poet of old time, whose name is Lord.

After a half hour Simon Peter will be sleeping, and after a few more hours he will startle the angels who have been listening to this song, will shock them with his cursings. Simon Peter, also, will have to struggle and suffer and pray long and strenuously before he can write the words which we have just quoted from him—before he can say that it was the Spirit of Christ who testified and prophesied beforehand, also in the psalms of the Hallel which Peter and John sang at Jesus' bosom. It always takes a long, long time before a person, and before even the Christ, learns to refer the psalms to the poet. In that fact is contained the whole of church history, and of the history of doctrine. We can say nothing opprobrious of Peter — we must admit that we ourselves had to *learn* to understand it.

What we must do is to listen attentively to Peter. Simon Peter *learned* that the Spirit of *Christ* made this Hallel, and Peter wants to tell us that he has learned that. And we—"we have also a more sure word of prophecy, whereunto we do well that we take heed, as unto a light that shineth in a dark place."

Repeat those words, will you? *A light that shineth in a dark place.*

The dark place is the room of the Passover. The *darkness* of it consists of Jesus' human voice, of the frailty of His lungs, of the limitations of the flesh, of the much that must be concealed.

1. We can also think of Mark: see Chapter 26.

And the *light* is the Spirit of prophecy, the Logos, the great Poet. It is the Poet (the Creator) absolute and unique.

The whole of theology, the whole of the mystical mercy of God, the whole teaching of the Scripture — that in respect to the Word and the incarnation of God also—is contained in the verse: *When they had sung an hymn, they went out into the mount of Olives.*

First Christ prophesied out of the body, in the Old Testament. Even then the Spirit of Christ was singing in the poets. That is the first moment.

Then the Spirit of Christ sang again; this time in the soul and by means of the tongue of Jesus. That is the second moment.

And years after this dark night of the Passover the Spirit of Christ caused Simon Peter to write the words, to which we alluded, about "the Spirit of Christ which testified beforehand." That is the third moment and it unites the first with the second.

For the Scriptures are one; and the Spirit is one; and time is one; and God one.

The devils heard Jesus sing, and they trembled.

The Hallel was an awful song, making the firmament shake, even though it was "altogether human."

Jesus' going to the Scriptures was, from God's point of view, quite the usual thing.

We often hear the word "mysticism" referred to, and many have made supposed mystical experiences of the Crucified One a pet subject of meditation.

There is a mysticism in Jesus' soul at this time. The Poet must return to His hymns and to His prophecy, because, although as Servant of the Lord He is the object of these, as Poet He is the subject of them. True mysticism consists of a living relationship between subject and object; a relationship, that is, whose life consists of *communion.*

In that way an unbroken *mystical* relationship exists in Jesus between the Scriptures and His soul. He is continuously in living contact with the Scriptures; it is simply impossible for Him to take that living union "for granted," be it for but a second. Similarly, on the other side, His whole soul clings to the Scriptures. The subject penetrates into its own object. The object enters into its own subject.

Again that is all we can say of it. But if anyone cannot feel that the dogmas of the church also allow a poet to sing, he must not blame the church and the dogma for lacking the appeal of beauty. He must blame himself.

All of us, for that matter, all of us, not as poets or thinkers, but as *believers,* as needy, lost souls need to know and experience the truth that Jesus *sings* the Scriptures. The Word made flesh is Jesus; the Word made Scriptures is the Bible, including the Hallel. These extend a hand of fellowship to each other *and do it for our atonement.* We should have done that; we should have reached out for the Scriptures, for the Word. But we did not do it. Hence the singing of the Hallel signifies more than the great joy of the Poet who is allowed to sing His own hymns. Besides, the singing includes more than the profound shame of the Saviour-in-humiliation who experiences His authorship under limitations. This singing includes another significance; namely, *mighty obedience* for our benefit. It represents the active obedience of the Mediator of God and men, who sings while others are silent, who sings with perfect tones the notes which stuck in Adam's throat . . .

Finally, this: The Jesus who sings the Hallel exhibits to us the charming features of *mature manhood.*

As a child Jesus heard these psalms sung; as a child He joined the "grown-ups" in singing them. When He attended the feast of the Passover as a lad, the Hallel fell upon His ear. Who can tell? Perhaps the questions the twelve-year-old Jesus put to the teachers in the temple concerned texts and issues drawn from the Hallel and from the hymns which the pilgrims sang upon entering Jerusalem. As a child, then, Jesus grew up by the psalms; as perfect man He grew *towards* the psalms. And as a man He has now grown into maturity *with* the psalms and before the eyes of God.

God tested the quality of the holy sacrificial lamb. While testing, He asked also whether the psalms resonated purely enough in Jesus' soul, whether He had been sufficiently sensitive to them *to fulfill them on the cross.* Only that poet, surely, can *fulfill* his own psalms who has understood them and fully responded to them. O, boundless mercy! O, unfathomable mystery!

This poet first sang of Himself. Thereupon, as a human being, He tried to understand Himself and to fathom His own significance. Now, the greatest thing must still be done. He must vindicate the psalms by *doing* what He witnessed concerning Himself beforehand. The autobiography of humiliation and exaltation consisted of prophecy only: the *deed* had to fulfill it.

Now the Christ comes to do the will of Logos and Spirit. The poet's human soul addresses the Divine Spirit of the Poet, as He bends to hear: Yes, I come to do Thy will; in the beginning of *my* book it is written of me . . . I am coming, I come. The time is at hand. It has come. It is coming. Now the Poet no longer *speaks* of Himself but *does* what He spoke of Himself before. Look, He is going out into the mount of Olives. He is looking for the humiliation, for the exaltation. He makes His own psalms come true. He writes His signature under His prophetic autobiography. By that He is saying: All that this hymn said of me is true; I am going out to prove that; God grant me my reward, Amen. — So the Christ swears to the truth of His own psalms. In this way heaven tests the lamb who realizes His own law, and experiences that law with the whole of His perfect being. And heaven names the lamb flawless, perfect.

You see—Jesus *sang* the hymn of praise *for our salvation also.*

To go on. Where would we end if we should inquire into the content of the Hallel in detail under this evangelical light?

Read Psalms 113 and 114 again, thinking as you attend to each phrase of "Jesus in the room of the Passover" and then ask yourself whether the designation "chief musician" was ever so meaningful as now. But you see so many glorious implications that you can hardly be specific about them. There is no boundary, no limit, to the significance of the lines, when you sense the Messianic meaning in terms of that comprehensive notion: Christ on the night of the Passover.

It begins very directly in Psalm 113:

Praise ye the Lord.
Praise, O ye servants of the Lord,
Praise ye the name of the Lord.
Blessed be the name of the Lord
From this time forth and for evermore.
From the rising of the sun unto the going down of the same
The Lord's name is to be praised.

That is the *Lord's Prayer,* is it not, which Jesus Himself composed? Blessed be the *Name: Hallowed be Thy Name.* May Thy Name resound from East to West, from the sun's rising to its setting. *Thy Kingdom Come.* Where are the servants of the Lord? *Thy will be done.*

You go on, and read that the Lord *dwells on high, that He beholds the things that are in heaven, and in the earth,* and raises the poor up out of the dust. Those thoughts again illustrate the central motif of God's self-revelation in Christ, the motif of transcendence and immanence. These two are conjoined in the Cross. We think about it for years: Jesus experienced it in one instant.

Or, read Psalm 114. *When Israel went out of Egypt*—that is the theme Jesus experienced personally as a child. As a man He appreciates the full content of it now. It is a theme which asserts that He is in perfection the Son who was called out of Egypt, but who later will be made a slave again in that same Egypt. (Revelation 11:8).

Listen to Jesus sing of God as He who

. . . turned the rock into a standing water,
The flint into a fountain of waters!

That was fulfilled this very night. Paul tells us later that the rock which issued forth water was Christ; the *stone* which poured out the water, it followed, *and* the water were Christ. Today, in the profoundest, most exalted sense, the stone will pour out water at the cross; today the living stream of grace will flow from a fountain which no force can avail to stop. The law of the Red Sea (verse 3) will be fulfilled today, just as the baptism of water "in Moses" will be fulfilled in the baptism of fire in Christ. The hymn of Moses (Psalm 114) will be fulfilled and will become a hymn of Moses *and the Lamb* (Rev. 15).

Again, listen to Jesus' voice in Psalm 115:

Not unto us, O Lord, not unto us,
But unto Thy name give glory.

Surely, the *Servant* of the Lord is saying this. And He alone can perfectly appreciate the fullness of its meaning.

In the same psalm Christ summons the house of Aaron to service and praise. But it must be that His soul weeps in the summoning. True the house of Aaron urges Him to sing praise to the priests of Aaron; nevertheless Aaron's house does injustice to His own psalms by the cross. Yes, He will sing to the house of Aaron until the end, for thus "it becometh Him to fulfill all righteousness to Aaron." Nevertheless, He will also assert Himself in the right and strength of Melchizedek, and in that way fulfill Psalm 115 (which treats of the difficulties of the annual struggles of Aaron that cannot come to rest) in Melchizedek's single, perfect, priestly deed (Hebrews 10).

We will go no farther. We would go out of bounds if we cited Psalm 115:

and:

I love the Lord, because He hath heard my voice;

The sorrows of death compassed me,
And the pains of hell got hold upon me...
Then called I upon the name of the Lord.

and again:

O Lord, truly I am Thy servant,
I am Thy servant and the son of Thine handmaid;
Thou hast loosed my bonds.

(In that last line Christ is prophesying deliverance from His passion beforehand.)

Then there is the 117th Psalm, in which *all the peoples,* the vast extent of the earth, confront Jesus' attention, and in which He gives a direct answer to Satan who once showed Him *all the Kingdoms*—but not in relevance to the Psalm, of course; you remember the event: it was the third temptation in the wilderness.

And where, pray, where would we reach an end in this treatise, if we were to think of Psalm 118 as Jesus sensed it. Think of

The Lord is on my side; I will not fear:
What can man do unto me?

and of:

They compassed me about like bees;
They are quenched as the fire of thorns
For in the name of the Lord I will destroy them.

Of:

I shall not die, but live,
And declare the works of the Lord

And, again, of:

The stone which the builders refused
is become the head of the corner.

No, we shall cite no more. All those passages constitute a unit in the soul of Jesus. His appreciation of the Hallel was Messianic throughout. These psalms represent prophecy looking to the *future*. The future was also in Jesus. There are liturgical hymns (113, 115) in this Hallel—but the greatest Liturgist was Jesus. One of the hymns, Psalm 118, represents a chorus for antiphonal singing: the one sings, the other responds. Perhaps the disciples sang it in reply to Jesus' first song. If so their meager expression of its rich symbolism must have hurt the pure soul of Jesus, which had sung and was singing perfectly. But when there was none to help Him, His own arm provided support. When no chorus could adequately respond, His own mouth replied to His singing. Jesus sang the song and the response *alone*. And, no wonder: the dialogue was a monologue for the Poet.

He sang "pro omnibus." Jesus, pray for us, sing for us! Holy Father, hear Jesus sing; listen to Him singing alone, His hand on the door of the palace of Thy holiness. Father, no salvation is possible for us, save in Him. He sings vicariously; He sings alone; but in Him all His own also sing: *Thou hast heard their voice.*

Suppose a poet had been present in the room of the Passover, or a psychologist, or a dramatist, or Bach, or Beethoven. Would they have sung better, been better aware of the soul, composed a more significant drama, given expression to better music? Perhaps—better, more artistic, more moving, perhaps. But, if so, the superiority would not be owing to their natural ability, to the externals of these matters, but because of *faith* and by reason of *revelation*.

And if they had not believed and had really been present, and had heard and seen in actuality—then they would have cursed, and gnashed their teeth, and have sounded diabolical chords on their organ.

After all, this miracle moves in a medium between heaven and hell. We are in it or we are entirely out of it. This is not a poet's benefit—but then by faith, by Him, alone.

We abide here. We should never dare to sing again, were it not for the fact that Christ's *Mediatorship*, singing for us vicariously, is included in this chapter next to the emphasis on the *perfect* Poet and the *pure* singer. God be praised. That Mediatorship is present in the chapter and ever will be. Hence we shall not try to sing "as beautifully as Jesus" (think of the vanity!) but, nevertheless, in His strength and by His grace. We were not present when He sang the hymn, did not attend the premiere, and were not spectators, students, "of the first class."[1] But we are not jealous of the disciples who were present. To *hear* Jesus the Poet-chanter, is a matter of faith. Whoever is internally, sincerely called—he it is who really hears with his soul, who really listens to God. He it is who not only was present but still is and if he listens to His Master's voice and then sings the Hallel of the feast of "spiritual" liberty, he is joined with Christ in his song by a *mystical union*. Jesus still remembers in heaven that He sang on that day of the Passover (Hebrew 5). His human soul as well as His Divine Spirit respectively bends towards and enters into each human heart which believes in Him, as a child, and yet as an "anointed" singer.

Through the Spirit Jesus still sings the hymn of praise each day in the corridors of our heart. This phenomenon is called mysticism. Use that word sparingly: Jesus and the Spirit, and the entire content of this chapter are back of it. Use the word sparingly.

But sing lustily. Sing by virtue of the blood; sing of the blood. Sing by virtue of the cross; sing of the crown. Quiet, Peter: just be quiet: we "have a more sure word of prophecy." And we have the hymn of the New Testament, for Jesus bore the Hallel from the Old Testament into the New while singing it.

Now we have the *true tabernacle,* for the Author of the psalms Himself became the Precentor of it. His Spirit has qualified us

---

1. Kierkegaard uses this phrase.

to sing through Him and with Him—to sing frailly, very imperfectly, but perfectly in principle.

In this true tabernacle the Hallel still searches out heaven; Christ and His Spirit still sing it to Themselves, for the Father's glory.

The mount of Olives has been left behind long ago; but just now an angel heard a Hallel arising from Java.

Christ's Sorrows Have Their Own Peculiar Origin

CHAPTER SEVENTEEN

Christ's Sorrows Have Their Own Peculiar Origin

- *Then cometh Jesus with them unto a place called Geth-*
  semane . . . .
  And (he) BEGAN to be sorrowful and very heavy.
  —Matthew 26:36a and 37b.

WE shall follow the Master out of the room of the Passover
now and into the garden of Gethsemane.

Gethsemane — people generally let their voices drop
when they reach that point in the story of the passion. The Bible
itself, however, *shocks* us by the use of the word; it does not put
us into a mystical twilight so much as it startles us by it.

It is as if the gospel of the passion simply lets us drop out of the
heights into the abyss. The transition is so abrupt that it almost
hurts us.

Certainly the contrast of what Jesus did in the room of the
Passover to what He is to experience in Gethsemane is sharp
enough to arrest the attention of everyone.

In the room of the Passover we saw Christ in His exalted
strength and in the beauty of the harmony of His life. How calm
His voice was when He spoke to Judas, when He took the bread,
when He sang the hymn; how quiet His voice, whispering when
they asked that He whisper, loud at other moments, engaging in
long discourses, even, when that was His pleasure.

The *restlessness* of Gethsemane is set in sharp contrast to that
picture of poise and calm.

He leaves the room and crosses the Kidron. He is looking for
the garden He had frequently visited. We know that He is familiar with the place. Its strangeness is, therefore, not the reason for
which restlessness suddenly enters into Him and seizes on His

soul. The place itself is not strange to Him. The circumstances, the exigencies of the place, cannot account for the turbulent passion arising in Jesus' soul.

In this we confront a riddle. A quiet voice almost engaging in recitative calm before God. That in the room of the Passover. And here in Gethsemane the black shadow. There He progressed from one act to another. Here He repeats the same act, He goes and comes back, He prays and returns to pray again.

In the room He engaged in an organized discourse; its structure, its artistic interrelationship of part and whole still amazes us. That high-priestly prayer, too, rising from the more ordinary to the sublime in a beautiful crescendo of significance — how artistic that was! That prayer reaching down to the bases of God's good pleasure, reaching up to communion with God, reaching out to include more and more, the gamut of His people, the apostles first and then the one holy, catholic, Christian church — how amazing the restrained eloquence of that temperately evolved prayer! And in its stead, in Gethsemane, there is the *repetition* of the same words, a constant returning of the same theme. Instead of the progressive prayer in the room of the Passover comes the retrogressive prayer in Gethsemane.

And those are not all of the contrasts.

We cannot name them all; we need not name them all, for they all arise from the same cause. We can concentrate the contrasts into this one: In the room of the Passover, Christ is He who *gives,* He who gives Himself to His own. Exalted and absolute, He performs His work for them. But in Gethsemane Christ is the poor and naked one who receives. He is a child; so very helpless that He cries for a few faithful friends, who, be it for but one hour, may watch with Him—

What is this, anyway? A riddle, of course, which arrests the attention of everyone. But what is the reason, the cause of it? What calls the stark contrast into being? What unseen hand smote Christ down from that poised assurance into this profound misery and undoing?

We shall have to discriminate carefully in this matter.

There are those who put the problem in such a way that their very formulation of it protests that the problem itself, not its solution, is the issue of contention between them and us. Their way of stating the question indicates that their notion of Scripture and their view of Christ is diametrically opposed to ours. The riddle *as they see it* does *not* startle, does *not* perturb us at all—although we dare not suppose that we can fathom all of the implications of what we think we know about the night in Gethsemane.

But there is another riddle which busies and baffles us, even when we separate ourselves from all who view the Christ in a way differing from ours.

Perhaps we ought to say first in what the riddle does not consist for us; and to say then in what it does consist.

Over against those who say that what baffles them in Gethsemane is the fact of Christ's being sorrowful and heavy even unto death, in other words, of His terrible suffering, we confess that His sorrow *in itself,* that the fact as such of His being sorrowful unto death does not constitute the riddle for us.

Let there be ever so many who can no longer "believe" because of Christ's "sorrow": our faith teaches us to reason in the precisely opposite direction. Wash those awful drops of sweat from the face of the Man of sorrows, retouch the outlines of the face which is wrung with sorrow, let the turbulent waters of His soul subside and become placid — but then Christ *is no longer our Saviour.* We cannot follow Him, cannot believe, cannot even see Him except as He is in this nameless anguish.

We know there are those for whose "faith" the *anguish* of Christ is the one great stumbling block. If only Jesus had not stumbled upon any stone they would gladly have accompanied and followed Him to the temple of worship, and have religiously identified themselves with this great example of spiritual nobility. And now, alas! They complain that Christ was not as great as that. He stumbled on the way. He trembled. He was heavy even unto death. Consequently they now fall over the stumbling Christ. A Christ who cannot maintain His poise is a rock of salvation for their own unintimidated haughtiness. But a Christ who falls over a rock of offense becomes a rock of offense to them.

They do not know that by that very attitude they are confessing their own essential smallness and, although unconsciously, are really *honoring* Him.

To say that the sorrows of Christ must make them surrender their faith in Him is to propose an argument which unbelief cannot justify on its own bases. If Christ by simply remaining always erect, and without ever creeping in the dust, can be our guide, and if we lift "ourselves" up by grasping Him — then His going before us is less His glory for leading than *ours* for being able to keep pace with Him. Our fitness for life is not His steadfastness in such a case, but is simply His illustration of steadfastness which we in our own strength can then proceed to emulate. There lies the inconsistency. If Christ were acceptable without suffering, without quailing under the wrath of God, and if everything depends, as it then does, upon *our ability* to lift ourselves — why, then, does our ability fail when His does? When I claim to be the hero, when I arrogate to myself the courage to judge or condemn His heaviness and sorrows, you may certainly expect me to *prove* my claim to such arrogance, my right to such criticism, my warrant for such self-trust by standing erect myself, by standing out above every storm with perfect poise.

But — if I cannot do that, I should have the good sense to begin on the other side: not on that where I illuminate the Christ with my own poor searchlight; but on the other, where I let Him explain Himself, also as He is in His sorrows, and in that way learn to tremble before Him.

That, over against the unreasonableness of all belief, would be the reasonableness of faith.

However that may be, this much is certain: If the stumbling Christ is an offense to me, if *His* falling causes me to stumble, *then His greatness is exhibited even by that fact.* If I really amount to so much, my heroism will be but the better illustrated in contrast with the smallness of Him who in Gethsemane called Himself not man but worm. However, if I can allow myself no such haughtiness, I must be honest and cry out before God that His misery proves mine far worse—or else, with a profound respect, *believe* on Him.

Obviously, this is a case of *choosing* or *sharing.*

Any comparison which puts Christ in a class with other men in an effort to measure and weigh His worth is a terrible analogy and is folly in God's eyes.

This artist, that psychologist, yonder philosopher, the expounder of revelation, the poet, the biographer who produces his "life of Christ" — these and many others almost invariably pause in the argument, introduce a caesura in their poem or soul-analysis the moment they come to Gethsemane, the place where Christ is depressed, is sorrowful, is heavy even unto death, and is sweating blood. It becomes tiresome, almost, to notice that this is the case again and again in the abundant literature of the world and of recent times.

One can hardly turn to an "essay" on Gethsemane without hitting upon that characteristic usage of bringing Socrates or some other hero of the spirit into comparison with Christ. It is so easy to find examples of people who died without a sense of dread, without the experience of intense anguish, or at least of people who approached death less anxiously than Christ. World history, national history, the history of culture, the galleries of great men dead will afford such examples. People read us their names and ask: What is your opinion? Are these who drink the hemlock courageously, who serenely approach death by the sword, in the arena, or by suffocation — are these not greater than the man Jesus Christ?

We should like to answer this question with a counter-question, for it is warranted "to answer a fool according to his folly."

We would ask: Why go so far afield? The dying chambers of philosophers, the battlefields of the world, the guillotines where political betrayers met death, are not the only places affording examples of people who faced death with a calmer mien than Christ in Gethsemane. *His own brethren, His co-heirs with God,* those whose redemption He purchased, have often confronted a martyr's death courageously, faced it with a sureness, a trust, a calm very different indeed from the turbulence, the humiliating misery, the quailing of the Man of sorrows in Gethsemane. How does it happen, we would ask in turn, that you appeal to all of those others, to philosophers, soldiers, political agitators in order to disparage the Christ, while you fail to scrutinize the equally interesting personalities of Jesus' own martyrs.

You do not *want* to see these, we should have to add. For if you would really look squarely into the martyr's eyes, your whole argument would *crumble* by the message you would read there. These Christian martyrs never asserted that their awaiting death calmly puts them in a position above the Christ. What they did say, the one thing they did aver, was that precisely the adequacy of Christ, and their eye of faith kept fixed upon the afflictions and sorrows of hell which He suffered, enabled them to stand firmly poised. Just because Christ was "a worm and not a man" they, judged by human standards, and in principle even by God's, were "men, not worms."

Hence, it must be admitted that any comparative study of Jesus' anguish, that is, any purely comparative study of it, is unscholarly, dishonest, and secretly antipathetic if it has not the courage to include Jesus' own martyrs, and nevertheless rests its case upon the comparison solely.

If anyone who has the courage of his own criteria will as objectively place himself before the urns that hold the ashes of the martyrs as he does before the biers of philosophers, generals, and political agitators who died serenely, then he must admit that those too did not suffer the anguish which Jesus suffered. The carefully formulated questions will disappear before those urns. The blood of the martyrs will spatter upon the dainty vellum on which this or that "scholar" compares Jesus with others and finds Him wanting. These martyrs are the very ones who proved, not in the comfort of a study, but in the gory medium of mud and slaver, of fire and battle, of wild beasts and fanatic people, that we must not *measure* Christ but weigh Him, to the extent that is possible — they, precisely, have said that we must not ask whether the "apparatus" of His humanity functions exactly as it does in other members of humanity, that there is another view according to which Christ is not merely "a member" of the body of humanity (that would have to function exactly as all other members) but that He is *the Head* of the body. That stipulation means that a different law of life lives in Him than obtains in people *not included in Him*. The *Head* must necessarily differ from the members. The Head must be thrust under the breakers of wrath in order that the members may remain standing in freedom and joy. In Jesus, the Mediator who is the Guarantor of a better covenant is punished and afflicted for the sake of the others. He must suffer all sorrows for them, must writhe because of awful anguish in order that the members of His body may without any dread at all see God's judgment seat standing behind the arena, the guillotine, or the deathbed.

If only the concept of *substitution* is brought into the argument, the *folly* of thinking the discovery that Socrates acted differently than Jesus in a similar situation a significant one, will become obvious.

The most superficial observer will notice a pronounced difference between these two, even in regard to peripheral aspects of their life and death. But there is an infinite difference between them in respect to the principle, the point of view, the life-secret of each.

Yes, it is obvious that even a casual observer will notice a peripheral difference in the "phenomena" of Socrates and Jesus. That difference alone names every comparison of the two a piece of folly.

Socrates calmly drank the cup of poison which had been concocted by misinterpretation and bad faith; he took and drank it serenely when legal coercion and the popular will extended it to him. But when Socrates entered into his death serenely, he did so at the cost of much that is lovely and beautiful. In him we can afford to lose the lovely and beautiful, but we may not dare to lose them in Christ. Socrates' scorn of the judges and people represents a haughtiness and arrogance which knows not love. Do we want to see Jesus as such?

Again: Do we want to think of Jesus as one who lives on a plane far above that on which one's wife and children try to get on, as an aristocrat of the spirit who is hardly affected by such domestic responsibilities? On the contrary, Jesus cries for and weeps about His disciples now and again, assigns His mother a son later on, engages in no abstract discourses about His right doctrine, but bears that doctrine in Him as His life, clinging to doctrine and life together and sealing them with His death.

We need not dodge the issue any longer: Socrates was able to face death fearlessly simply because he succeeded so enormously well in the art of suppressing. And we have seen repeatedly that Christ never suppresses anything. Therefore, it is folly to compare the serene courage (probably legendary at that) of Socrates with the sorrows of Christ, the "historical" one. Socrates lives only a half-life (in that he suppresses the bitterness of death) and consequently can die only a half-death. But Christ lives with all that is in Him. Therefore, He also dies in *entirety*.

Moreover, Socrates only lets us guess at his life-secret. Yes, his speeches were notated by his friends, but who can say what he experienced as he lay in his solitary cell awaiting the gaoler, the cup, and the last nod of the judges. But Christ permitted the anguish He felt to be recorded for us. In fact, He wrote the description of His sufferings Himself, through the Spirit. He took His disciples with Him up to a distance a stone's throw removed, and later He *revealed* His anguish and groanings to us in the Holy Gospel.

Whoever cannot see these differences, peripheral as they are, is blind. It is about time for Christendom to cease responding to such "comparative" studies by "apologetic" arguments supported with material borrowed from psychology and from religious-philosophical theories.

And we are certain that similar differences, even such *external* ones, obtain between Jesus in Gethsemane and those other figures who, according to report, approached death unafraid.

Enough of that, however. We must not forget the most important thing. We must *not* answer the fool according to his folly—that, too, is written in the book of Proverbs. And, remembering that warning, we wish by a few brief indications to point to the principal reasons which compel us to call such "comparative" studies the product of the devil.

a. Christ's *task* differs from that of any other human being. His task is to suffer the *penalty* sin has deserved. Hence, it is part of His calling to quail in anguish before our God. What sense, then, is there in making any comparisons if we accept this His own pronouncement concerning His work. *One would need to have been in hell for some time* in order to understand what it is that is tearing Jesus apart in the garden. Hence, because neither subject nor object of hero-worship has any sense of the reality of hell's temptation and pain, the problem of suffering for those others was never what it is for Christ. And therefore the two kinds of suffering cannot be spoken of in the same breath.

b. Christ is a human being *in a way very different* from that of other human beings. He is the sinless one. Who can say how intensely or in what manner the discharges of sin, of curse, of suffering, of Satan, and of death affected him? It would be difficult to compare the effect light has upon a photographic lens or plate with that which it has upon a stove-plate. We should call anyone mad who could seriously contend as follows: A stove-plate does not change its nature when light plays upon it; a photographic plate does change under such a circumstance: I conclude that a stove-plate is a useful article because it retains its character in contact with light; and that a photographic plate is a useless thing, a luxury, a piece of foolishness, for it cannot stand the light. But it is not less stupid for anyone who acknowledges Christ as the Sinless One to compare those stove-plate personalities who do not react to outside influences, or who are affected by the play of light and shadow but very little, with Jesus, who, like a finely prepared photographic plate, reacts immediately to every change of light and shadow, and upon whom God is today directing His carefully aimed arrows of righteousness, truth, and judgment. A human being who is himself suffocated by sin should not allow himself the luxury of talking about the reaction of light and shadow upon the sinless soul of Jesus. Or, if we may continue with the figure just alluded to, without becoming trivial, we can say that no one in the world ever "worked with" *this* particular photographic plate. This is the first time and the only time that *such* a light falls in this way through *such* a lens upon *such* a plate. Even the sensitive lens of Adam's soul in the state of sinlessness had a different law of reaction from that of Jesus' soul. The time was a different one, and especially—the reception was different. Neither sin nor curse, neither suffering nor death had a place on earth. And what shall we say of Christ's soul, which suppressed nothing, neither God nor devil. We who suppress so much cannot judge of Him. We must believe or be silent.

c. *The way which death takes in the life of Christ,* and consequently the way the threat of death takes, is *very different* for

Him than for other human beings. Those others who have to die and who bear the burden of it bravely—but without faith— subordinate death to their thoughts (the "suppression" referred to above has relevance here also). But Christ may not ride "rough-shod" over death. On the contrary, He must look death squarely in the face, must to a certain extent so master and draw out death's complication that He Himself, when the time comes, can work His way towards death and implicate Himself in it. He will do that the moment the imperative of death has appeared to be God's way for Him.

d. Other people who are about to die debate with themselves until the thought of death wins over the thought of life after death, or the thought of immortality wins over the dread of death. They play off life against death, and then laugh; or if so be they complain, because fate, or God, gives them death for life—in that case the skies re-echo their groaning. But Christ may never play off death against life. He may not wrench himself, or leap, over the river of death by a *tour de force.* If in His heart or His head He wants to chant a hymn in praise of the spacious Elysian fields of a life after death, He can do so. But He may never accelerate the motor of the hope that is in Him to such vehemence that its noise drowns out the sighs and groanings of His soul. There is only the one law for Him: He can achieve life only by losing it completely, by paying the whole of it as ransom, and only by experiencing this loss with full consciousness of it. The life to *come* may be a sedative, a resting-place, for others in confronting the present death, but because Christ is the Surety for His own, the life to come simply is another force compelling Him to die, and in no sense a compensation while death itself is swallowing Him.

e. And still another difference is related to that last one. Those other heroes of death which we designated conquer the death of the *body,* and do it with the soul, or better, with the *spirit.* Their bodies die, but their spirits do not in the way their bodies do. The spirit, in fact, often whets itself on the dying body. That spirit does not "taste" death. That spirit retains mastery of what it has not itself tasted or felt. Suppose we call the planes of body, soul, and spirit planes A, B, and C, respectively.[1] The situation in the case of these heroes, then, is this. They suffer, they experience death only on plane A (the body); little more than the smoke of the firing line on plane A reaches plane B (the soul); on plane C (the spirit), the heavy cannon of strong argument are put into action against the enemy on plane A; and this is done solely to keep that enemy from subduing plane C. The plane on which they prove to be heroes (C, the battle-ground of the spirit) is in essence different from plane A upon which the attack is directed. The *spirit* does not rejoice in keeping death from conquering it, for death cannot touch it, but the spirit comforts itself in its aloofness from body and soul. It comforts itself on plane C in thinking of an enemy which is destroying plane A. Plane B meanwhile feels only the shocks of the concussions going on below it. Really, then, *this is not* a conquering of death; it merely represents a kind of victory of the personality in itself, a personality, you see, which has discovered that it *does not have to die.* No blood actually flows in the sphere of the spirit. There is no man-to-man conflict in it. All speeches made by dying people at the hour of death, all speeches of comfort not deriving their content from Christ, have been motivated by the saying: *non omnis moriar*: "I shall not wholly die."

Christ is entirely different. When He sees death coming upon Him, He sees it coming upon every plane of His life. His body must die (plane A), His soul must die (plane B), and His spirit[2] must die (plane C). He must take full cognizance of death, and must experience it fully; He must know and He must sense temporal death (the separation of soul and body), spiritual death (the grievous, temporally experienced separation from God, in the sense of being forsaken by Him) and eternal death (the complete realization of the consequences of being forsaken of God according to the spirit). Who, pray, can now dare to undertake comparing Christ *with others?* Christ could not set up any cannon on plane C with which to stifle the firing on plane A, to the

---

1. It will not be necessary, I trust, to say that, in using these terms, I am using them simply as figures of speech, and that I refuse to be drawn into any discussion of the psychology of the matter, especially of the great issue of soul and spirit.

2. Not His person: for the person of the Son of God must also will to die in His perfect human nature.

extent He was bothered by its din on planes B and C. The vapors of death penetrate each part of His human being. God disarms Him completely because God Himself by means of that death enters into Him—and that Christ knows. To Christ, death is not an enemy which His spirit can avert as a bystander; death comes upon Him; no, death forces its way into Him. It completely enters into Him, and it enters into His whole being.

f. It is quite possible for people who must die to put themselves on guard against the fear of death and against its overwhelming effect, but such activity is always partial.

A man may act very bravely, may set up a great ado with his weapons against the great tyrant Death, and may succeed in suggesting to himself and to others that he is master of the situation: secretly, however, the one certainty nevertheless remains that nothing can be done about it, that he is going to die anyway. His poise could be taken seriously only if he could say: I have power (the qualifications) to lay it down and I have power (the qualifications) to take it up again (John 10:18). But *he cannot say that*; the thought does not occur to him. Hence the struggle he carries on is never perfect; he can act never so bravely, but he has not the chances of a lion in the woods; his chances are those *of the lion in the zoo.* He simply reconciles himself with a death which he must accept as his lot. He can exert himself actively over against it? Yes—but his activity is circumscribed within the boundaries of passivity. His activity has such an easy task, moving about as it does, and orientating itself in a room locked by a higher power. As long as people are still alive and well and in full possession of all their desires, the distance between passivity and activity is as wide as life itself. But the moment a person discovers that the door giving access to liberty and the ability to move about freely, *has been locked,* and that the cell will never open again, then a limited activity exerts itself within that small bourne as in an arena ever getting smaller and smaller. The race which the soul then undertakes to run with itself is confined to the tiniest course which life was friendly enough still to afford.

Jesus Christ is not that man. His door has not been locked behind Him. The awfulness of His griefs can only be seen properly against this ideational background: I have the power to lay down life, and to take it up again. His race-course does not get smaller and smaller. His responsibility never diminishes. The tension remains. Passively and actively, His task is equally exacting. The pressure is never taken off. He cannot "rest" in the fact that He has to die "anyway" and accordingly conclude: Since the door of liberty is locked to me, I shall undertake once more to move about freely within the bounds of my fixed limitations. For Him the tension between *passive* and *active* obedience persists to the very end. If it had been so that Christ first had to see the passion approach Him up to a certain point, and that He then could have done the deed of obedience within the limited pale still left Him—then the awful tension would have decreased progressively as the end approached. That, however, is not the case: in Him passive and active obedience simultaneously grow stronger and stronger.

g. Human beings other than Jesus confront only an *individual* struggle. An individual man must die: he lives his own life first, and dies his own death then. And his death represents his own judgment alone. Christ, on the contrary, is not *"a man"*; He is *"the* man"; He dies very conscious of the fact that He is the *second Adam,* that He is the *Head* of the new humanity which is included in the covenant of grace. In His death, it is not a single chip which is broken from some rock jutting off the mountain of mankind; in it the shock of death is felt in the *base,* in the *foundation* of all humanity for whom He is entering into death. He stands solitary over against God, not as an individual but as the second Adam. Death separates them, and God says: *Take thou and eat.* Judged by human standards there is but *a step between Jesus and death,* for that is the sense, the tragic content of the statement of David and Jonathan, of everybody, of you and me, of anyone who has no command over death, no power over it; it is the grievous plaint of all who must suffer death as their *lot.* But Christ does not have to *suffer* death as His *lot;* He must accept it as His righteous judgment, because He is the Surety for His own, and because His suretyship, though it obligates Him to perfect passivity must nevertheless be *actively desired by Him* from moment to moment. Hence it is not true that there is but one step between Him and death. He must count His steps, but they are numberless because each one represents an act of infinite might. An infinity divides Him and death, even though that infinity is but a step. The way between Him and death is as long and heavy as the way from His forsaken soul to the strict, and silent, and condemning God. A whole *eternity* is between Him and death. He must take death in full awareness of the fact that He is the second Adam, who as the very image of God, and in full possession of His powers, takes it over from the first Adam for all those whom the first Adam conferred upon the second for salvation. The *Mediator's* passion, *vicariously suffered* anguish—who can dare to compare that with the suffering of a faithless *debtor?*

h. Another matter is related to this last one. Other people, to the extent that they have a comfort in death or suppose they have one, are always dealing with the problem of death in terms of time and space. For example, they comfort themselves with examples like these: *Here* I must suffer *a little while; there* I shall live an *eternity;* or: *Here* a light affliction—*there* a "more exceeding and eternal *weight* of glory"; or: On *this* side of the grave I must suffer *this,* on the *other* side I shall enjoy *that.* So when time comforts itself with the thought of eternity at all, it does so as seen from the viewpoint of time, and in that way eternity is so much more readily set in contrast to temporal suffering. In such comforts the weight of the glory to come always weighs heavier in itself than the burden of suffering itself.

This is not so for Christ. The limitations of time and space are not valid references for Him. True, according to His human soul, which is finite and created, He suffers in time and space, but according to His Person He is infinite. The burdens He bears, the weights He sees lying in the balances of His scale— both of these have infinite worth. The contrast for Him is not that of a little time confronting an eternal life, but of an *eternal* life. The contrast is not that of a light affliction over against a more exceeding weight of glory but one of an exceeding weight of misery opposed to an exceeding weight of glory. Christ's conflict is not conditioned by any play of force against force going on outside of Him. He must bear these two eternal weights in His own hands, must freight His soul with the heaviness of both. Who can say anything about that? Who would venture a comparison?

i. The sense of serenity that others have is either the fruit of Christ's suffering or else the unnatural fruit of a vaguely conceived idea of redemption. But Christ Jesus cannot pluck the fruit of a tree that has been planted by another person. He must produce His own fruits, must *produce* them. He suffers the griefs of the sower; hence He will taste the joy of the reaper. There is but one absolute *sower*: He is Christ. Therefore He is the only One who absolutely "sows in tears."

j. Hence others, when their ship arrives in port, may fasten its ropes to the pier; the pier will not recede from him who really seeks. Others may throw out their anchors; these will bite on solid ground for all those who want to anchor in God. And Christ also wants to fix His anchor in God, to moor His ship to the solid pillars of the fidelity and justice of God. But the awfulness of His situation is that God recedes from Him. God forsakes Him at this time. The solid ground recedes from the anchor that would bite on it, the pier recedes from the ship that would be fastened to it. Only after He has been entirely forsaken, after His ship refuses to hold to anything save to God alone, only when His faith, abandoning everything, has infinitely deepened itself—only then will He be accepted, and will He arise from bondage of death.

Once more, and finally, who can venture to make "comparisons"?

We return to our point of departure and repeat that the *fact* of Christ's sorrows and afflictions does not constitute the riddle for us.

On the contrary, without that anguish *He is not our Mediator.* The "back" that is beaten for the sins which mankind has perpetrated by means of Adam's hand, must necessarily feel the pain of the beating.[1]

Nevertheless, *another* difficulty exists for those of us who confess Christ's mediatorship. For us the difficulty arises from the fact that there is a *beginning of* this anguish for Christ, that He sinks down so *suddenly* out of the poised confidence of the room of the Passover into this oppressiveness and anguish. Not the

---

1. The figure is that of Dr. A. Kuyper and in *E Voto.*

fact of its existence, but the sudden genesis of the anguish baffles us, even when we observe from the viewpoint of faith.

What can be the cause of this sudden release of the fountains of suffering which bury Christ's head under their own turbulence?

Does the answer lie in the nature of the life of Jesus' soul? Is His soul really un-steadfast, fickle? Is the apparent inconstancy the product of His own self? Does He throw the beams of His searchlight this way now and that way next, leaving the rest in darkness?

To reply affirmatively would be to do injustice to the soul of Christ. His soul combines in itself the firmness of a controlled life with the serenity and harmony of an equilibrium which is never disturbed, or confused, or thrown out of balance from within. Even though Christ were placed in the chaos of hell, where sirens shriek, and devils scream, and every storm breaks abruptly into the quiet, His soul would not lose its equilibrium there. As long as He moves and stands *with God* His harmony continues. The pauses and intervals of life outside of Christ cannot be the cause of the variations within.

No, the sudden retrogression from the quiet of the Supper to the anguish of Gethsemane cannot be ascribed to the nature of Jesus' soul. Consequently, it cannot be explained in terms of that.

Since we must look for the cause of the change outside of Christ, can we discover it, perhaps, in what *Satan* or *what the people* are doing?

We shudder at making any too definite declaration in reply. Faith so easily goes beyond the boundaries of reverence and caution.

Nevertheless we venture to say something of the matter. The solution to our difficulty can be found in this *in part*. Christ's sensitive soul felt Judas approaching and sensed the coming of the party with sticks and swords to take Him captive. Impending dangers, the immediate approach of "bulls and dogs" (Psalm 22) really were new pricks to His sensitive feeling. For Him, too, the griefs are of graduated intensity; when the storm's violence outside of Him increases, the experiences in His re-echoing soul increase proportionately in intensity. Jesus' soul was purer than that of a telepathist; it was more finely aware of things than a clairvoyant. Hence, in proportion to the extent to which the murderous mob give stronger emphasis to their intention by their deed, the suffering of Jesus increases. They are interfering in this moment with—His prayer; and He must immediately include that disturbing power *in* His prayer. Jesus' impressions respond perfectly to the expressions made outside of Him.

However, that does not fully account for the sudden change in Jesus' soul. For we have repeatedly observed that Christ's passion before this time was very intense *precisely because He saw everything coming beforehand.* Jesus has seen long ago what Judas is at the point of doing now. What Satan has Him experience in the present He anticipated realistically before. He Himself conceived and executed the portrait of His passion and death: This is the terrible outline of Christ and of Him crucified.

Yes, the gradual approach of danger and death, the sneaking up of hell and the devils would suffice to account for a *gradual* aggravation of Jesus' anguish; but this does not adequately explain the sudden intensification of it. Judas and his mob, hell and its spawn, these explain a great deal, but not all.

Now it is our turn to leap for joy. There is only one other way which our trembling thoughts can follow to a solution.

We cannot explain the sudden change by reference to the nature of Jesus' soul, for it can be disturbed by nothing within.

We cannot explain it *entirely* by reference to Judas and the mob and the devils.

Therefore we shall have to find the answer in *the Lord our God.* And hence, as we suggested, there is good reason and even a binding command to leap for joy when Jesus plunges into the abyss, suffering nameless grief. Paradoxical as it may seem, we can shout for joy, for we have seen God.

But a Gethsemane, explicable *solely* in *God's* terms, one which is a perpetually baffling riddle, a repulsive offense and a shocking incongruity, *except* to the person who thinks *theo*centrically— that is *characteristic of the line which is drawn* throughout the Scriptures; that is organically part and parcel of the miracle of God's harmonious plan of redemption; that kind of Gethsemane enables us to escape from the confusion of "psychology," philosophy, and spiritual anatomy; that keeps the law of *faith* unadulterated, unbroken—the law, namely, *that God alone is,* and *that God alone gives, the explanation of His self-revelation in Jesus Christ.*—I thank, Thee, Lord God of heaven and of earth, that Thou hast hid the things of Gethsemane from the wise in psychology, and from the understanding in philosophy, and from the learned in biology, and hast revealed them to the children of believing obedience. Even so, Father, for so it seemed good in Thy sight!

O man, return to your Bible. It is God who explains the significance of this event. He does it by way of His own counsel, and by His own deed, or even by His own refusal to act, by His withholding Himself from communion with Jesus.

The biblical account of Gethsemane tells us in so many words that we may seek the explanation of it only in God Himself. We read in it that God sends an angel to sustain Jesus. Certainly that means that heaven is regulating Jesus' pulse beats.

We hope to consider that particular emphasis again in a later chapter.

But we are pointing to the angel of Gethsemane now solely to indicate that the explanation of the riddle of the garden cannot be given only in terms of Judas and the devils, but that in the final analysis it can be given only in terms of what heaven does or does not do. The energies passing from God to Jesus, from heaven to His tormented heart, from the trinity of God to the man Jesus Christ, those energies, being sent out now and recalled then— they alone can explain the sudden alteration in Jesus' attitude.

That gives our roaming thoughts a point at which they can rest. For it is a terrible thing to see a worm squirming about blindly in God's wide universe. But hope rises again the moment the worm can refer itself to the firm vault of heaven and to the eternal Counsel of God as its standard of direction. Then the firm plan of God's eternal pleasure is still ours and the world has not thinned out into one miserable worm, a worm into which a *Man* has shrivelled. Then the pattern remains with us, fixed and firm in definite outline; it is the pattern, the form of God's faithfulness, of His justice, of His one will, of His wrath and love, of righteousness and judgment.

Thus the secret of Gethsemane is pointed out to us, although not at all discovered to us in all of its far-reaching implications.

Now we know that Jesus' sudden fall from the heights to the depths was as sudden and acute as it was because God began forsaking Him then. My God, my God, why dost Thou begin forsaking Him?

The beginning of Christ's sorrows coincides with the beginning of God's departure from Him.

Again the reaction to what the triune God does and does not do is a perfect one.

This is God's hour to forsake. Up to this time Jesus had to *work*. He had to administer the Passover, to give the Supper; He had to deliver prophetic discoures, to preturb Judas, to impel Satan, to wash the feet—He had to give, always to give. As Mediator He had to perform His daily work calmly.

But the clock of God is striking now.

Now the Father thrusts Him into the abyss of perfect long-suffering, thrusts Him back from the luxury of the Mediator's *deed,* which *gives,* into the pain of the Mediator's forsakenness, which can only cry for help.

Now wrath flares up against Him, for He must know what it means to represent a host of condemned and yet be forsaken of all. God withholds the comfortings of the Spirit, the helpful whisperings of love, the assurances of faith. These He withholds in order that it may become manifest that the Lamb, in spite of His being forsaken, still peers into the darkness, looking for God. To have no voice other than the one voice of the eyes, and with that voice to ask, tremblingly: Where is my God? To be a prophet and to groan with the genuine groanings of all created beings— that is Christ in His awful solitude.

For the present we shall not penetrate farther into these mysteries. Later, when revelation cautiously draws the curtain aside, we shall consider them again.

However, if we are seeking a resting-place for our thoughts now in this consideration of Gethsemane, we must find it in this thought: Any attempt to understand the meaning of Gethsemane is sacrilege and folly *unless it discovers the explanation in the almighty God.*

Gethsemane is not a field of study for our intellect. It is a sanctuary of our faith.

Gethsemane, knowable to Jesus' soul and to ours *only* in reference to God, has a voice for him who can listen. And, because God is its sole interpreter, a radiant light from heaven plays upon the dark obscurity of the garden.

Our feet, now, can stand firm upon the rocks of eternity. In the company of the Word we pass from Christ's depths to our heights. We know that the change in Christ's soul-sufferings put no hiatus there; that the *one* soul which for our lives' sake must preserve its unity unimpaired responded perfectly to what God in the awfullest hour sent over it.

Lightning struck this time. But God released the bolt. Gethsemane witnessed the first test of strength. And the record reads: The whirlwind which blew from heaven did not push the Man of sorrows a hairbreadth over the line God had drawn for Him.

At this point our thoughts return to the conclusion of the first chapter of this book. There, too, we observed that a whirlwind blew out of hell but could not prevail against Christ's equilibrium.

In Gethsemane the whirlwind comes from heaven and beats against Him. But even when God sends the force from heaven the Son of man falls to the ground only in the place where Justice would find Him.

Before we probe farther into the sombrenesses of Gethsemane, we must reverently fold our hands, and say: I thank Thee, Lord, that Thou wast the first to open the way for me into these holy places. I thank Thee that Thou alone dost interpret God to us, through the Word, in Christ. Storms rage, the winds blow, clouds lower, sins scream aloud—but there is an ark. Yes, Lord; see, I go.

The *Lord* closed the door behind me.

To view things Christocentrically is in the final analysis to see them theocentrically.

"We all believe in our hearts and confess with our mouth, that there is one God."

This is for us an awesome but certain beginning. But when Noah discovered that the Lord had closed the door behind him, no one in the ark cared to comment on the necessary ventilation. They held their peace—there, behind the door.

Christ's Sorrows Have Their Own Peculiar Cause

CHAPTER EIGHTEEN

Christ's Sorrows Have Their Own Peculiar Cause

● *Father, if thou be willing, remove this cup from me;*
nevertheless, not my will, but thine, be done.
—LUKE 22:42.

THE burden of the preceding chapter was the necessity of seeing Christ in Gethsemane solely in reference to God. Not what the people do, and not what arises in His own human soul, but what God, from His side, does and does not do —that, we discovered, is the first cause and the quintessential motivation of the experiences, the sorrows, the heaviness which Jesus feels in Gethsemane.

We must cling to that truth. Only the person who holds tenaciously to that fact can succeed at all in becoming aware of the terribleness of Gethsemane.

The event in Gethsemane can come but once. The world could be created only once, and only once be destroyed. Once a human being is born and once he dies. The work which God accomplishes by His special grace happens "once" only. In grace (in distinction from nature) there is only one spring (the sprouting), one summer (the ripening), and one autumn (the harvesting). Precisely so the passion in Gethsemane is unique. It occurs *only once*. It is never repeated; never in history is it repeated. It has no sequel; not in history has it a sequel. No one may say, as someone once did,[1] that Gethesmane and Golgotha are part and parcel of actual life, belonging to it as evening and night belong to day. The extraordinariness of Gethsemane arises from the fact that it took place on one particular day, one not to be counted

---

1. Wittig, Joseph, *Leben Jesu in Palastina, Schlesien, und anderswo,* Munich, 1925, II, p. 253.

as a day among days. Gethsemane took place on *the one day,* the one day (of the Lord).

Remember the *one* great *day* courses through all the days of time. That is the *one day of the Lord.*

The prophets know, and are in hearty agreement with each other in asserting, that the day of the Lord is one day. That day extends itself over all the centuries. Or, to put it more accurately, that day is the day of all the ages taken as a unit. A century, an epoch, is only a subsidiary part of the one "day of the Lord." A century elapses—the timepiece of the day of the Lord ticks its single, dry tick. In fact, the humanly designed and mechanically conceived subdivisions of time into "centuries," and, consequently, the coming and going of these, have preciously little relevance for heaven's timepiece. God's day has its own, distinctive subdivisions. It reckons with epochs, yes, with processes, with periods of growth, maturity, and decay, with the substitutions of one culture for another, with reformations and revolutions—but it reckons with these *in its own way.* Whenever an epoch of world, ecclesiastical, or cultural history has developed fully, the clock which marks the time of the day of the Lord from the origins of Genesis 1:1 to the consummations of Revelation 22:21 strikes the hour loudly, forcefully. For that day of the Lord is the day in which God executes the plan of His counsel. And this plan is one which includes all the centuries in one immense decision. This day's dawning appears in creation as soon as it rises to the plane of redemption as expressed in that promise of Paradise in reference to the seed of the woman and the seed of the serpent.[1] And the morning of that day of the Lord is the calling of Abraham. The time of the grasshopper-plague of Joel's day, of the captivity and the return from captivity, and of the rebuilding of the temple in Jerusalem—that time represents the late hours of the morning of the day of the Lord. That day has its noon in Christ's advent to the world and in His being impelled by the relentless coercion of the ticking of God's clock to the cross and the resurrection. That day's afternoon is completed when the

---

1. Note that the "day of the Lord" is the day of redemption; the "day of God" refers solely to the day of creation. After the fall the "day of God" becomes the "day of the Lord."

Spirit of Pentecost comes to the world.   And that same single day moves to its close during the centuries following.   It will be completed when Christ opens the graves, raises the dead, establishes His seat upon the stars, and leads a regenerated world back to the Father.

Hence it is folly—no, we may say it is blasphemy, to assert that Gethsemane and Golgotha belong to every day as do the evening and the night.   Such blasphemy asserts that there are numerous analagous days in the realm of grace.   If the Preacher who said that in *nature* days come and go, suns rise and set, and that all that exists comes, and goes, and returns again in unprofitable repetition—if he could have raised the same plaint against the history or developments in the realm of grace, the statement made above would be quite true.   Then every man would have his "mount of olives" and every man his "golgotha."

But the startling truth is that in the kingdom of heaven there is but one day, the day of the Lord, the one "jôm" Jahwe."

The conclusion of this?   The clock can strike twelve only once on a single day.   Therefore the clock of Gethsemane can strike only once in the world.

Lift the word once out of the title-page and text of the book of God's counsel—then Christianity is no more, and all that teaches us faith and hope and love becomes vain.   If Christ be *not* raised, says Paul, we are of all men most miserable.   And to that we may add, for this, too, is written in the Bible: if Christ had been raised *twice,* if He had done any single thing twice, we should be the most miserable of all men.   That would have meant that grace had been made subject to the law of nature, that special grace had mingled itself with common grace.   Then the tedium of grace would have fatigued the Ecclesiast even more than that of nature.   We may as well drink the cup of dregs with a Jesus, if he is one who repeats his actions and must drink the cup more than once.   For such a Jesus is our companion in misery, but not our Lord in *redemption.*   Take "once" out of the books of redemption and that writer referred to is correct in saying that any person can experience his gethsemane at a study-table.

Leave the word "once" where it is written and you will see engraved over the gate to Gethsemane and mingled with the leaves of those trees of God this secret truth: "It is appointed unto the *Son* once to die, and *in* this *the* judgment." Then you will appreciate, will have a full sense of the blasphemy of the assertion that Gethsemane could have obtained in the world before this and after. Gethsemane is meaningless except in relevance to Christ and His *specific* work, His *specific* relation to God, His *specific* task as Mediator, and His *specific* cup. Whoever chooses to strike that *specific* character from the record of the garden of Gethsemane will retain nothing but vanity and emptiness. Is Gethsemane "a" place of a cup? On the contrary, it is the place of *this* cup, of this *one*.

THIS cup!

Father, Father, *this* cup. Father, this unique cup; there it is . . . the hand that extends it comes from the hills of eternity.

THIS cup.

Hence, we will care to *believe* Christ. I say that we want to *believe* Him. We shall not prove, not demonstrate, not point out the fact that the little word *once* ignited the atmosphere and seared itself upon His soul. What comes but once leaves us no time for "demonstration." We can only apply scholarship and critical methods to such events as come again and again. If only one star had fallen in the world, only one meteor crashed through the atmosphere, and if only once a person had died, we should be unable to make a study of the phenomena of stars, meteors, and death, or to write a description of them.

If you cling to the truth of that, you will feel—and this is true of our own Christian argumentations also—how blasphemous it is to dissect, rationalize, demonstrate, or point out the plausibility of Christ's sorrows in Gethsemane.

Exorcise such blasphemy; put it far, far away from you.

There is the Christian thinker who likes to compare the experience of Jesus' soul with that in the souls of others, and who prefers to stop with comparison as if to say: My psychological sermon is finished now; I have enabled you to stop trembling; God be gracious to your soul; Amen. But such a thinker does injustice to his soul. He calls that edification (a building up of things) which really is a breaking down. He does not eat the bread of heaven in the temple of God's justice, but he simply nibbles at his own little biscuit while sitting on the tomb of a certain Jesus. And while there he carves his own initials into the wood next to that of other visitors. From the vantage point of that monument he looks out pleasantly upon life. But his argumentation insults the redemptive event, both superficially and essentially.

No, no—we choose to believe; to believe that Jesus experienced the extraordinary experience of the word *once*. We will believe, simply believe, that He keenly sensed how on the one day of the Lord the hands of the clock, built solely for that one day, gradually moved towards twelve.

And in that faith for which—God be praised!—we have no quantitative evidence whatever, in that faith, whose very imperviousness to evidence is the very glory of all, we accept the fact that Christ in Gethsemane trembled before God who sent over Him that one time what He could only once subject Him to.

Had it not been *revealed* we would know *nothing* of it. Because of revelation, however, we know that the cup was prepared. The hand appeared and wrote on the wall: mene, mene, tekel, upharsin. Only the *Surety* could read; only He could not fail to understand it.

The Cup.

The Hand.

The Surety.

Consequently we cannot explain the *individual*, the *characteristic* quality of Gethsemane by reference to a conclusion in some paragraph of a psychological treatise (supposing such conclusions were available). And we cannot discover that peculiar characteristic either by reference to any utterance made about the life of our mind, the life of our *days*, of our *experience*.

Even the Bible does not give us a single statement derived from human suffering and life, by way of saying: Look, this is the key to the *explanation* of Gethsemane.

If the Bible had given us principles derived from human psychological experience to serve as a light in our hands by which we might illumine Jesus Christ in Gethsemane, and so investi-gate the character of His passion, the Bible would thereby have taken the crown and the terribleness of Jesus Christ and Geth-semane away from these.

For example, there is the biblical phrase which heightens the enigmatic character of the riddle of Gethsemane for numerous readers.

I am thinking of the statement in one of the letters of John: *There is no fear in love.* And I am thinking also of the utterance which follows: *Perfect love casteth out fear.*

Many assert that the *riddle* of Gethsemane arises from that first phrase. "In love," it says, "there is no fear." Christ—and in this consists the enigma—has love, has perfect love, and never-theless has a thousand fears.

Moreover, these troubled minds continue: *Perfect love casts out fear.* Is Christ, whose love, certainly, is perfect, unable to vanquish fear? Can He not cast out fear by the act of faith, and, by a sudden motion (as the text indicates), raise Himself again to the heights of poise and serenity? Alas, these are two riddles indeed, they complain.

The first of these is the query as to how it is possible for fear to enter into Christ's soul. The perfect love which is in *us* was imperfect before; of us, therefore, it can be said that fear had its opportunity to enter. But His love was always perfect—how could fear obtrude upon His soul?

And, indeed, from this point of view, that does constitute the first enigma.

And the second (for those who have the courage to proceed to a second over an unsolved first) is that Christ cannot cast out the fear, but constantly falls, rises, falls forward, rises again, goes, returns, and goes again, *repeating the words.* That, surely, re-presents a second "problem." Christ, these argue, does jerk at the ropes, but He is unable to sear them into pieces with the fire of faith and perfect love. Christ does battle against fear, but He cannot cast it out. If an angel had not come to support Him, fear would have exhausted, vanquished Him and laid Him low. Without an angel's intervention *His own soul* cannot cast out the fear. That is the second cause of bafflement.

In that way these observers try to distinguish the parts of Gethsemane, and formulate the question "in reference to" a text which speaks of people (plural) in general who in the days (plural) of their life are repeatedly fighting the fierce struggle of love and fear within the recesses of their souls.[1]

We may as well acknowledge immediately that such considerations also rob Gethsemane of its significance.

John's utterance to the effect that there is no fear in love and that perfect love casts out fear was written for *people* and for all *days*. The statement is not relevant to the one Man on this one day of the Lord.

In man love, when it is perfect, can cast out fear. Exorcising fear, he throws himself and all of his cares and sins into the arms of God. God is ready to receive him. Alas, for misery is his if he does not flee to the Father for refuge.

But God is not prepared to receive the Christ. God thrusts Him away.[2]

Such rejection of man by God, complete and conclusive, a rejection which even bars him from the sphere of "common grace," *never* occurred on earth. It represents the flames of hell licking their way up into Gethsemane.

And the winds of God's common grace do not blow the flames away from the Son of man. And that is why those flames of hell can actually reach the heart of the Son of man. Their tongues penetrate Jesus' heart. And this never previously occurred in the world.

It will never occur again as long as the world remains the world. We know that as long as the world continues, there will be no *unhindered* perseverance of wrath, and no *unhindered* exodus of the curse.

Christ is fully conscious of the fact that the Father does not accept Him. The sacrifice of His lips is refused. All the smoke of the altar of His soul beats down to the ground.

---

1. This is an erroneous way of explaining one part of the Scriptures by another part. Gethsemane cannot be compared, for example, with 1 John 4:18; but it can be compared, for example, with Hebrews 9:12, 26, 28 and 10:7, 10, 12, 14, 20.

2. As we indicated incidentally in the preceding chapter.

In spite of that He may not take His hand from the altar for a second; the sacrifice must remain; the will to sacrifice must continue unabated also.

For that reason Christ must struggle with what He calls "the cup." More particularly, with what he calls: *this* cup. Mark that demonstrative adjective. How often we have used it, and said *"this* cup"! Very often, however, the word "this" is a luxury unbecoming to our lips. For, although we continue to repeat such phrases as "this passion," "this sorrow," "this cup," can we be sure that we really *see the suffering as it actually is?* Often our use of the modifier represents overstatement; and such overstatement curses us when God prepares the cup of suffering, and tells us: Drink ye! In order to use the words "this cup" authentically and sincerely we should have to know what is in it; whether is be filled with curse or blessing. We should have to see, not "any" cup, but *this* cup which God has filled with His specific intention.

Our use of the phrase "this cup" too frequently is applied to a vague significance, and, in that sense, is unwarranted. But there is no hint of a sweeping statement in Christ's use of it in His prayer. His use of "this cup" is a reference to no other cup neither in the sphere of actuality nor in that of possibility. *This* cup grieves Him. This particular one wounds Him fatally. This cup does that in this particular hour of the one day of the Lord.

The meaning of "this cup" can be no other than the fact that Christ finds the door of His Father's house closed to Him. Now is the Son the lost Son.[1] He would arise and go to His Father, but the Father is not awaiting Him; the door of the heavenly mansion is closed. The *Judge* has barred Him from access.

"There is no fear in love." Love and fear, yes. There are two worlds. One is the world of heaven. There love is without fear. Casting out fear can have no meaning in heaven, for heaven is exalted above any need of it.

The other world is the world of hell. In hell there is no love in fear; there fear has sunk to a plane so low that it can not possibly communicate with love.

---

1. In the Dutch the Parable of the Prodigal Son is called the Parable of the *Lost Son.*

Christ Jesus is being bandied back and forth between these two worlds.

He fears, yes, and He dreads. But the will of love, the desire for communion, the longing for God inhere in His fearing. Hence He does not accept hell, and hell does not accept Him. True, hell desires to sift Him as wheat, for He must be quite different if hell is to swallow Him into its depths. Christ fears but His fear is not concerned to constantly cast out love, His fear does not sink down to that plane below the yearning for love. And such a Christ is simply incongruous in hell. Hell cannot accommodate itself to Him that way. He does not blaspheme love in each successive moment and that fact is incompatible with all that is demonic.

But heaven, on the other side, does not receive Him either.

This is a terrible hour; it represents a defeat of Satan but not yet a triumph for the victor. A terrible hour; hell refuses to receive this man, to envelop Him in its death; and He is also unwelcome to heaven. Present in this hour is a fear which still acknowledges love; absent from it, however, is a flourishing love which can rise above fear and abound there luxuriously. Therefore heaven has not yet arrived; therefore, heaven does not receive Him. Where are the friends whom this man befriended? Can they not see that He is in need? The answer is the same—they do not receive Him in the eternal tabernacles.

Christ is thrown back and forth between these two worlds. He is a man without a world. But can we, possibly, say that He is at least a child of the *earth*? No, there is not even that kind of naturalization for Him. The earth, and all things earthly, cannot maintain a separate position between the worlds of heaven and hell. All earthly things must conform themselves to the one world or the other; they are not self-sufficient.

Christ is the *perfectly isolated* one in this hour. That is why He cannot cast off the sorrow. He is living through the *one* hour that never obtained on earth, or in heaven, or in hell. He is experiencing the hour which never will be, neither on earth, nor in heaven, nor in hell.

O terrible hour! The casting out of fear *cannot take place.* Christ cannot leap into God's protecting arms by an act of faith.

And He *cannot* gruesomely blaspheme against God, deny Him, cannot haughtily, superciliously stride past Him who sends out the fears. Consequently, the anguish remains.

God Almighty sends His fears into Jesus' soul and does not want to be denied in these, not for a second, not for an eternity.

The one thing that is left for our faith to do is to acknowledge that Christ's *suffering* is as great as the *labor* of His soul!

To labor against God is the work of hell. That is not Jesus' work. To labor in coöperation with God is heaven. But in this moment the Father is not, at least not audibly, summoning Christ. The Father is silent.

Hence the *suffering*. Here is One whose *nature* desires to labor with God and for Him, and so achieve heaven's law upon earth. But His status is like that of the Man of Sin who opposes God and accomplishes the law of hell upon earth. From this tension Christ's suffering arises. The friction between the external and internal attitudes of Christ Jesus constitutes that suffering. That which is *in* Him is love. That which is *outside* Him draws Him away from the atmosphere, from the God, and from the sphere of love. A great gulf of separation is fixed between Christ's inner being and His *experience* of external things.

But, behold: He prays. The prayer comes at the appropriate time. And Christ's praying is more than an *attempt* to straighten what is crooked; it is itself the straightening. Christ's prayer in Gethsemane is not merely a *way* by which He arrives at a genuine acceptance of what God so relentlessly sends against the Son: it is itself the genuine acceptance.

Observe that there are three elements in Christ's prayer.

The first element is the name of the *Father;* the second is the petition: if Thou be willing, remove this cup from me; the third is the return of the will of God. And that return is not one of spiritual abstraction. It represents the concrete longing of the soul. Not what the soul by virtue of its own inner life might desire must be done, but that which the Father by His eternal counsels would have, that must occur: *Thy will be done.*

These three elements of Christ's prayer restore the proper balance to this completely warped and distorted world of suffering and sorrow.

By His use of the Father's name Christ proclaims the natural relationship between God and Jesus, and He does that above all and in spite of all else. That natural relationship is this: Jesus' desires and God's are one. They merge; they harmonize. What father is there who would give his son a scorpion, when he asks for bread? By this element of His prayer, therefore, Christ names as primary the quintessential, unintermittent communion of love between God and Himself. He prays, but does so in *faith*. The matter of first importance is faith.

From the general (the relationship of love between the Father and His human soul) He proceeds to the particular (the dire need of that human soul which His spirit cannot comprehend). He opposes one element to another in sharp contrast. He names the *great programme* drawn up for the *day of the Lord* since old times—a programme which cannot admit division between the Father and the Child; and, over against it, He places this particular hour in which actuality does not correspond to that programme. Father, Father, listen now: appearance is not reality now. The cup, this cup, is filled with gall, Father. Can love be gall? What father gives his child gall to drink? A law other than that of love which binds Father and Son together has placed this cup before me. Father, Father!

This testimony of Jesus is true.

Justice must accrue to Him; the cup of passion is extended to Him not because of the relationship of love existing between the Father and Son but because of the law of Mediatorship.

At this time the experience of Mediatorship rests upon Jesus' soul with a heaviness of sorrow. True, the consciousness of it had been present in His spirit for years. But now He discovers something not present before: *being forsaken*. Father, Father, why dost Thou *forsake* me? The Mediator's being forsaken of the Father affects *His office* also. Father, all things are possible. I am Thy Son; cannot that fact be united with the office of Mediator; does the relation of the Mediator rule out that of the Child? My Father——

Listen, for the third element follows: Not My will, but Thine, be done!

By this petition His trembling soul again builds the bridge of obedience and faith which can lead Him away from the passing experience of this one moment of the day of the Lord, and guide Him across it to the great programme of the one day of the Lord. And *justice* as well as love is a part of that great programme.

Love and—justice, yes. First, in the invocation of the prayer ("Father"), *love* is acknowledged and retained as the basic article of unity between Father and Son. Now, at the conclusion of the prayer, *justice* is acknowledged as the other basic article of the programme, and thus of all of the moments, of the day of the Lord.

Love—and—Justice. The Love of the Father and the Will of Justice, both are acknowledged. In this way Jesus interposes *"this* cup" (the passing experience) between the two fundamental principles of the day of the Lord: namely, *infinite love* and *infinite justice.*

He interjected the "moment" into the single "day"; He placed His personal struggle between the two pillars of love and justice; He interjected temporary experience into the eternally abiding. And this was for *our preservation.*

By this prayer Christ explained time in terms of eternity and not eternity in terms of time. He illuminated the moment by the day, and not the day by the moment. He brought that relationship about, not by the abstract erudition of the prophet, still less . . . in this instance—by divine prescience, but by living, vital humanity. He achieved it by a labor which had to achieve the task of obedience from its rudiments upwards, and had to proceed from the depths of essential humanity and limitation. Yes, he had to proceed from a basis of human limitation, of short-sightedness. To use such terms is not to compare Jesus with other men, but is designed to stress the fact that He is looking upon things with the eyes of man, and not with those of God. This genuine humanity in His distressing labor is our salvation. What the Son, what the Word as God, does from eternity, Christ does now as man, and *in time.* Eternity and time, that which *is* and that which is *becoming,* the static and the moving, God's virtues and the agonies of all time—these He is joining together in the one way that is pleasing to God.

Precisely because this task had to be performed *without God's assistance*, because He had to accomplish in a state of *forsakenness* what had ever been done in fellowship with God, therefore this task represented—suffering! Have no fear, however. We are looking upon Jesus as the Christ. Yes, the eternal pressure of wrath weighs upon Him; but the perfect strength of His human soul, and the personal will of the eternal Son assert themselves against that pressure and permit Christ to be buoyed up precisely there where it bears most heavily upon Him. This tension, arising as it does from the opposition between the power asserting itself from within and that oppressing Him from without, this is the suffering.

No, it is not "the" suffering but "His" suffering. *This* suffering, *this* cup, and *this* moment.

There is no alternative for us at Gethsemane; we can only *believe* that the cause of Jesus' suffering is the friction between time and eternity, between person and office, between the moment and time. At Gethsemane we witness a fatal disharmony between Jesus' *natural* longing for God and this *anti-natural* rejection from the presence of God. Such rejection is anti-natural because it asserts the holy law of justice in His flesh and blood, in His soul and body, asserts it over against the sin of others. Besides, is not sin itself anti-natural?

If that was the cause of Christ's anguish in the garden, Gethsemane is indeed a source of great blessedness to us. Take Jesus' anguish out of the picture, if you will. But then the "atonement" He preached to us was nothing but a dispassionate hurrying through of a programme upon which Father and Son had agreed since eternity.

That was not the case. That which the counsel of God between the Father and Son from *eternity* had, in the tranquillity of heaven, determined and fixed for this particular hour, now enters into the sensuous, living medium of *time*.

The hour in which the will of the Father and Son determined to lead the elect of God to Salvation was still the hour of the *counsel of peace*. Father and Son could treat to all that Gethsemane should be witness to, and could do so without any diminution of *blessedness*. Heaven and hell, grace and sin, blessing and curse, communion and forsakenness—all these the Father and Son considered, and without in any sense disturbing their blessedness.

This all entered into the medium of time and space in this hour, however. And we may ascribe our salvation to the fact that an exalted God did not in aloof and haughty abstraction run through a program mechanically and then announce the results from on high, but chose instead to enter into our human situation and to experience and suffer there the passion which He determined upon in a state of blessedness.

This complete humanity, this absolute restriction to the world of time and space, was a part of God's counsel, too, of course.

Whoever wants to consider the seventy times seven blessednesses of *God* in connection with the seven sufferings of the world must remember that the seventy times seven sufferings of the *man* Jesus were once *also obtained in the counsel of God*.

In the hour of His adoration God's static peace, exalted above the distress of actual life, and God's living restlessness, which He suffered among us *as man*, merge before His face.

Only by seeing this relationship between time and eternity, only by seeing God's absolute joy, and also His anguish as a human being, can we really get a glimpse of Jesus' passion and of the miracle of our joys; so only can we become aware of the great "mystery of godliness" (I Tim. 3:16).

Christ's Sorrows Have Their Own Peculiar Law of Revelation

CHAPTER NINETEEN

Christ's Sorrows Have Their Own Peculiar Law of Revelation

● *And he was withdrawn from them about a stone's cast.*

—LUKE 22:41a.

I N view of the many tremendous realities with which the account of Christ's sufferings in Gethsemane overwhelms us, beneath which, in fact, it almost buries us, so trivial a fact as Christ's removing Himself from His disciples *about a stone's cast* hardly seems necessary.

The Gospels in various ways indicate that Christ is being led into constantly deepening solitude in Gethsemane. These inform us that Christ left the room of the Passover and approached the garden in the company of eleven disciples. Once there, He has eight of them stay behind at a particular place in the garden, charging them to remain until He joins them again. The three intimates, the three especially trusted disciples, were permitted— or were they compelled? — to penetrate farther into the garden with Jesus. Finally, Jesus left even these behind. Although He stayed closer to them than to the eight, He separated Himself from them, and entered into deep solitude. There He devoted Himself to prayer.

Luke indicates that the distance between Jesus and the disciples was a short one. He denominates the distance that of a "stone's cast," that is, about fifty or sixty feet.

It is worth remarking that Luke's reference is not to the distance between Jesus and the three aforementioned, intimate disciples (from whom He also separated Himself); his designation must be taken *in a general sense;* it refers to the disciples as a group of eleven, without further modification. The whole group, then, was not farther from Christ than some fifty or sixty feet. The three intimates, accordingly, were even nearer Him.[1]

Again, therefore: This simple indication points to nothing extraordinary; is hardly worth dwelling upon; there is so much to consider, there are so many factors to weigh, we might as well neglect to pause over this one . . . .

Still, it cannot be that Luke's description in this matter is pointless. The Spirit does not record any trivialities in the account of the passion. The Gospel is not wasted upon what are called "insignificant details." Everything in it has a meaning; and the inclusion of peculiar details has its meaning also.

Obviously, Christ defined the distance between Himself and the disciples. When He left His disciples and sought out alone the place where He kneeled to pray, He did so *consciously*. Naturally, the conception of a Master who stumbles His way into the night unwittingly, and unconsciously segregates Himself from His disciples, is incompatible with everything that we believe about Jesus Christ. But, in this instance, the very phrasing of the text indicates that Jesus calmly and deliberately separated Himself from His disciples.[2] True, Luke in the phrasing of the text usually employed, used a word which might be construed to mean that a strong influence *impelled* Jesus to leave His disciples (a conception more or less permanently crystalized in the Vulgata[3]). However, it is also true that Jesus leaves the others, motivated by His *own will*. The word used by Matthew and Mark must be interpreted to mean a conscious and deliberate departure. Moreover, there are other versions of Luke's usage which employ a verb form which points not to a *passive* permitting oneself to be taken away but to a voluntary leaving.

Hence there is no doubt about Jesus' having voluntarily chosen to leave His disciples. Even the Roman Catholics, who, in their

---

1. Compare: Zahn, *Das Evangelium des Lucas*, Leipzig, 1913, p. 688, Note 74.

2. The reader must know that the Dutch text used by the author at the head of this chapter has the active rather than the passive form of the verb. In other words, the text preferred by the author reads not "he was withdrawn," but "he withdrew."

3. Avulsus est. Vulgata, the Roman Catholic translation of the Bible.

Vulgata, employ the word which suggests that Jesus was constrained, was wrenched away from His disciples, in the last analysis explain His going as an act prompted by the motivation of His own soul or by the influence of His own Spirit.[1] According to their view, His own inner prompting impelled Him to leave them.

It is certain, then, that Christ was not driven from His disciples by a force which seized Him, apart from His own will, but that He personally *willed* that some distance should obtain between the place of His anguish and the place where the disciples had to stay behind. That leaves the question: What significance has this matter for us?

Obviously it is not enough to simply say that Jesus separated Himself from His disciples a few paces. In a sense the distance between them was very short, and could hardly be called any distance at all. What do fifty or sixty feet amount to? But Jesus deliberately would have it so. The distance was so short that the disciples, doubtless, were able to hear Him in the restiveness of the anguish of His soul.

Just that perception imparts some meaning to the fact that all of the disciples were but a stone's throw removed from Jesus, at the most. Yes, it is true that those three intimate ones, Peter, James, and John, fell asleep, that they stood at the edge of the precipice without knowing it; but that gives us no reason to believe that *all* of them, *including the other eight,* fell asleep. If we remember that (according to *Hebrews,* Chapter 5) Christ offered Himself up *with strong cryings,* that the nameless anguish of His soul therefore also issued in plaints which broke the silence of the night, in penetrating cries shattering the darkness, then we can know that the apostles must have noticed something of the excruciating passion which moved His soul unto death.

That, then, is the importance of this matter.

It appears that Christ, even as He enters into the holiest of the temple of passion, does not withdraw behind curtains through which no sound can pass, but that, on the contrary, all those who have been with Him during these years of His oppression may be

---

1. Obviously, the issue has significant implications for the Roman Catholics. It affects the relation between the human and Divine natures of Christ as expressed in their dogmatics.

with Him now also. The *man* Jesus did not hide Himself from His *friends,* and the Mediator Jesus Christ did not hide Himself from His appointed office-bearers, His apostles, His missionaries. He did not segregate Himself behind the heavy curtains of those solitary souls who admit no one to their holy of holies. True, Christ wanted some little distance to separate them, but He desired that only in view of His prayer. Prayer is a confidential matter. There is such a thing as a public worship, also in prayers; there is such a thing as social worship, also in prayers. But there is a personal worship, too, solitary, intimate, confidential; and there is that in prayers. This is the hour in which Christ must personally pray for Himself. His human soul needs it. He wants to strengthen Himself in God. And this, His personal worship, is also an official ministration of the *Mediator*: He prays for all. Hence, this prayer exacts a complete consecration. To this extent it is not extraordinary to observe that Christ wants to be alone. It is not the first time. There were other occasions on which He withdrew into solitude to pray. Nevertheless, His prayer is not made personally in this instance: His *office,* His *mediatorship* exacts it of Him.

It is in view of that *official work* that Christ's conduct becomes significant in this instance. Christ does not withdraw into a solitude in which no eye can see Him, and no ear can hear Him. He lets the heaviest official duty that was ever required of Him be *seen* (to the extent possible in the night) of all who were constantly with Him, and lets all of these hear it.

Christ is entering the most holy place. And, in that holy of holies, there is, it is true, a mystery no one can understand.

But what of that? The mystery is *not* being sought out; nor is it being proposed, externally, as a riddle. The mystery is an *inner* reality.

And, precisely because the mysteries of God, of which we tremulously saw something in the preceding chapters, are contained in the essence of Christ's *official* work, in Gethsemane also, therefore this essential mystery needs no external display of secrecy but discovers itself unreservedly to the true lovers who would *see* with their eyes. Moreover, it discloses itself presently to the ears that would hear, for it fills the ears of the disciples with the grievous plaints and anguished cries of its terrible suffering.

Whoever calls these concerns trivialities in the Gospel story which are best left alone, forgets that the ground on which he is standing is "holy ground," is, in fact, a temple floor.

We are so indisposed to call this a "triviality," a little feature which had better be ignored, that, on the contrary, we want to see in it especially how the temple of God's justice and grace remains faithful to its pure and exalted style not only in broad, general outlines, but also in detail.

A connoisseur of architecture is able to describe the style and pattern of a building, after he has studied some segment, some part, some subsidiary piece of it; that is, he can do so if the architect of the building was sufficiently an artist to manifest his stylistic principle even in the little details.

Zoölogists, when they find the bone of a skeleton, are able very frequently to reconstruct the whole skeleton by reason of it. They proceed on the principle that the relationships of the whole are those of the part in its detail; thus they infer the design of the whole from the nature of an individual part.

May we, then, when we hit upon this or that detail in the temple of the passion, call it a triviality and say of it: This is an accidental part of what is essentially a severely artistic structure? To say that, certainly, would be to insult the great Architect of this temple of passion: His name is Lord of Lords.

Or, inasmuch as only a subsidiary part of the divine *scheme* of Gethsemane apparently comes to our attention, shall we *pass* by and say: It is impossible to determine or recognize the pattern of the whole from this little part? Surely not, for that would be an insult to a God who makes the spiritual temple of Gethsemane, terrible as it may be, infinitely more beautiful, more harmonious, than the skeleton of an animal, the structure of a plant, or the movement of His stars.

Again in this instance, you see, faith reverses the situation. It must be a matter of conviction with us *beforehand* that this particular "detail," too, has a weighty significance.

Consequently if we proceed from the vantage point of this *preconception* and try to find the pattern, the design of God's architecture in every detail of His perfect building, we shall discover that all the lines of God's *revelation* converge at a point in that reference at the distance of a stone's throw. Then we shall be able to read from this specific detail also the adequate, rich, artistic thoughts which are being expressed by God Himself in the redemptive work of Christ.

We alluded just now to the word *revelation* and did so designedly, for, to a person who believes the Scriptures, revelation is a *discovering* of mysteries, a disclosure of them. In revelation God Himself makes it possible to know Him and His thoughts. True revelation, therefore, *discloses* mysteries; mysteries which we should never become aware of except as they were discovered to us by grace. We should never become aware of them ourselves, for we should have to attain the awareness at the cost of our lives.

Now that which is revealed will eternally and in the deepest essence of its being retain the character *of a mystery*. Man will never *comprehend* his God. The dream of those many mystics who believed they had peered so far into the depths of God's being that they actually had *exhausted* it was just that — a dream. And not a particularly pleasant dream at that. For it is precisely the *glory* of all flesh that is nourished by the Spirit to know that the finite can never comprehend the Infinite. And that we can never let the plumb-line out into the depths of God so far that it reaches the bottom. Indeed, always there is a distance between God and us; our eyes will never penetrate to the farthest essence of His being. A space of distance separates Him from us. The space is as wide as the distance between finitude and infinitude; the distance is greater than that between heaven and earth; wider than that between East and West.

Nevertheless, God, on His own part, reveals *Himself* to us. He comes to us to reveal Himself to us, to *give Himself away*, to satisfy us more and more with the pure waters of the knowledge of the Lord, and, to *curtail* the distance between Him and us so much at least as to make it as short *as is possible*. True, as far as the essence of God's being and ours is concerned, the distance between Him and us is infinite. But, next to that fact is the fact of God's will to come to us, to remove what conceals Him from us as far as such is possible, and to have us see and enjoy Him to the extent that we can sustain the sight and endure the joy in our *enlightened* condition.

For that reason those forms have been chosen for the revelation of God which speak to us in our own language, appear before us in guises susceptible to our eyes, and make themselves heard in this world of space and time in a manner our ears can apprehend. The distance between God and man obtains nowhere unless fellowship in revelation is desired and commanded there.

For that reason God brings revelation as close to us as is possible. He knows that we shall never fathom His depths; nevertheless the forms by which He makes Himself known to us are brought very near to us.

This general law can be discerned as operative also in the comparatively trivial particular of the distance of a stone's throw which separates Jesus from His disciples.

Yes, there *is* such a distance. According to the *essence* of what is being achieved and suffered in Gethsemane, that distance is as great as . . . as . . . a stone's cast. Absurd! As great as infinitude! No one can fathom what is happening here; not even these disciples can. Disciples are not mystics. The world now pouring its flames through Gethsemane is of so patently *different* an order that the disciples can sleep while the enormities are taking place; or, to the extent that they are awake, they can only, like children, stand spellbound, with mouth agape, and, wide-eyed with amazement, look on, and listen to the penetrating cries of the Master in His dire need. Indeed, there is a distance separating them. This very night they will all be offended because of Him. A stone's cast removed, you say? Yes, a stone's throw; but also an infinitude. The mystery of God's counsel and work is hidden here in the conflict of Jesus' soul and in the convulsion of Jesus' body; He is being tossed to and fro between two worlds—those of heaven and of hell. But was any onlooker struck blind by the spectacle? They fell asleep. The mystery was too . . . incomprehensible. But the fact that there is a mystery here Jesus impresses upon the memories of the disciples by *withdrawing from them*. By that act He seems to say: something is about to happen now which you cannot understand; a whirlwind will come, out of which

I alone shall be able to raise my head, waiting for what God has decided to send over it.

However, this mystery, on the other hand, *is directed to man*. The distance will remain because no one can restrict infinitude. Nevertheless God, by means of the forms of His revelation, comes as close to His people as He possibly can. Hence the distance remains as short as possible. Think! Is it not a wonder: to be but fifty or sixty feet removed from heaven? To be only twenty paces away from infinitude?

And it *is* a miracle, it is a wonder of *seeking* grace, of that revelation-urge which forcibly causes God to go out to us in a will-to-fellowship, in the election of approach and of entrance to His people.

In order to actualize this communion as really as possible, to show that nothing is being withheld or tempered of that which God can shriek into our delicate ears without rending them, Christ *takes people with Him as close to the place as He possibly can*.

Nothing more overwhelming than this ever took place in the world.

This was nothing less than the beginning of the descent into hell. That is saying: He who came from above goes down, down to the bottom. He who dwells amidst His eternal luxury sinks down into the most abject impoverishment. He who is from heaven turns toward hell. In this moment revelation itself passes from the highest height to the deepest depth.

But the people are allowed to be present — some fifty or sixty feet removed. Yes, the people are allowed to be present. Many prophets and kings have desired to see those things which they see, and have not seen them; and to hear those things which they hear, and have not heard them (Luke 70:24). But the fishermen of Jesus are allowed to be present, and they may see and hear.

A mystery moves through the night of Gethsemane and it is a mystery greater than that of Jacob when he came to Bethel. The disciples may witness its passing. Jacob had a ladder; its end rested against heaven; and angels climbed up and down. But that was only a dream. In this case the ladder extends not merely from heaven to earth but reaches down through the earth to hell. Those who move up and down it are not only the angels: the devils also are there. And this is not a dream; it is an awful, bloody, oppressive reality.

But people — people were allowed to witness it. Those who are called of God may approach not only up to the fountains of bliss rippling out in the inner court of His palace, but may come to the inner room, to the place of profound concern, where the will of the Almighty proves the ground to find a foundation for His temple.

Separation . . . distance!

And *communion.*

A stone's throw, a short distance — but its two ends extend out on both sides and reach into infinitude. And, in another sense, this is an infinite distance which is conquered by God's desire for fellowship, His will to communion, which discloses to the hearing and souls of a few fishermen the conflicts of God. That is a little thing, is it not? And also a very great thing?

Has the style, the pattern of God's building, even as manifested in a "detail," not some significance for you now?

The nobility and authenticity of the Christian faith are closely related to this. In fact, faith in the atoning strength of Christ's passion and death depends on these matters.

We have several times referred to the difference between the mysteries and mystery-cults of heathendom, on the one hand, and the Christian faith with its redeeming content, on the other.[1] The difference is one of essence. But it is a difference of concrete manifestation just as well. We think of that again in this connection.

At the time when Christianity came into the world there were many preachers of pagan or semi-pagan origin. All these preached saviours, redeemers, Messiahs, who had to lift the world out of its distress. And, irrespective of the differences in these many, they were all alike in two important respects.

---

1. It is impossible to go beyond mere suggestion in this book, which is designed for popular use. This is not the place for the science of theology, particularly in controversial matters. Only here and there is it possible to point out how a Reformed view of the Scriptures affects theological problems, also in relevance to the passion of Christ, and that maintaining a Reformed conception over-against the views of Bousset, Reitzenstein, Heilmuller and others, affects definitely the Christian life and faith.

This is the first difference. These saviours are not "worms"; they are men, heroes, the sons of gods. Nectar drips from their locks. Wisdom creates a halo around their heads. They have been wedded to heavenly wisdom. The translucence of their human form, their airy moving over their heights of earth is merely a pleasing fancy. They are not under the compulsion of partaking of the flesh (Hebrew 2:14). They are half god, half man. They can leave and enter heaven at will. They differ greatly from Jesus as He is here, who exists in the flesh because necessity demands it, and who cannot enter heaven except by blood.

And a second difference is that their life-secret is the same as the secret of their office. They all have what is called their great "Messianic secret." Occasionally a very little of their work may shimmer before the astonished eyes of the people, but their elevation is such that they withdraw behind many curtains. Their evangelists are mere allegorists who understand the language of mysteries. They themselves are wandering myths; their secretiveness looks for no fellowship; does not allow itself to be seen with the eyes, heard with the ears, or touched with the hands (I John 1:1). Their heart is not laid bare. The mystery to them is a delight by which they lord it over the people without *exercising fellowship with* them. How different these are from a Jesus who must elicit the confession *My Lord and My God* from Thomas by letting him probe His wounds with a finger.

Such is the double and always dominant characteristic of the image of the false Messiahs. Glamour and secretiveness. Those two are always present and are constantly supporting each other.

Christ Himself, we remember, pointed to that fact. He told us that false Messiahs will come who will go to and fro upon the earth, not exercising fellowship with the people in a priestly, humble, patient way, but trekking across the world, high, and lifted up, like living miracles, like wandering wonders. Today, He said, they will be in the desert. And tomorrow they will be in the inner room.

In the desert? Can they exist there? Yes, indeed, for they do not eat the bread of ordinary folk, are not dependent upon a loaf bought at the shop as ordinary mortals, and as Jesus is, who promises the woman of Samaria living water, but has in the meantime sent His disciples into town to *buy* some bread. No, these others are giants all, heroes whose lives are self-sufficing: they are not worms, but men, children of miracles, demi-gods. The first feature of the false picture of the Messiah, therefore, characterizes them completely.

They embody the second feature of the false Messiahs just as fully. For they can be found in the inner rooms. To the extent that they do condescend to come to the people and "make" fellowship with them, the little ones, they do not mingle with the crowd in the market-place, and they do not, as Jesus did, daily *sit* in the temple, or play with the children, or lay hands upon the leprous head. No, no. These enter into the inner chamber. A cloud of mystery envelops them. Their official conduct accords with their personal conduct. So far from feeling *burdened* by the feeling of *distance* separating them from others, they delight in the sense of it. There is only one thing of which they are mortally afraid: of the distance of a stone's throw.

You ask why they cannot bear the familiarity implied in being but a stone's throw removed from men? Because of their essential poverty. Because they are *essentially* poor, appearances must save them.

They do *not* really have the great mystery in their *being;* for they are not filled with the same satisfying abundance with which, in the Gospel according to John, the *man* Jesus is filled by God and by the Spirit. These pseudo-Messiahs do not come from the perfect eternal heights. They are not being driven by the absolute and sovereign-*eternal* Counsel. And *because* they do *not* possess *the* great mystery in their essential being, they look for it in *externals*. That remove of a "stone's cast" simply goes against their grain; the poverty of what is really their profane being requires a show of mysterious forms designed to conceal the absence of genuine mystery.

That is just a suggestion — by no means exhaustive — of the truth about the false Messiahs at which the sentimental imaginations of the world gaped, while Christian slaves and day-laborers preached the Crucified One.

May our souls in response to this fall down and worship the Man of sorrows.

In Gethsemane He appears to be the *true* Messiah. And He proves Himself such, especially in the so-called "trivialities." If the actual shedding of blood is all that can make us exlaim *Lo, there! Our Messiah! There! Hallelujah!* we do Him an injustice.

Our soul must make many amends for Him. For we must learn to see and honor Him as Messiah also as He expresses Himself in what we carelessly called "details which could as well be ignored."

We must remember that Christ (the true Messiah), and the pseudo-Christ (pseudo-Messiah) eternally are and will remain different. That proved to be so throughout Jesus' official work. And He proves it again as He achieves His peculiar work now — a stone's cast removed.

Christ Jesus!

No, He did not reside in the desert in order to live by miracle. He does not call down manna from heaven. He *buys* bread and promptly pays His taxes. He lives *in the city* of man, and rubs shoulders with each and all daily. And this common, genuine humanity He asserts in Gethsemane also. He, O church, is your true Messiah. He does not, like the son of a god (recall the first feature of the pseudo-Messianic figure), feel disgraced by those weak moments in which people can see Him in His littleness. He takes the disciples with Him. He *cries* for company. He beseeches, He implores that they watch with Him one hour. He cannot bear being without love. He is not the son of a god, subsisting on His mystery. In His last hour even, He says, without making any effort at concealment: *My soul is sorrowful to death.* They may see Him; *they may look on and see* — as He lies there, crushed, naked, exposed to the whole universe. He makes no attempt to smother His sobbing in the folds of His garment, in order to prevent the children of earth from seeing His brokenness. Instead He fills the air with His cries: the stone's cast! The stone's cast! That is manifesting genuine humanity, and is doing it, not in the desert, but in the world of men — of fishermen.

Besides, He is not found in the inner room. He takes no delight in seclusion. *The stone's cast! The stone's cast!*

Our Lord Jesus Christ can disclose His nakedness to the searching eyes of the Galilean fishermen, because it is *precisely in His nakedness* that He is beautiful and strong! He is so completely filled with the essential mystery in the real being of His existence, that He has no need of taking recourse to the appearances of the mysterious. He came just in order to discover all that God had concealed. To that end He has come to "this hour" in Gethsemane also. Hence He takes His children, His brethren with Him, keeps them as close to Him as He can.

This was done for our salvation. This *will* to preach the distance separating us from God and nevertheless to effect communion with God was the secret of every act of revelation, and became the cause, became the real motive of the cross.

What is beautiful in this matter is that the true Messiah, while redeeming *our* soul by perfectly ministering the service of His Messianic office, is simultaneously able to prepare perfectly *for His own soul* exactly what it needs in each moment of its conflict. For whom are those words written? For oxen only, or for missionaries also: *Thou shalt not muzzle the ox, when he treadeth out the corn?* Was the law that the wages are contained in the labor preached only in reference to animals and men?

Certainly not! In the final analysis that law was written for Christ's sake. Look — see how He treads, how He labors and sweats. But it is exactly that labor which gives Him a chance to breathe, which takes the muzzle off His panting mouth.

Just for a moment, imagine the impossible. Imagine that He had to conceal His sufferings like a pseudo-Messiah, that He had to sustain His "integrity" by taking recourse to an *external* appearance.

Then His suffering would have been false before God, and for that reason, condemned. But, more than that, He would not then have *been able to express His own soul;* he would have had to thwart His desires.

Now, however, He can express Himself unrestrictedly, just as He is, and just as He is *as a man* also. If He desires human companionship, He may ask for it; shame does not keep Him from it. When He has need of some to watch, whose souls' prayers can pour new strength into Him, no false haughtiness, no false pride keeps Him from the plaint: *Can ye not watch with me one hour?*

Such is the glory of the true Messiah. The false Messiah lives behind a mask; the true has authentic integrity. Whoever lets God speak unhamperedly is able to speak freely himself.

For us, then, again on this occasion, Christ manifests Himself as rich and adequate in mercies.

Nietzsche drew a picture of His "Messiah," Zarathustra. Just another redeemer, he was, and another false one. In fact, his features resemble the figure of the pseudo-Christ less than they do those, in principle, of the Antichrist. Zarathustra, the creator of new morals and of a new philosophy, also withdraws into the mountains; he, too, cannot believe in "the law of a stone's throw of distance." But He refuses to believe in the law because of *disdain* for the people. He seeks the greater disdainer. He despises the fishermen of Galilee, the simple folk, the docile creatures who simply accept things and believe them. He would rather tread every growing thing, in the neighborhood, into the dust than spare the broken reeds or endure the burning flax within the radius of a stone's cast.

Not so the Christ. In His suffering, *disdain* had no part. Who despises the day of small things? All the false Messiahs must answer: I do. But Christ does not despise the day of small things, for this day makes small things great. That was a long distance, was it not, that of the stone's throw. Infinitude was contained in it. Yes, the mystery has been *revealed,* but it has remained divine.

Now we ask all men: Who despises the day of a small distance and of small things? Christ, in His direst need and in the weightiest task He had to perform, allowed His disciples to stand by; first, because the law of revelation required it; and, secondly, because His own soul yearned for companionship with them.

Such, surely, is a personal insufficiency which shows us the extent of His humiliation; moreover, it makes us blush deeply in shame. The *great* disgrace is indeed taking place here. Think: The intimate ones of Jesus, but a stone's throw removed from Him when the greatest drama that ever perturbed a soul moved Him — fell asleep. That is the worst disgrace, the most painful humiliation that can conceivably be recorded in the records of history.

John, even John slept. He is the evangelist of the Word made flesh.

Nevertheless we are grateful and give thanks, for we know definitely now that his Gospel is not written in terms of what he saw, is not based on a personal view of the facts and their significance, but is solely the product of the impelling of his soul by the Spirit of God.

You ask how this matter affects us. We need not imagine for a moment that we shall escape from the strictures of Gethsemane, from the awe-inspiring, dread-engendering proximity of the miracle. True, this seemed an *exceptional instance,* this being but a stone's throw away from the other world — and what have we, ordinary people, used as we are to ordinary distances, to do with such exceptional incidents?

True. Nevertheless, remember that this situation in the garden obtains just so for you and me each day. By nature we also are but the distance of a stone's cast removed from eternity — and we are asleep, and are unaware of it.

The fact that we are so close to eternity is not owing to us but is due to the revelation and to the coming of the Kingdom which is the Kingdom of Heaven.

That is, consequently, the great lesson which this narrative has to teach us. The mystery of God's eternal thoughts are contained in the external circumstances of Christ's passion and express themselves through these. Yet, no one will ever discover this truth except the person who by faith learns to see the meaning of external things in the light shed upon them through revelation by the Spirit of God.

We are by no means sure that everyone wants to be obedient to the concept of revelation which expresses itself in the law of the stone's throw of distance. Have there not always been those mystics, masochists and others, who preferred to regard the suffering of Christ primarily, and sometimes solely, in terms of its externalities? They shrank back at the sight of the blood, they shuddered as the nails were driven through the hands and the feet, but they did not penetrate to the profound Justice of God, nor to the laws of the revelation of God.

Such is, as a rule, in fact, the response of all those who do not *believe* revelation. Unfortunately, the same response sometimes is the rule rather than the conspicuous exception among those rightly-disposed ones who always have the word *revelation* at the tip of the tongue.

We must, of course, fix our attention upon the bowed *soul* and the struggling *body* of the Man of sorrows. And we may — no, we must come up to this human suffering, must come as close as the space of a stone's throw. But we must remember at the same time that a mystery, entirely hidden, is contained in this matter, and that we are in a different world here, a world we cannot become aware of by thinking. Only *faith* can grasp that world; only faith can accept it.

And if that faith operates in love, only one effect can ensue. Then the great confusion to which he is prey who sees that distance of a stone's throw stretching out into an infinitude of space will be restored to order by faith, by childlike faith. He must have faith in the fact that God honors His Word and acknowledges it. He must believe that God *came* to us to reveal Himself; in other words, that while keeping *distance* and separation between Himself and us, He seeks *fellowship* with us in the one Christ who suffered and died, but now lives and triumphs.

If Christ is not the false Messiah, who in celebration of Himself turns his back upon mere human beings, but is the true Messiah who, even in His most tragical moment, *seeks* His own— then we should certainly always seek Him. Indeed, we shall care always to seek Him anew, because we know that He who, while maintaining distance and separation, nevertheless bought the privilege of *communion* from the Father, also teaches us to believe in God as Father, *in* and *through* Himself.

The "stone's cast," in the last analysis, you see, is the law of eternity and time; it is the whole fact of revelation which teaches me to say: Abba, Father, from Thee comes strength and power; but from Thee also comes loving-kindness:

Though the Lord be high, yet hath he respect unto the lowly.

That is the confession of the believer who at a distance of a stone's cast has learned to find his Father in Christ.

To our conscience, however, He who is the Father also remains the Judge. It will never be forgotten, not even in heaven, that Jesus' most intimate disciples slept but a stone's cast away from the great arena of combat. Yes, yes, it was to be explained —the characteristically human in us will raise arguments by way of excuse. But enough of that. They who are above, all know that the frailty of the flesh closed their eyes, and they willingly confess: The Church, which is the bride, slept while the Bridegroom wooed her—that is and will remain a disgrace to the Church. Nevertheless light breaks into the darkness of this shame. The law of *grace* is there to console, and it reads: Redemption has taken place, with us, above us, without us.

What the eye did not see a stone's cast away, what the ear did not hear at a distance of fifty feet, what the heart did not feel in the immediate neighborhood of Jesus' struggling soul—that God has prepared for those who love Him.

For those who love Him it overcomes even the distance of a stone's cast, in the form of the mystical union.

Union, yes; and also: *mystery*.

Christ's Sorrows Have Their Own Peculiar Law of Severity

CHAPTER TWENTY

Christ's Sorrows Have Their Own Peculiar Law of Severity

● *And there appeared an angel unto him from heaven, strengthening him.*
—Luke 22:43.

THE sorrows which Christ suffered in Gethsemane have their peculiar essence. We have been observing that for some time now. The griefs suffered in the Garden of Olives have their peculiar origin, their peculiar content, their own language in which to *express* themselves.

They also have their peculiar intensity—for so we must conclude as we see the advent of the angel, coming to strengthen the Son of man during—and for—His passion.

The appearance of this angel represents a peculiar combination of *comfort* and of *humiliation*. In fact, we shall not venture to say whether the comfort which the angel brought outweighed the humiliation for Christ which He must have felt as He saw one of His Father's servants coming to strengthen the Father's Son as one needing assistance.

The prodigal son of the parable was severely humiliated also. But at least he was spared a message of a *servant*. It was by virtue of his own resolution that he returned to the father. That father did not send a servant to fetch him, for he, the *son,* the heir, would have succumbed to shame had he been compelled to see his father's servant — from his position among the swine.

And here? Here, in Gethsemane is *the* great Lost Son. He is terribly aware of His misery. But before He can, at His own prompting, turn to the Father, saying *Father, into thy hands I*

349

commend my tired spirit, an angel approaches Him. In other words, the servant of the house approaches Him; the *servant* meets the Son and sees Him smitten, dismembered, a worm and not a man.

Surely, every message coming *from home* still has its comforts for the Son. But a message which compels the Son to show His nakedness to the servant also represents a gruesome humiliation.

Indeed, we do not know which weighs the more heavily, which is the greater: the comfort in the disgrace, or the disgrace in the comfort.

As a matter of fact we have never known it in the whole history of the Church. So manifest is our embarrassment on this account that this single text in Luke's narrative of the gospel has been a bone of contention between the conservatives in the old-Christian Church and the more heretical element of the first centuries. The orthodox (conservative) element and the heterodox (heretical) took turns bandying this text back and forth between each other, and each in turn told the other that its theological disposition and its dogmatic construction concerning the human soul and the divine nature of Jesus Christ were supported by it.

This is an historical particular which is something more than interesting. It shows that the appearance of the angel in Gethsemane colors the misery of Christ darker and makes the heavy curtain behind which His divine majesty conceals itself less transparent. But it also shows that, in spite of all, a certain fellowship continues between Father and Son even in Gethsemane and that the unity of the throne of highest majesty and the deep valley of Christ's brokenness continues in force.

Surely, those are contrasts which can keep us busy.

Now the enigmatic in this statement may have induced thinkers to take one course this time and another the next, but we believe we can do justice to the text only by not passing "verdict" upon the issue of whether the sense of comfort and of the experience of fellowship outweigh that of the humiliation he feels with acute bitterness, or whether the awareness of humiliation overshadows that of comfort.

We *can* not make a choice.

And we *may* not make a choice.

Both are equally strong: the keen sense of humiliation, and the certainty of the coming promotion. They are equally significant: the Son's being forsaken by a Father who sends Him a mere servant, and the acknowledgment of the Son, who, though never so forsaken, gets a message from His Father's house none-the-less.

Because both truths are equally significant and strong, the wonderful, the paradoxical[1] character of *all* of Christ's suffering fully informs that short account concerning the *strengthening* angel.

Accordingly, we acknowledge first of all that this event means gladness for Christ. He is in Gethsemane; there He has been undone by suffering and anguish. In the fierce distress of His Soul, He took refuge in God. See, He bows, He prays. He prays repeatedly, each time pronouncing the same words. During the prayers—between the first and the second—He sees an angel, imparting strength to Him. This angel approaches without much ado. He is not, as on Christmas night, surrounded by heavenly hosts. Hence, he cannot for a moment change the night of Gethsemane into day—nevertheless, he comes from above.

It was but one angel, just one. But for Christ that one was very important. A ray of light entering a dark place is always conspicuous. That *one* was a gift, a greeting, a stretching out of the hand—and it came from home. His Father's house has not forgotten Him. The Son is not yet a pariah whom heaven gloriously ignores; not yet a wastrel whom angels pass by or allow to bleed to death on a cross. Heaven still concerns itself about Him, and Jesus' soul takes cognizance of that right soon. As quickly as His soul becomes aware that heaven has not yet cut it loose, it gives rise to a quickening of confident trust.

Do you remember the speech of Job, the smitten one, who once exclaimed (16:18): *O earth, cover not thou my blood, and let my cry have no place?* That is the plea of a man who does not want to be forgotten in God's wide universe. His blood must be seen of God; God must remember it; it must become the great question mark inducing the whole universe to place an excla-

---

1. Paradoxical: not in the sense of irrational.

mation point after it. Job's blood, that precious blood, may never be forgotten. It would rather be the obstacle in the way of the pacification of the universe than ever be forgotten. O earth, do not cover, do not bury, do not hide the blood of Job. His plea? His cry? His life-purpose? His individuality? These, too, crave acknowledgment. Job's plea may not be smothered within the four narrow walls of his own house. The cry of Job's spirit and soul must have "no place" in the whole universe. It means that every mountain-side must send it echoing back. The universe must be at its wits' end, must now know what to do with the afflictions of Job. And God especially must listen to the call of the blood of Job, and to the plaint of his questioning spirit.

Listen to that, Jesus Christ, and behold it.

What Job craved is still being given Thee. Thy blood which is being demanded of Thee in Thy last bitter hour, is not covered today. It is being brought in an open vial; it is being brought before God. Heaven is concerned about Thee; it is fixing all its attention upon Thee. Perhaps it rejects Thee, perhaps exacts Thy blood, but Thou art not yet forgotten. That one thing Thou still hast: Thy blood is not covered; God is still busy over it. Thy blood is not something which can be ignored. Look: an angel. All Thy blood is remembered of God.

And Thy cry, O Son of man?

Thy cry, too, finds *no place* in the universe. Disciples may sleep and friends be silent, but heaven takes note of it; the Father hears it. Look: an angel. That means a message from heaven. The cry of Thy soul and Thy spirit reaches the ears of the Lord Sabaoth. Irrespective of what happens, of how justice may knead and shape Thee, at least God remembers Thee. Thou still hast individual dignity.

It is true, is it not, you who read the Bible reverently, that joy must have leaped within Him, when the Son of man by means of that angel again established contact with the Father's house? Even though it was very painful to Him to have an angel find Him weltering in His own blood, it was a consolation to know that heaven was extending fellowship to the Son anew.

To Jesus the angel's appearing was especially a cause of joy because that angel gives Him what the people, who were really first designated for the task, withhold. That is a sharp, a shaming contrast: man *had to* give, and did not; angels gave what men withheld. Those men could have and should have *watched* with Jesus. Their watching would have imparted a strength to His human soul which would have been a great boon to it. But men have nothing to give Jesus. Their flesh is very weak; their spiritual energy does not flow out to Jesus. And now that human *souls* have nothing to give to Jesus' *soul* the *spirits* from heaven come. These have no soul. An angel is pure spirit and has no *human soul*. Hence, something is always lacking in their fellowship with the *man* Jesus. This is not a case of a soul speaking to a soul. But when souls are silent the coming of spirits is a gladdening thing. Jesus felt that and He acknowledged that it was so.

Thus His soul is strengthened by the spirit from heaven. The Son of man takes courage again. For that which is strengthened by the angel's coming is His *Messianic consciousness*.

When Jesus began His work, His official work, in Israel, He Himself uttered in the circle of the disciples this pronouncement: *Hereafter ye shall see heaven open, and the angels of God ascending and descending upon the Son of man* (John 1:51).

By that statement He meant that in reference to His *office* as Messiah He is quite sure of the special providence of God. Providence will sustain Him during His official ministration on earth. The angels of God, who are always busy as messengers in the world-task of the Father, will accompany Him from moment to moment. They will keep His foot from all offense as long as the hour of the great offense had not struck. Heaven will unintermittently and attentively share in the conflict of soul which the Messiah is suffering. Jesus is so completely assured internally of heaven's sympathy, manifesting itself in the service of angels, and in His Messianic task, that He beforehand prophesies of it; beforehand, that is, before He puts His hand to work, He prophesies, and with a double "verily" affirms with an oath, as it were, that His Messianic consciousness does not for a moment doubt the living, lasting relationship—between Himself and heaven's interest.

And now, at the opportune time that Messianic consciousness is again strengthened by God.

Verily, verily, He sees the heavens opened. Now, in this unique moment, He sees and experiences that the angels of God still ascend and descend for the Son of man. Yes, God forsakes Him, God yields Him to Satan's grasp, God does not shock these sleeping disciples awake—in fact, God Himself, as it seems, closes their eyelids—nevertheless, God is still there, and is speaking, is making Himself heard. Jesus has not yet fallen into the hands of chance. And this to Jesus is proof of the fact that—however it may be—this enigmatic suffering *must* have a relationship to His Messianic task and calling, and—to the eternal justice of God.

Indeed, this is consolation. He is not yet quite alone in the awfully spacious cosmos. This moment, since it allows Him a glance at an angel from heaven, cannot be the darkest moment. After awhile, at the cross, it will be worse. Simon Peter is sleeping just now, yes. But presently he will deny, and will curse, and will swear. One who sleeps bars his soul from another; but one who curses bars his spirit. There is an angel here; then there will be none. Presently the Sanhedrin will meet; and the angels will allow that to happen. Caiaphas and Pilate and Herod will witness no invasions of heaven. And at last, certainly, every angel will completely withdraw himself from the cross. Then the Son's isolation, hanging over against the whole universe, alone, will be perfect.

Hence this moment, in which the angel comes to visit Him in Gethsemane, is not yet that of complete suffering. Some light is playing on the darkness. Heavenly fire still radiates from the cloud of hell. He who seeks God can still live.

Hence the angel who imparts strength to Jesus is a gift of consolation. God, who comforts the lowly — comforts Jesus by means of this nameless one.

You say: But the angel only remained a moment.

Yes. But is Jesus one to despise a moment, and a moment of joy, of strengthening of the faith? Would He despise a moment which breaks the hours of God-forsakenness and of wrath? True, the appearing was but a ray of light; it was not at all the day's dawning. It was but a moment of comfort, not a continuous consolation. But who despises the days of small things? Who despises a ray of light on a dark night? Who could fail to see a white spot on a black screen?

Jesus saw the angel, and leaped for joy in God.

He fell down again, yes; and His fall was severer this time than before.

Nevertheless, He leaped for joy.

His joy was the gladness caused by the uncovered blood and the unthwarted cry of His exalted Spirit.

There is, however, the other side of the matter. We may not forget for one moment that the coming of the angel is and remains a subsidiary part of the account of the passion.

A nameless suffering accompanies the angel. Not only does that angel represent suffering for Christ: it also represents an aggravation of suffering.

We already pointed out the nature of that suffering in our allusion to the prodigal son who gets a message from the servant and not directly from the Father. To think of a servant meeting his master's son in utter humiliation gives us a sufficiently vivid conception of suffering—we need not add to the picture. Just so the service of the angels comes to the Son in His humiliation. Jesus once in His life experienced a service of angels—in the desert, after the temptation. This service gave him a foretaste of the glory to come. When Jesus had triumphed, heaven opened itself to Him: the angels ministered to Him. This ministration in the desert did not represent a joint attack upon the threatening death, but a joint celebration of a festival, a prophesying of His own strong life. It was indeed a foretaste of the coming ministration of angels, in which the angel ministers to the Son of man from eternity to eternity, not because He needs it, but because He, the rich, the strong, the heroic, is glorified in it.

How very different the situation here in Gethsemane! Here Christ has not yet emerged successfully from the conflict. This is not yet the time to speak of triumph. He cannot do the work alone, He will almost perish—unless heaven itself fortifies His strength from heaven. This time the angel comes not to celebrate the life of Jesus but to ward off death, to avert and untimely, the futile death of Jesus.

This angel has no beautiful liturgy, no *jubilato Deo* in his repertoire. He represents so public an acknowledgment of the smallness and frailty of the Son of man that he can only amplify the *miserere* which is being intoned sonorously through space. Today the angel comes not to honor the King but to support the slave.

This is to Him a grievous sorrow. And it is inescapable. It follows from the law of the kingdom of heaven which read: *To him that hath shall be given, and from him that hath not shall be taken even that which he hath.*

When Christ has vanquished Satan in the desert, and has so achieved the victor's glory, then will something be given Him. Then angels will come to add their riches to His; then they will come to strengthen the strong who conquered and who therefore needs nothing. They will come to enrich the rich and to honor Him. To Him that had, had to be given.

But, in the dark hour, when Christ is weak, is a slave, and is humiliated, He "hath not," and from him that has not must be taken even that which he has. And, though He gives, the angel also *takes* something from Christ. This time the angel's service is not an adding of luxury to him that is satiated with it; instead, the angel this time lends support to one who would succumb without it, in order that He may not yield before the hour has come. He is "saving" the Son—for that hour. Hence that angel hurts the Son grievously. Never was Jesus' poverty so graphically delineated, so ungainsayably affirmed as fact. O, piteous consolation—the Lord is being reckoned with criminals who are also "saved" for the evil hour.

This is what the Church calls the *state* of Christ's humiliation. It is a proper designation, for the spirit is indeed "in prison" now. A prison is the place where one is retained for the irretrievable sentence.

Moreover, the *condition* of Jesus' actual suffering is exceptionally aggravated by this "strengthening" which the angel gives.

That Christ's suffering was aggravated by the strengthening angel is a fact which we can learn from all of the Scriptures. The very word used in the original and translated *strengthening* in our version of the text points to the fact that the ultimate aim of the Lord of the angels was not the encouragement or consolation of Jesus Christ but only the preservation and sustenance of His capacity for *endurance*. The fortitude of His human nature—that it is which is being strengthened from above, precisely because without such support it would succumb. And—it is being strengthened so that it may suffer again.

No, the coming of that angel represents no interlude in, no respite from, Jesus' passion. On the contrary, his coming prevents the possibility of such respite.

In order to suffer, one must have strength. All suffering takes place by virtue of the strength of the sufferer. Two forces are active in every instance of suffering, an oppressive force which is external, and a force which exerts itself against that and comes from within. A suffering person is like the bellows-organ. The wind blows into it causing the bellows to expand it, but steel weights immediately depress the bellows again. If only the wind is blown into the organ——

Hence, among us, human beings, suffering is always a transitional condition. It leads to recovery or to health. The weight bearing down upon the bellows gains the victory. That means death. Or, it may be that the buoying force within overcomes the weight overhead. That means health, normality, life. Suffering on earth is always operating between these two poles. Suffering never idles. It gets worse or it gets better. The tension cannot persist. Suffering on earth is always a matter of "becoming," never one of "being."

Now think of the Christ of God. The strength residing in Him has expanded as much as possible. But the force which curses Him, which weighs down upon Him, threatens to conquer Him. His body has only a limited potentiality; even His soul cannot eternally endure the pressure. The burden is too great. The strength of humanity cannot bear up against this pressure.

If only that were all. But, at the very moment that the external pressure was increased, the internal strength was dimin-

ished. God forsook Him. The forces that want to assert themselves against Satan and against the threatening death must relax, for God, who can only send a servant, as Elisha once sent
Naaman, is forsaking Him.

Hence, had not heaven intervened, had the increasing external
pressure and the decreasing internal response gone on side by
side, Christ would have succumbed before it was time. Then His
soul would have yielded before it could have borne the eternal
wrath of God. Then He would have fainted, swooned, been defeated. Then suffering would have the apathy of death, the las-
situde of unconsciousness rather than the joy of life as its way
out. The end would have come before the clock reached the hour
in which could be said: *It is finished*.

Not for our life's sake may this be so for Him. If the Man
of sorrows had succumbed before eternal death had overtaken
Him, we could say that the cross had been laid upon His
shoulders, but not that He had *taken* it. Then the curse would
have *overtaken* Him, and we could never have included in the
Form[1] for the Holy Supper that precious statement: "(He) took
the curse upon Himself in order that He might satisfy us with
His blessing."

Only after He has said *It is finished* may Christ yield to death,
or let His flesh relax or stiffen in inactivity. Until then He must
go the whole way without a pause, without a hiatus.

How terrible the angel becomes from that point of view. He
intensifies the pressure but in the direction of severer suffering.
He works towards death. He presses blood out of Jesus' pores.
He does that — the angel does that. Not before, but *precisely*
after his coming, Jesus began sweating His own blood. His angel caused that. He sees to it that the Son of man regains the
strength of a lion; for only in that way can He die the death of
a lamb. If the Son of man be as defenseless as a lamb of what
profit is it that He also dies as a lamb — what reward is that to
Him? Do not the lambs die just so? But if He is a lion who
can shake His mane, who can rise to assert Himself, whose
blood courses lustily through His veins in whom the latent Samson is aroused, and if He then gives Himself up to death as voice-

---

1. As given in the Confessions of the Reformed churches.

less as a lamb, then we can speak of the mediator's strength and the mediator's reward. This angel strengthened the activity of the man Jesus which threatened to lapse into unconsciousness in order that His *active* obedience should keep pace with the *passive*. Jesus' suffering is never allowed to become His fate; it always remains His deed.

How terrible the angel, then!

In the desert where He was tempted Christ told Satan—it was His Messianic consciousness again which prompted the statement —that God should give His angels charge concerning Him, to attend Him on His way, lest at any time He dash His foot against a stone. But that is only half of the truth about Jesus and His angels. For this angel comes not to keep Jesus from hurting His foot, but, on the contrary, to keep Him from dashing on something without feeling the pain. He must ever be active in dashing Himself, for the rock of offense is in the way. The hour of stumbling has struck. And lest Christ stumble over the stone cut by Bashan, the angel opens His eyes. The angel recalls Him to full consciousness; He is given an injection which requickens the lagging pulse of His awareness. When the blood begins flowing again, when He clearly sees the road God has laid for Him again—then the question comes: Art Thou still willing? Wilt Thou go the way God has pointed out? Art Thou prepared?

We cannot appreciate half of the intensity of such suffering. Such passion can be measured by no known standards of comparison. We can at best use our strongest word, and say: *eternal* death is throwing open its doors.

It is in this way, however, that the suffering becomes a power unto salvation for us. If the way had been changed, or if Christ had succumbed on the way, before everything had been finished, He could never have been our Mediator. But since the afflictions of Jesus are the way by which we must enter, the angels have seen to it that the way was not prematurely removed and that He who walked it did not cease walking prematurely.

> The driver's powerful rod
>   Drives Him relentlessly on;
> He walks, and grows very tired,
>   He runs, but can hardly go on.

> The driver's powerful rod
> Drives Jesus still on, on His path;
> The driver who smites Him is God—
> God drives Him and smites Him in wrath.

God smites Him for our salvation.

No, there is no incompatibility between what Christ said about the angels who would descend and ascend for the Son of man at the beginning of His official career, and the absolute solitude, the sheer misery, which He suffers now. *Then* and *now* are co-existent for Him. For the angels first attended Him on His way lest someone or something break up Jesus' path before He Himself saw His hour approaching. But, now that the last steps on the way of obedience must be taken, now the same extraordinary providence of God sees to it that the One on the way does not succumb. He must not stumble to the end half unconsciously: He must stride thither, He must look into God's eyes and say: See, here am I!

Well, this strengthening from heaven attained its sad purpose.

We have referred to the fact already that the face of the angel appeared between the first and second prayer. Now note the words of the text. During His first prayer Jesus fell forward upon the earth (Mark 14:35; Matthew 26:39). He fell on His face, His eyes turned to the ground. When He prays the second time, however, His prayer may be more vehement, more weighty, and full of greater tension, but then He does not fall upon His face. He remains in a *kneeling* position, and is able presently to go away, having mastery of Himself (Mark 14:39; Matthew 26:42). For that reason He is qualified, after a while, to employ the ironical, the extremely severe phrase: *Sleep on now*. And in this way that power grows strong in Him which can make Him encounter and greet the company of murderers presently with the words: *Whom seek ye? I am He*. Thus He again becomes the self-assured one, who can cause the murderers to fall down, before He lets Himself be bound by them.

He must—that first. He wills to—that next. And, therefore, He—*can*.

Gethsemane, Gethsemane — sorrows of Christ. These have their own secret, their own beginning, their own intensity. Heaven and earth coöperate. Powers from above and powers from below coöperate. The angels contribute. Men sleep. And we who are numbered with the sleepers, whose flesh is so weak, we reverently, tremulously say:

We thank Thee, Lord of heaven and earth, that Thou didst lead the Son of man to the foot of Jacob's ladder, to the very foot of it. Angels descended, angels ascended, when Jacob's great Son, the little one, the humiliated one, lay in misery, an exile from the earth, a wanderer of God. We thank *Thee,* Lord, that His angel saw the face of His Father which is in heaven. We thank Thee, Lord, for that one thing: for that *contact.* There was communication. O God, how great a thing that was. We thank Thee for that one great thing. For this we thank Thee, Lord, that though Jacob said, *Surely, the Lord was in this place, and I knew it not,* the Son of man found the Lord in His place *and knew it.* Lord, He saw the angel. How could He still demand: Show me the Father? He who has seen the angel has believed the Father again. Believing is seeing. We thank Thee, Father, that, although Jacob merely *dreamed,* the Great Son of Jacob *watched* in sheer reality.

He watched through God.

He watched for God.

He watched when we slept.

He watched as Mediator in our stead.

Truly, this is indeed a house of God. Gethsemane is Bethel. No—it is more than that. It is the fulfillment of Bethel. Bethel is the place of many angels. Gethsemane is the place of the Great Angel who saw the lesser angel, and was satisfied. Blessed is the greater Angel who is not offended by the lesser.

Lord, even though all should be offended in Thee, Thou canst not be offended in all eternity.

Gethsemane, Gethsemane! Anguish of Christ!

Christ's Sorrows Have Their Own Peculiar Law of Sacrifice

CHAPTER TWENTY-ONE

Christ's Sorrows Have Their Own Peculiar Law of Sacrifice

● *And his sweat was as it were great drops
of blood falling down to the ground.*
—LUKE 22:44*b*.

THE sweat of Christ, or, as some, and that incorrectly, like
to put it, the sweat of God,[1] has impressed the *soul* of the
church more than its *spirit*.

This can be explained readily but cannot be justified.

True, sweat is the soul's concern the moment it proves to be
the sweat of passion. But after that it should also concern the
spirit. Sweat concerns the spirit because passion does.

And the sweat of Christ, particularly, shall become the concern of the human spirit, especially of the thinking spirit of the
church. In the sweat of the Christ the church recognizes the
form (not the essence) of the price which the Bridegroom gave
for the bride.

Besides, the sweat of Christ is blood. It is His own blood
concerning which the church and many outside of it have written books, and which mysticism has accepted as the motif of utmost surrender. That is therefore so much more reason for
saying that the church should concern itself with the sweat of
Jesus' passion which fell from Him in the garden.

Finally, if we consider in addition that the blood-sweating
man, Jesus, is perfectly united with the very God who is in Eternal Life, then we know that the indifference of the spirit of the
church is quite inexcusable.

---

1. Giovanni Papini, *L'Histoire du Christ*, Payot, Paris, p. 323. Dieu est couvert
de seuer, comme s'il venait d'accomplir quelque extenuant.

The thinking spirit of the church should have concerned itself anxiously about the blood which is sweat and about the sweat which is blood. The spirit of the church, so to speak, might well have sweated anxiously in considering the problem of the sweating Bridegroom.

But the fact is that the spirit of the church has been less concerned with that problem than has the soul of the church.

Yes, the soul, the believing soul soon busied itself with the sweating of blood. **Think** of mysticism, for instance. Think of Francis of Assisi, and of the lesser stars of mysticism around him. These all wanted to force Christ's sweat out of their own pores. Indeed, some among them succeeded in sweating blood.

But—such mysticism must be named a labor of the soul rather than a work of the spirit.

And others there are who in great perturbation and with tremulous voices spoke of the sweat which is the blood-sweat of Gethsemane. They pondered how terrible must be the suffering that draws sweat out of blood and drives blood out of the pores like sweat. They shuddered before the affliction so severe that it is nameless among men, and then, with eyes half-closed in fear, they listened to the scientists who said that nameless agony could, indeed, force blood out of the pores like sweat. There is such a condition, the scientists assured them, as an excessive sweating which makes huge drops of sweat look like clots of blood.[1] Fact is, these people were very glad for a moment when their souls which regarded and wanted to regard this suffering as unspeakably excruciating were given the support of scientists who, as guardians of the faith, now came forward to assert that the expression Luke employs in our text was not a hyperbole but a description of actual fact. Why—they hastened to ask—do you suppose that Luke, who was a physician, would not have discriminated painstakingly in this matter? And, is it not remarkable that Luke is precisely the one who emphasizes Christ's sweating of blood?

So men searched, and pondered—but, when it came to the point, it was always *the soul* which wanted to keep its eye upon

1. Groenen, *op. cit.*, 1, 1.

this terrible suffering. The soul assigned a task to the spirit of the scientists only inasmuch as it told the spirit of these to *argue for* the possibility of respectably retaining the terrible description of the sweating Christ. Meanwhile, the essential mystery of the Christ who sweats blood was far less the concern of the spirit than of the soul of the church.

It will be unnecessary for us to establish the fact that Luke's account of the drops of blood which were pressed from Jesus' pores so abundantly and so heavily that they fell to the ground is not hyperbole but matter of fact. Even though we felt unable to say more about such a phenomenon than we are assured of by those specific investigations of men of science, who tell us that in human life such a thing as the sweating of blood is indeed known to accompany awful anguish of soul, we would take Luke's word for it. Gethsemane is and remains the place which alone can *explain itself*. Consequently we accept Luke's description as evidence for the awful oppression weighing on the soul of Christ; we shudder at each drop which falls to the ground. Why do we shudder, you ask? Because in those falling drops of sweat we see the drawing force of the angel, of the angel who strengthened Jesus and who accelerated the motor of Christ's heart and soul again, when it threatened to stop.

And does that, then, suffice for us? May we be satisfied the moment scientists courteously assure us—as they do assure the weak—that Luke was right "indeed"? And, for the rest, may we then withdraw into a corner reserved for mystical meditating, acknowledging there that Christ's agonies must have been most extraordinary?

As though we had not always known that! As though it had not been told us repeatedly.

Indeed, we always knew Christ's anguish was exceedingly severe. In fact, the sweating of blood cannot even tell us that, cannot even preserve the truth for us that Christ's passion was extraordinary. For, if it is true that other people also can sweat blood under the pressure of awful distress, then such sweating of blood is included in the human round of possibilities; it may be above the plane of our bourgeois level of humanity but not above "the" human plane.

It is good for us to see the situation thus and to express it.

For that which transcends our capacity for suffering in the sorrows of Christ is not something perceptible in the *forms* His sorrows take. That is something contained in what we cannot see. It inheres exclusively in the conflict of His *soul,* in the passion of His *spirit.* In these is contained the extra-human in Jesus' suffering. In these and in His divinity, the sweating blood, though perhaps known only at the outer margins of human possibility, does take place within the human bourne. The truth, therefore, that Christ suffered by virtue of *other* laws and because of *other* forces than those known to men, is a truth we believe not on the ground of the blood which He did sweat; but that we believe because of the Word. We *believe* it, and without drawing the slightest suggestion of evidence from the sweating of blood.

.Hence, we insist that this sweating of blood must give our believing *spirit* great concern, and that this biblical datum must lead us back from the solitary cell of nebulous personal meditation and emotional affection, to the lecture-room of the Highest Wisdom, where our spirit may be taught. And we have a strong argument in favor of this insistence in the very history of the church. Church history itself supports the demand that spirit as well as soul should be active in the matter of Jesus' sweating blood.

Think: How long has the church busied itself now with the blood that was pressed out of the Christ at Golgotha? Volumes have been written, the whole problem of the exegesis of Scripture has been read into the issue in several treatises on *the blood and water* which flowed from Jesus' side when the centurion's spear tore the dead body open. Not only did Roman Catholic mysticism put the *soul* to work upon the wounds of Christ on the cross; it put the spirit to work also when it conjured angels into existence who caught up the blood of Christ in vessels as it flowed from His side, in order to pour it over all souls later, even over those in purgatory. And those who were not Roman Catholics have also repeatedly considered the blood which was forced from Christ *at His death* an important subject for Christian *thinking.*

What, pray, in comparison with that, has the spirit of investigation in the church done with the drops of blood which the ground absorbed from the foliage and moss of Gethsemane?

In comparison with what Christ's blood *on the cross* has meant to the inquiring spirit of the church, we must confess, certainly, that the blood which came as sweat in *Gethsemane* has interested the spirit and the mind of faith very, very little.

Who are we, that we may so accentuate one incident and ignore another? Who gives us the right to make an issue of the one, and not of the other? Who gives us permission to cut the account of Christ's blood and of its movement, its expulsion, into two? And to give one part of that sacred page to the *spirit* to *think* about and to reserve another for the sourly-disposed ones to shudder at?

The whole Christ must concern soul and spirit together. Each movement of His blood speaks the same language, addressing the soul only if the spirit is willing to listen simultaneously.

Hence, Christ's sweating of blood is an issue for us *spiritually* also. It is an issue of revelation. It is no less that than is any of the parts of the suffering on the cross, of the sorrows, and of the temptations of the Man of sorrows.

It seems to us that as we try to understand a little of the element of revelation in the sweating of blood, the right trail to follow is precisely that of the contrast between the sweating of blood in Gethsemane and the vehement expulsion of that blood in the death on Golgotha.

Each of these incidents constitutes a kind of terminal point. The blood of Christ was driven out of Him twice: first at Gethsemane; then at Golgotha.

The first time, at Gethsemane, the blood was expelled from within. It was expelled as sweat. The second time, at Golgotha, the blood was forced out by wounds inflicted externally. Thorns had been impressed upon Jesus' brow, lashings fallen upon His shoulders, nails had been driven through His hands and feet, and these all culminated in a thrust of the centurion's lance which caused blood and water to flow from Jesus' wounded side.

Christ's blood, which is the stream of His active life, can, therefore, be driven out in two ways: the way of an *internal agony of soul,* and the way of an *external physical affliction.*

The sweating in Gethsemane is the culmination and acme of the first way. The flowing of the blood and water at Golgotha is the culmination and acme of the other way.

In Gethsemane the blood is forced out organically; at Golgotha it is made to flow by mechanical means.

Jesus sweats blood in Gethsemane but it was not a *human* weapon which forced it out. He sweats the blood before the eyes of God. God and Satan—but Satan only as seen in the light of God—draw that blood out of His body.

At Golgotha, on the contrary, *earthly* weapons exact Christ's blood and let it flow away.

Taken *together,* these two final and high points show us that Christ's blood is being demanded by the *whole* system of the universe. Heaven draws it out, hell drives it out, and the earth forces it out. From every side Christ's blood, which is the bearer of life, is demanded of Him.

From His own side also there is a contrast between these two incidents of the shedding of blood. True, the suffering of Gethsemane and of Golgotha affect the whole Christ, and in body and soul; nevertheless there is a difference between the two.

In Gethsemane no one touched Him except God alone. Hence in Gethsemane His own soul sacrificed itself to God. There He found peace with God, with Him who exacts blood. Christ said *yes* to the Chief Requisitioner of blood. He puts all His powers into His *yes.* He swore the oath of fidelity to God who made Him sweat blood. He did not stint one drop, nor begin to want to recall a single drop. Therefore, it is truth: He sacrificed that blood as an offer. He *gave* it; and He gave it from within. Christ's own sorrows of soul forced out the blood in Gethsemane. In those sorrows He fully justified God. The angel who called Him to life, who recalled Him to the possibility of sacrificing blood, did not avert His vehemently-pulsing blood from him, not even when Christ's spirit understood the angel's heavy demand. The lion was voiceless. In shedding His blood in

Gethsemane, He is *offering His soul.* In Gethsemane He offered His soul as a sacrifice. And on Golgotha He sacrificed His body.

In Gethsemane the blood was forced out by powers none can name. But at Golgotha it was forced out by the weapon that can wound us also.

Gethsemane is therefore the sacrifice of Christ's *blood-soul*[1] as it confronts the invisible world. And Golgotha is the sacrifice of Christ's *soul-blood*[1] as it faces the *visible world.*

The mystery of each of those culminating, final incidents is equally great, however. Gethsemane, where the soul offered itself before the body, and Golgotha, where the body offered itself after the soul, are *united* by the invisible work of the Spirit. By the eternal Spirit Christ offered Himself to God blameless.

When *men* require His blood at Golgotha, He allows them to take it. For He has subjected Himself to their service.

But before He allows mankind to take His blood He gives God that privilege in Gethsemane. In the final analysis it is God alone who forced Christ's blood out at the pores in the Garden of Olives. Only a God-engendered conflict[2] of spiritual forces wrought this extreme crisis in Jesus' life, and injected into the life stream of the Son of man the virus of death.

This is a beautiful mystery: Gethsemane has its own peculiar law of sacrifice. The hour of sacrifice is not determined by grasping human hands; it was determined by Father and Son in God's own time.

Hence, this final, culminating point in the internal way of the shedding of blood shows us the love of Christ Jesus in its highest form. This moment in Gethsemane is as permeated with love as is the other moment at Golgotha.

Human blood is described in the Scriptures as the bearer of life, is it not? *The soul is in the blood.* That means, then, that Christ's blood and His soul are not only taken from Him but also forced out of Him by His own effort.

---

1. Play on the statement concerning sacrifice in the Old Testament: *the soul is the blood* and *the blood is the soul.*

2. Compare Chapter 17: "Christ's Sorrows Have Their Own Peculiar Origin."

If Christ's blood had been shed simply because it *had* to *flow* by reason of human pressure, His soul would have gone out with the blood, but it would not have been given as a *sacrifice*.

Inasmuch, however, as He Himself forces His blood out by means of the soul, His soul becomes a sacrifice. His soul then, like His blood, is moved by the pressure of His own whole human nature.

The act of the priest on this occasion is a perfect one. In the highest sense of the word, Christ lost His life, here in Gethsemane. He lost it to God. Hence He can also receive it again from God, for He who has lost His life shall gain it.

Now that He has lost His soul to God, and has manifested the sign and seal of the losing in the expulsion of His blood, He receives the soul which is life from God in return. He can arise, be master of Himself, arouse the disciples, meet the band of murderers, and hold out His hands to those who bind Him. Soul and life are returned to Him by God, in order that soul and life and spirit may sacrifice themselves to God, but, this time, for the sake of mankind.

For the life and the *blood-soul* which He first gave God, He can now let men take as a testimony for them, and, if they believe, for complete salvation.

This culminating moment of Christ's passion in Gethsemane shows us also the *majesty* of His grief.

Surely, Christ's suffering on account of the invisible world was not less severe than His passion owing to the visible world. In Gethsemane He suffered from the actuality of invisible forces in the spiritual world which attacked Him there. But He also suffered from a full anticipation, a sensitive premonition, of the passion which would descend upon Him at Golgotha. He suffered as severely because of the idea as because of the actuality.

This Saviour can bear mankind now. He withstood and overcame them in the invisible struggle. He withstood them in *idea* before their *actuality* caused Him to groan with convulsions.

Beforehand He saw all those madding people who move against Him now. In the presence of God He saw them. He can resist them all now, for in the labor of His soul He has already reckoned with all of them.

In this fact inheres the majesty of Christ's passion. From this fact it becomes plain that God alone can bruise His Son. Men cannot do it, for them He has already defeated in the arena where God was the only spectator.

The breaking of the body on the cross later is folly and an offense only inasmuch as God is operative in the breaking. Not the external side of the passion on the cross, or of the suffering in Gethsemane, but the spiritual conflict represented in it is the essence of Christ's grief as expressed in the sweating of blood.

Nevertheless, there is folly and offense in the blood-sweating Christ as well as in the crucified Christ.

To Jews and Greeks, says Paul, the *crucified* Christ, peculiarly, is offensive and foolish.

For these can *see* the cross. They simply cannot tolerate the fact that men, mere thugs, can triumph over one who claims to be a world-redeemer. How can one whom ordinary soldiers are able to nail to a cross be the bearer of the world's burdens? Externalities annoy Jews and Greeks and therefore the cross annoys them. The people, the men who are active at Golgotha, are so large and so busy that they rob the Jew and Greek of a vision of the Mediator, Jesus.

But we sense the problem more profoundly still when we have seen Christ sweating blood all *alone before His God.*

In this instance the offense is not external but internal. Christ lay before God alone. The riddle of the event is not that the victim of men is the Saviour of men but that He who was smitten of God receives His great Commendation from God. Whoever sees Christ's blood forced out at the pores by God Himself must think the Gospel of such a Saviour offensive and foolish. As long as nails and hammers manipulated by *human* hands are causing Jesus' blood to flow, we can clench our fists in protest against the men who wield them. And that is to many a welcome substitute for the acquiescence of faith which they do not covet. But when I see God, and the Holy Ghost, and all the angels drawing the blood out of Jesus in Gethsemane, I clench my fists in vain. Then all I can do is to *believe.* Then all that is in me must either rise in rebellion or bow in faith.

The great difficulty does not arise from the bound hands nor from the crown of thorns, for only men are to be blamed for these.

The great difficulty is the blood-sweat. The sweating of that was the work of God. It is the riddle of Abraham who was about to kill his own son, but it is that riddle transferred to the clouds, and to the abyss of perfect knowledge. For Isaac, the son of Abraham, nonchalantly climbs the hill of sacrifice. "Father," he casually asks, "where is the lamb?" He does not sweat one drop of blood. But Christ *knows* everything. The abysses into which the Highest Wisdom is descending today do not make the Son a naive Isaac. Therefore He sweats blood: "Father, I am the lamb."

That God could have treated His Son thus in the last moment before men were permitted to beat Him, that the farewell of Father and Son required the sweating of blood before men came to do their work—that, my heart, was thy fault, thy work, because of thy sins.

Otherwise it were impious, ungodly, to believe a word of this.

Now, therefore, a deeper note is sounded for all who *believe,* in the admonition to have patience: you have not labored to the point of sweating blood! For the blood of Jesus and that of none besides Him was ever taken by outside forces or ever pressed out from within by an invisible power as was His.

In the full, complete sense He alone strove to the point of blood. His struggle proceeded from within outwards, and from without inwards, and all the while it demanded and took the unique, noble blood of our Surety and Mediator.

All that we have written so far would be foolishness if Christ had merely *undergone* the suffering; if Christ's agonies had placed Him before us only as a *passive* sufferer. But Christ does not suffer in that way only.

Once we read: *Jesus wept* (John 11:35). He wept at the grave of Lazarus. But He wept because He "groaned in the spirit, and was troubled." Would He have wept in Gethsemane, then, do you suppose, without having "groaned in the spirit"?

In Gethsemane God *took* His blood. But in God's taking it and through it Jesus also *gave* it Himself.

His blood was taken, His blood was given: Blessed be the name of the Lord.

His soul was taken, His soul was given: Blessed be the name of the Lord.

Christ's Sorrows Have Their Own Peculiar End

CHAPTER TWENTY-TWO

Christ's Sorrows Have Their Own Peculiar End

> ● *Then cometh he to his disciples, and saith unto them,*
> *Sleep on now, and take your rest; behold the hour is at*
> *hand, and the Son of man is betrayed into the hands of*
> *sinners.* —MATTHEW 26:45.

THE agonies of Christ in Gethsemane have their own peculiar origin, and their own peculiar career; naturally, then, they also have their own peculiar victory.

And they manifest that victory in their own unique manner.

This unique, this peculiar victory of the suffering Christ in Gethsemane, as well as the unique announcement of it, must have our attention now. For that is the message of the statement with which Jesus, raised from the dead, as it were, arouses the disciples to *their life*: "Sleep on now, and take your rest: behold, the hour is at hand, and the Son of man is betrayed into the hands of sinners."

Indeed, this statement voices a cry of victory.

This victory already has been achieved in the conflict of prayer of which we were told in preceding verses. We noticed that an intensification of the conflict which perturbed His soul entered into Jesus' prayer. But in proportion to the intensifying conflict grew the possibility of release. It is impossible to compare Jesus' soul with a battlefield on which two opposing armies meet, and on which one can win only when the other retreats. On the contrary, if Jesus Christ is to attain to victory, He must devote full and fine attention to both forces, to both powers active in the life of His soul. He must conduct Himself to victory, by uniting in God what was divided on the battleground of His soul. Time and eternity, desire and need, nature and spirit, the wishes

of love and the demands of law, human experience and divine decree—these He will join together in God.

Thus Christ's prayer in Gethsemane achieves the victory.

The form in which this repeated prayer is described to us indicates that Jesus was gradually coming nearer to His triumph.
His first petition was: Let this cup pass from me. That, according to the phrasing, is the main clause of the sentence. True, it
is modified by the addition "Nevertheless not as I will, but as
Thou wilt." And, although this last thought may be the one in
which Jesus' soul comes to rest as the truth towards which He
inclines, and in which His faith and love here already imbedded
themselves firmly in principle, nevertheless this modifying clause
is not the main clause.

But when Jesus prays His last petition, He formulates it thus:
"O my Father, if this cup may not pass away from me, except
I drink it, Thy will be done." In this instance the phrasing as
well as the content indicates that the words, "Thy will be done,"
constitute the main clause. Jesus is not merely approaching it:
He takes *His stand in* the one will of God.

He does it solely by faith. Jesus cannot by means of His human intellect and earthly apperception completely understand
what God is doing. He still confronts the problem: *If* this cup
may not pass away from me, He says.

Irrespective of the fact that it is not clear to Him, however,
He has taken His stand on the will and on the decision of God,
and that is why victory has been achieved. He announced this
victory as such. Christ does not continue lying on the ground,
waiting for what is to come, but gets up, rouses the disciples and
prepares things in Gethsemane for the reception of—murderers.

The absolute character of the Victor's restfulness manifests
itself also in that other statement to the disciples: *Sleep on now,
and rest.*

We cannot deny that these words leave a strange impression
at first. So strange, in fact, that they have frequently been translated so as to convey a different meaning from the one to which
we are used. Some interpret the adverb "on" in such a manner
as to make the phrase suggest *Sleep later on* or *Sleep after a while
(but just now you must get up).* Others by their translations

give the sentence the meaning of a question: What, do you still sleep on and rest?   And some, although they retain the usual phrasing, inflect it so as to suggest a demonstrative declaration rather than an imperative one: You sleep on and rest.

We, personally, believe the version and meaning given in the Revised Version should be maintained as correct: Sleep on now and rest.

Now the question, of course, becomes: *What does Jesus mean by that statement?*

It cannot be taken to mean that Jesus was seriously giving His disciples permission to rest—for the statement is followed by the command to arise, inasmuch as the enemy is at hand.

The only interpretation left us, therefore, is to accept the words as irony.   Those who wrote the marginal notes of the Dutch Bible must have felt the truth of that to some degree, for they indicate: ". . . He says this in a tone of reprimand such as is used towards a person in allowing something which can no longer be prevented anyhow, and against which one has futilely warned beforehand." This explanation of Christ's remark, and it is a very old one, leaves room for the thought that Jesus' words, which often, and often before this time, had been ironical, are that again on this occasion. Jesus means: Just go on now; you have slept so long and so deeply that you may as well go on. My words addressed to you in the hour of my need, beseeching you to watch, could not keep you awake. So you may as well sleep on now— now that it is quiet here and the whole garden is immersed in stillness.

Irony it is, irony suffused with grief.

The statement, however, is also the expression of a soul that has achieved a condition of peace. We shall comment on that presently.

First, however, another matter. Some people object to this explanation which we are accepting. Against the conception that Christ spoke these words ironically, says one of them, "we can raise the objection that such an ironical inflection—hard as it is to associate with Jesus at any time—is especially unlikely in this very tragic moment of Jesus' terrible passion in the garden. In addition to that, however, such an ironical thrust would imply a bitter disparagement of the apostles, a criticism they had not deserved, inasmuch as their sleeping could not be blamed to indifference or apathy, but was owing to attendant circumstances. Of these, in fact, not the least was their *sharing the grief of* Jesus: *He found them sleeping for sorrow*. And, although it is true that the irony in question is interpreted by some in a way which excludes even the slightest suggestion of sarcasm, still that irony seems out of place here. In view of Christ's personal attitude as revealed in all of His words and actions during these last hours in the room of the Passover and in the garden, it seems hard to believe that Jesus, immediately after vanquishing His awful anxiousness, and while His enemies are at the gate of the garden, could have been blaming His disciples for a certain apathy by His words 'Sleep on and rest'."[1]

This objection, which we have included in full, can be understood, naturally, and deserves our complete and respectful attention.

However, we do not believe that the objection is tenable.

In fact, we choose to reverse the argument. Whereas this writer believes irony has no place in the given connection, we believe it fits there peculiarly. We believe that the power of Jesus' triumph in prayer can be understood rightly only if we see Him rise to assert Himself and to assert Himself also in this utterance of exalted irony.

We may not overlook the fact, in general, that Jesus made ironical statements more than once. The Gospels are very clear about that. In this respect Christ is like His own prophets and apostles. Yes, like His *prophets*. The form of irony occurs again and again in the prophecies of the Old Testament. And like His *apostles*—for Paul, too, adopted the ironical tone at many a holy moment. Hence, if Christ could speak ironically on other occasions, why should it be impossible for Him to do so now? We surely do not have to accept the thought that Christ's "seriousness" is more thoroughgoing at one time than at another.

Besides, we must remember that there is an essential difference between irony and sarcasm. The aversion sarcasm arouses in us is not justified in the case of irony.

---

1. Groenen, P. G., *op. cit.*, p. 198.

Finally, we must bear in mind also that irony is the gift of the truly sublime. Irony is a glimpse of God's own blessedness showered upon us. God is *always blesséd* and, even though it is incomprehensible to us, He is that even in connection with the misery in the world. In God's awareness, contrasts are ever simultaneously present: light and darkness, praise and cursing, repentance and hardening of the heart, the humility of the one who bows before Him and the foolhardy haughtiness of the one who clenches his fist against Him. And, in the same way, on occasion, a *human being* can suddenly be struck by a singly-focused view of *diametrically* opposed things.

At such times the human soul feels an upsurging of intense relief. For the human soul is not God. Being finite, it cannot concretely reconcile opposites.

Besides the grief, however, such a soul also sees vaguely a glimpse of divine *rest*. The soul suffers, but does not perish in suffering. It achieves a state of poise again. Yes, indeed—the human being who sees contrasts, opposites, in the same moment of attention, suffers, but in such a way that, instead of engulfing him, these contrasts keep his mind busy in peaceful equilibrium. The fact is that the contrasts impart a sublimity to his thoughts; they give them a distinction, limited of course to the capacity of a creature, but nevertheless savoring of blessed, divine insight.

Irony is a part of the *image of God in man*.

We have been speaking of God. Concerning that exalted God we read in the Bible: He that sitteth in the heavens shall *laugh* (Psalm 2). That, also, is an expression of irony, and it is surrounded by words of divine love, divine justice, divine holiness, and divine wrath.

Just as God laughs because He *continuously* sees the folly of men over-against His wisdom, and the impossibility of victory in an attack upon God, and the foolish, feverish activity of men and devils who pathetically try again and again to overcome the Almighty, so, occasionally, it can happen that a human being momentarily receives, shares, experiences something of that divine insight. The smile which appears on the face of that human being is a dim and momentary shadow of what in God Himself is perfect—and everlasting.

No, such a smile is not sinful.

It represents rest, poise, equilibrium.

Even as God, the Lord, exists *in* the peace and quiet of His perfect blessedness, and also is moved to have fellowship in love with the fallen world; yes, even as God in the man Jesus Christ weeps, and at the very same hour in Gethsemane also laughs in the blessed poise of His divine existence, even so man cannot be blamed for an irony which is moved to sympathy at the same moment in which it sees the perverseness of the world. On the contrary—only he who has seen the irony, has seen how foolish sin is, and how ludicrous recalcitrant dwarfs are in God's sight, how laughable the feverish activity of hell is—only he can, in a state of self-constraint, go into the world to blast the dwarfs into nothingness or to raise them up and stretch them into their normal length. Only he can by his sublime laughter destroy the incongruous fools who are playing before the threshold of God's palace of holiness, or teach them the seriousness of life. Irony is an expression of a sublime condition of equilibrium; but it, in no sense, excludes profound sympathy, heavy sorrow, or loving sensitiveness to suffering.

The soul of a human being, because it is human, is capable of such irony.

By this very capacity the human soul demonstrates that it holds a position between God and Satan.

We just heard concerning God that He in His heavens *laughs*. His laughter is an expression of the equilibrium, of the perfect experience of blessedness of the God who constantly fixes his attention upon the contrasts of the life of the world.

On the other side of the world lies Satan. Of him we read that he *trembles* (James 2:19). This trembling of Satan is the perfect antithesis to God's *laughter*. Satan, too, can *see*. He has a clear eye and a vitally sensitive attention for the existence of the same contrasts, which God sees. We have discussed that before. With his own eyes Satan sees his own dwarfish figure leaping up against the immense gate of God's awful grandeur. Like God, Satan is aware of two things simultaneously: each moment of his existence, he is fully aware of the impossibility of overcoming God and of the obstinacy of his own restless will in persisting in the assault upon Him. But Satan does not look upon these contrasts from the point of view of the equilibrium and blessedness of the God who *laughs*, but, on the contrary, from the vantage point of the utter misery of Satan and of hell. Hence he trembles: his trembling is the perfect antithesis to God's laughter.

As a general rule, we human beings do not notice the sharp contrasts of our complicated life; wo do not observe one part in its opposition to another. It is as though man were in a valley looking up against a mountain range, of which one mountain hides the other from view. One impression crowds the other out. One point of view prohibits the other, and neither of the two is central. Hence irony—in the case of the sublime man— and sarcasm—in the case of the plain man—are rare, are always the exception. Although God, who is always seeing contrasts, laughs *continuously,* man can express himself ironically only at intermittent moments. Satan trembles continuously, but the sarcastic man can be rid of his sarcasm only at periodical intervals. The instances in which human beings can see simultaneously both elements of the contrasts which exist in reality are exceptional instances.

But if a human being does see both of the contrasting elements in one glance, and if he is one who manifests the image of God, he will use irony in his speech in that moment. His smile then is a faint image of the laughter of the sublime God. And, over-against this, he whose spirit is akin to Satan and allied with evil will express the contrasts he observes in sarcasm. This sarcasm, too, will be a reflection of the wild furor, of the unabating restlessness, and of the self-consuming zeal of the Evil One.

Now we must give this general law the most specific possible application in the human, satanic, and divine confluence of forces in Gethsemane. Here Jesus is bleeding for the sake of and by reason of His . . . *sleepers.* Here the devils are marching against God in parade-formation. Here Jewish authorities seek to elongate pompous phrases and liturgical formulas into staves and swords. And here the contrasts are so numerous and so sharply antithetical, that any observer, whose soul is in a state of equilibrium, must certainly express himself *ironically.*

And there is here a soul in a condition of perfect equilibrium. This soul is *the* soul, is the great, the one, the holy soul, the soul of Jesus. It achieved its equilibrium definitely by prayer. The prayer preceded the poise.

The contrasts present on this occasion were first experienced by his *trembling* soul when it was in a state of restlessness. These contrasts were suffered even to the depths of hell's afflictions, but sinlessly. Hence all those agonies and tremblings, owing to sharp contrasts, in Christ lead to *prayer*. He trembled, but He trembled as one *without sin*.

And now? Now those same contrasts come again before Jesus' soul and spirit. But now He has regained His poise, His equilibrium, and again has done so sinlessly. He can laugh sublimely now; He has prayed, and now He is walking on the heights. "Though I should walk through the valley of the shadow of death, I should fear no evil," but continue treading on My heights.

This irony, then, represents the zenith of Jesus' restfulness and poise in contrast to the nadir of restlessness in the hour of hell's temptation just experienced. He sees the same contrasts both times but from different points of view; first, from the agony of excruciating pain; then, from the viewpoint of the superior calm of a second Adam who conquers in God's strength, from the balanced poise of an image-bearer of God, of the expressed image of God's laughing self-sufficiency, the reflection of God's exalted glory.

It may be well to consider that last point more specifically. We said Jesus' irony harmonizes with the depths of His prayer. In truth Christ's praying was a struggling with the sharp contrasts which broke into His human and His official life. There were the mountain-tops. They lay over-against each other, as grand and exalted mountain-tops can. One of these was the peak of His own *communion with the Father*. The other was that of His rejection by the Father. Yes, there were those towering mountain-tops. The one was that of His human love for life. The other was that of His official obligation to prepare His limbs for His dying.

Christ, in His praying, had to labor so strenuously because He had to conquer by faith, and by faith see the essential oneness of

the two mountain-tops. This He had to do, not by abstract specu-
lation and in a condition of divinely isolated grandeur, but by
means of a human labor of faith in which He had to be afflicted
in all the afflictions of His people. So He had to learn to believe
and to see the oneness of the mountain-tops, and to leave the remainder, the great remainder, to the God who is His God also.

In the labor of that prayer Christ was purely a human being.
He who as God gave expression to the sublime laughter of the
second Psalm now lay low in abject humiliation as man. He saw
the contrasts but could not discover the oneness of these. He
suffered, He sweated, He groaned. Father, Father! He was
pressed hard, for a great chasm divided the two peaks of time and
eternity, of desire and destiny. He could not harmonize the contrasts from *on high,* for He lay in the deep gorge of humiliation
and undoing. His prayer was a struggle to see *as one* what He
saw *as two.* His struggle was not a struggle of mind but a conflict
of faith.

He does not come down from the heights of heaven in order
to see in bird's eye view how those two peaks which He somehow
could not draw together were really one in the thoughts of God.
No, no. He does not descend from those heights in order to
draw recalcitrant peaks together *as a laughing God.* No, no. *Lord,
out of the depths I cried to Thee.* Out of *our* depths, the depths
of man, out of the deep chasm of our shortsightedness, O fellow-
man, He had to labor upwards, and by faith plant His feet on the
extremity of the jutting crags of time and eternity, of desire and
destiny, of the prayer to live and the command to die.

Christ *wrought* this victory as a human being and by faith.

Because He did this we may call His irony His state of rest
and equilibrium in contrast to the restlessness which preceded.
For, because Christ is standing on those two peaks now, both feet
firmly planted on them, and because by faith He has reconciled,
has seen as one, time and eternity, desire and destiny, love and
justice, He now beholds from the vantage point of *rest* the very
contrasts which a while before filled Him with an unrest unto
death. Now it is His irony which can see the dwarfs who are
the apostles in all the pathos of their frailty, in the indifference of
their fatigue. Ironically He looks upon these who are able to

sleep amid the alarm which hell is sounding against heaven, amid the ringing of bells whose heaven-sent sounds reverberate through the spheres. Jesus endures it now, without toleration, but with perfect calm, without perturbation. He knows now: For such as these I shall die. He knows His death will not be the futile sacrifice of friendship for friendship, but one born of the perfect will to fulfill the demands of justice, through love. He knows now that Gethsemane and Golgotha are so awfully sublime because the Bridegroom can only give Himself to a bride who can give nothing, but can only receive. He knows there is a heavenly irony; He knows that, as He looks upon those sleeping disciples. The covenant of grace, like every covenant, has two parties; and yet, in a sense, there is only one party, for the church is the sleeping beauty who cannot even remain awake in the hour of the Bridegroom's coming. Now He knows that He is the Bridegroom who will buy His bride; but He knows, too, that only by purchase can He make her His bride.

Sleep on now and rest . . . .

The phrase expresses a unification of desires by virtue of the fear of God's name. It expresses a unique victory on the part of the perfect man who labored in prayer as man never labored before. With these words He who was undone in the depths strides to His heights again.

In this way Christ attained His restfulness, His poise, His balance.

That is another way of saying: Now His suffering will grow severer.

For, in looking fully in the face the contrasts which will cause His suffering and condemnation, He passes out of the *moments* of *acute* sorrows into the *chronic state* of passion.

Gethsemane, therefore, occupies a unique position in the story of the passion. It raises Christ from the depth of suffering in which intellect and will cannot yet join hands to the upper plateau of passion where He regains equilibrium, and where the passion and its causes receive His even and uninterrupted attention.

The ironical statement uttered on the other side of His prayers sharply outlines the transition from the abyss to the plateau. True, Christ gave expression to the statement as one who had achieved poise and attained balance, but also as one who, so far from being rid of His suffering in that state, precisely *continues* it. Christ has achieved a state of equilibrium, has reached the plateau of calm, but He has not yet climbed to those heights from which He can laugh as God does. His course continues to wind its way on earth; the contrasts which He will continue to encounter will also continue to grieve Him, precisely because He sees them now in their sharpness and in their life-size, and because He sees them continuously.

Therefore, we can say that the end of the sorrows in Gethsemane is the transition to the second phase of suffering, in which Christ, who could not be silent in Gethsemane, can be silent before Caiaphas, before Pilate, and before Herod. And, in this second phase, He can speak to God later, and can do it in His *strength;* He can be the intercession for murderers, can unlock paradise for a lost soul, and assign a home to His oppressed mother.

The ironical statement "Sleep on now and rest" marks the transition from this first to this second phase of His suffering.

Yes, rest has come to Him; but it has increased His suffering.

His suffering becomes chronic suffering now. Now, from beginning to end, it will be a conscious, deliberate deed, one of which He is always sensitively, fully conscious — and the deed not of a poised God but of a poised human being whose poise and calm is owing *solely to faith.*

Precisely because of His equilibrium, the human part of Jesus' suffering will be more alien to us than it has been. That will now increase in strength and sublimity from moment to moment. In the presence of it we grow afraid, feel insignificant, are embarrassed. Then, however, He lifts us up to His heights in His priestly arms. A Saviour who can endure the "costly folly" of disciples who sleep near God's hell fire, and then is willing to die for them, is the *supreme* Priest.

This ironical sufferer is *the Surety.* He is that in His use of irony also.

Sleep on now and rest.

By that humiliating statement Jesus puts before His eyes and expresses with His lips the truth that His human soul received no benefit in His suffering from His disciples. "The disciples proved that they could not be one with Jesus in His suffering; they place no value on it; no strength passes out of them; they sleep and rest; Jesus gets no help from them." They were as dead men in this hour; as dead men good enough to bury their own dead, but who did not prove strong enough to take an active part in the struggle for *life*.[1]

Jesus knows and proclaims that in the struggle of His soul He has had no support from the best and the first, and from the representatives present here of those whom the Father has given Him. He knows they have left Him quite alone, and that they can never enrich Him because they are mere fragments of misery. And now, fully aware of that, He goes to take up the cross for them. Knowing that they have nothing to give Him, He gives Himself to them! That is the Mediator's passion and the will to achieve it in utmost perfection.

Let the dead bury their dead—that is a serious utterance, for who is not "dead" in himself? But Christ who lets the dead stay at their grave-digging, proceeds to *achieve life,* and to lay it after a while upon the corrupted spirits of the dead. So the path well-worn with the feet of many pall-bearers becomes the playground of those God has called to life and light.

A Surety who can make such ironical utterances is a perfect Surety. How the sense of this enhances the word of the Scriptures, the comforting word about God who (in Christ even now) gives generously and does not blame!

In this way Christ's sorrows had an end. Their own peculiar end. At any other place in the whole world irony would have been excluded in such a moment.

May everyone subject himself to the Man of sorrows, then. May everyone admit Him who perfectly utters irony, in order that He may judge of man; and may no one suppose that he from his side can judge of Christ.

By the grace of God this Ironicus is too exalted and sublime. Confronted by such grandeur of humanity our bravest words are not worth expressing. We can only listen and believe.

---

1. The quotation and the striking allusion to Matthew 8:22 is taken from Dr. F. W. Grosheide's *Kommentaar op Mattheus*, p. 324.

But when we *believe* we see Him *stand* there. Thereupon we see Him *go* His way. He *goes* to die, He, the ironical man of ironic, peace-bringing sufferings. The sublimity of heavenly rest enlightens His face; nevertheless, He covers the glow with the mustiness of an arid death. The cross does not only cover His divine but *also His human* majesty and rest.

He laughed, but only with a sad smile. *Sleep on now and rest.* But the face which gave expression to the smile is dearer to us now, for we see that it is covered with tears.

The *man* Jesus — who can suggest more of what that means. He is much more beautiful than the children of men. He is much more beautiful than the most gifted poet laureated by men. His irony is of a different order, of a higher character, than that of the *poet laureate,* for it is holy. Besides, He Himself is entirely without sin.

He is also very terrible.

For He whose lips phrase speech more finely than a poet's mouth, whose spirit is richer than the most genuine poet's soul, has taught us that genuine souls and celebrated artists cannot redeem the world: that the *Poet* God has crowned with laurel becomes the thorn-crowned Surety. His spirit proves to be more *human* and delicate than that of the most refined connoisseur, more beautiful and artistic than any spirit among the children of men. But without sacrifice that pure soul cannot redeem us. He has everything that can charm us. The phrase "cultural refinement" as a characterization of Jesus' soul would be ridiculously inadequate. It says too little about the perfect harmony of the purely organized soul of Jesus Christ. The most sensitively constituted man holds his breath in witnessing such irony.

Hence, O Son of man, neither humaneness nor culture but *sacrifice* only can purge us and cause us to repent by faith; only sacrifice can draw us to God.

Because Christ knew that He yielded to captivity.

The mouth which pronounced the irony with a full sonorous sound, moving us to silence, closed after a while.

The hand which could raise those who slept gently, gives itself up to the handcuffs.

Therefore He is dear to us.

For had He not been such, we would have been bound. Then, instead of listening to heaven's irony, we would have to listen to Satan's sarcasm.

He is dear to us, using irony, bound.

This irony first of all declares itself blessed: Blessed, it says, is the pure in heart, who has laughed beautifully, for He has seen God. Thereupon it declares us blessed also. It purchases our peace. It prepares us, us, too, though we cry now — to laugh one day with pure, holy, sublime laughter. Blessed are they that weep now — for they shall be comforted. *Sleep on. And rest.*

The Harmony Profaned:
The Perfect Round
Is Broken

CHAPTER TWENTY-THREE

The Harmony Profaned: The Perfect Round Is Broken

● *And while he yet spake, behold a multitude, and he that was called Judas, one of the twelve, went before them, and drew near unto Jesus to kiss him.*
But Jesus said unto him, Judas, betrayest thou the Son of man with a kiss?
—LUKE 22:47, 48.

CHRIST is ready now to receive *the people*. He has fought the fight with His God. The sacrifice was placed before the court of God, when none were admitted. Now that the soul of Christ has been placed on the altar of God, that offer can be publicly presented.

Men may come near now: publicly, too, Christ will make a spectacle of the authorities and powers which oppose Him, and will triumph over them. First He vanquished them in seclusion, in secret. Now follows the great public Presentation: God is seated in the heavens; the thunder-storm breaks loose. *Men may come near now.*

And they are coming already.

They come with staves and swords, equipped to capture finally the prophet of Nazareth. They have found someone to point out the way for them. That someone is Judas.

And Judas is one of the twelve. We know that, of course. But the evangelists took the trouble to say it in so many words once more. Their readers knew it, too, for it was written in the gospel. Nevertheless the evangelists repeat it: Judas was one of the twelve. And this particular truth is the important one in this connection. Not one of the strangers, not one of the acquaintances, but one of the twelve, one of the specially gleaned group of intimate friends, delivered Jesus up into the hands of those who carried swords and staves.

The rest of the story is well known. We will not disclose the precise sequence of events (absolute certainty about that we probably will never have), but be satisfied with the particulars about which the evangelists are perfectly clear. While en route Judas and the group had agreed upon a sign of recognition, and Judas had conducted them to the place where Jesus generally stayed. Naturally, it would be difficult for this group of soldiers, partly strangers to the district, to capture Jesus if He should not want to be taken. It might very well be that in the general confusion the Nazarene would make good His escape. It had happened before. These men could not have surmised a hint of the fact that Jesus has "an hour" in which He does *not* give Himself up, and "an hour" in which He *does* give Himself up into His captors' hands. But the uncertainty about the chances for a successful capture are reduced to a minimum by Judas. He promises them that he, as usual, and as though nothing were amiss, will step up to Jesus and kiss Him. We know that in the Orient students were wont to greet rabbis so.

The kiss will be the sign of recognition; he will give it; they can capture Him then.

In passing, we should say that it is not correct to state, as some do, that Judas repeatedly kissed Jesus. The form of the verb employed in the original does not warrant that interpretation. We can speak of a hearty kiss but not of a repeated kiss.[1]

It requires no contention to assert that Judas' kiss hurt Jesus severely, that it burned His soul and spirit much worse than His face showed. It would have wounded Him, even if we thought Jesus none but a man having the usual responses to such stimulus.

But we can understand Christ's suffering as evoked by Judas' kiss correctly, only if we see Him in this connection also as a Mediator.

---

1. Compare Dr. F. W. Grosheide's commentary on Matthew 26:49. The word of the Greek text used here is also used in the Septuagint; whereas the Hebrew has the simple verb *to kiss*.

Jesus Himself has pointed our thoughts in this direction. His question has not the connotation of "Dost thou betray a *friend* with a kiss?" but denotes "Dost thou betray the *Son of man* with a kiss?" The designation *Son of man* has its unique position here. Taken as such this name indicates only that "Jesus was born of man, and thus was a man among men." The expression has no Messianic content, simply refers to Him as man. But when Jesus prefixes the definite article to it and refers to Himself so often in the third person, He reveals Himself as a particular Son-of man; in fact, as the one indicated in Daniel 7:13 . . . . Jesus uses the name specifically when He refers to His suffering and to the qualifications that suffering implies, because these are the *qualifications of the Messiah*. Jesus uses the phrase in order to call the attention of the people to Daniel 7:13, which He is approximating all along, in order that so, too, He may teach them that He is the Messiah.[1]

If we keep that in mind we know that Jesus is emphatically pointing to the heart of the betrayal of Judas and to the essence of His own suffering when He speaks, in this connection, of the Son of man. We may not, in considering this event, limit ourselves to the relationship of a friend to a friend, of a teacher to a student, of a man of refinement to an uncultivated man, of the bearer of an ideal to the fanatic supporter of another ideal, of a reformer to a rebel, of a person devoted to improving the world to a chauvinist, of the peacher of a new doctrine to a representative of sectarian "orthodoxy."

The relationship obtaining here is this one: On the one side, the *Son of man;* on the other, *one of the twelve.*

In these two terms the contrast reaches its climax; these terms alone define the contrast correctly. Those other matters have some connection with these, yes; but they do not touch on the essence.

A corollary of that definition of terms is that we have no business combing the literature of history, not even the Bible, for examples of "other" friends who were treacherously deceived and killed. One can find analogous instances, even in the Bible. These have been pointed out at length. Men have pointed to the case of

---

1. Grosheide, Dr. F. W., *Kommentaar op Mattheus*, pp. 387 and 388.

Joab and Amasa, and to others. Such analogies are virtually irrelevant. Such comparisons represent a departure from the straight line, and one which is dangerous for orthodox thinking. For these comparisons are made in the manner of those who see in this event simply a relationship of friend to friend.

The matter is profounder; it concerns the Son of man in relation to one of the twelve. The office of the Messiah is relevant to it. He who holds that office is the One, who, as the Son of man, fulfills and perfects all the histories of His *types* in Himself. Instead, then, of looking for an "analogy" in the older and newer chronicles of friendship, we must look to this episode for the perfection and fulfillment of the conflict which has existed throughout the ages, but which expresses itself in he kiss of Judas. It is the conflict between the spiritual office of the Son of man and of the fleshly distortion of that office by those who do not believe and have not love.[1]

If we think of that, we know that Christ's suffering is terrible because He as the Son of man fell into the hands of murderers through the agency of a traitor's kiss.

The title *Son of man* proclaims that His office as Mediator at no time weakened or ignored His *true humanity*, His being genuinely, perfectly human.

By sending Christ to earth God revealed Himself in human form. Everything divine, His divine demands, His divine Son, He expressed in a man, and that man is the Son of man. He is not a stranger, who cannot be trusted among men. He does not strut around as though He were the great Exception, making everyone automatically profane except Himself. He is not a ray of light beaming across the darkness of night simply to make the darkness more conspicuous. No, no. He is the Son of man; nothing human is alien to Him;—in fact, instead of putting it negatively, we can say that everything which is essentially human is His.

The essence of the suffering on this occasion is not that Judas, by means of his kiss, sells God as God, but God Himself in the

---

1. It would be more in harmony with the Reformed interpretation of the Scriptures to allude to Ahithophel's relation to David (though the specific particular of the kiss is no part to it) than to Joab and Amasa (even though the kiss could be included in the analogy for these).

form of the Son of man. Its terribleness inheres in the fact that Judas deceives in the very hour in which God has partly concealed His glorious being as expressed in the Son of man, but has concealed it without deception, simply to give Himself to men as one they can trust, as the Son of man.

Christ's humanity, however, is not the only part of Him that is being insulted and profaned by Judas' kiss.

The Son of man is an office-bearer; hence Judas also profanes His office. Until this moment the kiss of Judas is the cross for Jesus' official life. As is the cross, so the kiss is folly and an offense in the Messianic, official life of Jesus Christ.

The sharpest point of the contrast which pained Jesus was that Judas was one of those given Him by the Father, and that Judas nevertheless betrayed Him. "Those that Thou gavest Me I have kept, and none of them is lost, but the son of perdition."[1]

This is the comforting way in which Jesus puts the possession of the eleven over-against the loss of that one. The Saviour, obviously, is viewing the question of the loss of that one from the human side. He is not talking about the gift of the Father from the vantage point of God's counsel, but from that of His own appreciation of it as a man, living in time. But from this human vantage point the fact is a problem to Jesus: one of those "given" Him by the Father has been lost. He knew it all along, it is true. But Judas' kiss seals the fact. And Christ's suffering inheres in His awareness of this loss.

The difficult problems begin revolving in His mind again: In the mutable oscillating appearances of time, He must believe in the immutable faith and firm counsel which exists yonder in God's eternity. He can believe in the relationship between these two but He cannot see it. Jesus prayed before He called the twelve; we have pointed that out before. And because one of these twelve who came to Him *in response to this prayer* is lost to Him now, that loss becomes a painful problem to Him. O, yes, we can quickly "solve" it for Him by distinguishing between a "narrow" and a "broad" sense in speaking of the Father's *giving*. That is an easy solution; too easy, sometimes. We can assert that Jesus

1. John 17:12.

really lost none of those "given" Him in the narrower sense. We can establish a relationship between election in eternity and regeneration in time, and add: only where both of these elements are found can we speak of the Father's giving. And of these the Son of man loses none.

We can make such distinctions. We must make them; at least we must move in that direction. Now, too, we may not be satisfied until we have considered this statement carefully. For we are not dealing with the discoveries of men, but with the revelations of God.

But our concern just now, we must remember, is the suffering soul of Christ. And He did not merely rationalize from a dogmatic and prophetic point of view what was happening before His eyes and slipping out of His hands. On the contrary, He suffered this loss, felt it acutely, experienced it, by means of His human appreciation. A part of His struggle was to throw a bridge from the passing events of the day to the Word which is eternal. Between the one and the other, between the dogmatic explanation and the personal experience we wish to fix no antithesis. But we do want to distinguish between the two. Hence it is correct to say that Jesus' human soul suffered severely when one of those *the Father had given Him* proved lost.

This problem becomes particularly significant in its relevance to Christ's office. Not only as man but also, and especially, as the Mediator of God, Christ likes harmony. He likes what is well-rounded, complete, beautiful, and harmonious.

But He must conclude by seeing fragments, by seeing piecework. Wrestling with God in prayer, in Gethsemane, He has just sensed the harmony between the distorted things of time and the straight lines of God's eternity. Now Judas' kiss places Him before the question how He can possibly believe in harmony, when He must leave Gethsemane, sure that the line is broken, the perfect round disturbed, that the twelve have been reduced to eleven.

We must linger a moment over that last assertion. Christ, as all will know, had *twelve* apostles, and exactly that number not by chance but on purpose. That specific number was designedly chosen. It reminded of the twelve tribes of Israel and also of the twelve patriarchs.[1] That the number twelve was not accidental, but necessary, to the holy *order* of His Messianic work becomes obvious the moment we pay attention to His Messianic consciousness. At the time of the calling of the twelve apostles the clear and self-assured consciousness of the Messiah is very certain that He is the Father of *Young Israel,* just as Father Jacob and his twelve sons, the twelve patriarchs, is the father of *Old Israel,* the Israel of the flesh. When Jesus chooses twelve, Christ, that is, the Messiah, as is His privilege, tears another life out of Israel's life, and emancipates it. He gathers around Him, He *bears* out of the womb of His *will,* a new Israel, Young-Israel, the Israel of the Spirit, whose appeal is not external, whose beauty resides within. He does not derive His strength from a fleshly ancestry of the twelve patriarchs, but from a spiritual building based upon the foundation of the twelve apostles. So Jesus sets the twelve patriarchs who are the beginning of the Israelite dispensation of the covenant of grace over against the twelve apostles as the beginning of the dispensation of the covenant of grace for the New Testament. The calling of the twelve was a reference backwards to the generations of father Jacob. It represented a quake in the Kingdom of Heaven. Jesus Christ, in virtue of the qualifications given Him, and full of Messianic consciousness, chose twelve apostles, as a foundation — the "foundation," you remember, "of apostles and prophets"—on which to build the whole communion of the New Covenant. Yes, Jesus referred to Jacob, to Israel, and to his twelve fleshly sons, in order to set Himself over against him as one who has gained twelve spiritual name-bearers. But he also looks ahead to the throne of the Almighty, saying: Father, I will; I will, Father. My strong will is placing the twelve thrones of the New Testament next to those others around Thy throne, those of the Old Testament. I will, Father; I will. My Messianic will would now place next to the twelve tribes of Israel the twelve times twelve thousand, the hundred forty and four thousand sealed saints of the New Testament.[2] The twelve patriarchs have their names written in the foundations of the city of father Jacob, and on the earthly house of Zion. And I, as the Father of the new

---

1. Grosheide, *op. cit.,* p. 122.
2. Revelation 14.

Israel, would write the names of *My* twelve apostles in the foundations of the new Jerusalem.

Indeed, the choosing of the twelve was the forceful deed of the Messiah, the deed of jurisdiction and of strong faith.

Yes, it was an act of strong faith also. These twelve represented a repetition, but also an expansion. The Old Testament had its twelve patriarchs; Jesus has His twelve apostles. That is repetition.

But there is an imperialistic tendency, an eagerness for expansion in Jesus' *twelve*. *Twelve?* That is *three* times *four*. *Three* is the number of God; *four* is the number of the world. By means of His twelve Christ hopes to bring God into relationship with the world.[1] He wants to penetrate the world. By the apostleship of those twelve He, through Himself, will gain the world for God.

That was strong faith, was it not? In this the Messiah puts over against the desire for expansion of the fleshly kingdom that of the spiritual kingdom. Old Israel, too, was eager to dominate the world: it still wishes to do so. But, from His side, Christ puts over against that the mission, the world-mission of His kingdom. He does that by appointing the twelve.

His whole soul, all of His strong spirit was attached to those twelve, also to their number. His pretention as Messiah must rise or fall with those twelve, and with their number, *twelve*. A strong, a firm, a conscious usurping of His will is manifested in the choosing of those twelve. His will is a thousand times stronger than that of Israel's father, the father of the twelve patriarchs. Twelve sons were born to him, but he obtained these sometimes by illegitimate means. Moreover, it was not really his will, but God's from whom they were born. And he himself did not fully appreciate what these twelve would mean in the world. But when Christ comes, He bears these twelve Himself, out of His own will. He draws them to Him. He takes them. He constrains them in a moment. The choosing of these twelve, therefore, was one of the brilliant apices of His Messianic task. He cannot spare those twelve; He needs them. His office, His kingdom, His prophecy, His filling of the Old by the New Testament

---

1. Grosheide, *op. cit.*, p. 122.

must rise or fall with the preservation of His beautiful, symbolical, and therefore also His necessarily unalterable *twelve*.

Those who think such symbolism is arbitrary, or that it has no relationship to the pain Jesus feels, now that the number has been broken, should read again the *genealogy* of Jesus Christ as it is recorded in Matthew 1.

There, too, and before the Messiah appears in the world, a series of names (by no means all) are selected from the generations of the Old Testament and are so arranged that the symbolism of the numbers is put into the service of prophecy, which, as we know, illuminates the whole of history in its own peculiar way. The names are selected and the numbers drawn up in such a way that the writer of the chapter on that basis prophesies about the history of the Old Testament, out of which Jesus has legally descended.

He distinguishes between three epochs of time: from Abraham to David; from David to the captivity; from the captivity to the birth of Christ. Each of these epochs comprises fourteen generations. Three times fourteen, therefore, is the number which symbolizes the history from Abraham to Christ.

Those *fourteen,* of course, suggest at once the number *seven,* which is half of fourteen. And seven is the holy number, the number representing completeness and representing also the communion between God and the world. Over-against *twelve* as the product of *three* and *four* is placed the number *seven* as the sum of three and four. In Israel, therefore, God and the world are united. The seven represent God (*three*) and the world (*four*). Hence the law of Immanuel can be found in Israel, for Immanuel means: God with us; *three* plus *four*. In this is contained prophecy: the history of Israel issues in Jesus Christ as the true Immanuel, for He is the crown of Israel in His person and His work. He is the fulfillment and the interpretation of the number-symbolism of the perfect harmony which is the mystery of God's kingdom.

But the first chapter of Matthew goes farther than that.

In each epoch of Israel's history the number *seven* returns twice. Each period has *two* times *seven* generations. The law of Immanuel, consequently, appears in its completeness (twice).

This again issues in and tapers into a point in Jesus Christ. He is harmony in its extreme perfection.

Even that does not exhaust the number-symbolism. We are told of *three* times *fourteen* generations. That means *six* times *seven* generations. When six groups of seven have gone by, therefore, the *seventh* group of *seven* will come. That will come in the person of Jesus Christ. Just as in Israel after *six* units of time the *seventh* unit arrived as a Sabbath-period, so the Sabbath-rest perfectly begins with the New Covenant. And just as the *seventh* group of *seven* years arrives after *six* groups of *seven* have passed, to usher in the year of jubilee, of the emancipation of slaves, of the blessing of the poor, of the enriching of the miserable, so Christ's coming into the world will represent an enrichment of the poor, for these will be given goods. That year, too, will emancipate the slaves, and will bless the exploited and down-trodden.

See how informed these matters are with a number-symbolism which Jesus points to as the first rule of action and source of rest.

These truths are reinforced by the thought that the sequence of names in the first chapter of Matthew (*three* times *fourteen*), besides representing a number-symbolism, is also a way of naming. In the Hebrew language *letters* of the alphabet can also be read as numbers. And if you read the letters in the name of King David in terms of their corresponding figures, the result, the sum, is *fourteen*. Hence *fourteen* means David. And *three* times *fourteen* generations, then, means *three* times the glory of David.

The first epoch, from Abraham to David, represents David's rising. The second epoch, from the kings of the house of David to the captivity, represents the period of his flourishing. The third epoch, then, extending from the captivity to Christ, represents David as the stem of Jesse.

Then as the crown of all will come the Christ, who is the rod out of the stem of Jesse, David's fulfillment, bringing peace to the house of David, and manifesting the beauty of His glorious being there.

Such thinking is not the product of illegitimate allegorizing, or of a false juggling of figures. The scientific researches of believers of the Scripture[1] confirm the fact that these are the implications of the grouping of names and their being limited to the chosen number in the first chapter of Matthew.[2]

It is certain, then, that even before His birth, Christ was announced in the world as the one in whom the laws of the kingdom of Heaven will find rest. Especially if we remember that the number-symbolism of the genealogies recorded in Matthew is not arbitrary but *prophetic,* do we know that Christ Himself, when He comes to interpret His family-record by means of His official work, does not act arbitrarily but purposely when He chooses His twelve. When, at the beginning of His Messianic work, He appointed those twelve, He proved that He understood the meaning of the book of His generation Himself; and by the same token He proved that He was the true giver of peace, of rest; as Immanuel He was appearing to give Israel its real sabbath-rest.

Now recall the kiss which Judas gives. Surely, you feel the brutal pain which it inflicts. And the enigma presents itself: But this breaks the perfect round of twelve. This interferes with the harmony. Judas' kiss goes cutting its way through the spheres; a laugh of derision echoes somewhere in God's universe, a laugh so loud that things quake because of it; the laugh is in derision of the number-symbolism of the whole Bible and also of that of Jesus Christ Himself. Judas simply draws a line through Jesus' precious number-harmony; this he does for murderers and sword-bearers, and in the presence of the devils. He reduces the twelve to eleven. The number of completeness becomes a foolish number which seems to sing the praise of folly.

Jesus must die now looking upon that fragmentary number, upon that "stem."[3]

1. In particular Dr. F. W. Grosheide (*Kommentaar op Mattheus*) who, for the most part, also adheres to this interpretation of the number-symbolism.

2. The chapter must not be regarded as an exhaustive citation of fathers and forefathers. It is not designed to be that. Above it we read: *The book of the generation of Jesus Christ.* This chapter is the Genesis of the New Testament. It reveals the spiritual laws of God's harmony as the prophetic spirit discovers them in the history of the generation of Jesus Christ.

3. Compare "The Stem of Jesse" of Isaiah 11:1.

The number *eleven* danced up and down before His eyes when, at Golgotha, it was dark for three hours. Eleven—eleven—broken harmony! Is this David? The David of Matthew 1? Has not the stem out of Jesse been broken again? He who yearned for a holy and round number, and expressed His Messiah-spirit in it, He is stumbling over Judas, is He not? The whole Old Testament is stumbling over him. The whole of Christian preaching is. This, is this not an offense, a stumbling block to Jesus' Messianic consciousness? Eleven — only eleven — the perfect round is broken!

Truly, this is to *suffer*. How this wounds me, Father above, Father of round numbers! Jesus' suffering is as severe as Abraham's was when he was called upon to sever a harmony finally discovered, with the stroke of a knife. Jesus' suffering is worse. It is the "stem." It represents failure; to all appearances, it represents failure. The year of jubilee is called into question by Judas' kiss. The whole doctrine of revelation and the whole body of Christology is very closely related to that traitor's kiss. And, as it seems, Christ has not only failed as *King,* as the great David (*three* times *fourteen*) but also as Priest. Aaron, at least, may carry his breastplate with its twelve precious stones, undefiled, into his grave. But when Christ dies, one of those *twelve* stones, which the Father has given Him, is lacking.

O yes, the kiss of Judas is something more than a sinister act of treachery committed by one friend against another.

In order to say that, we need not agree with the foolish self-assurance of that so-called religious-historical school which sees revealed in the twelve apostles a kind of symbolical expression of the idea of the pattern and of the holy, cosmical order in the laws which can be read from the stars. Members of this school have asserted that the choice of *twelve* was owing to the fact that the light of the world distributed its domain among so many lords; and these members, naturally, have not failed to identify the twelve apostles with the twelve signs of the zodiac, all surrounding *Christ,* as the light of the world. As eager as we are to stay far away from these untenable and unwarranted speculations, so eager are we to cling to the *prophetic purpose* of the number-symbolism in the Bible itself, also as it applies to the *twelve* apostles.

This last consideration makes the problem more difficult for us. The religious-historical school which we named just now, believes that only *gradually,* decades later, these symbolical explanations occurred to the Christians, by way of giving expression to the thoughts outlined above.

These, then, care very little whether the historical Judas did, or did not leave the circle of twelve. For—so the argument goes—that requisite twelfth individual was restored to the group, anyway, in the person of Matthias, or in the person of Paul. What matter if Christ Himself lived before these people? For "Christendom" as a composite of pagan and Hebrew elements drew all these mythologies within the pale of its holy books in its own peculiar way, fancying it so that the astral idea—signs of the zodiac—was embodied in twelve fishermen, who became apostles. And to these interpreters Judas' falling out of the circle of twelve, and Jesus' having to die with His eyes fixed upon broken number, are not catastrophes.

To those of us, however, who believe the Scriptures, and believe them in their *historical* records, too, both these matters are very serious. The moment we look upon Judas in the light of Christ, and upon Judas' falling out of the circle in the light of the deliberate, symbolically prophetic choice of twelve by Jesus, the kiss of Judas becomes a tantalizing enigma. We know that Jesus has actually lived. The notion of *twelve* apostles was not a product of the pagan-Jewish fancy of the first Christians, but existed in Jesus' own soul and spirit. The notion of the *harmony* of the twelve did not arise in the mind of the Church *after* Jesus' death, but was present in His soul at the beginning of the fulfillment of his Messianic task. The calling of the twelve and the completion of the number *twelve*, does not begin after the Pentecost; the official appointment of the twelve disciples to the office of apostleship is described in Matthew 10:1.[1]

The plain fact is, then, that Christ must die with His eyes fixed upon a profaned harmony; and that fact enhances our sense of the suffering which Judas' kiss caused.

---

1. Grosheide, *Kommentaar op Mattheus,* pp. 121-122.

Behold how severely God tries His Son.

See how Satan tempts Him.

He began with twelve; may He end with as many? He felt Himself to be the Messiah; can He sustain His pretenses? The kiss of Judas, the broken round, is as painful and as enigmatic to Jesus' spirit, and to ours, as is the nail driven into, or the crown of thorns impressed upon, His flesh. He must assume the full burden of the law of the "stem of Jesse." In its external splendor, the house of David passes into decay. The result, the effect, of Christ's work, externally considered—that, too, passes into decay. Not only the Christ Himself in His human nature, but also the *work* of Christ as symbolized in the *twelve* is being profaned this night. This Mediator has no compensation to glory in, saying: "True, I shall be destroyed, but they can at least see My work!" For if His work and His personal glory are defiled, then He has not even these to compensate for His death.

This is an acute trial for Jesus. Now He will have to manifest whether or not He believes in God. There is only one avenue He can take now, the avenue of Abraham, the father of all believers. For, when Abraham must slay his own son, when he must cut his own tree down to a "stem," he derives his comfort from God, knowing that God is able to call life into being even out of death.

God puts the same question to His Son, now, when He lets Judas kiss Jesus. God profanes His harmony, disturbs His nicely rounded number, throws His precious mosaic into a heap of ruins. How that kiss burns! But it is God's voice which is asking: Dost Thou believe now, Thou Son of man, that God is able to call Thee into life from the dead? Dost Thou believe that Thou shalt have a future, that although it is necessary for Thee to see Thy twelve profaned now in Thy death, the twelve thrones of the New Testament shall remain standing over against those of the Old, shall ever remain, surrounding the one throne of God and of the Lamb? Hast Thou faith in God, O man!

Yes, Father, He believed in Thee. The great David of the New Covenant has faith. The Head and Mediator of the covenant of grace has faith. He holds out His hands to be bound: He lets Himself be conducted into death before He can restore completeness to His twelve, and believes, and comes to prove to us, that His cross is not a pause in His task. The cross will be followed by the resurrection, by ascension, and by Pentecost. Christ Himself will return to the earth in the Spirit of Pentecost. Then, by the designation of His own Spirit, He will restore completeness to His twelve, and will present it, perfect, to God and the world.

Christ can die with His eyes fixed upon a torso because He knows that His perfect harmony will in its own time complete its expert sculpturing.

Because of this *faith* which Christ has, He is not an offense or a stumbling block to us, but the power and wisdom of God. Only such faith can defeat the kiss of Judas in this oppressed world.

Faith teaches us to see Christ as a greater than Aaron, although, a while ago, He seemed a lesser one. It is true that Aaron can transfer his breastplate, studded with the twelve stones, to his son, but he cannot in his own strength preserve one of these stones. But Christ's death made a distinction between false stones and true; Christ, by passing through His death completely rounded out the true stones till they were twelve—and these He laid upon God's heart.

Faith teaches us that Christ is not an unsuccessful King, a rod, which, arising from the Stem of Jesse, like that stem is a failure. On the contrary it teaches us to see Christ as one who by enduring Judas' kiss can in His own strength overcome the offense of it. Now He will go to prove that His work cannot be completed in the cross, but must be perfected in the resurrection and glorification, and that it will return in the person of the Spirit.

All men will be judged by the kiss of Judas, not because of Judas' lips but because of Jesus Christ. The whole question of faith and unbelief lies between those lips and Jesus' face. In this matter people irrevocably go opposite ways.

Only one conclusion is possible.

Say that Christ's Kingdom is of this world; that His choice of the twelve was not an act of Messianic power but of excessive imagination; that His death ends the matter; and that Christendom does not live by virtue of an *historical* Jesus, who was put

to death in full sight of a broken round of twelve, but who arose
to restore it to its perfection.

Then Judas is indeed a man who is tainted with the traitor's
infection, but that is all. He is nothing worse than that. Then
Jesus was "unfortunate" in His friendship and an "unsuccessful" prophet. But then the kiss of Judas is not an act of betrayal
over against the other world, the world of God, the world of the
Kingdom of Heaven.

Then we can call Judas' kiss unpalatable, unaesthetic, and
repulsive, but we must admit that essentially he was right. A
Jesus, who calls Himself the Messiah, must rise or fall with His
twelve, the number of Messianic perfection; and He who cannot preserve His twelve *really deserves the kiss of Judas.* That
is putting it bluntly, but why mince words in the Kingdom of
Truth, in the night of darkness? If everything depends on the
twelve of His Messianic awareness, everything depends on a kiss
of Judas. If Jesus is not the Messiah, Judas is as great as He.
Then Judas is just another of Satan's moves (really of Me-
phisto's) on the chessboard of history—a move in response to the
unfortunate one God made in Jesus. Then Judas has pricked
the balloon of the Nazarene's phantasy—and kept us from de-
ceiving ourselves.

But in the other case; that is, *in the only case?*

Jesus truly is the Christ. Christ had to die with His face
fixed upon a profaned harmony, for that was the law of His
kingdom. His kingdom has no external appeal. He endures the
disgrace of His broken body and of His broken harmony. Such
is the law of the cross, and it is binding throughout.

Thus only is the way to the resurrection and glorification prepared. This only can make room for the Kingdom of Heaven,
and for the possibility of breaking through to victory.

Precisely by dying, and by reigning in death, Jesus established that better kingdom in which the external calling finds the
internal one and retains it as its being. In that realm *election* is
made the basis of calling in time, and the internal calling of man
by the regenerating Spirit is achieved by Christ Himself as a gift
of grace. It becomes the great gift of grace which gives a dur-
able being to the calling of His church, unified and gathered in

harmony as it is. Not only by His work upon earth, but by all of His work He has achieved the *right* to establish a relationship, by means of the Spirit, between the election of God's good pleasure, on the one hand, and the gathering of His hundred forty and four thousand, on the other hand.

Presently the achievement of the Spirit will by His death be accomplished, and Christ will be Lord of God's Spirit also. Then that Kingdom will arrive in which the Kiss of Judas is *basically impossible* simply because in that realm those who have been called internally cannot fall from grace. Then—when the harmony of the spiritual Kingdom of regeneration and of internal calling has come to be, then it will be impossible, within the pale of true faith, to betray Jesus. That Kingdom will gather together a community of genuine believers who can kiss the Son in obedience and in faith only. Whoever lives by virtue of the Spirit of Christ cannot in all eternity betray Him.

One must take the problem of the kiss of Judas to Dordrecht.[1] For, from the viewpoint of Christ's resurrection the doctrine of *the perseverance of the elected saints* gives an answer to the question of the profaned number of twelve in Jesus' death.

But—and this is even more important—the problem of the kiss of Judas must be solved at the gate of that other city which is called the *New Jerusalem*. There one can find the number of those gathered and called of God. And that number is not a fragmentary or defective total, but is *perfectly* whole. The Revelation of John is the eloquent peroration to the dull gospel of the offense of Judas' kiss and of the broken round of twelve. Listen to the sounds: 12,000 furlongs, 12 gates, 12 pearls, the 12 names of as many apostles in the foundations of the gates of the city, 2 times 12 thrones surrounding the one throne, 2 times 12 elders, 12 times 12 cubits, 12 times 12,000 saints. Christ Jesus is here and His twelve are here, and from all sides these praise Him with their heavenly hymns of praise for His unprofaned harmony. "Father," He says, "*now* of those whom Thou hast given Me from eternity, in the communion of the Holy Spirit, *I have lost*

---

1. The great synod of Dordrecht, a city in the Netherlands, where in 1618-19 the famous Five Canons or Heads of Calvinistic doctrine were formulated in opposition to five points held by the Arminians. (H. Beets.)

none. Among those *really* given Me there is not one child of perdition."

Thus Jesus died. His hands were bound; His work lay in fragments. Clubs swung in the air. His cheeks burned.

But in the distance His eye saw a new Jerusalem having twelve gates. His holy longing, His strong faith, seared twelve names upon them. This Christ who is bound is the glorious One. As a matter of fact, *nothing has been profaned;* He Himself *drove Judas out.*

We must not forget that behind Judas' kiss lies Jesus' statement, that impelling statement made in the room of the Passover: What thou doest, *do quickly.* If that word of Jesus serves to prune Judas as a dead branch from the tree which Jesus planted, that tree has not been hurt. That tree, on the contrary, is saved from decay by just such action; now it can stand, and flourish, ever flourish.

Anyone who wants to see Jesus in this faith can shape only one prayer upon leaving Gethsemane: that he himself may belong to the perfect number, 144,000, and to the congregation which manifests the number twelve, twelve times; that is, 12 times 12 in all the multiple forms (1,000) of our abundance of life and of our breath-taking, glorious mutiplicity.

Such a person does not dare to refuse conversion. From his personal point of view—not from God's, such refusal is as culpable as Judas' kiss, and is an effort to destroy the harmony not of the twelve, but of the 12 times 12,000. If he refuses, he must suffer condemnation.

For Christ *was not kissed by Judas in vain.*

Christ's Last Wonder In the State of Humiliation: The Liberator of Slaves in the Form of a Slave

Christ's Last Wonder in the State of Humiliation: The Liberator of Slaves in the Form of a Slave

> ● *And one of them smote the servant of the highpriest, and cut off his right ear. And Jesus answered and said, "Suffer ye thus far." And he touched his ear, and healed him.* —LUKE 22:50-51.

WE observed in the preceding chapter that, according to the number-symbolism of the Gospel, the great symbolical "Year of Jubilee" in the history of the world begins with Christ, and that it impinges upon the world at all only by virtue of His strength.

The Year of Jubilee is the year of the *slaves*. It represents the emancipation of bondmen; first (inasmuch as the shadow-services of Israel are concerned), literally; later (in the New Testament), figuratively. Those in distress and in the darkness of prisons were released from oppression in that year. The sun of freedom must dawn upon the field of the Messiah, must shine upon it for *all*. Slavery is essentially incompatible with the Messianic kingdom. That realm is peculiarly the Kingdom of Perfect Freedom.

We remind ourselves of this prophecy concerning the Christ, which takes its course throughout the whole of the Old Testament, now, as we watch Christ carefully healing the ear of a *slave* of a priest. Christ goes about it very tenderly. While the band of Jewish police scream and yell, and while the Roman authorities manifest their cold animosities, Christ devotes subtle attention to doing full justice to one of God's slaves. In this He is reverently obedient to the law of the year of jubilee, to the law of the right of slaves. Indeed, Christ fulfilled the shadows, which manifest His image in the Old Testament, on the cross; but He also fulfills these shadows, these symbols, by putting his hand to the ear of one of the slaves of Israel's priesthood.

The circumstances of the incident as such we know very well. In the dead vast of night a band composed of Jews and Romans moved upon the Nazarene who was tarrying in the garden, in order to take Him captive. They expected to confront resistance, but in this they were mistaken; for Christ who has fought Himself into a state of peace with God is able now to give Himself up to death voluntarily. Unsummoned, He steps towards them out of the darkness and asks: Whom seek ye? The poised majesty of His unruffled figure standing there in the lurid glow of the torches is so astonishing that the ruffians of the Jewish police force and the adamant Roman soldiers fall backwards, overwhelmed by fear.

Thus the majesty of Christ immediately manifests itself. He does not conceal Himself, for He knows neither the sense of guilt nor the sense of fear. Asserting Himself simply as the Son of man, He strikes fear in those who oppose Him. So Gethsemane, at the moment of His being taken captive, figures forth that other hour when He will appear as King, and when every mouth which will dare to oppose Him will straightway be stopped.

But this aspect of the matter really is not the one demanding our attention. We want to speak of what Jesus did for that slave of the high priest.

We are told that one of the group which was sent out to take the Nazarene captive was a man who functioned as the personal servant, as the valet, of Caiaphas. This man must have led a hard life. Slavery is always hard for the slave; and it must have been especially so in those days of decadence. Truth to say, this man — Malchus was his name — led a very tragic life. Every day he had to walk in the shadow of the last high priest to whom the Old Covenant assigned a seat.

Now it is the will of God that this high priest, both as a man and as an *official,* must also let the light of Israel's *evangelical* existence fall upon his slaves. To do that is a priest's work. He must let the divine, Christological grace, which has conceived of a year of jubilee, glory in an assault upon the judgment which makes the

pare it with the number of times confessors have given special attention to this particular wonder. We would find that the miracle performed upon Malchus has had far less attention than the other signs of Jesus.

Nevertheless, this kind of appraisal is *worldly*. It judges internal worth according to external manifestation, and hidden significance in terms of visible forms.

We may not promote such standards of appraisal.

A miracle which Christ performs is always a miracle. Whether He removes a mountain to the sea or heals an ear, whether He dams up rivers or blood-vessels, does not affect the quality of the miracle. The force, the energy, the concentration of will, the faith, the spiritual puissance which exercises itself in each instance is altogether the same. Is wind less vehement when it blows a house down than when it twirls a bit of paper from the wastebasket into mid air? And is Jesus' power to perform miracles less powerful when He calls the dead from the grave than when He heals a gaping wound. The faith of Christ is *faith* and it remains that; the power of Christ is power, and it remains so. As Mediator He must concentrate His whole soul upon His Father when He lets power go out of Him, and this He must do irrespective of the object upon which He directs His power.

Moreover, we must remember that this miracle is the last which Jesus performed in His state of humiliation. From this time forth men will see no more of His miracles until He has sent out His Spirit. And may we forget, or minimize the worth of, this last miracle? Would that be "edifying"? Does it prove that we have grasped the conception of the *drama* of Christ's life? Surely, anyone who has felt anything of the exalted style and divine harmony of the life of Christ knows better. This last miracle represents the culmination and close of His prophetic teaching and self-revelation. This last sign which He adds to His spoken word should be much more accurately written upon our hearts by faith, than it was described in the minutes of the commandant of the company that night. We, especially we, may not say: "He was only a slave, and it was only an ear." We must confess: "Here is the King, and this is the power — the King and power of the world to come are here revealed. Amen!"

Many a ray of heavenly light is reflected upon this precious act of Jesus by the prism of faith if we look at the matter from this point of view. These rays fall upon the hands of the careful physician of Malchus — our brother, if he and we believe.

In the first place, this miracle represents the fulfillment of the law of the *sign of Cain.* Cain killed Abel. The seed of the serpent persecuted the seed of the woman. The flesh of Cain drew the word against the Spirit of Abel. And in that day God did not wreak vengeance upon Cain by destroying him, or by declaring him quite free. Instead God protected Cain from arbitrary violence on the part of men. "The Lord set a mark upon Cain, lest any finding him should kill him." Some think this sign was actually visible upon Cain's body. Others that Cain *saw* a sign assuring him of the promised protection of God. Irrespective of which view is correct, however, it is certain that the sign upon Cain definitely and emphatically protected him against every sword, even against the swords of the impetuous Peters of that day. The blood of Abel is not avenged by a sword, for that blood has a voice. It has a voice, and that means that the matter is a spiritual one and cannot be settled by the stroke of a blade. Neither the blood nor the voice can come to rest until One comes whose blood speaks better things than Abel's. His blood, too, will embody a voice, and with it the strength and the right to make itself heard. That One will be able not only to call aloud against Cain, but also for him. In contrast to Cain's arbitrariness, this One will first of all re-establish justice in the world.

Now that One has come. Christ exerts Himself in Gethsemane to *apply* and to *fulfill* the law of the sign of Cain.

Christ *applies* that law; Gethsemane, too, must witness the power of Cain, of the seed of the serpent, of physical force, as it asserts itself in opposition against the great Abel, who is the seed of the woman in the *most* specific sense of the phrase. And, although Christ can summon the hosts of the angels to destroy the bonds representing the spirit of Cain, nevertheless He puts a sign upon him. It is a sign which they all can see. It is a sign applied to the body of a hanger-on, a number of the band of Cain. That sign is evidence for the fact that Christ will not let arbitrary impulse battle against Cain and his cohorts. He reserves for Himself the right to open the bar of justice and there to judge of the spirit of Cain and of his deeds according to right. This act of Jesus is just another manifestation of Christ's active obedience, therefore. As a greater than Abel, He has gained from God the privilege of occupying a judge's bench, and He has achieved this privilege in part by this very act of rejecting anarchy over-against the band and by ministering holy justice there. Christ vindicated His right to establishing His judgment seat upon the clouds, by healing the ear of Malchus. Nothing in the shadow of Gethsemane is insignificant. Time there becomes eternity.

In the second place, Christ also *fulfills* the law of the sign of Cain. The first Abel did not himself protect Cain. By no means. Abel merely let his blood cry out against Cain. It was God who set a mark of protection upon Cain. But from Gethsemane where the blood of the *greater* Abel has cried unto God and still implores heaven — from Gethsemane God *withdraws Himself.* He lets the great Abel shift for Himself in the presence of the steers of Cain. For this is the hour in which Abel's superior must move in His own strength. As a matter of fact, He *is able to do that.* Even though this great Abel is entirely forsaken of God, He will nevertheless continue extending to "Cain" every cup of cold water as long as God Himself includes that "Cain" within the pale of the law of common grace. Even though Christ's, which is "Cain's," mouth, is parched with thirst, and even though His flesh is drying out, He continues handing the water to Cain. He is one who is greater than Abel: see, He who in one person is God and man, Himself takes Malchus' ear and affixes His sign on the armor-bearer of Cain's army of enemies to Christ. This He does in order that Cain may not be destroyed by any who might find him. Hence it is not only God who is protecting Cain against the vengeance of Abel's blood, but "Abel" is now Himself shielding Cain. You may well tremble now, Cain: when in God's time Abel undertakes to shelter you, you *fall into His hands.* Tremble, indeed: The cure of Malchus is the beginning of the last day! *Dies irae, dies illa* . . .

That which is happening here is exceedingly important. The sign which Christ affixes to Malchus' ear is of much greater moment than that which God once set upon Cain. It proclaims God's long-suffering to the world, a long-suffering which spares Cain throughout the days in order that he may be preserved (this is a biblical idea) until the day of the great retribution of the greater Abel Himself. The sign set upon the ear of Malchus proclaimed the law of *common grace* which meted out to Malchus and his company the full measure, renewing his power, regulating his pulse, *until the day of Jesus Christ.*

A ray of sunlight falling upon a perspiring slave in an eschatalogical phenomenon. When, indeed, does grace come without obligations? When is Jesus' friendliness not a judgment? *"Dies irae, dies illa."*

Yes, when does grace come without judgment? The line leads from Cain past Malchus to the Antichrist, that beast—*"whose deadly wound was healed."* In this the law of Malchus' ear attains fulfillment. *"Dies irae, dies illa."*

One other element of this event proclaims the glory of Christ to us. In this last miracle which His hands perform before they are bound together He exposes to men the holiness and the Messianic character of His wonders. The miracle performed upon Malchus is a miracle of *revelation.* It is foolish and offensive to the flesh. The miracles which Christ performs, as He intends them, as they are revealed to us in the Holy Scriptures, are always in essence and effect quite different from any miracles which men devise, and which nebulous phantasy (and "pious" phantasy) ascribes to Christ.

True, men have, in their own fashion, pondered upon the law of the miracle. The apocryphal gospels, for instance, those so-called gospels, written and conceived by men and without the inspiration of the Holy Spirit, also indicate that their writers have pondered upon the miracles of Christ, and have conjured up many a wonder and sign designed to enhance the apocryphal image of Jesus. Whoever reads these apocryphal gospels, however, is painfully struck again and again by the peculiar daring of human imagination where it interprets miracles. For the miracles ascribed to Jesus in these human creations do not aim at *redemption* and they do not serve to set free the enslaved. These miracles are merely a dazzling display by which a humanly fabricated Messiah pompously makes his bow as a magician, doing miracles by virtue of himself. These miracles are always done for their own sake, and these signs are always ended in themselves. The miracles of the apocryphal books *do not* serve *a purpose*. They do not prophesy. They are not instinct with fervent love, not permeated with an evangelical purpose. He who performs them is simply the chief of the magicians. They are designed simply to set mouths agape. Really they are designed simply to show that the Jesus who performs them is an *aristocrat*. His dazzling magic is so overwhelming, despotic, arbitrary, that it aids no one. The *little ones* are not blessed by it.

See now what Christ does for Malchus. He is the Christ of the canonical gospels. His last miracle is due. It is His *last* miracle. In view of that fact, the apocryphal gospels would say that the pyrotechnics of Jesus' miracles should end with a dazzling finale. But Jesus, the Jesus of the canonical gospels, does not set off any "fireworks". He comes to minister, not to be ministered unto. And, irrespective of whether a crowd of five thousand witness it or only one slave, He will bring the invisible forces of God into play in order to do justice also *to a pariah among His dying beggar-folk,* and so to complete the service of love and also the service of judgment. This miracle *accomplishes* that. It serves both God and man. It is not an end *in itself;* it is a *means.* It prophesies to men; as well as to the friends who must abandon their swords, as to the enemies who must learn that it is beating the world's Physician, not its Destroyer, to death. This miracle serves a purpose. The Physician of Gethsemane is God's Liturgist. He exposes the depths of heavenly compassion and of superhuman majesty to an astonished slave. His miracle is not a piece of fireworks; it is a fire which gives warmth and a light which points out and discovers the way. It is fire which consumes the ungodly and a light which blinds the enemies of God. It consists of the perfect obedience of the servant of the Lord. As the servant of all, He is this day assuming the form of a slave. Nor does He say to any servant anywhere: "You, I do not know." The entire Saviour reveals Himself in this deed performed upon Malchus. And it manifests itself both as a blessing and as a judgment. This healing represents the crisis in the life of Malchus, not the end of it.

Finally, by way of a third emphasis, we want to consider the *contrast between Christ's ministering signs as these culminate in this last miracle and the miracles of the Antichrist.*

Of the Antichrist also we read that he will perform *miracles* and show signs. These wonders will be intent upon three things: **to** lead the world astray; to prove himself the arch-aristocrat, dominating over all of the dwarfs of the world; and thirdly, to conceal the real character of the Antichrist from sight. For Paul names these miracles "lying wonders". They will be the great masquerade. He will conceal the chaos of sin under an apparent cosmos ("ornament") of wonders and signs, which he will presently stamp out of an earth which is fast dying. He hides his lie under the false glow of dazzling signs intended to prove real his claims to authority and truth. He drapes the thin disguise of a father's and shepherd's kindliness over the wolf-like character of his being. He promises by his signs to change the arid pastures of the sheep into a luxuriant garden. The miracles of the Antichrist are the great *ap-ousia* of the revelation of the Antichrist.[1]

The Antichrist will end his activities upon earth by means of such false wonders and deceptive apparitions.

Contrast Christ's last publicly performed wonder upon earth with these. It is not a concealment. It is not an ap-ousia but a par-ousia[1]. He is part and parcel of His deed; He reveals Himself in it just as He is. He acts without hesitation and yet—how often we have seen these two converge—His spontaneous response to what confronts Him is also an entering upon the symmetrical completion of the course of His perfect obedience. Christ, the physician to Malchus, reveals Himself as He is, and by His act pulls the forces of the world to come and of the sacrosanct privileges of the last day straight through the world. This is His conclusion in the name of the Father, and of the Son, and of the Holy Spirit, Amen.

The wonder by which Christ, just before He is bound, finishes His public earthly course, does not lead the people astray, but calls upon them to repent. Moreover, this act is not a dazzling emblem of His exalted aristocracy, by which He blinds the eyes of the people. True, He did strike the authorities of Rome and Jerusa-

---

1. Read the 13th Chapter of Revelation and the 2nd Chapter of the 2nd Epistle to the Thessalonians. Ap-ousia means absence and is used in contrast to Par-ousia or apparent presence. The name Par-ousia (in reference to Christ) points throughout to His glorious return. But par-ousia can also mean simply: The appearing.

lem blind, for they fell prostrate before Him. But at this particular moment, His eyes are blind; He washes the blood from Malchus' face very carefully. The miracle proclaims aloud the character of the entire Christ and does so according to the truth. Men carry chaos to the fore in this night of sin; but Christ reveals God's cosmos to a slave. Man fell on lies, but Christ preaches the whole truth; His last sign is declared obedient by the accompanying Word.

The Antichrist may make an effort in the eleventh hour to change the decaying world into a paradise. Christ while performing His last wonder is moving towards His own curse-laden death, and towards the desert of the sufferings of hell. But He ministers the word and sign of the coming paradise to a slave.

The signs of the Antichrist may lead astray, but Christ's signs disclose their meaning by the word of preaching.

Finally, Christ is not an enemy who is hiding the character of a wolf under a friendly approach. He is the true High Priest and He whispers this message into the ear of a false priest's servant: "Am I not He who is willing to deliver you from the bonds of death and from the yoke of everlasting slavery? Listen, my son; listen, Malchus: I am the priest who would become a slave in order to convert servants into lords."

The Antichrist and the Christ are two, and they prove to be two by their concluding signs and wonders upon earth.

One more beam of light falls upon this miracle, and discovers another important implication.

As we think of this event, we must also think of Jesus' kingship and of Christ as the Son of David.

Once before, the God who shapes history arranged a drama which at a distance resembled this one in Gethsemane. For on this occasion, the true King of the house of David is in great need. God places Him before a slave and tells Him: Do justice to this slave; let him see the Messianic light; let him observe it unhindered.

That has happened before and in a time of need; and in time of crisis. Some centuries before this, the God of the history of revelation tested the house of David by presenting slaves to it to be reverenced.

Do not forget that such testing was appropriate to the house of David. That house had to be different from the house of Saul. Saul laid waste the kingdom by exercising tyranny and manifesting haughtiness. He sought his own gain and he used his people to enrich himself. Then God took the kingdom away from him. For Israel is a theocracy in which the lesser must be served by the greater, and in which the king, consequently, may not prey upon the slave. On the contrary, the king must function as a Messianic message to the slave; for in this manner, also, the kingship must be an image of the Christ, who is the coming exponent of the year of jubilee and the first and greatest Emancipator of the slaves.

When, in history, it appeared that Saul was treading the theocratic Messianic laws under foot, the action of evangelical grace pushed that devourer of slaves off the throne, accepted David, and gave him the keys of the house of Saul.

In David's house things at first are acceptable. David dances before the ark of the Lord in the company of his slaves, and does not drink the water which slaves must fetch for him at the cost of endangering their lives. As first, therefore, David's kingship is in harmony with the Messianic purport of Israel's theocratic existence, which promises all of the people, including the slaves, their freedom. It leaves room for the law of the jubilee-year.

But gradually decay enters into David's kingship also. The decay increases, and threatens at last to lay the house of David waste. And the last king of the house of David, King Zedekiah, is finally removed by God Himself, precisely because of an injustice done to slaves. That is not an accidental event. It is a significant moment in the history of special revelation.

Prophetic light falls upon Zedekiah's downfall from two sides. First in the 17th Chapter of Ezekiel; then, in the 34th Chapter of Jeremiah. In both chapters the prophet proclaims the wrath of God against Zedekiah because he *has broken the oath*. He treads upon the laws of the oath, and profanes them in reference to the *great* on *earth* as well as to the little ones among *his* people. And his people are God's people.

Zedekiah first broke the oath in his dealing with the king of Babel. That was one sin. If the royal house of David, in the person of Zedekiah, was chosen to profane the oath in relationship to

Babel, that is, to the great enemy, to Cain, to the power of Anti-christ, then that same Babel will come to destroy the house of David. Because Zedekiah has broken the oath in his relations with Babel, he himself will die in Babel (Ezekiel 17 : 16, 18 and 19). That was one term of the sentence pronounced upon Zedekiah, of the verdict read to the house of David.

And that was severe enough, we might be disposed to add. Furthermore, inasmuch as the men were concerned, this was the principal cause of the fall of David's house. That is all that is written in the records men have kept of it. Zedekiah broke his oath in his dealing with the mighty on earth, of whom Babel was one. Therefore, he fell.

But there is such a thing as a divine record of history and this includes in its account the injustices and infidelities done to and manifested towards the little ones on earth as well as the injustices committed against the mighty. In the sight of God, Zedekiah sinned grievously when he broke his oath in relation to the *mighty* of Babel and of Cain. But he profaned the oath much worse in his dealing with the *little ones* of Jacob, that is, of Abel. We read of that in Jeremiah 34. The prophet is there alluding to the fact that King Zedekiah, when in distress because of the approaching war, decided to set free the slaves among the people. For the old and venerable institution of the year of jubilee, which had been established by the law, and which provided that slaves who by reason of pecuniary stress had sold themselves should be given their freedom again after a time — that institution had long been ignored. The royal house of David had played fast and loose with the fetters of servants and with the lives of slaves. But when Nebuchadnezzar threatened, King Zedekiah as a last resort decided to emancipate the slaves, and a decree was issued and covenant made "with all the people which were at Jerusalem, to proclaim liberty unto them; that every man should let his manservant, and every man his maid-servant, being an Hebrew or an Hebrewess, go free; that none should serve himself of them, to wit, of a Jew his brother (Jeremiah 34 :8-9).

Yes, when danger threatened, the slaves were set free. The voice of conscience spoke. Apparently it was known that this privilege of the slaves was sustained by God's own law. But the threat had hardly receded, the Chaldean troops had scarcely departed from the walls, before the covenant of emancipation with the slaves was broken. With the permission of the *last* king of David's house, the people broke the oath and the slaves were put in chains.

Is this a trivial circumstance, and are we perhaps putting things together which do not belong together?

Whoever thinks so is foolish.

The prophet Jeremiah himself asserts in the 17th verse that this infidelity to the slaves, including the slaves of the priests, that this breach of faith in corrupt Jerusalem in the days just before the captivity is the principal reason for which the Lord delivers His people, and the royal house of David, and the priests into the hands of the kingdoms of the earth. David's fall was caused by his stumbling over the lives of slaves, not over the chariots of war sent against him by the mighty powers of Babylon and Cain.

It is not surprising that this breach of faith should be the cause. God had introduced and fixed the year of jubilee into the law precisely because in it a Messianic light fell upon Israel and because by it His people were proclaimed to be a people who in principle were free. When the royal house of David withheld from the slaves the light of freedom, which in Christ would sometime fully dawn, it thereby became like the house of Saul; it profaned the theocracy, robbed God's heirs of their liberty, offended God's "little ones" and thus forfeited its right to a place under the sun. Now, three centuries later, and here, in Gethsemane, three parties are again witness to the incident: the slave of a priest, a Roman (Cainite) band, and the uncrowned king of the house of David, Jesus Christ.

The Roman still rules over the house of Caiaphas and of David. He rules by reason of the same judgment which Jeremiah proclaimed in chapter 34. God uses the whip of the Romans to beat the faithless slave-drivers who have stood in the way of the freedom of their bondmen; the whip of Rome is merely an extension of the whip of Babel, which Jeremiah saw coming down upon the backs of the mighty in Jerusalem, upon the backs of Caiaphas' slave-driving predecessors. That is one side of the tragedy. And this is the other side: there is no one here who sees it. Caiaphas gives no attention to it, and Malchus does not. They kiss the rod of Rome in order to be rid of Jesus. Moreover—*homo homini lupus*: the priest himself is a slave-driver. What more can sin accomplish?

Here are the slave-drivers of Rome. They are organically related to those of Babel. In fact, they establish a new Babel in the city of the Beast. Here are the slave-drivers whom the Bible almost depicts as the image of the Antichrist, of the great Cain. And there are Caiaphas and his slave, who together, are again the slaves of Rome. And between them stand Christ Jesus. As the true Son of David He bends tenderly over the slave of a priest. He withholds His disciples from violating the rights of bondservants. This king forbids His servants to offend one slave of Abraham voluntarily. Besides, in a positive way, He ministers to this slave the privileges which, in Abraham, are his due and He does that at the very moment in which Rome and faithless Israel are prepared to beat Him. See to this, He tells His church, and Himself first of all, that you offend not one of these little ones. As long as Malchus is incorporated into the body of Israel, he is, according to the covenant and the oath, one of the little ones of Israel. Take heed that you despise not one of these, as Zedekiah did; for I say unto you, that in Heaven their angels do always behold the face of my Father which is in Heaven. Yes, Lord — but Thou art the great Angel who dost ever see Thy Father and His slaves. Thou seest God and the slaves at the same time.

We bow our heads in reverence. The healing of Malchus' ear is as sublime as the coming of the last day. At this moment the house of David in the person of Jesus Christ returned from its last transgression. Christ averted the curse of Jeremiah 34 and Ezekiel 17. For He kept His oath with a slave and remained faithful in His dealing with the power of this world. He did justice to a Roman centurion. He did justice to Malchus in His great obedience. This healing proclaims common grace and also special grace. It vividly presents to us Christ's just relationship to both the world and His church. The house of David, broken as it was, is restored to continuity by Christ's grace to Malchus. All the issues of the Gospel, all the ultimata of the last judgment are laid bare before us in this healing. The earnestness of the preaching in this event is inescapable. The roaring turbulence of the waters of God's justice and grace, the thunder of the coming judgment and of the present plea of grace — these resound in Malchus' ear.

When, indeed, is Christ not sublime and overwhelming? When does He slight the year of jubilee, and when does He withhold the greatest reward from the least of His little ones?

Truly, such a King is meet for us; for He is merciful, tender, just, and He ever sees the Father and the slave, ever looks into Heaven and over earth, at one time.

O res mirabilis: salutat Dominum pauper servus et humilis.

Who is the slave, pray, who would not greet this King? He heals those in bonds, for such is the theocracy. The greater was served by the lesser. Saul has forever been replaced by the great David.

The people which sat in darkness have seen a great light.

Christ In Bonds

CHAPTER TWENTY-FIVE

Christis in Bonds

- *But this is your hour, and the power of darkness.*
  —LUKE 22:53*b*.

- *Then the band and the captain and officers of the Jews took Jesus, and bound Him.* —JOHN 18:12.

CHRIST has performed His last wonder. His hands have done their service. What in the world could keep those hands out of the bonds now? He came into the world to be bound. Only the calling which gave His hands work to do could thrust aside the fetters. But now the series of wonders has been completed. And now the hour strikes in which Christ is to be bound. The privilege of unhampered passage through His own city and His own world is taken away from Him. The Lord of the vineyard must go about in chains. He is delivered into the hands and fetters of the faithless keepers of that vineyard. In other words, He is given into the hands of those who have profaned the oath. He who kept the King's oath in His dealing with slaves, is surrendered into the hands of slaves who broke the oath in their relations with the King.

Ah, God, what can be done with hands for which Thou hast no more work, but to bind them? Alas, Jesus has done His duty to Malchus and is dismissed. That is His tragedy.

Christ is in bonds.

But I can hear Him speaking. *For the Word of God is not bound.*

I hear Him speaking. His words are awful, but also very comforting. Christ tells the Romans and Jews who have clasped Him in the bonds of death: "This is your hour, and the power of darkness."

435

The utterance, we said, is one of awful import. For the statement does not mean as some have contended that Jesus was pointing merely to the fact that these came upon Him in the dark simply because the night was the only appropriate time for them to do their work. According to this explanation, Jesus would be saying to them: "I have always worked in broad daylight; even in these last weeks. I was publicly and openly instructing My disciples in the temple where everyone could see. Then you undertook nothing against Me. But, now that it is dark, now you come to the fore to take Me captive. I am not surprised: to you the darkness of night is the appropriate hour." According to this interpretation, Jesus had nothing more in mind than to point out the contrast between His own unconcealed activity and the secret plotting of His enemies.

We have objections to such an explanation of Jesus' words.

In the first place, it is impossible to determine, on the basis of that, just what Jesus means by the *power of darkness*. The original of the text really means the *authority* of darkness. And some think that by using this word Jesus is saying: This particular spot on which we are standing now is the province of darkness. According to this version of the matter, there would be a *time* of darkness (the night, not the full day) and a *place* of darkness (the secluded garden of Gethsemane, and not the temple). Others maintain that Jesus in speaking of the *power of darkness* is referring to the *powers of Satan*. These interpreters, therefore, do accept the phrase, "This is your hour," literally, but look upon the second part of the utterance as a figure of speech.

We feel that the uncertainty attending each of these theories should admonish us to be very cautious. For if we compare this utterance of Christ with the very similar ones in Matthew 26:55-56a, and in Mark 14:48-49, we observe that in these the expression, "This is your hour, and the power of darkness," is replaced by another: "All this was done that the Scriptures (of the prophets) might be fulfilled." It is obvious that in this second statement, Christ plainly points to the fact that in the events of the moment He sees the fulfillment of what has from eternity been proclaimed. The hour of His captivity spends itself according to a holy, sovereign schedule: not one second of it is left to chance. Inevitability governs these events: they *must* come. God has for centuries proclaimed all this through His prophets; behind the Scriptural proclamation lay the counsel of God which from eternity willed and fixed what is taking place here.

The comparison of the statement in Matthew and Mark with the one we have read in Luke teaches us, accordingly, that the hour in which men put Him in bonds *has been determined by* God's counsel. Why are they *able* to bind Him now? Because it is *their hour*. In the structure of the pre-historic decrees of the sovereign God this particular moment of time was fixed as the hour of God's great *active permission*. Because He has willed it from eternity, He will reserve that province for the enemy. He will give them the full measure of their hour. God has arranged all of the preceding centuries, all of the intervolutions of time, all of the events from Genesis 1 :1 up to this moment— has arranged, has moulded them, has had them converge in such a way that there would be a place for this hour, the hour in which His Son will be bound. The hour had to be born from the womb of night. God had to shape the history of peoples, their coming and their going in a way which would leave room for this hour. He allowed neither the forces above nor the forces below to tamper with the clock of history. He directed the battles of Ceasars, the conflicts of kings, the migrations of peoples, the world wars, the courses of stars and sun and moon, the change of epochs, and the complex movements of all things in the world in such a way that this hour would come and had to come. God *reserved* this hour for Satan. He is the prince of darkness. Hence this is "his" hour. God's counsel has fixed it as the hour of Satan.

Hence the darkness referred to in the passage refers to nothing other than the power of sin: to the entire composite of hell; to the whole conglomeration of devils and demons which is poisoning the atmosphere of the Garden of Olives and pouring the curse between the luxuriant leaves and into the thick foliage of the Garden of Olives.

Of course, it is quite in keeping with the character of the devil and of those in his service to choose the night for their work.

But to say that the appropriateness of the nocturnal setting for the activity going on in it was all Jesus meant by His statement would be to miss the profound meaning of His utterance.

Furthermore, our interpretation of the statement is confirmed by the similarity existing between what Christ says in Gethsemane and these other passages of the Scripture in which He speaks of *His hour having not yet come.*

Again, then: How awful this statement is! It means that *the hour* has come. The hour of *darkness* has come. God gives Satan free rein in this province. Trembling angels, nervously fluttering their wings in their eagerness to administer God's justice in the world, can do nothing about it; they must stand back. God's will is permitting all this to accrue to Christ. Yes, as far as having the power goes, Christ, as He says Himself, could call down more than twelve legions of angels. But more important than what He can do is what He *wills* to do, and what He *may* do according to the justice of His God. And according to that justice He may not call down twelve legions of angels, or persist in summoning them. If His voice had implored the Father to send them, if His strong spirit had drawn them down from Heaven, He would have asked for another fulness of time than that which His Father had eternally willed. But God's programmes are absolutely imperative for all things alive. They are being carried out at all places in all times up to this moment. How attempt to achieve anything against the God of Koheleth?[1] Hence the angels must fold up their wings, must step back, and be quiet. The law of isolation, to which the Son is now being subjected, begins to be binding throughout the universe. First of all the angels of God must be obedient to it, and declaim its magnificat. *This is the hour of the devils.* Michael must put up his sword; Gabriel may not unsheath his; neither of these two may move against Satan. Just as there had once been an hour of darkness in Heaven itself when the storms of the evil angels began to blow it, so there is now "the hour and the night of darkness." All of the angels are held back in order that all of the devils can move upon Gethsemane and Golgotha freely.

The devils come. They beat against the Master with the vehemence of mighty waves. They are keenly aware that this is the white-hot center of the fires of time. They come. This is

---

1. See *Ecclesiastes.* The word means: Strict inevitability by reason of God's will.

their hour. On the one hand, this their hour is related to that other one, the original hour of darkness, in which sin first manifested itself in the world of angels, and in which these made their first attack in an effort to cause God's throne to totter. And, on the other hand, this hour of darkness is related to that last hour of the world, in which the devils, when the "thousand years" (the time of the perfecting of God's Church) have elapsed (are reaching their culmination), will for the last time be given free rein, be released from their bonds, in order to do their sinister work in the world.

The hour of Gethsemane—the release of the devils! They are coming now, for now they *may* come. Their privilege is not, indeed, the most pleasing application of God's justice but, nevertheless, they come with His *permission*. This is the hour of high noon in the great world-day. They come; they have their hour; they have their authority. God allows them to come, for they must begin the battle against the Son of man. And they find Him, laden with sin. That is why they are authorized to let judgment accrue to Him. *God* is blowing the flames of judgment against His son, because He has made Him to be a curse. Hence, those who fan the furnace in God's universe may employ their arts to blow the flame into a whiter heat, to drive the hot vapors of the Wrath of the Eternal quite up to and against the heart of Jesus. This is their hour and their province. God's permission is absolute. The divine activity represented in that permission is also absolute. God Himself throws open the doors of the prison-house of hell; and all the ominous demons creep out of it and rush to Jesus, to hiss and sting Him into death.

In Revelation 8:1 we read that there was silence in Heaven about the space of half an hour. That occurred in the crises when the *seventh*, the final, the definitive seal was opened. God's angels had to be quiet then, for God kept them from activity the while.

The apocalypse wants to tell us that when the history of the world approaches its dénouement in the seventh and perfecting seal, God first silences the angels. For the whole of the great world must know that even the most catastrophic judgment does not impinge upon it by an invasion of heavenly hosts, as though these introduced the alien ingredient into it, but that forces actively inherent in the world itself cause that judgment and "hour" to come.

It is just so at this unique hour in Gethsemane. By a glance of His eye God causes the angels to fold up their wings. The catastrophe is at hand; they in heaven may retire into God's counsel-room.

A half-hour of silence weighs burdensomely upon Heaven; heavenly ears can detect the breathing of sighs under the wings of the angels, who keep their perturbance covered with them. Never had there been such complete silence in Heaven as now. Only one hour will supersede this one in the strictness of silence, and that hour is coming fast. That will be presently, when the Son will be forsaken, hanging, bleeding in darkness.

While Jerusalem is sleeping, and while in the lowlands by the sea, the Batavians and other tribes are whetting their hunting knives for the chase, and while the little world lightly goes on its way over the course of the centuries, a crisis is being realized in the spiritual world. *The devils approach, while the angels are held back.* Each has been given up to the power of hell. From now on it will be impossible for earth to escape from the heavy burden of its *awful* calling: in a spiritual sense to be the center of the universe.

For this is the hour and the power of darkness.

But in the kingdom of Heaven, the most awful and the most comforting things are found side by side. The very fact that this is the hour of darkness may be called the great manifestation of grace and the chief comfort—provided, of course, we only remember *that God determined this hour.*

The hour happens to the devils; but He who sent it to them lives. He is God.

Had hell disposed matters, it would have selected its *own* hour and by its own will have determined its authority. The satanic yearns for a formula such as this: *Satan by the grace of Satan.* But God writes instead: Satan, *servant by the grace of God.* God *designated* the hour Satan could have, and all that hell undertakes in it is at bottom only that which God allows it to do.

Hence, this particular space of time may be called Satan's hour in one place and Christ's in another. Nor is this a contradiction; it is simply looking at the same thing from two sides. This hour is Heaven's; it is also the authorization of light. Why does Heaven give Satan free rein? Surely, in order that He can then vanquish Satan, after the devil has poured all of his venom into the body and soul of the Son of man. The volcano of sin must be exhausted before the angels may plant gardens of delight on its peak for the blessedness of God, and for the congregation of the first-born. That is why the hour of darkness is also the hour of light. And that is why the earth can no longer escape from the burden of its *glorious* calling, but, after its eternal election, must, in a spiritual sense, be the center of the universe.

Our salvation, accordingly, lies contained in Christ's statement. The fact that He *expressed* it and that it actually *lived* in His soul is also our salvation.

Jesus is perfectly conscious of the fact that this hour is the great hour of crisis, in which God's permission is simultaneously a mystery and a revelation. In His awareness of that fact we may observe a confession of His Messianic consciousness.

If Christ had *doubted* that this was the great hour, if His silent perseverance had been compelled to keep suspicion or doubt grimly down, He would have made Himself an exception to the silent angels, whose ability to be still is born from *careful attention to God* and from a sensitive knowledge of His will. Then Jesus would have doubted the crucial significance of His own hour. Then to His mind everything which was happening here would from this time forth no longer be fully informed by the counsel and foreknowledge of the heavenly Father. All this would then be a mere play of uncertainties and vacillations. Christ would then lose His faith in the firmness of God's counsel and providence at the very moment in which God's counsel was discovering its firmest bases and in which His providence was demonstrating its greatest certainties. If, in such an attitude, He had yielded up His hands unto death, and permitted Himself to be bound of men, He would have done so not as the great Fulfiller of God's counsel but as the horrible defeatist—the great blot on God's universe. By not resisting He would have proved to be the coward who turns both cheeks to the enemy, but only because He averts them from God who at this time wants to strike both of them. Indeed, if such had been His attitude, the Author of the sermon on the mount would have contradicted His own word.

In the sermon on the mount He does speak of turning the other cheek also when the enemy smites the first. But the implication of His utterance is that in turning both cheeks to the enemy, we must keep our eyes fixed upon God. Unless I keep my eyes fixed so, my non-resistance is a purely negative attitude. But if I turn my cheeks to the enemy *coram Deo,* that is, squarely facing God with my whole being, my non-resistance becomes positive in character. My attitude then is the most vigorous resistance which I can possibly give to the animosity in my enemy. Such resistance represents overcoming evil with good, and a reference of the eternal to every particular which arises in life. The word Jesus spoke on the mount demands more than mere non-resistance and keeping silence. Everything depends upon whether we have first allowed ourselves to be introduced into the atmosphere of eternity. For in His sermon on the mount Christ placed all things in an eternal light. In that sermon He gave the citizens of Heaven the great, life-consuming charge to see all things which happen in time in the light of the Kingdom's laws. Every dynamo in our human life must be charged with energy by the eternal God, before it can be of use.

Now imagine the impossible. Suppose Christ had not known or had neglected to become sensitively aware of the truth that this shocking hour of injustice was an hour which God was sending upon Him. Then His silence would have been despicable, and His surrender and act of disobedience. He would have been stepping out of the atmosphere and possibilities of the sermon on the mount, a sermon of which He Himself was the Author. Then His putting the kind hands which had just performed a miracle into the hand-cuffs of the Jews and Romans voluntarily, would have been the act of a tired man who—we say it reverently —was letting God's ocean inundate God's field.

Again, everything depends upon a single word. If Christ's surrender is to be the deed of the Messiah from the very beginning, He must be able to determine the momentous worth of this moment perfectly, in accordance with the Scriptures.

Therefore we thank Him for giving expression in His Messianic consciousness at this moment also, in order to comfort us greatly. Just because He has His eyes firmly fastened upon His father, He is able to really turn both cheeks to His enemies. To Him the whip of Assyria——to use the style of Isaiah—is the rod of God. His Messianic self-assurance deepens His joy in the beautiful moments of rejoicing in His God; it also makes more intense His trembling before the Chief Musician of death. Hence *His* non-resistance is the *most vigorous resistance possible*. This hero reserves His strength until Satan has time to enter the field, to sharpen his weapons, to take account of the situation. But afterwards these two will meet in a struggle of life and death.

This is your hour, and the power of darkness.

The Giants are coming.

Hence, we shall not ask, as a familiar line in Bach's *Passion of St. Matthew* has it: Where does the thunder stay, and where the lightning? For the God who restrains the angels from acting also keeps His own hands *from hurling out the lightning*. God strains hard not to do so—we speak of it after the manner of men; He has given us the *right* to do so. If God had issued His bolts of lightning at this time He would have been unfaithful to Himself. His justice would have become an arbitrary whim. Then the *biblical God* who never hurls His bolts arbitrarily would have become an image of the Greek Zeus who plays wantonly with his lightnings. The activity which Greek imagination ascribed to the aristrocratic gods on high Olympus certainly was a wanton, a wild and arbitrary disposition of the fires of Heaven. What Greek hero, pray, could in reference to it speak of *the hour and power of darkness?* But our Gospel presents to us the holy God who has consumed the whole, blasphemous, aristrocratic swindle obtaining on Mount Olympus in the one concept of *mediatorship between God and man.*

That is why no lightning *may* fall at this place. Bach is not theologian enough.

What could bolts of lightning achieve? Smite Malchus whom Jesus healed? A stroke of lightning directed at Malchus now would have struck the heart of Jesus. And Jesus' death at this moment would have been untimely: the world would not have been redeemed by it. If God had forcibly interfered with Satan now, God would have been doing Satan an injustice. For He has reserved this hour for hell. Hence, if Heaven had begun to protest by means of lightnings, these would have struck not only the Jews and Romans, not only the devils and the watchers of hell, but also the faithful soul of my Saviour and (this is saying the unreasonable again) the great faithful heart of God. For, now that the word of permission has been spoken, the fate of the world depends upon the emancipated slave of a priest and upon an unstartled band of Jews. If these are not given free rein in the "hour" of darkness, then Jesus superfluously lifted His hand over His people when He said: *Let them depart in peace.*

Therefore we thank God for the fact that Jesus not only reached the time of crisis but also *knew* it was that. "Surely, the Lord is in this place and He knew it well." It is His keen awareness of it which makes every deed He is to do savor of a conscious Messianic act. He imparts the power of redemption to His work, and does it with the consciousness of the highest love, a love which proceeds to the sacrifice, well aware of its meaning. Not only in His passive but just as energetically in His active obedience, this keen awareness converts His captivity into liberty.

In this manner my King goes to captivity. So Christ, your King, goes handcuffed. The Lord of the world, who no longer has free passage in it, gives that privilege to move freely to the demons of the night. He who pays the ransom and purchases the year of jubilee for all of the oppressed is Himself made the servant of others. As soon as Malchus could go on, God declared Jesus an alien in this province. And God would issue no more passes.

This represents an altogether new experience for Christ. Until now He could go where He wished, and could escape from the snares of enemies as frequently as He chose. But now, in the hour of darkness, He is *bound.*

Whoever remembers this last emphasis will not put the foolish question: "But *could not Jesus break His bonds?*" For we must spontaneously reply: "No, *He could not.*"

Do not regard that statement as one which subtracts something from the omnipotence of God, or as a disparagement of the enormous strength of Jesus' human nature. Oh yes, *speaking generally,* God can break all bonds; and, again, speaking generally, Jesus' human will is able to tear fetters apart.

But note well that such knowledge is inert and unfruitful. It is a mistaken way of talking. It concerns what is irrelevantly possible, *generally speaking.*

You who are mortal: do not mention this poor objection again —not in Gethsemane. For, *generally speaking,* Gethsemane does not even exist. It is fatal for Christian theology and philosophy to talk anything "in general." *Nothing* happens "in general." Everything has specific bearing. Everything which occurs in Gethsemane is *unique*: it happens once and can happen only once, in Heaven and on earth. The things occurring here are all specific; they are all special; they are all peculiar. And *that* is why we dare to say that Jesus' bonds can not be melted in any fire; not in God's own consuming flames, and not in those of Jesus' *human* soul, powerful and overwhelming as it is.

We have been naming two powers: *God's* power, and that of the *man,* Jesus.

Whoever confesses the omnipotence of God, thinking of it as something independent of His other attributes, is blaspheming God. The omnipotence of God inheres in the fact that He can do everything He wills to do. But His will is one of perfect justice; and His justice is part and parcel of all his attributes. Therefore, if God's justice, God's love, God's truth, God's revelation, and everything included in God, has designated this hour as the one for the binding of Jesus, then God cannot break those bonds. How could a God who has no jurisdiction over His lightnings possibly sear the slightest ropes? His only means for igniting them is the lightning; even the frailest flames that sear the tenderest souls on earth, are, if the burning takes place according to divine justice, as potent as lightning, for the majesty of the Almighty does the burning. O painful miracles: the ropes which were twisted together in a street of Jerusalem and are now used to bind His wrists cannot be broken by all the powers of Heaven. The suction of God's whole being draws them tightly around those wrists; the will of the Almighty has tied the knot; the power which is above joined with the power which is below in the act of weaving the strands of this particular rope together. Those souls simply cannot be removed. Nazarene, say yea. Let your yea be yea and your nay, nay, for whatsoever is more than these cometh of evil. To say more would be to place the loom of the rope-maker in Jerusalem outside of the sermon on the mount which you derived from God. A mere rope suffices, Thou Preacher of the mountain. Whatever is more than that cometh of *evil*.

As for the strength of the *man* Jesus: that, too, cannot break these bonds. It would be folly to say that Jesus can do everything *He wills* to do, unless we add that Jesus wills to do only what is compatible with the will and programme of His Father. The man Jesus performed all of His miracles by faith, by looking firmly to God, with exalted self-assurance, by annexing to His own human capacity the strength of God. Take away His faith, and you take away His power to perform miracles. The moment it is certain that Jesus has no "faith" in a matter, the question of being able or unable to do it becomes irrelevant.

And now we return to His own word: *This is your hour and the power of darkness."* Jesus knows this is true; He is perfectly sure of it. Therefore it is quite impossible for Him to believe that God could give Him the strength to break those bonds. His human strength weakens, at least in respect to these bonds, because of His sure sense of the fact that His Father is binding His hands.

In this manner, then, Jesus is bound. God has bound the mighty Samson, even though He has not touched Jesus' hair, and even though He will not in all eternity thrust out Jesus' eyes. Now Jesus must set free all the Philistines who have been given Him, even though these must fall upon Him first in this temple of Dagon, which serves at the same time as the grinding-mill of sin, and as His prison-house. This—is—*your hour*.

Jesus is being bound. And these three are tying the knots: the devil, man, and God. In personal language this means that the three who are doing it are I, the devil, and God. But I shall not succeed in making that personal way of expressing it my own until I put my own flesh, which bound Him, in bonds. The bound Jesus is the beautiful King only to the *spiritual* man. To the flesh Jesus' band is just as "offensive" and "foolish" as are the cross and His being forsaken. But to those who have learned to see and "distinguish" from the vantage point of the Spirit, the bound Jesus, who knew His Father's hour and therefore the hour of the Tyrant of His Father, Satan, is lovable only because of the bonds. In Him they look up to their God. Precisely by not playing wantonly with His lightnings, and by doing injustice to the *rights* of *devils*, the God of the Scriptures proved to be different from the God of the world. Let the gods of Greece and paganism clothe themselves in the garments of whim: The God and Father of our great Shepherd of the sheep, together with His Son, appears in the strict bondage of justice and truth, even in the. moment when the devils are loosed.

To those who believe, therefore, the bonds of Jesus are the power of God and the wisdom of God. The ropes which are cutting deeply into Jesus' wrists are a visible manifestation of the bonds within which God is bound by Himself; the bonds, that is, which limit His infinitude in all of its virtues, including his *justice, omnipotence,* and *love.* To us Jesus' bonds are a symbol of the unity of God and of the trinity. For the joyous limitation by which God restricts Himself to His own Being is the restriction which fettered His Son in the bonds of death. This was done in order that the Father, Son, and Spirit, who limited each other in the counsel of peace, might strive together for the peace of the world. *Together,* remember, and on the night in which "He was bound in order that He might set us free," *these bonds maintain the counsel of peace.*

This is your hour and the power of darkness.

We human beings will never be able to repeat those words unless we do it by faith. To anyone who has no faith in the unity of God there can be no offense greater than the bound Jesus. But to those who have the faith the bonds of Jesus will "utter abundant speech" and abundant knowledge.

As long as we are in the present we cannot know what will happen in the future. Hence we can say of no coming hour: This is the unique hour which is solely the province of darkness. It pleased God—and this, also, we call *common grace* — to bind Satan. And only at the time known to God, as we have observed before, will Satan be loosed once more.

Hence we may and hence we *must* oppose the satanical, in the power of the cross. And we must persevere in this opposition until the days of the Antichrist; for we can never be sure of when the definite crisis of the last day is at hand.

How should we who are mortal determine the time of God's unique *hour*. For we can read the history of the world only from our human point of view.

That is why we want to take rest in the Christ of God, who, when He was bound, *knew* God's hours, and who still knows them. For Christ, *as man, experienced* history, and again as man, by His strong faith in God and by His communion with the Father, illuminated it. Thus He shows what is a paradox to the unregenerated mind: that the bonds of Jesus are the devising of human arbitrariness but also the product of the fixed system of God's all-wise counsel.

Jesus is bound: He is wonderful in counsel, and mighty in deed.

In His bonds He did see *God*. Therefore, He is *fully aware* of what is happening as God forsakes Him.

When Jesus was being bound, the angels kept silence the space of an hour. For this was the hour and province of darkness.

> Patriarch Abraham, it pleased thee once to say
> That hell and paradise too far apart did lay,
> And a redeemed sinner ne'er near to it would stray.
> But these are wonders which surpass our thought
> That Heaven so close to the abyss is brought.
> To show us the great patience Jesus wrought.[1]

---

1. Heiman Dullaert (translation of H. Beets).

Christ In Isolation

CHAPTER TWENTY-SIX

Christic in Isolation

● *And they all forsook Him, and fled. And there followed Him a certain young man, having a linen cloth
about his naked body; and they laid hold on him. And
he left the linen cloth, and fled from them naked.*
—MARK 14:50-52.

ONE additional incident attending the capture of Jesus
requires our attention. We refer to the flight of the disciples and also to that of the anonymous youth, who followed Jesus into the night, but who was beaten back from the
Saviour by the ruffians of the band.

The question might arise: Why give any consideration to the
flight of the disciples? That was a "characteristically human"
thing to do. And is the fact that an unknown lad who followed
the events at a distance, and who, perhaps because of a fight with
the soldiers, had to flee, important enough to warrant separate
consideration?

Many reply negatively at once, and do so unequivocally.

And it has been maintained that the last incident, particularly,
has no special signifiance for the course of events, and that it is
quite irrelevant to the suffering of the Lord.[1]

We cannot be satisfied with this interpretation. Jesus' large,
sensitive heart was susceptible to *every* influence coming to it
during His life. He is directly responsive to every stimulus.
Moreover, the Gospel never tells anything that is irrelevant to
the synthetic whole of the Scriptures.

---

1. Dr. J. A. C. Van Leeuwen, *Het Evangelie Naar Markus*, Korte Verklaring

Therefore we have the right—yes, and the duty—to give separate attention to the flight of the disciples, and to the young man who was brutally wrenched from the soul of Jesus. We must consider these and must do so all the more because we are concerned *not* with them as such but with the Christ.

We must know at once that the flight of the disciples and of the youth constituted *suffering* for Christ. We may not call these incidents trivial and colorless. On the contrary, the whole Bible and all of prophecy has bearing upon them. Just because prophecy was always fully informing the Spirit of Christ, He was able to point to this isolation Himself. He stated beforehand that all of His disciples would be offended because of Him, and that their forsaking Him would be a fulfillment of the prophecy of Zechariah: *I will smite the shepherd but the sheep of the flock shall be scattered abroad.* And it is for this fact that the flight of the disciples, typically human and readily understood as it may be, is included in the large context of prophecy which makes the little incident one of great importance. This is not a case in which some putterer has added a small feature to the great canvas of the Gospel. Prophecy is involved in it. Everything that is taken up into the stream of prophecy, everything buoyed up and propelled by the Eternal Spirit has its importance. The flight of the disciples has its *function* in the history of the passion.

We can easily infer from Zechariah that the scattering of the sheep was originally intended as a punishment with which God wanted to chastise His people for their unbelief.

We have given attention to the prophecy of Zechariah before in our considerations of the suffering of Christ. We observed then that this prophet likened Israel to a flock which refused to accept the good supervision of the shepherd. Israel wanted to arrogate to itself the spiritual privilege of shaping its own picture of the ideal of a good shepherd. And because the shepherd of God's choosing does not conform to the image which the people have shaped, these people withdraw themselves from His cares. Hence, Zechariah concludes, God will remove His shepherd and scatter the sheep abroad. Obviously, then, the scattering of the sheep is a penalty "visited upon" the people because of their sin of "unbelief." Are the sheep pushing aside God's shepherd? Then God will remove that shepherd of His election, the only one who could possibly keep them together.

At this point our difficulty begins.

If the flight of the disciples were nothing more than the natural effect of the capture of Jesus, the incident would introduce no new element into the history of the passion.

But now we notice that we are required to observe a *visitation* in this scattering of the disciples. And that changes matters; it makes the situation very painful. The prophecy of punishment which Zechariah pronounced upon the *unbelieving* people is fulfilled in and applied to the disciples of Jesus. How astonishing to think that Zechariah's judgment must accrue to this circle of disciples. On the threshold of Gethsemane God lifts this sombre passage out of the prophecy of Zechariah, writes it upon a piece of paper, and addresses this threat *against an unbelieving people* —to the eleven faithful ones of Jesus. In other words, He is addressing it to the last ones still left to Jesus, to the called office-bearers, who are to extend and support His kingdom.

In this fact inhered Christ's great suffering. He had suffered when His perfect round of twelve had been broken by Judas' betrayal. But now His suffering is also very great, for the eleven who are still His are scattered by a judgment which Zechariah pronounced upon those who ignored *the shepherd*.

He wants to rescue the little bark of the church from the turbulent waterfall. And as He plunges into the stream, a tidal wave rushes against the vessel and dashes it into pieces. Here wreckage and a raging storm of *judgment!*

There is no escaping it; we shall have to look behind the external appearances of matters, and shall have to believe that *sin* is lurking there. For judgment comes only to the place where sin dwells.

That the scattering of the disciples is really a "visitation" which accrues to the disciples because of their sin becomes obvious at once from the manner in which Christ announces it. He uses the word "offense": *All ye shall be offended because of me.* By that He meant that the disciples would stumble, and by stumbling, fall into sin.

454 · THE SUFFERING CHRIST

What was the sin? We may be disposed to ask. Can it be that it was not quite natural for them to flee? Did something remain, still, for them to do? And putting it the other way, would they not have been tempting God if they had haughtily braved the danger? In fact, Jesus Himself had said: *If ye seek me, let these go their way.* How, then, can their leaving be called sin? Jesus Himself desired that they should go.

You see that questions abound.

But whoever asks these questions forgets that the disciples did something quite different from what Jesus asked for them. Jesus said: *Let these go their way.* But "to go one's way" is by no means the same as "to flee". "Going one's way" is a neutral phrase. A person can "go his way" calmly, trustingly, peacefully, of course. But he can also go restively, anxiously, nervously. And the disciples, in their going, manifested none of the firm poise and strong faith which characterized their Master. They *fled.*

Jesus had asked for them the privilege of going where they pleased. They could still have chosen, therefore, to follow Jesus, to continue their confession of Him as one who, although He was in *bonds*, was a shepherd who was conscious of His purpose, and a good pathfinder and protector. But they fled: they went into every direction save into that towards which the band was leading Jesus.

Flight, sheer flight, is never a religious act. On the contrary, it is always an irreligious act. The flight of a person who flees only because of weakness is certainly not an appropriate expression of the will of God. Mere fleeing as such is never the response which faith gives to the Word of God as it addresses itself to us in the Scriptures and in history.

True, there is a kind of "fleeing" which may be called "flying" (Revelation 12). This is a retreating, conducted in the strength of God, by faith, and to His glory. Accordingly, the word "flee" is also included in the Heidelberg catechism. But it may never be wrenched out of the context in which it is used there. It is used, you remember, in Lord's Day 33, which speaks of true repentance. The discomfort of the sense of "fleeing" is contrasted there with joy in the quickening of the new man who aspires to keep the law, and to do that by virtue of the *promises*.

But that is not the meaning of the word in this connection. The fleeing of the disciples is caused not by keeping their eyes fastened upon God, but by fixing them upon the enemies. That is why their flight takes place without faith. Christ is to die in order to procure for them the privilege of *walking*. But He is required to atone for their sin of *fleeing* first. They did not use their privilege: not even after He had obtained it for them. Should they not have trusted Him? And should their going away not have been a manifestation of their faith in the strength of Christ? Indeed, if they had trembled before the majesty of His Word, before the strength of His will, and before His poise, they would have recognized immediately that His command swept the course clean for them, that the Red Sea was passable. But they did not tremble. They belong to the baptized of Moses, but they do not baptize themselves in Christ. *They do not cross their Red Sea.* O Moses! O Lamb of God, you will have to enter the Red Sea *alone*.

For a long time the disciples have known the Master as one who can stay the storms, and can tame men, as one whose will is law. But that does not help them now. Staves and clubs such as those of this band are stronger than the stars at times, are they? Bonds and fetters of men are stronger than the Word? Jesus has been bound, has He? Then the same thing can happen to them. So do their souls instruct the disciples and so they prove to be unaware of the unique meaning of the binding of Christ. It does not occur to them that *He is binding Himself,* in order to purchase the freedom of the world. As their spirit perceives the matter, Gethsemane still stands outside of the sphere of prophecy, and is not subject to the pressure of the plan of redemption. Their way of looking upon this night is worldly. Therefore they ignore His keeping on the very night in which the good Shepherd is making the supreme sacrifice for them.

Hence it is for this sin of unbelief and faithlessness that the letter of prophetic judgment written by Zechariah reaches the disciples. The meaning of it is not that God wanted to take this means to tell them that they were outside of the pale of love. But it does mean that God was complaining against it, and weeping bitterly in the earth because of it. The great Shepherd of the sheep, left completely isolated in His calling, performed the supreme act of care for His sheep, the act which had to explain and make valid every other act. And because the sheep did not even recognize that, the earth was amazed exceedingly. To give all of His words full credence when swords are flashing and handcuffs rattling around Jesus' hand——

We need ask no longer, then, whether the flight of the disciples pained Jesus. Alas, there is ever that *fulfilling of the Scriptures!* Did you observe that Christ emphatically requested *free* passage for His disciples, in order that *His own experience of prayer,* or *thanksgiving,* might not become vanity. Before the darkness of Gethsemane swallowed Him, He had knocked at His Father's door, and *given* Him this specific praise: *Those that Thou gavest me I have kept, and none of them is lost* (John 17:12). *Father, Father, Thou hast not isolated me!* There are the soldiers, the swords, the brutes! May Heaven rescue the prayer of the Son——

. . . Listen to that and notice how Christ fights for the preservation of His own doxologies. He says it; He implores it; He commands it. Let them go free, he says. I am willing to lose Myself, but not my sheep. And he prays, in order *that the saying might be fulfilled, which He spake: Of them which Thou gavest Me have I lost none.* (John 18:9).

Now the *chasm* opens itself. For what could appear more futile, more vain, than the doxology of Christ? In the room of the passover He prayed, and He has thanked God and has sung a new hymn into God's ear because He had not been segregated from His sheep. Today, however, an old hymn — a hymn of Zechariah — clashes with His new one. Alas, Lord, He *is* being segregated! The sheep are fleeing! They are subject to the ban of isolation read over them by Zechariah the prophet. Lord, my God, dost Thou accept everything, then, save the prayers and thanksgivings of Jesus, the Nazarene?

You who read the Bible, do you see the friction which exists between the first instance and the second in which the words "might be fulfilled" are written? Christ's word was fulfilled? But so was Zechariah's! And that is a gnawing, chafing, painful truth! The sheep have been kept? No, they have been scattered abroad . . . . being outside of the province of faith! My Saviour, what didst Thou do amiss to warrant God in causing Thee so much grief — in Thy Prayers?

What didst Thou do to warrant the Almighty to make Thee doubt Thine own doxologies by means of a prophecy of Zechariah? Must Thou suffer everything, *literally* everything . . . . hailing from the nethermost abysses? Is God unwilling to accept even appropriate praise from Thee? Must Thou fight for the privilege of praising? Lord, art Thou so *basically alone?*

Yes, so absolutely, so strictly alone is the Christ. The best offer He has to give is the offer of prayer. But the incense of His sacrifice is beaten down. Cain, Cain: Nevertheless, His name is *The-Greater-Than-Abel.*

Christ, you see, is being drawn into His isolation from two sides: from God's side and from that of His trusted ones.

The fact that God is isolating Him is obvious from the expression: *Smite the shepherd.* God Himself is summoning the sword against the shepherd whom He first appointed. It is God who puts Jesus in bonds, thrusts Him away from the sheep, and lets Him feel that the scattering of the sheep is a dispersing of His own prayers. Cain, O Cain! Nevertheless His name is — the great Abel.

If only the sheep had accompanied Him to the end. If only they had simply "gone their way," calmly, with the consummate poise of faith, and as warriors who, although they are defeated by a fleshly power, gratefully and trustingly make use of the privilege which their captain has negotiated for them! O, if only this dispersing of the sheep had been purely the result of God's act in taking Christ, the shepherd, away from them, then the scattering of the sheep would not have added at all to the grief which God was causing him. But their *unbelief* causes a segregation of the sheep from the shepherd. Sheep of my flock, what have I done to you deserving of such infidelity?

Two things, then, God's justice and the infidelity of the sheep, divided the Shepherd from the flock and set Him in isolation. What could this shepherd possibly do? The owner of the flock is silent; no, He wrenches Him away from the sheep. My God,

my God, why didst Thou take His charges away from Him?
Was there nothing to warrant Him in laying down His mandate
over Thy flocks? Must this Laborer proceed blindly in His task?
Looking backwards, He sees the sheep leaving Him. They, too,
place Him in isolation. Sheep of God's pasture, why did you
remove your trust in Him? Spirit of the Lord, why dost Thou
harden their hearts, why not grant Him a few arms for support?
Why must the Holy Trinity blow away the incense of that prayer: I thank Thee, Father, that I have lost none? Cain, awful
Cain! But He is called the fulfillment of Abel, is He not? A
voice was heard across the Jordan. Where does the Spirit stay
who hovered over this baptized head? The dove has flown long
ago. This sound is the screeching of demons. Who teaches Him
Israel's songs of praise? God is among them. And His soul
searches for God in the morning.

Christ in isolation!

The owner of the sheep, the sheep themselves. These thrust
Him aside. And Thou, my soul, Thou especially dost push Him
away. And the great Shepherd must, in His isolation, give His
life for the sheep. Surely, the tenderness of John 10, the tenderness of the hymn of the Good Shepherd, never sounded so
terrible as it does in this awful moment. For this moment gave
birth to the utterances which Paul weakly repeated later: *All
men forsook me: I pray God that it may not be laid to their
charge.*

And now, in order to achieve that last result, in order to *purge*
the isolation, the shepherd takes upon Himself the burden of His
own segregation as the penalty for their act of isolating Him.
Thus He removes the sheep from the judgment and leads them
to the meadow of communion. He bites His teeth in His effort
to bear their blunt confusion and nervous activity as they dispel
the incense of the sacrifices of His far-reaching Passover prayers. For this they do until the sacrifices of His prayers begin
to resemble the sacrifice of Cain. He bears, He endures everything, everything, ... amen. *A greater than Abel is here.*
In seeing the remnants of the old man in them, of the Cain in
them, He has not ignored or rejected the new man in His disciples.

He will die for them in spite of everything. The voice of His blood will cry louder than that of Abel.

But never again ask whether or not this is causing Him pain. Isolation is always painful, for a human being instinctively seeks company. There are solitary souls who invite the companionship of some animal, when men forsake them. This they do because they cannot exist without communication and fellowship. Here you find a childless man and wife who keep a dog; there a dying soldier cries for his mother in vain, and clings to the hand of the nurse instead; yonder sits a poor old woman with a canary in a cage. A hidden tragedy hovers over all these people. They cry for fellowship, brush aside a tear, keep back a choking sob.

And could you suppose that this was not so for Christ? Nay, precisely His sensitive heart craved company, yearned for understanding, for sympathy, for someone sharing His experiences, someone fully understanding His soul. But Jesus must watch them go, one by one. See, there goes Peter. And now John. James, too, is leaving. One by one they tear themselves away from Jesus' soul. And His soul is more delicately responsive than the most sensitive telepathic plate. Very finely it responds to the presence and to the absence of loving thoughts and heart's passions designed for Him, caressing Him in friendliness and faith.

This, then, is the *first attack* of the tragical conflict in the solitary Christ, who is left in solitude by His twelve confidants as well as by all of the silent heavens.

Nevertheless a new light seems to dawn upon Him for a moment. True, the eleven who have long been faithful to the Master leave Him now. But another makes his appearance, shyly, bashfully he comes, it is true, but he comes to comfort and strengthen the human soul of the Man of sorrows by his presence — that great and precious human good.

The newcomer is the anonymous youth in the garden of Gethsemane.

It looks like a promise. When twelve giants fall in battle the arrival of a dwarf to take their place can be definitely encouraging. When eleven great oaks have been felled in the forest, the discovery of a little flower, shyly lifting its head from the grass, can be a beautiful find. Just so the anonymous lad is a lovely flower by the side of the road on which the eleven have deserted the Saviour. Can it be that this unkown youth who followed Jesus with love and not without courage *is going to break the ban of isolation?* Father in heaven, art Thou going to send a little one? Wilt Thou cause Jesus' hand to turn itself to the little ones? Of those whom Thou hast given Him, He has lost all. Wilt Thou give Him another, and may He keep this One? Thou withholdest the disciples; wilt Thou grant Him this embarrassed novice? The students of the first order have been repulsed; may the Son know that His solitary soul has the companionship of a "student of second rank"? Heavenly Father, dost Thou proffer grace in this moment?

The question is a significant one. It touches upon the *suffering* of Christ directly. And, in reference to what has occurred before, it also touches upon *prophecy*.

Just what has God in mind by sending this youth? And just who is he?

As a matter of fact, we do not know who he is. His name has been withheld from us. It is apparent that he left his home in haste. He must have gone to bed already, for he is wearing a linen cloth over his naked body. Nevertheless he came down from his chambers to follow Jesus shyly. Apparently he saw what took place, was moved by feelings of love and sympathy,[1] and followed after Jesus. Moreover, he persevered in the pursuit — so much is obvious from the Greek text — he persisted in following even after the disciples fled. The first onslaught of the enemy was not enough to repulse him. He followed after, and when he followed, Jesus noticed it. The same delicate perception which had noticed Nathanael sitting under the fig tree, and informed Him at once when the faith of a suffering woman drew her life out of Him by touching His garment, is active now also. Jesus' soul tasted and fed on the love of this young man

---

1. This becomes apparent from an element in the original text which some of the manuscripts include. Compare P. L. Groenen, *op. cit.*, p. 221; also Mark 5:37 and Luke 23:40.

as it affected Him, strengthening Him. His presence was a gift of God to Jesus; it seemed designed to destroy the isolation.

You ask again, who was this young man? Jesus knew, but we do not. Some have ventured to suggest names, have alluded to John, for instance, and to James, and to Saul. One interpretation deserves attention, because it is not an arbitrary one. And that is the interpretation of those who link the name of Mark, the evangelist, with this young man. Much can be said in support of this view. In Chapter 10 we discussed the possibility that Mark lived in the same house in which Jesus kept the Passover, and we ventured to suggest that Mark attentively followed everything which happened in the room where Jesus and His disciples had sat at supper.

And if this Mark, whose father (or mother) belonged to the circle of Jesus' friends, had occasion to be impressed by Jesus' holiness, it is easy to understand — perhaps it was one of the first blessings to issue to the outside world from the first Supper — that a more than magnetic force drew him after Jesus. Some commentators prefer to think that the band of soldiers who were guided by Judas, first went to the house where the Passover had been kept, in order to make sure whether or not Jesus was still there. It is possible that the young man was awakened by the noisy vehemence of the soldiers, and that he, gripped by a sense of anxiousness and love, immediately arose and followed after them. We read that he wore a linen cloth, that is, a garment made of precious Indian stuffs, or possibly from cotton; and this fact tells us that he belonged to the well-to-do. And this particular feature fits appropriately into the structure of what we know of Mark.

All of these particulars, to say nothing of other data, make the thesis that Mark was the anonymous lad a very plausible one. From such a point of view, for instance, we would easily see why Mark alone records this incident in his narrative of the Gospel, and why the name of the youth is modestly withheld from us in it.

But why should we care to find data which would determine more definitely the identity of this young man? Would that be an especially significant discovery?

Of course not. The question of his identity may be interesting but does not affect the central significance of the incident. And we wish to state here emphatically that we have no certainty about who he was.

But no certainty is necessary.

The important fact is this: The companionship of this proselyte was quickly snatched away from the Christ. The soldiers threaten him, because they recognize in him a follower of Jesus, and because they are annoyed by his boldness. A free-for-all ensues and in the commotion of the fight, the young man leaves his coat in the hands of the soldiers, and flees to his house naked.

For Christ this event serves to *confirm* His absolute isolation and to enhance its application.

We must not forget that the situation of the young man in relation to Christ was different from that of the eleven disciples. He never belonged to the narrow circle of the disciples; the evangelists indicate plainly that these all had fled. To this extent, then, he did not share in the freedom to go where he pleased which Jesus had procured for the eleven. The fact that in spite of this he had the daring to follow and to see what should become of Jesus is an indubitable indication of courage. He followed after Jesus without a single promise, without a bodyguard.

His courage put to shame the fear of the apostles who had indeed received the protection of Jesus' word. This young man accompanied the band and clung closer to Jesus than Peter and John later would dare to do. And this conduct on his part looked at first like a new hope and a new beginning; a new bud was burgeoning forth in the garden of the expectations of Jesus, the Nazarene, the genuine *man*.

But now God, who put Jesus in bonds, appears to be so brutal, so harsh, that He forcibly slashes off the new shoot arising from the broken stem of the hope of Jesus. God permits the sword of the soldiers to drive this young man away also. For the darkness of night must bear down upon the Son of man from all sides. Not merely the old, but also the faint beginning of this new fellowship must be snatched away from the Son in this moment. Student and apprentice, the advanced in Jesus' school and those just beginning, the twelve of the past and the first-born of the future Pentecost, the new patriarchs and the bashful proselytes, the remnants of the Old Covenant and the novices of the New — all, all must be taken away from Jesus. *Yea, Father, for such has been Thy good pleasure!* The isolation must be absolute!

Now it is true that the tender bud of love for Jesus, which sprouted in the souls of bashful novices, later blossomed out and bore fruit to the glorification of Jesus Christ, and it is also true, assuming that this young man was Mark, that the lavish love of this new-comer proved abundant, and strong, and prophetic later in its efflorescence for the glorified Christ. But in this moment, nevertheless, God takes everything away from Him: the old and the new, the familiar disciples and the strange novices, those who have been satisfied with wisdom, and those who are craving a single word from the Wonderful Prophet who takes souls captive. All of them must be torn away from Jesus, the guests seated at the table as well as the spectators standing at a distance. Be silent, ye heavens, and forbid that the synthetical spirit should assert itself upon any heart which is seeking Jesus. Stay back, ye winds of love, and withhold your dews, ye morning-clouds of youthful hearts: steel your countenance against Jesus, the Nazarene, O earth, nor let a benignant, sympathetic smile fall upon Him. In this way He must learn the art of "setting his face like a flint." O angels, ye who bear the candles, and make coldly calculating discriminations, thrust Him into abysmal solitude. Cause all the heavens to know the cruel secret: *Christ is in isolation, for such is the judgment.*

Do you want to taste of this judgment? Then you will have to live in hell. For only in hell is isolation perfect and complete.

There are two worlds ultimately.

There is, first of all, the world of *heaven*. In Heaven souls melt together without losing their individualities. There the unexpressed hymn born in the heart of one is immediately taken into the heart and upon the lips of the other. Heaven is the place of perfect fellowship, of perfect harmony of thoughts and of ideas.

But the Bible places over against this picture that other one of *hell*. In hell one person desires no fellowship with another. The soul-expression of the one is as a dagger-thrust to the other. Thoughts and desires are as stabbing knives in hell.

The bound Christ is now passing between these two worlds.

The unbelief of His disciples sets Him apart; they isolate Him. Ah, how their thoughts do stab at His heart like knives!

And here is this modest young man. He wants to go along; love draws him; the future makes its just demands in him, the anonymous one, known only to God. He is the flower and the hope of what is almost the Christian fellowship—— But he, too, is torn away from Jesus. God is isolating Him. Ah, how like sword-thrusts the thoughts of God are now! All that the Judge of Heaven and earth ponders in His heart on this very night which is also going to inspire a Form for the Holy Supper—all is as a two-edged sword to Jesus. God's sword is being aroused against the Shepherd, and it even drives the trembling lambkin which is stumbling on behind the flock, away from the good Shepherd. O, how consuming, how terribly devouring this sword is!

May we never again say that anything included in the narrative of the passion constitutes no real suffering for Jesus. May we leave Gethsemane with our eyes solely fastened upon the surety of our souls who fulfilled His office as Shepherd, even when the flock was removed from His sight, and who did this simply and solely because God required it of Him and because He was moved by unspeakable love. The Shepherd, who could not even see the sheep, placed His soul in their stead, trembled before God, and put Himself, together with the sheep He had to purchase, into the Father's hand. For he had *pondered* in His heart the *idea* of the shepherd and the sheep. When He had once really grasped that idea, when His shepherd's heart moved by virtue of faith and not by virtue of things visible, then He conquered reality, creatively and omnipotently. Only he who has the idea *has* the *reality*.

Therefore my Jesus deserves to be called the *King* of His church and the chief Shepherd of the sheep. He had the idea of the church in His heart, even when everything mocked that idea.

Remember, *two* forces drove Him away from His own.

First, there was a force which operated from within outwards. This force was their unbelief and fear. They fell to pieces; in themselves they could not achieve fellowship and communion.[1]

Besides, there was a force which proceeded from without inwards. God drove them away from Him, and the devils drove them, and men. There was no external force present to draw them together, to force them, to hold them, to gather them together.[2]

And when the situation was so desolate that no force proceeding from within outwards along organic channels, and no force entering in from the outside by mechanical means could unite the communion of believers with Jesus, then He Himself achieved it. He *created* His church. He did it by an omnipotent deed, by a tremendous will. For is the *Creator* conceivable except in *isolation?* The creating God is necessarily alone. O Christ, Prince of the church, *Father* of the church.[3] My Lord *and* my *God!* Because Thou didst have the Church in Thine idea, therefore Thou dost gain it in reality.

Some have said that Mark's inclusion of the incident of the anonymous young man in his narrative may be likened to the monogram which a painter sketches upon his canvas when he has done with the work by way of indicating that he is the artist of it.

Perhaps this comparison is true to fact.

Be that as it may, so much is certain. In the personal account which each of the sons of God writes of his fellowship with God, the part which tells of his having forsaken Jesus is surely the most personal monogram with which he can prove his account of his conversion and fellowship with Christ *his own personal experience.*

Fix your heart upon the isolated Christ and tell him: Yes, I have forsaken Thee. My Saviour, my Bridegroom, I have for-

---

1. Coetus: Communion, proceeding from within outwards.
2. Congregatio: Communion externally realized.
3. Coetus (active) and congregatio (passive): The name for the Church in the Confession of Faith in the Netherlands.

saken Thee. From me the soldiers took the garment, me they molested when I sought the Bridegroom, whom, nevertheless, I isolated by my unbelief (Song of Solomon, 5).

I, I have done it.

Be silent now and listen attentively to Him. For now He Himself will proclaim that He has accepted you, not only as a forsaken one but also as one who forsakes. Such an one is my love, O daughters of Jerusalem.

For if, when we were still forsakers, we were reconciled to God by the death of His Son, much more, being reconciled, we shall be saved by His life, after we have been borne into communion with Him. If, while we were isolating Christ by sin, we were nevertheless accepted of Him who, though broken in isolation, drew us unto Him by the irresistible force of His life, then is redemption perfect. All doubts and uncertainties which must creep into the soul as often as it fosters the illusion of an unisolated Christ, are dispelled as soon as we return to a Reformed outlook upon this unspeakable wonder: Christ was isolated in order that solely by sovereign grace He might break the isolation and establish the communion of God with those whom He has purchased.

Indeed, when John wrote that he had seen with his eyes and handled with his hands the Word of life, he included in it the visible image and tangible misery of Christ, isolated, *also by John.* Hence grace surges up in the words which follow: That which we have seen and heard we declare unto you, that you also may have fellowship with us: and truly our fellowship is with the Father, and with his Son, Jesus Christ. And these things write we unto you, that your joy may be full (I John 1:1-4). Indeed, fellowship thrice multiplied by Christ's three-fold isolation! And joy fulfilled by His profound grief. Please give me again the form for the Lord's holy supper.

We now leave Gethsemane with our eyes fixed upon the isolated Christ. We know that in God and in the eternal good pleasure our redemption is sure. For *nothing* man could give, not even the aspiration of a passionate longing for Christ which trembled in human souls, qualified Him for the sacrifice. He ignited all His incense alone. He dwelt in His absolute isolation, and His own flame alone reached up to Heaven. His own arm alone acquired salvation.

Moses, Moses! You lifted your staff over the Red Sea and your faith coerced the wide expanse of her waters. Behind you was a yearning people, and these pushed on; they had to cross it and they would. Aaron watched you anxiously; Miriam wrought hard for you in prayer. All the available energies of prayer wrought with you, Moses; together these supported the arm that held your staff, the staff which clove the waters. Yes, yes, it was your faith but you were faithful and believing *amidst a cloud of witnesses.* You were not isolated.

But Christ——

He stood before the Red Sea, looked around, and saw that no one, no citizen of any of the worlds, was accompanying Him. Israel was scattered. The night was dark. Ah, how hard it is to cleave the waters of a sea if the people are *invisible!* But, isolated as He was, Christ did enter the Red Sea. Never was anyone in such solitude as He.

The Law of the Kingdom *willed* so; hence there was no alternative in all the world.

But if my soul may one day sing the song of *Moses and of the Lamb* (Revelation 15), the Lamb will be more important to me than Moses. And that too will be in conformity with the Law of the Kingdom.

In His isolation is contained all *my* strength. Before long I shall praise Him as one of a *great host.* That host will be the gathering together of all those who fled from Him.